Before Internment

ASIAN AMERICA
A series edited by Gordon H. Chang

The increasing size and diversity of the Asian American population, its grow-ing significance in American society and culture, and the expanded appreci-ation, both popular and scholarly, of the importance of Asian Americans in the country's present and past—all these developments have converged to stimulate wide interest in scholarly work on topics related to the Asian American experience. The general recognition of the pivotal role that race and ethnicity have played in American life, and in relations between the United States and other countries, has also fostered this heightened attention.

Although Asian Americans were a subject of serious inquiry in the late nineteenth and early twentieth centuries, they were subsequently ignored by the mainstream scholarly community for several decades. In recent years, however, this neglect has ended, with an increasing number of writers exam-ining a good many aspects of Asian American life and culture. Moreover, many students of American society are recognizing that the study of issues related to Asian America speak to, and may be essential for, many current discussions on the part of the informed public and various scholarly communities.

The Stanford series on Asian America seeks to address these interests. The series will include works from the humanities and social sciences, including history, anthropology, political science, American studies, law, literary criti-cism, sociology, and interdisciplinary and policy studies.

Yuji Ichioka. *Akahata*, Tokyo, December 1999.

Before Internment

ESSAYS IN PREWAR JAPANESE
AMERICAN HISTORY

Yuji Ichioka

EDITED BY GORDON H. CHANG
AND EIICHIRO AZUMA

STANFORD UNIVERSITY PRESS
STANFORD, CALIFORNIA
2006

Stanford University Press
Stanford, California
Printed in the United States of America on acid-free, archival-quality
paper

Library of Congress Cataloging-in-Publication Data

Ichioka, Yuji.
    Before internment : essays in prewar Japanese American history /
Yuji Ichioka ; edited by Gordon H. Chang and Eiichiro Azuma.
        p. cm.—(Asian America)
    Includes bibliographical references and index.
    ISBN 0-8047-5147-1 (cloth : alk. paper)
        1. Japanese Americans—History—20th century.   2. Japanese
Americans—Study and teaching.   3. Ichioka, Yuji.   I. Chang,
Gordon H.   II. Azuma, Eiichiro.   III. Title.   IV. Series.
    E184.J31415   2006
    973'.04956—dc22   2005032978

Original Printing 2006

Last figure below indicates year of this printing:
05   14   13   12   11   10   09   08   07   06

Typeset by BookMatters in 11/14 Adobe Garamond

To Emma

Contents

Note on the Translation and Transliteration of Japanese Names and Words

In this volume, the names of Japanese persons and Japanese immigrants (*Issei*) are written with family name first, followed by the given name. The only exceptions to this rule occur when their names are provided in the customary Western form in original source materials. For the American-born Japanese (*Nisei*), the given name precedes the family name. All translations from Japanese-language sources are the author's unless otherwise noted.

E.A.

Preface

Even in the last few days of his life, as he was fighting cancer, Yuji Ichioka was thinking about how he might complete this volume, an anthology of previously published and unpublished essays that examine the experiences of Japanese Americans between the two world wars. It had been a project that had absorbed his attention intermittently for several years. But his passing in 2002 came suddenly, and the task of completing the compilation fell to others. Before you is substantially what Yuji intended to publish. His unfinished introduction, which he had wanted to complete and expand, is included essentially as he left it; we have labeled it Chapter 1. He included Chapters 3–10 in his working manuscript. Added posthumously are Chapters 2, 11, 12, and 13. Yuji published Chapter 2 in Japanese in 1991, but it has never appeared in English. Chapter 11 was first published in the *Pacific Citizen*. Yuji's working bibliography is also included as an appendix. The editors located this item in his office after his death and included it because of its scholarly importance. Yuji may have been reserving it for a future publication of his own, or he might have been using it as a research guide for a projected study of the war years, but we hope that he would approve of its inclusion here. Sources that are listed in the bibliography appear in the notes in their short citation form. We would like to mention that because of the way the material for this volume was compiled, occasionally some text is repeated in the essays. The editors, wanting to limit tampering with Yuji's own composition, chose not to eliminate such redundancies and ask the reader for indulgence. Eiichiro Azuma's introductory essay, completed after Yuji's passing, provides an expanded historiographic and biographical context for the anthology. The essay gives an overview of Yuji's scholarship and the immense contributions he made to the study of history, Japanese American history in particular. The volume ends with a personal reflection by Gordon Chang about Yuji as historian and friend.

We are also including one of Yuji's last published works, "A Historian by Happenstance," as Chapter 13, which *Amerasia Journal* published in 2000. In this essay Yuji tells us in his own characteristically lively and occasionally acerbic language how he came to the craft of history; he also presents his own vision of the present state and future of Japanese American history. He included little biographical information, however, so we provide a few bits here: Yuji was born in San Francisco in 1936 to modest circumstances. He and his family were interned in Topaz during the war, settling in Berkeley afterward. Yuji's record at Berkeley High was a mix of application and indifference, depending on whether he thought his teacher merited his attention. After graduation he entered the United States Army and was stationed for a time in Germany. After his discharge he entered the University of California, Los Angeles, and graduated in 1962. He briefly attended graduate school at Columbia, intending to study Chinese history. After working as a youth parole worker in New York for a short while, he made a fateful trip to Japan in 1966. The trip inspired him to take up the study of Japanese history and language. He moved back to Berkeley and participated in the civil rights and anti-war movements. He attended the University of California, where he earned a master's degree in Asian Studies in 1968. He coined the term "Asian American" in graduate school. The next year he helped found the Asian American Studies Center at UCLA, where he spent the rest of his professional life. His best-known book, *The Issei: The World of the First Generation Japanese Immigrant, 1885–1924* (1988), was nominated for the 1988 *Los Angeles Times* book prize for history and was awarded the 1989 Book Award from the Association for Asian American Studies. In 1999–2000, he was a visiting professor at Tokyo University. At the time of his death he was adjunct associate professor of history at UCLA. He never pursued a doctoral degree.

If Yuji was living, he would have wanted to acknowledge the help, collaboration, and support of colleagues, institutions, archives, friends, family members, and funders in Japan and in North and South America over the years, but he is not here to identify them. Regretfully, we, the editors, are unable to reconstruct such a list. We trust that those who would constitute it will understand. The following journals kindly allowed the editors to reprint Yuji's previously published articles in this volume: *Amerasia Journal* (Chapters 5, 7, and 13); *California History* (Chapters 3 and 8); *Pacific Citizen* (Chapter 11); and *Pacific Historical Review* (Chapter 10). In the production of this volume the editors wish to acknowledge the help of Russell Leong, Don Nakanishi, and the staff of the UCLA Asian American Studies Center, especially Mary Uyematsu Kao and Tam Nguyen. We also thank Muriel Bell, senior editor at Stanford University Press, who had been in conversation with Yuji for many years about this project, and the staff of Stanford University Press, especially Mariana Raykov and Joe Abbott, who supported this complicated posthumous effort with understanding and patience. Most of all, we thank Emma Gee, Yuji's lifelong companion and comrade. She provided essential help and direction for the completion of this volume. Emma herself has been an important figure in the inception and development of Asian American Studies, and it was Yuji's intention to dedicate this volume to her. And so it is.

Gordon H. Chang
Eiichiro Azuma

Editor's Introduction

Yuji Ichioka and New Paradigms
in Japanese American History

EIICHIRO AZUMA

Yuji Ichioka was a pioneer historian. During a span of over thirty years, from the establishment of Asian American Studies in U.S. universities in the late 1960s through the beginning of the twenty-first century, Ichioka was unarguably the most influential figure in the field of Japanese American history. Having been involved in the antiwar and civil rights movements in the 1960s, his life as a professional historian began as something inseparable from his ties to "community" and deep concerns for social justice. Not only did he revolutionize the practice of research and writing, which gave birth to Japanese American scholarship, but Ichioka also challenged long-standing interpretations, prompting "paradigm shifts" in the field. This volume, which explores the Japanese American experience of the hitherto neglected "interwar years," is no exception. The significance of *Before Internment* is best appreciated if it is read in light of Ichioka's overall scholarly trajectory from 1971 to his sudden passing in September 2002.

Through his many publications, including those collected in this volume, Yuji Ichioka called into question the master narrative that had been constructed over the years by white academicians, *Issei* intellectuals, and *Nisei* writers. Infused by the modernizationist assumptions of linear progress and the dominant "immigrant paradigm" of U.S. history, much of the existing literature on Japanese Americans structures historical narration around the question of assimilation (or the lack thereof), based on the polarizing notion of "America vs. Japan." However differently they explain such processes, orthodox histories have much in common in the privileging of exemplary

Issei and Nisei individuals (usually male entrepreneurs and intellectuals), in the emphasis on their "contributions" to U.S. society and economy, and in downplaying the force of racial restrictions in shaping the lives of Japanese Americans. One of the most extensively cited historical works, Yamato Ichihashi's *Japanese in the United States*, is representative of that master narrative, and Ichioka's critique of that book in Chapter 10 exemplifies the best of the "revisionist" thrust in his scholarship.[1] Ichioka unravels the basic assumptions and biases that underlie Ichihashi's work, but he does so with an understanding of the social conditions in which the Issei intellectual had to operate, as he also tries to historicize the production process of Ichihashi's study by bringing to the foreground the political agenda that influenced it.

Published in 1988, Ichioka's first book, *The Issei: The World of the First Generation Japanese Immigrants, 1885–1924*, was to change the established academic discourse on early Japanese immigrant history once and for all. Based on a collection of pathbreaking essays crafted between 1971 and 1985, *The Issei* centers the focus of historical research and interpretation on race, labor, and, to a lesser degree, gender. First and foremost Ichioka declares that Japanese immigrant history is "a history of a racial minority struggling to survive in a hostile land," which was "far from being a success story."[2] Rejecting the familiar scheme of acculturation and economic achievement, Ichioka illuminates the political disenfranchisement of the Issei, or the plight of "aliens ineligible to citizenship"—the legal status that kept them outside the American body politic and social life until the early 1950s. In his painstaking construction of various aspects of Issei history this theme occupied a central place after 1977, when he first took up *Ozawa vs. U.S.*, the case of Ozawa Takao, a longtime Japanese resident in Hawaii who in 1922 had taken his ultimately unsuccessful case for naturalization to the U.S. Supreme Court. Ichioka's study of the Ozawa case was so crucial that it has become a staple for Asian Americanists, immigration historians, and Critical Race theorists, among others, in discussing racial formations and processes in early-twentieth-century America.[3]

The Issei also emphasizes the importance of labor issues in the study of Japanese immigrant history. Since Ichioka characterizes Issei experience as "labor history," much of his narrative revolves around the explication of the activities of immigrant workers, labor contractors, and leftist dissidents.[4] For the first time in the history of Japanese Americans, Ichioka shifted attention from what white racism did to these "political pariahs" and "cheap labor" to how they fought and negotiated racism and exploitation. Some scholars in the 1970s called for a "history from the bottom up," but none were able to unearth the "buried past" of the Issei as substantively as Ichioka did, since the task of reading and interpreting Japanese-language materials was too onerous. His ability to take advantage of the rich collections of immigrant sources also allowed him to mitigate the male-centered nature of the existing scholarship. *The Issei* incorporates two articles on Issei women—prostitutes and immigrant wives—that he produced during the early years of his career.[5] Ichioka's insistence on bringing all these marginalized figures to the center of our historical consciousness signifies his radical politics, which not only sought to overcome the myth of Asian Americans as a model minority but also to connect Japanese immigrant experience to the struggles of many other people inside and outside the United States.

For all intents and purposes, *Before Internment* is a continuation of *The Issei*. Like its predecessor, *Before Internment* is a compilation of articles—published and unpublished—that Ichioka authored after 1985, though his untimely death prevented him from weaving these articles into more of a narrative, as he had done with the earlier volume. In 1986 he published one of the most important works that appears to have set the basic tone and direction of his scholarship after *The Issei*. In "A Study in Dualism," which is the fifth chapter of this volume, Ichioka led yet again a discursive shift in Japanese American history. Looking into the dilemmas on identity and politics of an early Nisei leader and newspaper publisher, James Y. Sakamoto, he introduced new paradigms—generation and dualism—into research on a Japanese American past from 1924 to 1941. As he expounds in his unfinished introduction to this volume, "historians have treated this period as an interlude between the Japanese exclusion movement . . . and the outbreak of the Second World War" or "as an incidental backdrop to mass internment" (3). No serious scholarly attention had been paid to the interwar years, which Ichioka saw as key to properly understanding what took place during the 1940s, especially the mass internment of Japanese Americans. As readers will be quick to perceive, the problems of generation (distinctions between the Issei and Nisei) and dualism (dual identities, affiliations, and loyalties) inform the discussions in this volume. Generation and dualism form the organizing grammar for Ichioka's narration of the collective experience of Japanese Americans during the 1930s.

New paradigms also called forth a reconsideration of the periodization of

Japanese American history. Ichioka chose to punctuate the second phase of Japanese American history with the transition of the 1930s not simply because the decade was when the Nisei came of age or because it was situated between the two distinct events that scholars have studied extensively. His periodization is suggestive of a more profound reconceptualization of Japanese American history. The first phase (and hence the first book) concluded with the passage of the Immigration Act of 1924 by the United States Congress, which Ichioka describes as the culmination of anti-Japanese racism and the end of mass migration, including common laborers and Issei women. In light of his interpretation of the early immigrant experience, then, the year 1924 marked a logical break in history. Here Ichioka's genius was also to find at the same historical moment the emergence of generational differences among Japanese Americans and growing ambiguities in their consciousness and practice. Therefore, in the context of post-1924 community formation, *Before Internment* concentrates on the contentious relations between the Issei and Nisei, the dilemmas for the Issei of educating their American-born children and for the Nisei of growing up as a racial minority, and the challenge of balancing ties and allegiances to America and Japan within a context of exacerbating bilateral relations.

In this volume Ichioka operates on the premise that the boundaries of the Issei and Nisei were forged as a matter not of simple age differences or cultural divides but of historical exigencies in the aftermath of racial exclusion. In the very last paragraph of *The Issei* he had already set up that scheme, discussing the ramifications of the 1924 law in this way:

> Japanese immigrants came to attach extra significance to the American-born generation. They transferred their hopes and aspirations onto the Nisei generation. The Issei could not escape the liability of being aliens ineligible to citizenship; the Nisei were American citizens who, in theory, had all the rights and privileges that came with their American citizenship. Since the Issei no longer perceived any real future for themselves, the Nisei's future, however precarious it appeared in 1924, suddenly loomed all-important to them. The future of the Japanese in the United States now depended on how their children would grow up and fare in their own native land.[6]

Generations, according to Ichioka, were fundamentally political constructs. The production of differences between the Issei and Nisei rested with their citizenship status, which was in and of itself a product of racial formation under white American hegemony.[7] As it was racism that arbitrarily distinguished "aliens" and "citizens" in the Japanese American population, *Before Internment* duly employs race as the key variable in the analysis of how the two generations of Japanese Americans thought, acted, and lived in the complex political spaces between the two nation-states prior to the Pacific War.

With the lens of generation, Ichioka was the first historian to examine the lives of both Japanese immigrants and their American-born children in an encompassing and integrated manner. As he notes in his brief introduction, several studies that treat the 1930s as their subject matter tend to look only at the doings of the Issei or of the Nisei but not both. The articles included in *Before Internment* indicate that Ichioka divided his attention almost evenly between the two groups; put together in one volume they provide a fuller and more nuanced picture of Japanese American intergenerational experience during the decade than is available elsewhere.

Ichioka also includes in this narrative yet another political construct, the *Kibei*, even though the coverage is not substantial. Born on United States soil but educated mainly in Japan, these second-generation youth formed a distinctive subgroup with a unique experience of their own. They added to the intricate entanglements of the generations in post-1924 Japanese America that Ichioka unveils in this book. The categories of the Issei, Nisei, and Kibei were so essential in the numerous studies of the wartime internment that our understanding has been structured in accordance with their alleged differences, rifts, and struggles that became manifest inside the camps. But contrary to conventional wisdom, as Ichioka shows in his introduction, division and contention already existed during the 1930s. The matter of generational differences serves as a good example of what he means by "significant continuities and discontinuities between [what transpired in] the 1930s and the 1940s," for without "taking into account the former," as he insists, "the latter cannot . . . be properly understood" (3). In this sense *Before Internment* is indispensable for substantive reevaluations of internment history.

Since Ichioka's interpretations necessitate historicizing the production of generational differences in the context of interwar American race relations, one may wonder why this volume offers only a limited discussion of the Kibei, who increased in number during the 1930s as a result of the Issei resolution to pass on to the second generation their tradition and language despite the prevailing racist denial of a Japanese heritage in the United

States. As Chapter 2 ("*Dai Nisei Mondai*") reveals, Ichioka was quite mindful of the topic, intending to write more about that subgroup after the publication of this volume—an idea he shared with this writer on numerous occasions. Yet Ichioka never realized his plan to organize a conference on the Kibei, where invited scholars would present academic papers while ordinary Kibei men and women discussed their personal experiences. Based on that conference, he envisioned editing a special issue of *Amerasia Journal* dedicated to the Kibei.

This is the strategy that he had employed to promote the studies of the interwar era and its relevance to the internment when very few had yet recognized the importance of, or cared to take on, such research. A 1985 "Coming of Age in the Thirties" conference he organized provided a forum for the unveiling of "A Study in Dualism" (Chapter 5), which was subsequently published in a special *Amerasia* edition on "Japanese Americans in the 1930s and 1940s." In much the same way, "The Meaning of Loyalty" (Chapter 7) came out of his 1995 symposium and a 1997 *Amerasia* issue entitled *Beyond National Boundaries: The Complexity of Japanese-American History*, which includes memoirs of some Kibei and Nisei residents in Japan. Following another academic conference in 1988, Ichioka also edited *Views from Within*, an anthology of essays that critically examines the meaning of social science research conducted in the camps and beyond, which subsequently helped compound slanted views on the three groups of Japanese Americans according to such sociological categories as "Americanized versus unassimilated." Ichioka interrogated the relationship between power and knowledge production because their entanglement made the studies of internment inescapably prejudiced and oppressive under the façade of scholarly objectivism. Common biases against the Kibei (unacculturated, pro-Japan, and disloyal), which the public now tends to wrongly accept as historical truth, were perpetuated, if not produced, by academic explanations provided by liberal social scientists in the camps. Ichioka was among the first historians who systematically scrutinized the manner in which Japanese Americans had been studied, which generally subjected the people to the objectifying gaze of white scholars, and to the theories and frameworks they constructed in the name of detached scientific research.[8]

Ichioka was always the trailblazer, and the articles in this volume mirror a critical historical method that is unparalleled in existing scholarship: to let the Issei and Nisei speak for themselves in their terms with all their faults and problems, including internal exploitation and racism against other minorities. Had illness and death not cut short his endeavor, he would have continued to rattle historical "common sense" and complicate our understanding with new discoveries and eye-opening arguments. But what is in *Before Internment* already shows younger generations of scholars what else needs to be undertaken, including an in-depth study of the Kibei experience. In particular, Chapter 2 provides a useful overview of the Nisei's generational dilemmas and challenges that the Issei conceived as "Dai Nisei Mondai" before the Pacific War. Published in Japanese in 1991, it contains overlaps with other chapters, as the treatise was not part of the original manuscript Ichioka had been preparing. Having revised the essay several times between 1984 and 1987, Ichioka appears to have relied on it as guidelines for research and writing in producing most of the chapters of this volume. The editors have elected to add "*Dai Nisei Mondai*" to this volume without modification in respect for the integrity of its narrative and arguments, since we believe that the chapter provides an invaluable window into the complexities of interwar Japanese America, which would certainly "stimulate future research" as Ichioka wished (4).[9]

The second paradigm around which *Before Internment* is organized, dualism, too, has profound implications for the future direction of Japanese American Studies and history writing. Ichioka first introduced this notion into his 1986 article, in which he explored the seemingly conflicting agendas of "full-blooded" Americanism (the Nisei as loyal citizens) and internationalism (the Nisei as a bridge of understanding between the United States and Japan), in the ideas of a key Nisei leader, James Y. Sakamoto. Placing this dualism in the context of ongoing white racism in the 1930s, Ichioka probes the strategic use of identities for survival among Japanese Americans. The idea of dualism debunks the established definitions of nation and culture (categories of "American" and "Japanese" as polar or incompatible opposites), as well as bounded notions of political identities and affiliations.[10] Building on this problematic, Ichioka goes on to tackle the thorny and highly sensitive issue of loyalty. Examining different responses of Issei and Nisei individuals, the chapters in Part II of this volume elucidate that "the question of loyalty was never black and white," especially when white society "overwhelmingly rejected the Nisei [and the Issei] on racial grounds" (171). As he argues convincingly, the experiences of marginalized people defy the "simplistic wartime categories of loyalty versus disloyalty" (156).

The problem of dualism accounts for what Ichioka calls "discontinuities between the 1930s and the 1940s." As Chapter 3 ("*Kengakudan*") and Chapter 4 ("*Kokugo Gakkō*") demonstrate, the internationalist ideal of the Nisei as a bridge of understanding constituted an important part of the intellectual current in the Japanese American community of the 1930s. Both Issei leaders and older Nisei embraced the idea, even though they differed in the practice. Their dualism, in the form of the bridge concept, nonetheless became "untenable" by 1940. Nisei leaders, like Sakamoto, "began to espouse Americanism exclusively and refashioned [their] original Americanism into a flag-waving form of 200 percent patriotism" (110) that naturally came into conflict with the Issei's continuous identification with Japan. Nisei expressions of cultural and political identity became so one-dimensional that it hardly entailed any trace of previous dualism. Internment history, as we know, is only an extension of this shift, which had already taken place around 1940.

Laying its focus on the questions of political identity and loyalty, *Before Internment* takes readers to highly controversial and sensitive terrain. Ichioka confronts the greatest "taboo" of Japanese American Studies: discussion of possibilities of espionage and subversion among some Japanese Americans before the attack on Pearl Harbor. While Chapter 7 traces the trajectory of Buddy Uno from a naive Nisei journalist to a propagandist on the Japanese side, Chapter 9 looks into the activities of Issei members of the Japanese Naval Association of Southern California in the 1941 Tachibana espionage case. Whether or not one agrees with his contention that the arrest of the implicated Issei in the Tachibana incident was justified, it is certainly courageous of Ichioka to problematize the biases embedded in Japanese American historiography that have categorically excluded the so-called disloyal.

In Ichioka's view the ongoing treatment of the disloyal as persona non grata in history represents an enduring legacy of white racism and the mass internment, which has disallowed recognition of complexities or ambiguities in our understanding of Issei and Nisei lives. Ichioka was fully cognizant of the political implications of history writing, as well as the danger that his revisionist endeavor might entail, in light of the dogged attempt in segments of white America to rationalize wartime internment even at the present. It is precisely for this reason that his article on Issei pro-Japan nationalism (Chapter 8) remained shelved until after the successful conclusion of the redress and reparations movement in 1988, even though it had been ready for publication for several years. In the post-redress era, when historical research and writing are no longer inseparable from community movements for justice, Ichioka stressed that it was high time for historians to grapple with controversial problems of political identity and so-called loyalty that they had hitherto dodged or neglected consciously or unconsciously. Buddy Uno, Furusawa Takashi and Sachiko (Chapter 9), and Honda Rikita (Chapter 11) are examples of such historical amnesia or denial.

While tackling the Tachibana espionage case was his way of being true to history's ambiguities and shades of meaning, Ichioka would nevertheless have little tolerance for a political exploitation of Japanese American history, just as he lambasted Page Smith's attempt to absolve America from the blame for the mass internment.[11] Now in post-9/11 America, conservatives have once again advocated the detention of "anti-American" elements (Muslims this time around) for "national security" without due process by citing historical precedents of alleged Issei and Nisei "treachery," including the activities of the Furusawas.[12] Had he observed such a distorted use of Japanese American history for "reactionary" politics, Ichioka would have been the first to fight it and insist that the individual allegations not be construed as representing the behavior and thinking of the entire group, let alone constituting any sort of justification for the indiscriminate suspension of their civil rights.

Finally, transnationalism is another important theme that infuses *Before Internment*. Because he appreciates the transnational nature of Japanese American lives, practices, and ideas, Ichioka was critical of single-nation frameworks that characterize U.S. scholarship on ethnic minorities and immigrants. In a fundamental sense his entire career could be described as a commitment to debunking nationalist narratives. As early as 1971, when it was still unpopular and even stigmatized among scholars of both the United States and Japan, he brought a transnational perspective to Japanese American history, calling for empirical research that would transcend national boundaries. In his very first published essay Ichioka declared, "Japanese-American history must be studied alongside the history of modern Japan." He made it clear, however, that this "does not mean the two are synonymous" because "Japanese-American history after all is an integral part of American history, the essential larger context from which its basic meaning derives."[13] More than thirty years ago, in simple language, if not articulated as theory and devoid of trendy academic jargon and convoluted expression, the pioneer historian already ventured into questions of the global versus the local, as well as of the tensions and entanglements between Asian American (ethnic) Studies and Asian (area) Studies that have drawn critical considerations in both fields in recent years.

Ichioka also spearheaded internationalizing Japanese American history by attempting to extend the scope of research and analysis from the confines of United States society to the entire Americas, an ongoing development that has led to several publications.[14] While personally traveling to Brazil, Peru, and Mexico for networking and research, he invited Latin American scholars, like Mary Fukumoto of Peru, for lectures during the 1990s, and he also encouraged U.S. scholars to take up comparative studies of Japanese experiences in the Western Hemisphere. Prepared for a public lecture in 1999, "The Future of Japanese-American Studies" (Chapter 12) succinctly explains Ichioka's rationale for transnational perspectives on *Nikkei* (people of Japanese ancestry) in the Americas, and as one can see, his primary interest remains the same as three decades ago. Ichioka continued to focus on "the essential . . . context from which [the] basic meaning" of a collective experience "derives," that is, a society in which Issei and Nisei lived their everyday lives as Nikkei under the constraints of a hegemonic power. To Ichioka, being Nikkei takes many shapes and forms, but their differences are bound to the specific manners in which political economies operate in various countries. In a comparative setting, then, juxtaposing Nikkei histories in different societies ultimately serves a pivotal goal of deepening an understanding of Japanese Americans' racial position in the United States, and of the impact of American racism on their identity formation that set them apart decidedly from others, especially those in Brazil.

Although Ichioka was unable to produce a comparative historical study in his lifetime, *Before Internment*, in its own light, offers an excellent example of a transnational history based on substantive archival research. All the discussions here deal with aspects of Issei and Nisei lives that overarched the Pacific Ocean, in consciousness or actual practice. Critical of ahistorical abstractions, Ichioka was insistent on appreciating the complex agency of the people in the context of their times with the help of the vernacular documents that they left behind. His transnational approach naturally entailed the collection and organization of Japanese-language source materials from inside and outside the United States. When teaching this writer how to do Japanese American history, Ichioka stressed that it should not only involve telling a story from one perspective or another but also help preserve the remains of the people's activities and thinking—the primary sources that would allow other historians to tell different and perhaps more informed stories in the future.[15] Archival research was central, he asserted, because that is where historians would be able to establish meaningful connections to the people they study. Theories would be meaningless unless they are predicated on the analysis of the people's voices—however fragmented. Thus, an important aspect of Ichioka's professional life was devoted to the development and expansion of the Japanese American Research Project (JARP) Collection at UCLA, the best archives of Japanese immigrant materials in the nation, soon to be renamed the Yuji Ichioka-JARP Collection.

His sophisticated approach and methodology notwithstanding, Ichioka would have hated to be associated with any theoretical school or position. His essays are full of fascinating conceptualization and interpretation, but he was impatient of fuzzy theorization without consideration of concrete social realities and historical contexts. Ever committed to social justice and the interest of his community, Ichioka knew too well where he stood first and what he was concerned about most. "Although bilingual and bicultural," he notes in his last published article (Chapter 13), "I identify myself as an American committed to politically changing our country for the better" (296). This political impulse characterizes his style of writing, which values clarity so as to be able to also reach ordinary readers outside academia. Thus, Ichioka declared that he still believed in "the old-time practice of doing narrative history, of telling a story in ordinary language based on substantive research in primary sources" (296). As readers will see, *Before Internment* indeed does all that, but it is hardly "old-fashioned." With new paradigms and a transnational approach to uncover interwar Japanese American history, this book no doubt opens up new horizons for research and learning. *Before Internment* is another milestone built by Yuji Ichioka, the pioneer historian in Japanese American Studies.

Notes

1. Other prewar English-language works that helped define academic discourses on Japanese immigrant experience include Sidney L. Gulick, *The American Japanese Problem* (New York: Charles Scriber's Sons, 1914); Harry A. Millis, *The Japanese Problem in the United States* (New York: Macmillan, 1915); Karl K. Kawakami, *The Real Japanese Question* (New York: Macmillan, 1921); E. Manchester Boddy, *Japanese in America* (Los Angeles: E. Manchester Boddy, 1921); Eliot

G. Mears, *Residential Orientals on the American Pacific Coast* (Chicago, IL: University of Chicago Press, 1928); and Jean Pajus, *The Real Japanese California* (Berkeley, CA: J. J. Gillick, 1937), among others. Most of these works were produced in the context of anti-Japanese agitation, with the specific goal of either refuting or supporting racial exclusion. Before the war Issei intellectuals were also active in the construction of specific historical narratives in search of national inclusion. Their vernacular publications are too numerous to list, but for a detailed analysis of Japanese immigrant history making see Eiichiro Azuma, "The Politics of Transnational History Making: Japanese Immigrants on the Western 'Frontier,' 1927–1941," *Journal of American History* 89, no. 4 (March 2003): 1401–30. After the war Nisei writers joined the process of history making. The most prolific writer is Bill Hosokawa, whose works have contributed to the emergence of orthodoxy on the Nisei. See Hosokawa, *Nisei: The Quiet Americans: The Story of a People* (New York: Morrow, 1969); Robert A. Wilson and Bill Hosokawa, *East to America: A History of the Japanese in the United States* (New York: Morrow, 1980); and Bill Hosokawa, *JACL: In Quest of Justice* (New York: Morrow, 1982). Other postwar metanarratives of Japanese American history are Bradford Smith, *Americans from Japan* (Philadelphia: Lippincott, 1948); William Petersen, *Japanese Americans: Oppression and Success* (New York: Random House, 1971); and H. Brett Melendy, *The Oriental Americans* (New York: Hippocrene Books, 1972).

2. Yuji Ichioka, *The Issei: The World of the First Generation Japanese Immigrants, 1885–1924* (New York: Free Press, 1988), 1.

3. Yuji Ichioka, "The Early Japanese Immigrant Quest for Citizenship: The Background of the 1922 Ozawa Case," *Amerasia Journal* 4, no. 2 (1977): 1–22. This article went on to occupy a key place in Ichioka's first book.

4. See Ichioka, *The Issei*, 2. With an interest in labor issues, he also edited an autobiography of a Kibei communist-union organizer, Karl G. Yoneda, *Ganbatte: Sixty-Year Struggle of a Kibei Worker* (Los Angeles: UCLA Asian American Studies Center, 1983).

5. Yuji Ichioka, "*Ameyuki-san*: Japanese Prostitutes in Nineteenth Century America," *Amerasia Journal* 4, no. 1 (1977): 1–21; and Yuji Ichioka, "*America Nadeshiko*: Japanese Immigrant Women in the United States, 1900–1924," *Pacific Historical Review* 48 (1980): 339–57.

6. Ichioka, *The Issei*, 253–54.

7. Students of "assimilation" usually understand generational divides as a natural manifestation of cultural clashes between "America" and the "Old World."

8. See, e.g., Lane Ryo Hirabayashi, *The Politics of Fieldwork: Research in an American Concentration Camp* (Tucson: University of Arizona Press, 1999); and Henry Yu, *Thinking Orientals: Migration, Contact, and Exoticism in Modern America* (New York: Oxford University Press, 2001).

9. For the Japanese version see Ichioka Yūji, "Dai-Nisei Mondai, 1902–1941," trans. Sakata Yasuo, in *Hokubei Nihonjin Kirisutokyō Undōshi* [History of Japanese Christian Activities in North America], ed. Dōshisha Daigaku Jinbun Kagaku Kenkyūjo, 731–84 (Tokyo: PMC Shuppan, 1991).

10. Clearly this idea has influenced how Lon Kurashige (Nisei "biculturalism") and Azuma (Issei "eclecticism") analyze their subjects in their respective works. See Kurashige, "Problem of Biculturalism"; and Eiichiro Azuma, *Between Two Empires: Race, History, and Transnationalism in Japanese America* (New York: Oxford University Press, 2005).

11. See Ichioka's review of Page Smith, *Democracy on Trial: Japanese American Evacuation and Relocation in World War II* (New York: Simon and Schuster, 1995), in *Pacific Historical Review* 65 (August 1996): 498–99.

12. For example, see Michelle Malkin, *In Defense of Internment: The Case for "Racial Profiling" in World War II and the War on Terror* (New York: Regnery, 2004).

13. Yuji Ichioka, "A Buried Past: Early Issei Socialists and the Japanese Community," *Amerasia Journal* 1, no. 2 (July 1971): 15.

14. On his early formulation see Yuji Ichioka, "Nikkei in the Western Hemisphere," *Amerasia Journal* 15, no. 2 (1989): 175–77. For an example of comparative Nikkei studies, albeit not historical, see Lane Ryo Hirabayashi, Akemi Kikumura-Yano, and James A. Hirabayashi, eds., *New Worlds/New Lives: Globalization and People of Japanese Decent in the Americas and from Latin America in Japan* (Stanford: Stanford University Press, 2002).

15. Ichioka was fond of characterizing Issei history as a "buried past," for scholars have neglected to use the immigrant-language material—the best source of historical information in his opinion. To help unearth it, Ichioka believed in historians' responsibility for the preservation of primary source documents. On his philosophy of combining history writing and archival development see Yuji Ichioka et al., *A Buried Past: An Annotated Bibliography of the Japanese American Research Project Collection* (Berkeley: University of California Press, 1974), 3–15; and Yuji Ichioka and Eiichiro Azuma, *A Buried Past: A Sequel to the Annotated Bibliography of the Japanese American Research Project Collection* (Los Angeles: UCLA Asian American Studies Center, 1999), v.

Before Internment

PART ONE

Introduction

Yuji Ichioka died before finishing his introduction. Although it is incomplete, the editors have included the author's draft, including the endnotes, with some minor stylistic revisions. Editorial additions are in brackets.

Until recently studies of Japanese American history have paid very little attention to the decades before World War II. As a general rule, they have treated the interwar period as an interlude between the Japanese exclusion movement, which culminated in the enactment of the 1924 Immigration Act, terminating all Japanese immigration, and the outbreak of World War II and the ensuing dramatic wartime mass internment of Japanese Americans. Historians understandably have been preoccupied with the internment of Japanese Americans and, consequently, have paid and continue to pay extraordinary attention to this topic. If they examine the interwar years at all, they tend to look at the period simply as an incidental backdrop to mass internment.[1]

The result has been to obscure significant continuities and discontinuities between the 1930s and 1940s. What happened in the interwar period had a definite influence on events during the internment period, so much so, indeed, that the latter cannot, in my judgment, be properly understood without taking into account the former. In other words, the mass internment of Japanese Americans cannot be fully comprehended without an understanding of the historical continuities and discontinuities between the 1930s and 1940s.

Clearly not comprehensive, this anthology of essays covers selected topics in prewar Japanese American history. Of the eight essays, six have been previously published, and two are new, unpublished pieces, "*Kokugo Gakkō*" [Chapter 4] and "National Security on the Eve of Pearl Harbor" [Chapter 9]. The published essays are reprinted here with minor changes and additions. All of the essays here are a sequel to my book *The Issei: The World of the First Generation Japanese Immigrants, 1885–1924*. I hope that these essays will stimulate future researchers to link the interwar period to studies of wartime years.

Several noteworthy studies devoted to the prewar period have been recently published. Eileen Tamura examines the *Nisei* [U.S.-born, second generation] in Hawaii and their acculturation under pressures to Americanize while forging a distinctive ethnic identity during the 1920s and 1930s.[2] Jere Takahashi analyzes the shifting political perspective of the Nisei and *Sansei* [third] generations during the prewar, wartime, and postwar periods.[3] David Yoo looks at the complex social, cultural, and religious milieu in which the Nisei came of age in the 1930s.[4] Valerie Matsumoto probes into the prewar lives of young Nisei women.[5] Lon Kurashige studies the history of the Nisei Week Festival in Los Angeles in terms of changing Japanese American ethnic identity.[6] In all of these studies, however, notwithstanding the *Issei* generation's relationship to and influences on the Nisei generation, the Issei are conspicuously absent.

To broaden and deepen our historical understanding of the wartime years, the Issei generation should be studied in much greater depth. Many research topics remain untouched. Here the problem of language presents itself. Past and present researchers, with few exceptions, have failed to examine available Japanese language sources.[7] To redress the imbalance caused by the almost exclusive reliance on English-language sources, future researchers must equip themselves with the necessary language skills to conduct research in Japanese-language sources. The best collection of such sources is the Japanese American Research Project Collection (JARP) at UCLA, which affords an unrivalled opportunity to explore almost every aspect of prewar, wartime, and postwar Issei life.[8]

Five of the essays in this collection cover one aspect or another of the Issei generation during the prewar period. Taken together, they mark a small beginning in highlighting some of the significant continuities and discontinuities between the 1930s and 1940s. The essay "*Kengakudan*" [Chapter 3] examines the origin of organized Nisei tours of Japan and the Issei concept of the Nisei as a so-called bridge of understanding between Japan and the United States. Nisei tours began with the first two sponsored by the *Nichibei Shimbun* in 1925 and 1926 and continued through the 1930s under the sponsorship of various community organizations. The purpose of the tours was to give the Nisei firsthand exposure to Japanese society and culture in order to stimulate their interest in their ancestral land so that they would eventually assume the role of a bridge of understanding. Once war clouds began to hover over U.S.-Japan relations on the eve of Pearl Harbor, however, these tours were discontinued abruptly. At the same time, the concept of the Nisei as a bridge of understanding became an untenable ideal.

The next essay, "*Kokugo Gakkō*," presents the Issei debate over the role of Japanese-language schools after the enactment of the 1924 Immigration Act, when Issei leaders and educators, in assessing the future of the Nisei generation, earnestly debated the pros and cons of maintaining such schools to educate the Nisei. The Issei did not operate Japanese-language schools to mold Nisei youngsters to be loyal "subjects" of the Japanese emperor as alleged by anti-Japanese exclusionists. There were considerable differences of opinion among Issei leaders and educators about the role of the schools; some even favored abolishing them altogether. In the end those in favor of the preservation of the schools prevailed over their opponents, and by the 1930s no one questioned the value of their continued existence.

The third essay on the Issei, "Japanese Immigrant Nationalism" [Chapter 8], covers the pro-Japan activities of the Issei after the outbreak of the Sino-Japanese War in July 1937. Apart from a few Issei who ideologically opposed Japan's military aggression in China, the majority of Issei, regardless of class, gender, religion, or locale, overwhelmingly rallied behind their homeland. The United States Department of Justice arrested and detained all Issei who were classified as so-called dangerous enemy aliens in the immediate aftermath of Pearl Harbor. These Issei included officers in local Japanese associations and chambers of commerce; Japanese-language school principals and teachers; newspaper publishers, editors, and reporters; religious leaders, especially those of Buddhist and Shinto sects; and heads and officers of cultural organizations and women's societies. The government's classification of "dangerous enemy alien" was based on surveillance reports compiled by the FBI and military intelligence agencies on the Issei. Thus the wartime arrest and detention of Issei leaders classified as dangerous enemy aliens were directly related to their prewar pro-Japan activities.

This essay documents how the Issei supported their homeland during the Sino-Japanese War without comparing their pro-Japan activities to intelligence reports. It should be noted here that such activities were *not* criminal offenses punishable by law. Separate from acts of espionage, sabotage, or subversion, they were simply expressions of Issei nationalism and patriotic identification with their homeland's cause in Asia.

In the fourth Issei essay, "National Security on the Eve of Pearl Harbor" [Chapter 9], covering the Tachibana Incident of 1941, which did involve espionage, I probe into the activities of the Issei members of the Japanese Navy Association of Southern California, look at the surveillance reports of the FBI and Office of Naval Intelligence, and conclude that the arrest and detention of the implicated Issei were warranted [but not the denial of due process of law]. Future research should further explore and demonstrate how the pro-Japan activities of the Issei, contrary to that of the implicated Issei in the Tachibana Incident, wrongfully led the FBI to classify them as dangerous enemy aliens and to their wartime arrest, detention, and imprisonment.

Issei nationalism caused splits within the prewar Japanese community that resurfaced in the wartime internment camps. First, it created a deep rift between the Issei generation and segments of the Nisei generation. This rift was caused by the cooperation of the Japanese American Citizens League (JACL), the principal civic organization of the Nisei generation, with American intelligence agencies. The FBI and military intelligence solicited information from JACL leaders about Issei leaders in investigating the Issei political activities. Although the exact extent to which the JACL cooperated with the FBI and army and naval intelligence is as yet unclear, it is a fact that some leaders did act as informants. For example, the Anti-Axis Committees of the JACL in Los Angeles, formed on the eve of Pearl Harbor, actively cooperated with Lieutenant Commander Kenneth Ringle, naval intelligence officer of the Eleventh Naval District of Southern California. The information supplied by JACL informants served, in part, as the basis for the dangerous enemy alien classification, earning the JACL the reputation of being a "stoolie" organization before Pearl Harbor. In 1942, protest demonstrations, often of a violent and anti-JACL nature, erupted at Manzanar and other internment camps. The wartime expressions of anti-JACL sentiments had their origin in the JACL's prewar collusion with the FBI and military intelligence.

Issei nationalism was behind another split within the Japanese community.

Dating back to the early 1920s, there was a small but vocal left within the community composed of a handful of Issei, Kibei, and a few Nisei, many of whom were members of the American Communist Party. Ideologically opposed to Japanese militarism and expansion onto the Asian continent, these leftists were always at odds with Issei leaders who patriotically backed Japan in the Sino-Japanese War. In Southern California Fujii Sei, Issei publisher and editor of the *Kashū Mainichi* and Shuji Fujii, Nisei editor of the *Dōhō*, a leftist weekly, engaged in heated exchanges over the Sino-Japanese War. Fujii Sei rabidly supported Japan and exhorted the Issei to do likewise, while Shuji Fujii denounced Fujii Sei and his patriotic Issei cohorts as pro-Japanese militarists. On the eve of Pearl Harbor, in accord with the Comintern's policy of a united front against fascism, the leftists urged Japanese-Americans to rally behind the JACL and its espousal of Americanism and allied themselves with the JACL through the war years.

"'Attorney for the Defense'" [Chapter 10] is devoted to Yamato Ichihashi, longtime professor of Japanese Studies at Stanford University and author of *Japanese in the United States*, published in 1932. Ichihashi was appointed to his Stanford professorship under special circumstances. After the enactment of the 1913 California Alien Land Law, the Japanese Foreign Ministry launched a "campaign of education" as a countermeasure to the anti-Japanese exclusion movement. The purpose of the campaign was to educate Americans about Japan and Japanese immigration. To accomplish this purpose in American higher education, the Foreign Ministry provided initial funds to Stanford University to enable it to hire Ichihashi in 1914 and subsequently endowed his position as a permanent chair. This essay covers the special circumstances of Ichihashi's appointment at Stanford, analyzes how he had to maintain a delicate balance between his obligations to the Japanese Foreign Ministry and to Stanford University, and examines how this sense of obligation influenced the writing and content of *Japanese in the United States*.[9]

The balance of three essays is on the Nisei generation. [One is on a Slovenian observer of the Nisei in the late 1930s and 1940s.] The other two essays are devoted to specific individuals, two Nisei contemporaries in journalism. The essay "'Unity Within Diversity'" [Chapter 6] is on Louis Adamic and the Nisei in a Eurocentric America. Adamic was a forerunner of today's advocates of diversity and multiculturalism. In 1940 he came to the attention of Japanese Americans with the publication of his book *From Many Lands*, an anthology of stories about different immigrant groups, including a portrait of an alienated Nisei under the title "A Young American with a Japanese Face."

"A Study in Dualism" [Chapter 5] is on James Yoshinori Sakamoto (1901– 1955), publisher and editor of the *Japanese American Courier*. An English weekly newspaper, the *Courier* was published from 1928 to 1942 out of Seattle, Washington. Sakamoto was one of the founding fathers of the JACL and an ardent advocate of the Americanization of the Nisei generation. He was also an enthusiastic adherent of the ideal of the Nisei as a bridge of understanding between Japan and the United States. The ideal of a bridge took on a new political dimension in the wake of the 1931 Manchurian Incident and the establishment of the puppet state of Manchukuo by the Japanese government in 1932. From this time the Nisei were expected to explain and justify Japan's policy toward China. Throughout the 1930s Sakamoto consistently defended Japan's military actions in China. In sum, the *Japanese American Courier* served as a vehicle throughout the 1930s for Sakamoto to promote and advance his brand of Americanism and to practice the ideal of the Nisei as a bridge of understanding as he understood it.

"The Meaning of Loyalty" [Chapter 7] is on Nisei Kazumaro "Buddy" Uno. [A controversial figure to this day, Buddy Uno (1913–1954) sided with Japan during the Pacific War. His case "raises a fundamental historical question. What is the meaning of loyalty in a racist society?"]

[Ichioka's incomplete introduction ends here].

Notes

1. See, for example, Sandra C. Taylor, *Jewel of the Desert: Japanese American Internment at Topaz* (Berkeley: University of California Press, 1993).

2. Eileen H. Tamura, *Americanization, Acculturation and Ethnic Identity: The Nisei Generation in Hawaii* (Urbana: University of Illinois Press, 1994).

3. Jere Takahashi, *Nisei/Sansei: Shifting Japanese American Identities and Politics* (Philadelphia: Temple University Press, 1997).

4. David K. Yoo, *Growing Up Nisei: Race, Generation, and Culture Among Japanese Americans of California, 1924–1949* (Urbana: University of Illinois Press, 2000).

5. Among Valerie Matsumoto's contributions are "Desperately Seeking 'Deirdre': Gender Roles, Multicultural Relations, and Nisei Women Writers of the 1930s," *Frontiers: A Journal of Women's Studies* 12 (1991): 19–32; "Redefining Expectations: Nisei Women in the 1930s," *California History* 73, no. 1 (1994): 44–53, 88;

and "Japanese American Women and the Creation of Urban Nisei Culture in the 1930s," in *Over the Edge: Remapping the American West*, ed. Valerie J. Matsumoto and Blake Allmendinger (Berkeley: University of California Press, 1999): 291–306.

6. Lon Kurashige, *Japanese American Celebration and Conflict: A History of Ethnic Identity and Festival, 1934–1990* (Berkeley: University of California Press, 2002).

7. There are a few notable exceptions to this generalization: Brian M. Hayashi, *"For the Sake of Our Japanese Brethren": Assimilation, Nationalism, and Protestantism Among the Japanese of Los Angeles, 1895–1942* (Stanford: Stanford University Press, 1995); Yukiko Kimura, *Issei: Japanese Immigrants in Hawaii* (Honolulu: University of Hawaii Press, 1988); Eiichiro Azuma, "Interethnic Conflict under Racial Subordination: Japanese Immigrants and Their Asian Neighbors in Walnut Grove, California, 1908–1941," *Amerasia Journal* 20, no. 2 (1994): 27–56; and Eiichiro Azuma, "Racial Struggle: Immigrant Nationalism and Ethnic Identity: Japanese and Filipinos in the California Delta, 1930–1941," *Pacific Historical Review* 67, no. 2 (1998): 163–199; and Eriko Yamamoto, "Cheers for Japanese Athletes: The 1932 Los Angeles Olympics and the Japanese American Community," *Pacific Historical Review* 69, no. 3 (2000): 399–430.

8. See Yuji Ichioka et. al., *A Buried Past: An Annotated Bibliography of the Japanese American Research Project Collection* (Berkeley: University of California Press, 1974); Yasuo Sakata, *Fading Footsteps of the Issei: An Annotated Checklist of the Manuscript Holdings of the Japanese American Research Project Collection* (Los Angeles: Asian American Studies Center, UCLA, 1992); and Yuji Ichioka and Eiichiro Azuma, *A Buried Past II: A Sequel to the Annotated Bibliography of the Japanese American Research Project Collection* (Los Angeles: Asian American Studies Center, UCLA, 1999).

9. See Yamato Ichihashi, *Japanese in the United States: A Critical Study of the Problems of the Japanese Immigrants and Their Children* (Stanford, CA: Stanford University Press, 1932). Ichihashi is the subject of a recent excellent study. See Gordon H. Chang's *Morning Glory, Evening Shadow: Yamato Ichihashi and His Internment Writings, 1942–1945* (Stanford, CA: Stanford University Press, 1997).

Dai Nisei Mondai

Changing Japanese Immigrant Conceptions of the Second-Generation Problem, 1902 – 1941

One of the recurring problems the Japanese immigrant generation faced was the vexatious question of the future of their American-born children, the *Nisei*. The Nisei became a recognizable element within the Japanese immigrant population from 1910. In 1900 there were only 269 Nisei children in the continental United States, but by 1910 the number of Nisei increased to 4,502. By 1920 the number multiplied more than sixfold to 29,672, and by 1930 the figure leaped to 68,357. Growing further to 79,642 by 1940, the Nisei outnumbered the *Issei* by two to one on the eve of Pearl Harbor. In the copious historical and sociological literature on the Nisei, very little, if any, attention has been paid to what the Issei called the "dai nisei mondai," or the second-generation problem. The Issei had many different expectations of the Nisei generation. Evolving over the years, these expectations reflected their own shifting orientation toward American society and the influences of the anti-Japanese exclusion movement, the maturation of the first-born Nisei, and the turn of political events in the Far East. This chapter will present a historical analysis of the Issei generation's changing conceptions of the second-generation problem from 1902 to 1941.

Nisei Education and Dual Nationality

In the late nineteenth and early twentieth centuries, Japanese immigrants recognized no Nisei problem. The immigrants landed in the United States with a *dekasegi* ideal. Their goal was to earn money and then to return to their homeland, where, ideally, they would enjoy a retired life of ease. Three common phrases embodied the *dekasegi* ideal: *toshu kūken*, meaning to be empty-handed, described the destitute state in which the immigrants arrived; *ikkaku senkin* expressed the dream of striking it rich overnight; and *kin'i kikyō* meant to return home as wealthy persons, the dream of dreams. A *dekasegi-rōdōsha* was an itinerant laborer; a *dekasegi-shosei* was a student laborer. To educate the first-born Nisei children, the immigrants established Japanese-language schools very early, the first one in Seattle in 1902, followed by others in San Francisco, Sacramento, and other locales. The purpose of these early schools coincided with the *dekasegi* ideal. The schools were supposed to educate the Nisei to enable them to enroll in the public schools of Japan. In 1932 an Issei educator succinctly described this initial orientation:

> In the past the majority of Japanese in America and Canada were under the sway of the *dekasegi* spirit. We crossed the vast Pacific in order to earn money. The land here was only a temporary place to earn a living, a travel lodge as it were, with our real home being in Japan where the cherry blossoms bloom. Hence we thought we had to educate our children accordingly. Some of us sent our children back to Japan to be cared for and educated by grandparents, siblings, or other relatives at home. For those unable to send children back . . . , we felt compelled to offer a "Japanese" education to them here. To achieve this end, we founded special schools—Japanese schools and language institutes. During this period, these schools mainly had the purpose of preparing the children to return to Japan.[1]

In California, a recognition of a Nisei educational problem surfaced in 1908. The first editorial on Nisei education in the *Shin Sekai* appeared in May 1908.[2] While not dogmatically opposed to the establishment of "pure" Japanese schools, the editorial questioned the value of such schools in view of the likelihood that school-age Nisei youngsters would be sent to American public schools. The *Beikoku Bukkyō*, official organ of the Buddhist Mission of America, carried an interesting article in September 1908.[3] The article was devoted to the ignorance of Japan exhibited by Nisei children. When asked about what they would like to become, some children replied that they aspired to become the emperor of Japan. According to the article this answer reflected the baneful influence of the American environment. Under the sway of the American folk belief that anyone could aspire to become the president of the United States, such children erroneously equated the emperor with the president. This example was an omen of grave problems that loomed in the near future. In 1908 the Japanese Association of America, the principal political organization of Japanese immigrants, conducted a survey to determine the exact number of Nisei children in the San Francisco area.[4] On discovering a sizable number of school-age children, immigrant leaders formed a special group to discuss the educational problems of the Nisei. Organized in early 1909, this group was called the Mokuyōbikai, or Thursday Club.

In the summer of 1909 the *Shin Sekai* raised a fundamental question regarding dual nationality.[5] Based on the principle of *jus soli*, all Nisei children had American citizenship by virtue of being born on American soil. At the same time, they were Japanese subjects based on the opposite principle of *jus sanguinis*. Since Japanese law determined nationality by paternal descent, all Nisei with Japanese fathers automatically had Japanese citizenship. The *Shin Sekai* editorialized that this dual nationality of the Nisei would become a thorny problem in the future, especially in view of the military service obligation in Japan. Rather than wait until the problem became a pressing reality, the newspaper advised immigrant parents to decide whether or not they were going to settle down in the United States. If they were settling down permanently, they should raise their children as Americans and, accordingly, seek to solve the problem of dual nationality. These first signs of a shifting attitude did not signify the erosion of the *dekasegi* ideal. They were simply an early recognition that the American-born generation had unique problems that warranted serious attention.

This realization soon manifested itself in a new educational plan. After studying the educational problems of Nisei youngsters, the Thursday Club drafted a plan for a new Japanese-language school to accommodate the growing number of Nisei children in San Francisco. "The cardinal principle" of the plan was that the education of the Nisei "must be principally the assimilation of American customs and manners, supplemented by education in other essential ideas so that they will not forget the motherland."[6] This plan called for a kindergarten and primary division. The former would accommodate preschool children to teach them English in order to prepare them for American public schools. To insure that they would learn "proper" English, the kindergarten division would employ white American teachers. The primary division would offer supplementary education in Japanese ethics, history, geography, and language to school-age children who were already attending American public schools. The Thursday Club submitted this plan in January 1910 to the Japanese Association of America for its consideration.

In January 1910 the Japanese Association of America convened its annual assembly with representatives of affiliated local associations. The Thursday Club plan appeared on the agenda, and the assembly adopted the plan without any modification.[7] To find a qualified principal for the future school, the assembly voted to seek the assistance of Nitobe Inazō in Japan and appointed a special education committee empowered to implement the plan. In June this newly appointed committee, using the identical language of the Thursday Club, affirmed that the education of the Nisei "must be the assimilation of American customs and manners." The Thursday Club plan embodied a definite change in ideas. In place of the simple notion, derived from the *dekasegi* ideal, that the Nisei should be educated to enable them to enter the public schools of Japan, it recognized the primacy of an American public school education and the importance of assimilating into American society. The adoption of the plan by the Japanese Association of America and its affiliated local associations indicated that this change in ideas was not limited to the members of the Thursday Club but was shared by other immigrant leaders as well.

Subsequently, a full-scale debate on the subject of Nisei education occurred within immigrant society. A speech by Consul Nagai Matsuzō of San Francisco sparked it. In July Consul Nagai delivered an address at Alviso, near San Jose. The occasion was the opening of a new Japanese-language school. As a Japanese diplomat, Nagai was an advocate of permanent settlement. He believed that Japanese immigrants had to discard their *dekasegi* ideal. He also believed that Nisei children should be educated exclusively as Americans. Nagai frankly expressed his opinions at the opening of the Alviso school, going as far as to assert that Japanese-language schools were not necessary at all.[8] Nagai's speech shocked his audience. After all, they had assembled to celebrate the opening of the new Alviso school. Shortly after, Takahashi Hōnen, principal of the new school, publicly assailed Nagai, and the ensuing publicity surrounding Nagai's speech produced a lively debate on the education of the Nisei.

As the debate was carried on, most participants did not see an irreconcilable conflict between a Japanese and American education.[9] The debate focused on the relative value of each. Some stressed the central importance of an American education; others upheld the primacy of a Japanese education; still others assigned equal weight to both a Japanese and American education. Special terms were coined to distinguish these different positions. *Beishu Nichijū* designated the first position, while *Nisshu Beijū* represented the second. *Setchūron* described the third position, *setchū* being the Japanese word meaning compromise. Notwithstanding these designations, however, the debate was never very clear, for no one precisely defined the meaning of a Japanese and American education. Those who favored the primacy of a Japanese education insisted that it should be based on the old Meiji shibboleth, *chūkun aikoku*. Yet no one bothered to elaborate on the exact content of such a Japanese education. Be that as it may, the fact that Japanese immigrants engaged in this debate indicated that they had begun to modify their views on the education of the Nisei as they themselves were casting off their *dekasegi* ideal.

Between 1911 and America's entry into World War I, the Japanese immigrants' perspective on the second-generation problem changed decisively. In accordance with the Thursday Club plan, in 1911, the Kimmon Gakuen or Golden Gate Institute was inaugurated in San Francisco. Headed by Kamada Masayoshi, who had been recommended by Nitobe Inazō, it was to become the largest school in northern California. The Thursday Club had been endorsed by the Japanese associations as a model for all schools in other locales, but no organization had been formed to unify the schools into a single system. The schools all functioned independently—they set their own goals, formed their own curriculum, and selected their own textbooks. One effect of the debate on Nisei education was to draw attention to the need to create a unified system under which all the schools could be operated. In 1910, and again in 1911, the *Shin Sekai* suggested repeatedly that a statewide conference of educators should be convened to consider this matter, but it was not until 1912 that such a conference was actually convened.[10]

Sponsored by the Japanese Association of America and held in San Francisco, the 1912 conference marked a watershed in the ongoing debate on Nisei education. For the first time, immigrant educators from throughout the state of California assembled together. Thirty-four educators in all attended the conference, which focused on the goal of Japanese language schools. The educators adopted three broad resolutions. Pertaining to the fundamental purpose of the schools, the first two resolutions read: "1) The main objective will be to educate future permanent residents of the United

States; and 2) Recognizing the necessity of an American education, Japanese schools will provide supplementary instruction in Japanese and education about Japan."[11]

The debate over the relative value of an American and Japanese education was settled. Declaring that the Nisei should be educated as permanent residents, the immigrant educators at this historic 1912 conference unequivocally accepted the primacy of an American public school education. In the words of Kamada Masayoshi, the educators' long-run goal was "to produce individuals who will be able to stand up for the rights and privileges of the Japanese people among Americans. To achieve this end, we must enroll Nisei children in American public schools and have them educated in the same manner as white children. To teach them about Japan and the Japanese language, we must provide supplementary education in Japanese schools."[12]

The Issei educators at the conference retained certain Japanese educational ideas. They made the distinction between intellectual (*chi*), moral (*toku*), and physical (*tai*) education. An American public school education, they believed, satisfied the requirements of an intellectual and physical education but not those of a moral education. The educators insisted that the moral education of the Nisei had to be based on the Imperial Rescript on Education. Some had misgivings and qualified their acceptance of the Rescript, however. Such educators were wary of promoting what they called "parochialism" among Nisei youngsters. The Rescript had been promulgated with the Japanese people in Japan in mind. If those aspects of the Rescript that were unique to Japan were emphasized unduly, the wary educators with misgivings about basing the Imperial Rescript for the moral education of the Nisei were afraid that they would create an insular mentality among Nisei children that would hinder the children's ability to adapt to American society. To avoid this pitfall, they interpreted the Rescript as broadly as possible and advised their associates to focus on its universal precepts, such as the exhortation to "extend benevolence to all."[13]

At this first conference, the educators also set down the secondary aims of the Japanese-language schools. With the growing number of Nisei children the language barrier between parents and children had become a matter of grave concern. By teaching the Japanese language, the language schools were to alleviate family problems by reducing the existing communication gap. Another secondary purpose was the inculcation of pride in Nisei youngsters. The educators feared that the children would develop "an inferiority complex" unless they were exposed to Japanese culture. Hence the language schools also served to instill a positive Japanese identity in the children. But whatever the secondary aims were, this first conference produced a much clearer perspective on the education of the Nisei. The educators committed themselves firmly to educating Nisei children as permanent residents of the United States.

In subsequent annual conferences, the educators changed their perspective on Nisei education. Held in June 1913, the second conference witnessed the establishment of the Japanese Teachers Association of America, a body composed exclusively of educators and persons interested in education, whose purpose was "to study and solve all educational problems pertaining to Japanese children in America."[14] The Japanese Association of America had convened the first two conferences. To divorce education from politics and to unify the language schools in California, the educators organized this association as an independent body. The educators also debated two important questions. First, they took up the subject of curriculum. Despite the fact that they agreed on the fundamental goals of the language schools, no uniform curriculum had been developed. All schools created their own curriculum, teaching many different subjects and using many different textbooks. To establish a uniform curriculum, the educators decided to limit instruction to three basic subjects: language, history, and geography, augmented by group singing. No specific classes on *shūshin*, or moral education, were to be offered. Rather, moral education was to be taught through the three basic subjects. This in itself was a departure from the standard practice in Japan, where moral education was always taught as a separate subject.

Second, the educators deliberated on the question of textbooks. Most schools used the textbook series compiled by the Ministry of Education in Japan. Was this series appropriate for the education of the Nisei? The educators answered that the series was inappropriate because it was geared specifically for Japanese children in Japan. The textbooks featured stories drawn from Japanese history, society, and culture. They also had didactic stories on the moral teachings of the Rescript on Education, most of which of course were alien to Nisei children. To be suitable for Nisei children, a textbook series had to be adapted to the American environment in which the children were being reared. This assessment reflected yet another change in the educators' perspective on Nisei education.

Events that preceded the second conference influenced the proceedings and the assembled educators. Right before the conference opened, the California State legislature had enacted the 1913 Alien Land Law. During the spring and early summer months of 1913, many prominent visitors from Japan arrived in California to observe the Japanese exclusion movement at first hand. Among them were two Japanese Diet members, Ebara Soroku and Hattori Ayao, who actually addressed the second conference and urged the educators to adapt their educational goals and practices to the United States.[15] At the same time, another eminent person, Shiga Shigetaka, published an article entitled "The Uselessness of a Japanese Education" in the immigrant press. In it Shiga claimed that a Japanese education, being insular and narrow, ill-prepared the Japanese people for overseas expansion.[16] Thus he advised Japanese immigrants to stress an American education for their children.

Subsequently, Japanese immigrant leaders turned to the problem of Nisei dual nationality. In 1914 this problem appeared on the agenda of the first meeting of the Pacific Coast Japanese Association Deliberative Council. The Northwest American Japanese Association of Seattle proposed that the Council seek revisions in the Japanese Nationality Law to enable the Nisei to renounce their Japanese citizenship. The council adopted the proposal, and in 1915 the Northwest American Japanese Association submitted a formal petition to the Japanese government asking for an amendment to the Japanese Nationality Law.[17] Two longtime immigrant leaders, Arai Tatsuya of Seattle and Tōyama Noriyuki of Los Angeles, lobbied in Tokyo on behalf of the Council working through Ebara Soroku and Shimada Saburō, two legislators who were familiar with the problem of Nisei dual nationality. As a result of the petition and lobbying, the Japanese Diet amended the Japanese Nationality Act in 1916.[18] This first amendment allowed the parents or guardians of Nisei who were fourteen years old or younger to renounce their Japanese citizenship for them and the Nisei who were fifteen to sixteen years old to do so themselves. Male Nisei who were seventeen years old or more, however, were subject to a precondition. They could forswear their Japanese citizenship only if they had fulfilled their Japanese military obligation. Complementing the Japanese immigrant educators' commitment to educate the Nisei as American citizens, this first amendment partially solved the problem of Nisei dual nationality.

External pressures influenced Japanese immigrants to modify their views of the Nisei problem further. After World War I, anti-Japanese exclusionists began to voice increasing alarm at the growing number of Nisei children. They leveled many charges, most of them utterly groundless. According to the exclusionists, by granting Japanese citizenship to Nisei children, the Japanese government considered the children as loyal subjects of Japan. Japanese language schools were indoctrinating the children with emperor worship or so-called *Mikadoism*. Unassimilable and alien like their parents, the children posed a threat to American society because they had American citizenship. Indeed, Japanese immigrants were evading the 1913 Alien Land Law by purchasing agricultural land in the name of their children. Thus, in 1919 the California Oriental Exclusion League proposed a constitutional amendment to deny citizenship to those children whose parents were "aliens ineligible to citizenship," regardless of whether they were born on American soil.[19]

This renewed agitation had an impact on the Pacific Coast Japanese Association Deliberative Council. The council convened twice in 1920, once in February for an extraordinary session and again in June for a regular meeting. In 1918 it had formed an educational committee to study the question of unifying all language schools and of compiling an appropriate textbook series for Nisei children. Only five textbooks had been compiled by 1918 to replace the Japanese Ministry of Education series that had been deemed inappropriate back in 1913. During the 1920 sessions of the council, the council discussed not the unification of the schools nor the question of textbooks but the very raison d'être of the schools.[20] Abe Toyoji opened the discussion. As a representative of the Japanese Association of Oregon he argued that the schools "contradicted" the policy of Americanization that had been adopted by all Japanese associations because the schools actually impeded the Americanization of the Nisei. He therefore proposed that the council adopt a public stand in favor of their elimination; barring that, he wanted the council to recommend that the schools be transformed into institutions to teach English to the parents of Nisei children.

The council delegates reacted differently to Abe's proposal. A few flatly opposed it. Some delegates suggested an amendment to the effect that the education offered by the Japanese-language schools must not conflict with the policy of Americanization adopted by the associations. Others felt that the council had no authority to abolish the schools, however desirable the goal may be. Such persons recognized that most schools were not under the control of Japanese associations, making them unwilling to endorse any public declaration that advocated their abolishment. In 1921 the council reconsidered the same question, with Abe reasserting his point of view.[21] No action resulted from these deliberations. Yet the fact that the council members entertained the idea of abolishing the schools indicated the extent to which the anti-Japanese agitation influenced the thinking of some Japanese association leaders.

The council did take action on other matters. Mindful of the campaign to deprive the Nisei of their American citizenship, it adopted the policy of promoting Nisei civic organizations. Such bodies were to teach the Nisei how to protect and exercise their American citizenship rights. Yet this was more easily said than done because the Nisei generation was still so young. In 1920 there was only a handful of adult Nisei. In 1922 a small group of Nisei formed the Seattle Progressive Citizens' League, and in 1923 an equally small group of Nisei launched the American Loyalty League in California. Both of these groups had the financial support of the Japanese associations and were organized at the behest of Japanese Association leaders.[22] The council also reconsidered the problem of Nisei dual nationality. To expedite the process of renouncing Japanese citizenship, the Japanese Association of America published a pamphlet on behalf of the council in 1922. This pamphlet explained to the parents of Nisei youngsters the 1916 amendment to the Japanese Nationality Act and the renunciation procedures.[23] To disseminate this information as widely as possible, local Japanese associations distributed the pamphlet to all Japanese residents living within their jurisdictions.

Still the 1916 amendment was not altogether satisfactory. Males seventeen years old or older had to fulfill their Japanese military obligation before they could renounce their Japanese citizenship. To eliminate this precondition, in 1922 the council again petitioned the Japanese government.[24] This second petition produced the 1924 amendment to the Japanese Nationality Act. Much more liberal than the first amendment, this one allowed retroactive renunciation of Japanese citizenship without any precondition. Moreover, it abolished automatic Japanese nationality based on paternal descent. In order to obtain Japanese citizenship for their children, parents were now required to notify the closest Japanese government office within fourteen days after birth that they desired Japanese citizenship for their offspring. Otherwise, the children would not possess it. Going much further than the 1916 amendment, the 1924 amendment removed the last legal obstacle to solving the problem of Nisei dual nationality.

External pressures also had a telling impact on Japanese immigrant educators. Japanese-language schools proliferated over the years. In 1914 there were thirty-one schools in California; by 1923 this number multiplied to fifty-five.[25] In 1915 the teachers of Southern California organized the Southern California Educational Society. This group adhered to the same goals as the Japanese Teachers Association of America, its counterpart in Northern California. In the words of President Shimano Kōhei, the educational work of the society was dedicated to "the Nisei who will live and work permanently here, not to those who will return to Japan."[26] In October 1920 the Japanese Teachers Association convened its annual conference as the California electorate was preparing to vote on the alien land initiative measure, which amended the 1913 Alien Land Law.

Japanese immigrant educators reacted to the renewed anti-Japanese agitation in several ways. Some schools used the Japanese term *shōgakkō*, or elementary school, as a part of the official name of their schools. Since such schools might be identified mistakenly as the same as Japanese elementary schools in Japan, the educators decided to designate all schools as *gakuen* or institutes. To reflect this change in name, they renamed the Japanese Teachers Association as the Association of Japanese Language Institutes. The same substitution of nomenclature occurred in Southern California. The educators also redefined the goal of the institutes to read: "Based on the spirit of American public schools, the purpose . . . is to supplement good civic education."[27] By civic education they meant the instruction in American citizenship offered by the public schools. The educators incorporated this redefinition of purpose into a new constitution and forwarded an English translation to the state superintendent of public instruction in the hope of mollifying the exclusionists.

In 1921 the California State Legislature enacted a law regulating private foreign-language schools. The law regulated the operation of schools, the certification of teachers, and the content of instructional materials. According to its provisions, no foreign-language school could operate during public school hours, and periods of instruction could not exceed one hour per day, six hours per week, and thirty-eight weeks per year. To be certified to teach in a school, all teachers had to pass a state examination in English competency (reading, writing, and speaking), as well as in American history and institutions in English. All textbooks and curricula had to be approved by the superintendent of public instruction. Finally, the superintendent was authorized to inspect any school and to withdraw the certificates of teachers at any time. This law became effective on July 30 as Section 1534 of the California Political Code.

All Japanese-language institutes became subject to this new enactment. The examinations in American history and institutions in English and in English competency were deferred until 1923. As a compromise, Japanese teachers were allowed to take the examination in American history and institutions in Japanese in 1921 and 1922. To prepare them for the 1921 examination, the Japanese Association of America and the Central Japanese Association of Southern California sponsored special Teachers' Training Institutes in San Francisco, Fresno, and Los Angeles. The program in San Francisco lasted for two weeks, with 127 teachers enrolled in classes on American history and institutions.[28] Various White Americans presented the lectures in these classes. Sam H. Cohn, assistant state superintendent of public instruction, personally appeared on the first day to explain what the state would expect from the Japanese teachers in the upcoming examination.

Japanese teachers took the examination in the fall under Sam H. Cohn's watchful eyes. In San Francisco the examination consisted of seven questions on history and seven on institutions. Five in each category had to be answered. The examinees pondered such historical questions as:

What two questions were definitely settled by the Civil War?

What was Washington's policy in foreign affairs? How has it affected the foreign policy of America?

What is meant by the Monroe Doctrine?

Discuss the territorial expansion of the United States from the original 13 colonies, explaining how each acquisition was made.

Turning to the questions on institutions, the examinees encountered such biased questions as:

Compare the form of government of the United States with that of Japan in regard to similarities and differences. Point out the strength and weakness of each.

Why is it essential that a teacher should be familiar with the institutions of the country in which he resides? Illustrate.

Instructing Japanese children in their relation to American institutions, what points would you consider most needful of emphasis?

In 1922 the questions on institutions were more slanted:

What restrictions are placed on immigration into the United States? Are these restrictions just? Why?

Explain your view as to whether the State should or should not have control of "foreign language schools."

Give the essential qualities of a "good" citizen.

How may these be developed in young children?[29]

These questions were patently absurd. Were the examinees to reply that the immigration restrictions against the Japanese were just? That the government of Japan was a terrible tyranny and that of America a wonderful democracy? Or that the state should require the examination they were compelled to take? Yet the examinees had no choice but to answer the questions to please their examiners. In 1923 the examinees took a similar examination in American history and institutions in English. As reference books for the Japanese teachers, the Japanese Association of America purchased two hundred copies of four American textbooks: Charles A. Beard and William C. Bagley, *The History of the American People*; Frank A. Magruder, *American Government*; Charles A. Beard and May R. Beard, *American Citizenship*; and *Civics for New Americans*, a manual on citizenship for new immigrants.

Assistant Superintendent of Public Instruction Cohn selected Kuno Yoshisaburō of the University of California to read the examination papers. Kuno was an assistant professor of Japanese in the Department of Oriental Languages. An Issei maverick, he was often at odds with Japanese immigrant leaders. He enraged them in October 1920 when he published a series of articles in the *Oakland Tribune*. Entitled *A Survey of the Japanese Situation*, the series alleged that Japanese consuls controlled the Japanese associations and that Japanese immigrants had managed to evade the 1913 Alien Land Law.[30] From the immigrant leaders' perspective, Kuno played into the hands of the exclusionists by giving the California electorate reasons for voting for the 1920 alien land initiative measure. As to the Japanese-language institutes, Kuno felt that Nisei children were being unduly forced to attend them. He disapproved of the institutes because, in his opinion, they were creating "hyphenated Americans" with "two loyalties."[31] On reading a batch of the 1921 examination papers, Kuno wrote to Cohn that he was "astonished" that "the majority of . . . teachers are unfamiliar with . . . American history and

American institutions." He condescendingly stated that "their average intellectual ability is approximately that of an 8th grade pupil in the United States." In his entire teaching experience he had "never before come across so many low-grade papers in a single lot."[32] Notwithstanding Kuno's harsh judgment, in 1921, out of 156 teachers who took the examinations administered in San Francisco and Fresno, 125 received licenses.[33]

To comply with the requirement relating to textbooks, the Japanese Association of America and the Central Japanese Association of Southern California cooperated to compile an acceptable new textbook series. Representatives of the two central associations formed a special education committee entrusted with the task of compiling it. Until the series was completed, State officials approved selected translations of the Japanese Ministry of Education series on an interim basis. The new alternative series took two years to complete. Consisting of sixteen volumes, the state superintendent approved it officially in August 1923.[34] This series was uniquely American; it neither had lessons in Japanese history or geography nor any reference to the Japanese emperor. The compilers drew on and translated from American textbooks. Stories about George Washington, Abraham Lincoln, Betsy Ross, and other American figures were so prominent that the series was overwhelmingly American in content.

Nevertheless, neither the 1921 legislation nor the Japanese immigrant compliance with it satisfied anti-Japanese exclusionists. In 1923 the California state legislature enacted a more stringent law. Authored by the rabid anti-Japanese state senator J. M. Inman, this measure limited enrollment into foreign-language schools to children who had completed the fourth grade. In addition, this measure included a provision outlawing all foreign-language schools by July 1, 1930. The United States Supreme Court indirectly nullified this new California enactment in a timely ruling. Just as the governor was on the verge of signing the bill into law, the high tribunal ruled that a 1919 Nebraska statute was unconstitutional. The Nebraska statute banned the teaching of a foreign language to any child who had not completed the eighth grade. In June 1923 the court rendered its decision in a case involving a person who had taught German to a ten-year-old in a parochial school.[35] Reasoning that the Nebraska statute exceeded the powers of the state, the court struck down the statute. In the light of this decision the new 1923 California enactment ended abortively with the governor never signing it into law.

The 1921 legislation eventually met the same fate. In 1927 the United States Supreme Court handed down another key decision, which invalidated a statute of the Territory of Hawaii.[36] The statute regulated the operation of foreign-language schools, the certification of teachers, and the content of instructional materials in the same manner as the 1921 California legislation did. Indeed, the California law had been modeled on the Hawaiian one. The high court declared the Hawaiian statute unconstitutional in its entirety, thereby nullifying the corresponding laws of California and other states. As a result, Japanese-language institutes could hire any teacher, use any textbook, and set any classroom schedule. The only restriction was that they were not allowed to open during the hours when the public schools were in session.

Post-1924 Aspects of the Nisei Problem

The Issei generation's conception of the Nisei problem underwent new permutations after 1924. One new concept that surfaced in 1924 was that the Nisei should be nurtured to become a *kusabi* or *kakehashi*, a link or bridge of understanding between the United States and Japan. Abiko Kyūtarō, a highly respected, if not *the* most respected, Issei leader popularized this concept. He was the publisher of the *Nichibei Shimbun*, the most influential Japanese immigrant daily. At its peak, during the 1920s, the *Nichibei Shimbun* came out in two editions, one in San Francisco and the other in Los Angeles, with a combined press run of twenty-five thousand with subscribers throughout California, the Pacific Northwest, and the Rocky Mountain region.

Throughout the exclusion movement period, Abiko adhered to his belief that the exclusion question could be solved amicably.[37] He never interpreted the problem purely in terms of economic competition, political demagoguery, or simple racism, although he acknowledged that all of these factors were involved in one way or another. Some degree of economic competition existed between Japanese immigrants and Americans, to be sure, but that was not sufficient to explain the anti-Japanese hostility. Occupying different sectors of the labor market, most Japanese were not in direct competition with white workers. Assuming that Chinese immigrants had been, Abiko believed that the Japanese were identified, wrongfully, with the Chinese by Americans, which conjured up the specter of economic competition.

Political demagogues were plentiful enough, but they were offset by other people who were sympathetic to the Japanese. The racial animus toward the Japanese, unlike that toward the blacks, included a white fear that Japanese had superior traits, which made them formidable opponents against whom Americans could not compete. Abiko always viewed the exclusion movement as a problem of ignorance. Americans were ignorant of Japan and Japanese immigrants, and their ignorance was at the bottom of the misunderstandings that fueled the movement. Abiko had an abiding faith that communication and education could dispel this ignorance and clear the way for a fundamental solution to the exclusion question.

Under his editorial policy the *Nichibei Shimbun* shifted its emphasis from the Issei to the Nisei from January 1924.[38] Attaching much greater importance to the Nisei generation, the newspaper began to declare repeatedly that the future of the Japanese in the United States lay with the Nisei. The Issei were already entering old age; the Nisei were about to come of age. Denied the right of naturalization, the Issei were "aliens ineligible to citizenship" and subject to numerous discriminatory legislation without a real future in this country; the Nisei were American citizens with a potential bright future. The Issei had to adopt their future as their own. To enable the Nisei to realize their full potential as Americans, the *Nichibei Shimbun* therefore upheld the view that the Issei had a moral obligation and duty to support the Nisei in every way possible. After the enactment of the 1924 Immigration Act, Abiko envisioned the Nisei playing a pivotal future role in United States–Japan relations. Being Japanese by descent but American by birth and education, the Nisei were suited ideally to become a future bridge of understanding between the two nations to dispel the ignorance that had been, in Abiko's opinion, the fundamental cause of the exclusion movement.

Abiko realized, however, that in order to assume this role, the Nisei had to be educated about Japan. After all, they had to be knowledgeable about Japanese affairs if they were to serve as an effective bridge of understanding. Thus the first task was to awaken an interest in Japan among the Nisei. From Abiko's perspective, the best method of achieving this was to let the Nisei see the country with their own eyes. In 1924 four Seattle girls seemed to confirm this conviction. These girls visited Japan in the spring and learned that their parents' native country was considerably different from what they had imagined it to be. They returned to Seattle deeply impressed with what they had observed and experienced and presented glowing reports of Japan to Issei and Nisei audiences in the Pacific Northwest. Influenced by newspaper accounts of these four girls, the Japanese Association of America invited them to California in the fall. The girls addressed many groups throughout the state, speaking in Japanese before the Issei and in English before the Nisei. Immigrant leaders who heard them were all elated. The *Nichibei Shimbun* was so impressed with the girls that it praised them effusively.[39]

These events formed the background to Abiko's decision to underwrite special Nisei tours of Japan. In November 1924 the *Nichibei Shimbun* announced its plan of sponsoring a Nisei excursion group to tour the country in the spring of 1925.[40] As members of this first tour group, Abiko selected Nisei who exhibited leadership potential. They had to be at least high school graduates and able to profit from a visit to Japan. Abiko secured the cooperation of Shibusawa Eiichi, a very prominent figure in Japanese business circles, who also envisioned the Nisei as a future bridge of understanding. Composed of eleven Nisei and led by Abiko's wife, Yonako, this group traveled throughout Japan for three months and saw the country literally from the top down. With Shibusawa's intercession the group had entry into places normally closed to ordinary tourists and access to upper-class Japanese society. Miya Sannomiya was a member of the second *Nichibei Shimbun* Nisei tour group of 1926. In relating the effect it had on her, she said that "the tour changed my entire life." Indeed, she herself became an actual bridge of understanding in 1934 as an English secretary of the *Kokusai Bunka Shinkōkai* [International Society for Cultural Relations], a Japanese educational society that disseminated information about Japan in Western languages.[41] Following the example of the *Nichibei Shimbun*, other immigrant newspapers and organizations sponsored their own Nisei tour groups from 1925, so that Nisei excursions of Japan became a widely practiced method of awakening an interest in the country among the Nisei by the late 1920s. In sum, Abiko Kyūtarō started the Nisei tour groups to facilitate realization of the concept of the Nisei as a future bridge of understanding between the United States and Japan.

The idea of the Nisei as a bridge of understanding was tied to another concept: the Pacific era. According to this concept, the Nisei were coming of age in a new epoch. With the decline of European civilization, the Atlantic era was drawing to a close. The center of the world had shifted from the Atlantic to the Pacific, and the United States and Japan had emerged as the two dominant powers at opposite ends of the Pacific basin. This heralded the

Figure 1. The 1925 *kengakudan* (Nisei tour group), in front of Japan's Inari Shrine, with Abiko Yonako, center, front row. Courtesy of Abiko Family Papers, Special Collections, Charles E. Young Research Library, UCLA.

beginning of the Pacific era in which the East and West, as represented by Japan and the United States, were meeting each other at long last. The result of this encounter would be a new Pacific culture combining the best elements of Oriental and Occidental cultures. The Nisei had a unique role to play in this historic encounter. By upholding harmonious United States–Japan relations, they were destined to make major contributions toward the peace and stability of the Pacific era. At the same time, they were destined to be creators and carriers of the new Pacific culture.[42]

International political events heightened the importance of the concept of the Nisei as a bridge of understanding. In 1931 a group of junior Japanese officers contrived the so-called Manchurian Incident and used it as a pretext to occupy Manchuria. The officers undertook this action in defiance of the high military command. Confronted by a fait accompli, the Japanese government defended the action by maintaining that its army had been provoked beyond toleration. To politically solidify its control of Manchuria, the government then recognized a political entity called Manchukuo in 1932. Ostensibly an independent state, Manchukuo in fact was a puppet state established under Japanese government tutelage and maintained under its control. The League of Nations dispatched the so-called Lytton Commission to investigate all the events and circumstances that had led up to the establishment of the state of Manchukuo. The commission branded Japan as a military aggressor, and based on the recommendation of the commission, the General Assembly of the League of Nations adopted a policy of nonrecognition of Manchukuo. Although not a member of the League of Nations, the United States also blamed Japan as the aggressor and likewise adopted a policy of nonrecognition. To protest the policy of the international community, Japan pulled out of the League of Nations in February 1933.[43]

These events gave the concept of a bridge of understanding a strong political coloration. Until 1931 the Issei mainly had the Japanese exclusion movement in mind when they applied the concept to the Nisei. The Nisei were expected to educate Americans about Japanese immigration and Japanese immigrants. They were going to remove one of the chief sources of friction in United States–Japan relations by dispelling the misunderstandings behind the exclusion movement. Now the Nisei were expected to explain political events in the Far East and present and justify Japan's side of those events to the American public. In this way, the concept of the Nisei as a bridge of understanding was expanded to encompass broader international political issues that affected United States–Japan relations. To enable the Nisei to learn about Far Eastern politics, Nisei tour groups during the 1930s, not surprisingly, often included Korea and Manchuria (after 1931) and North China (after 1937) on their itinerary.

Most Japanese government officials endorsed the concept of the Nisei as a bridge of understanding but prior to 1931 refused to support any program to promote the concept. Indeed, the Foreign Ministry refused to render any assistance in the education of the Nisei. In 1927 the Pacific Coast Japanese Association Deliberative Council petitioned the Foreign Ministry for financial aid. Aware of the paramount importance of education in the future of the Nisei, Japanese association leaders planned to establish a Nisei Educational Fund of five hundred thousand dollars for scholarships. Of this total sum, they hoped to solicit Issei donations amounting to one hundred thousand dollars and asked the Japanese government to contribute the balance of four hundred thousand dollars. The Foreign Ministry turned a deaf ear to the request because of its assessment of the post-1924 situation.[44] Anti-Japanese agitation had abated with the enactment of the 1924 Immigration Act. Inasmuch as Japanese immigrants no longer were a political issue, they could not expect any sort of aid from their homeland government. It was incumbent upon the Issei themselves to finance any educational fund for the Nisei.

The Manchurian Incident fundamentally altered this negative policy of the Japanese government. Much to the dismay of Japanese officials, the American press as a whole sharply criticized Japan for its actions in China. The adverse publicity made the officials realize in a concrete way the significance of the concept of the Nisei as a bridge of understanding. From the perspective of Seattle Consul Uchiyama Kiyoshi, James Yoshinori Sakamoto stood out as an outstanding, effective bridge within his consular jurisdiction. Sakamoto was one of the first-born Nisei of Seattle and a prominent leader of the Nisei generation. In 1931 he was active in the Japanese American Citizens League, a national civic organization formed by the Nisei in 1930. More important, Sakamoto was the publisher and editor of the *Japanese American Courier*, an English weekly published for the Nisei, which he had founded in 1928.[45]

In his capacity as a leader, publisher, and editor, Sakamoto actively promoted the Japanese case in China among his fellow Nisei and the local American public. Sakamoto was instrumental in organizing the Committee on Pacific Information in early 1932. Composed of a handful of Nisei and A. E. Holden, executive secretary of the Japan Society of Seattle, and his wife, Ruth Turner, this committee disseminated information favorable to the Japanese side on the Manchurian question. In the *Japanese American Courier* Sakamoto staunchly defended Japan in editorials and regularly reprinted the speeches of the Japanese foreign minister, Ambassador Saitō Hiroshi, and Consul Uchiyama, as well as the full text of Foreign Ministry press releases.[46] At Uchiyama's suggestion Sakamoto gave A. E. Holden space in the *Courier*. Utilizing the allotted space as a news outlet for the Japan Society, Holden wrote a column entitled "Notes of Japan Society." Members of the society were advised to subscribe to the *Courier* to keep abreast of the society's activities. Consul Uchiyama believed that Holden's column would induce many prominent Americans interested in Far Eastern affairs to subscribe to the

Courier, thereby increasing its circulation and influence. From 1934 Saka-moto also had a weekly thirty-minute radio program on which he aired news about Japan. According to Consul Uchiyama, Sakamoto was so cooperative in publishing and disseminating pro-Japan news, Uchiyama donated twenty-five dollars (later increased to fifty) per month in support of the *Courier.*[47]

Sakamoto himself was a firm believer and ardent supporter of the concept of the Nisei as a bridge of understanding. He encouraged young Nisei to study the Japanese language, to visit Japan, and to learn about the country and the Far East. There was no contradiction in his adhering to the concept and in his being an American citizen. Sakamoto identified the role of a bridge with being a loyal American. He incorporated it into his definition of good American citizenship. To be a responsible, worthwhile American citi-zen, the Nisei had to assume the role. Otherwise they would be shirking their duty. In enlightening their fellow Americans about the Japanese side of Far Eastern affairs, they would be fulfilling their civic responsibility as loyal, patriotic Americans. In other words, a good American of Japanese ancestry was a person who assumed the role of a bridge. Consequently, Sakamoto never saw himself as a propagandist for the Japanese government. In his own mind he was being a loyal American citizen when he disseminated pro-Japan information. In Consul Uchiyama's opinion Sakamoto vindicated the worth of the concept of the Nisei as a bridge of understanding to the Japanese government.

Japanese government officials endeavored to popularize this concept among the Nisei. In annual New Year's messages to the Nisei generation, Japanese diplomats regularly expressed their expectations of the Nisei. In 1931, for example, Ambassador Debuchi Katsumi emphatically declared:

> Being of Japanese descent, you are naturally expected to know more about the native country of your parents than does the average American. I urge you to live up to that expectation. You should study about Japan, about things Japanese, about the national spirit and ideals which are back of the marvelous progress achieved by that island nation in the last half century.
>
> You are expected to be the most effective of the connecting links between Japan and America. You can live up to this expectation only by knowing and understanding Japan as you know and understand America.[48]

In Southern California, the local consul sponsored annual speech and essay contests in Japanese from 1933. Nisei youngsters in local Japanese language institutes participated in these contests. In 1933 entrants in the advanced writing contest were required to compose essays on the theme "The Pacific Era and Japanese-Americans." The first prize was awarded to Mitsuko Yoshii, a student of the Rafu Dai-Ichi Gakuen. Her essay read in part:

> The Pacific Era—what does this have to do with us, the Nisei?
>
> We were raised in America, but we have Japanese blood. We stand between Japan and America. Lying before our very eyes is the great task of bringing Japan and America closer together and cementing our friendship.
>
> For us, this is the meaning of this era. We cannot dismiss it. Many years elapsed in the shift from the Mediterranean Era to the present Pacific Era. Gradually, the world stage moved eastward. Now the world centers on the countries of the Orient and the United States.
>
> . . . .
>
> Our mission is to strengthen Japanese-American friendship, to engage in mutual assistance, and to achieve the best possible understanding—all to eliminate misunderstandings in Japanese American relations. This is a monumental undertaking. Some doubt if we are up to the task. But we are. If everyone will cooperate and put their minds to this all important task, we will be able to carry it out.
>
> The Pacific Era is ahead of us. We must embark on our mission without wasting a minute. Let us begin our clear and monumental undertaking with steadfastness and enthusiasm.[49]

The second prize went to Shizuko Sasaki, a student of the Compton Gakuen. Also on the same theme of the Pacific era, her essay focused on the Nisei and the Manchurian Incident:

> After the Manchurian Incident occurred, I often read in the newspapers and heard in conversations that "this time there will be a war between the United States and Japan," and I always worried that such a scary state of affairs had come about.
>
> As Japanese-Americans, we, of course, cannot bear the thought of making an enemy of Japan, our parents' homeland. Nor can we, most of all, turn against our own native country, the United States. From our perspective as Japanese-Americans, we simply cannot afford to stand by idly. Somehow or another, we must study the Manchurian question in depth in order to dispel the misunderstandings Americans have and to preserve peace between the United States and Japan.[50]

These two essays rehashed exactly what Issei educators were teaching to young Nisei students in the Japanese-language institutes. Both embodied the concept of the Nisei as a bridge of understanding in the so-called Pacific era and in the aftermath of the Manchurian Incident.

In November 1934 the Foreign Ministry ordered all of its consulates in the United States to conduct a survey of the Nisei generation,[51] and each consulate filed a report on the Nisei who lived in its jurisdiction. Every consul agreed on the urgency of educating the Nisei about Japan, although there was some disagreement as to the precise means. Seattle consul Uchiyama was horrified that "some Nisei are fearful of and intimidated by Americans" yet looked down upon their own kind, to the point even of being "contemptuous" of the Issei. Such Nisei were afflicted with self-hatred. Despised by whites as being members of a colored race, they resented being born as a Japanese. Portland consul Nakamura Toyokazu bemoaned the fact that the Nisei were so "Americanized" that they, relying on anti-Japanese American press coverage, "are unable to understand Japan's position on the Manchurian question." Something had to be done to counteract the adverse influence of the American press. Consul Nakamura suggested the publication of an English newspaper as an alternative source of information for the Nisei.

Every consul applauded the efforts of Japanese-language institutes to educate the Nisei about Japan. Some wanted to unify the institutes into a better system to improve the quality of instruction. It is interesting that in 1935, according to a consular survey, 90 percent of the institutes were using the textbook series compiled by the Japanese Ministry of Education. This meant that the institutes had dispensed with the alternative series that had been compiled in California in 1923 and had switched back to using the Japanese series. Every consul also endorsed Nisei excursions to Japan. A few recommended that the brightest Nisei be sent to Japan for higher education and returned to the United States to assume positions of leadership among the Nisei generation. In order to expedite the admission of such Nisei into Japanese schools, it was advised that regular matriculation requirements be waived whenever they had the recommendation of any local consul.[52]

Study in Japan

As another way of acquiring knowledge about Japan, some Nisei actually went to Japan to study. A sizable number of Nisei were educated there.

According to statistics compiled by the Ministry of Home Affairs, there were eighteen thousand Nisei residing in Japan in 1933.[53] These Nisei were born in the continental United States and in Hawaii (a few in Canada). The vast majority had arrived in Japan as infants and lived in their parents' native village. Under the sway of the *dekasegi* ideal, their parents either had returned to Japan with them or, expecting to return eventually, had sent them ahead to the village to be raised by relatives. Both practices had begun in the years before World War I. These Nisei were educated as "Japanese" who became the *Kibei* on their later return to the United States. A second smaller group of Nisei arrived in Japan as adults after they had completed high school or college. Concentrating in the Tokyo and Kyoto metropolitan areas, these Nisei sought some kind of additional Japanese education, a few among them some sort of employment. Before 1931 there were fewer than one hundred Nisei in this second category. By 1932–33 the number increased approximately four times, and by 1934–35 it was in the neighborhood of seventeen hundred.[54]

Several factors were behind this sudden increase. First, the Manchurian Incident and its aftermath did arouse an interest in Japan among the Nisei. The appearance of Japanese athletes at the 1932 Los Angeles Olympic Games intensified this interest. Most Nisei did not expect the athletes from Japan to fare very well. When some of the athletes actually won medals, the Nisei felt an unexpected surge of genuine pride that reinforced their newly aroused interest in their parents' native country.[55] Second, many Issei thought that the Nisei could improve their employment prospects by studying in Japan. In the early 1930s, future employment emerged as another aspect of the Nisei problem as the first-born Nisei came of age. These Nisei faced formidable racial barriers in seeking employment outside of the Japanese community. Even with college degrees it was unlikely that they would be able to secure jobs in the larger society. As a result, many Issei believed that, if the Nisei acquired a good command of Japanese and combined it with their mastery of English, their employment options would be enhanced. Given the trade relations between the United States and Japan, this would be true particularly in the field of international commerce. Third, an economic factor made study in Japan attractive during the early 1930s. Prior to the 1930s the yen-dollar exchange rate was approximately two to one. Toward the end of 1931 this rate began to fluctuate markedly in favor of the dollar. At the beginning of 1932, $34.50–$38.00 could be exchanged for 100 yen. In November 1932 100 yen equaled only $19.00. During the first half of 1933, the dollar exchange rate of 100 yen fluctuated constantly but always remained below $24.00.[56] These fluctuations in the exchange rate favoring the dollar persuaded many Issei parents that it would be much cheaper to send their sons and daughters to Japan for higher education rather than have them study in the United States.

Specially created institutions in Japan that accommodated the Nisei further stimulated the practice of studying in Japan. In 1932 the Japanese government established an institute dedicated to the education of the Nisei. Known as the Kaigai Kyōiku Kyōkai and headed by Viscount Ishii Kikujirō, it was funded by the Ministry of Foreign Affairs. This institute operated a school and dormitory in Kanagawa Prefecture. The school was called the Mizuho Gakuen and officially admitted Nisei students from 1935.[57] In 1930 Buddhists launched their own institute to educate the Nisei. Called the Nihon Beifu Kyōkai, it operated a school and dormitory in Tokyo. The school, known as the Nichibei Gakuin, offered instruction in Japanese language and culture, as well as preparatory education for matriculation into other schools.[58] In 1935 the Waseda Kokusai Gakuin opened its doors and admitted many Nisei students. Staffed by people affiliated with Waseda University, it also provided instruction in Japanese language and culture and functioned simultaneously as a preparatory school for higher education.[59] In 1935 the Rikkōkai set up its own school and dormitory to accommodate Nisei from not only the Americas but also from Manchuria.[60] Established in 1897 as a Christian organization, the Rikkōkai had assisted many indigent students to immigrate to the United States at the turn of the century. In 1931 the Tokyo YMCA established a special program for Nisei in the Nichigo Bunka Gakkō, a school that taught Japanese and Japanese culture to foreigners.[61]

Some programs were geared specifically for Nisei girls. One was set up in the Keisen Girls' School, a Christian academy in Tokyo. This school was headed by Kawai Michiko. In 1934 Kawai visited the United States and discussed the educational problems of the Nisei with Issei Christian leaders. As her contribution toward solving these problems, she instituted a special two-year course of study for young adult Nisei girls at her school in 1935. The curriculum consisted of classes in Japanese, Japanese history and literature in English, Christian ethics, cooking, flower arrangement, and tea ceremony. Kawai arranged to have a screening committee in the United States select suitable high school graduates to take this course of study.[62] All of these special schools and programs—and many others in Tokyo and elsewhere—

served to help Nisei students adjust to school life in Japan and obtain firsthand knowledge of Japanese society. Their proliferation at this time reflected the growing number of Nisei who went to study in Japan from 1931.

Studying in Japan was not without its pitfalls, however. Three guides, written for parents who were contemplating sending their sons and daughters to Japan, warned of certain dangers. It was imperative for the Nisei to have clear and attainable goals in mind when going to Japan. Otherwise, they would not benefit from studying there. Some young men who had no set goals neglected their studies altogether. Such men often succumbed to the temptations of nightlife in Japan. They frequented dance halls and caroused in bars. The guides alerted Issei parents to this possible pitfall. As a precautionary measure, they advised parents to provide only money necessary to cover living expenses and school costs. Excessive amounts of money in the hands of young Nisei men could only lead to their moral dissolution. If parents desired their sons to have spending money, they should never give it to them directly. Instead, they should entrust the money to their guardians and authorize the guardians to disburse it at their discretion.[63] Interestingly enough, one early Japanese stereotype of the Nisei was that they were all disreputable. In 1933, for example, a Tokyo Metropolitan Police report noted that "very few Nisei are studying seriously" and that "in general they act in an undesirable manner." This report also suggested that the Nisei harbored subversive ideas. "Being adherents of Americanism," it said, "the Nisei are not in sympathy with Japan. Ignorant of the Manchurian issue, they are highly critical of the country as being militaristic."[64]

In 1935 the Japanese Association of America and the Central Japanese Association of Southern California started a campaign to encourage the Nisei in Japan to return to the United States. Association leaders had in mind the Nisei who had been taken to Japan in infancy. They estimated that, in all, fifty thousand Nisei were residing in Japan. The need to find successors to the aging Issei generation was the rationale behind this campaign. The economic foundation of Japanese immigrant society was agriculture. Yet few Nisei sons of farmers were willing to continue their fathers' occupation. They aspired to be professionals or white-collar workers; many were leaving their homes and moving to urban centers. If this trend continued, association leaders predicted that Japanese rural communities would be drained of Nisei youth, so much so that there would be no one to succeed the Issei generation in agriculture. Unless something was done about the situation, the

Issei stake in agriculture would disappear. Issei leaders deemed the Nisei in Japan as the best possible successors to Issei farmers. Raised and educated in Japan since infancy, these Nisei shared a common Japanese culture with the Issei. If such Nisei were induced to return, they could be groomed to take over Issei farms.[65]

To achieve the goal of the campaign, association leaders sought the cooperation of many groups. They appealed to prefectural associations in the United States and prefectural overseas associations in Japan, inviting them all to join the campaign. They even dispatched representatives to Japan. They appealed especially to the Foreign Ministry for assistance, but Japanese government officials were very wary of future adverse repercussions. In May 1936 V. S. McClatchy, the arch anti-Japanese exclusionist, issued a press release foreshadowing what might possibly happen. Issued in the name of the California Joint Immigration Committee, the release covered the alleged "dangers" of Nisei dual nationality and specifically voiced alarm at the fact that "the Japanese Association of America is planning to bring back at once to California all the Kibei . . . still in Japan."[66] Japanese officials disputed the estimate of fifty thousand Nisei in Japan. They placed the number at around twenty thousand. But regardless of the exact number, local Japanese consuls were fearful that, if any significant number of Nisei, suddenly and conspicuously, returned to California, they would become inevitably the object of renewed anti-Japanese agitation. As a result, the Foreign Ministry refused to help the campaign in any way.[67] Although this campaign met with little success, it did augur the eventual return of many Nisei in the late 1930s under different circumstances.

The Influence of the Sino-Japanese War

Much more than the Manchurian Incident, the Sino-Japanese War had a pronounced influence on the Issei conception of the Nisei problem. On July 7, 1937, hostilities between Japan and China broke out with the Marco Polo Bridge Incident, which rapidly expanded into a full-scale war. Most Issei quickly rallied behind their homeland with great patriotic fervor, establishing emergency committees to provide political, financial, material, and moral support. Set up in every Japanese community throughout the western United States, these emergency committees served four purposes. First, they disseminated pro-Japanese propaganda to counteract local publicity that blamed Japan for the war. To this end these committees published and distributed political pamphlets, sponsored public lectures, and promoted special radio broadcasts. Second, they collected money and goods to be sent to Japan. Funds were raised for national defense and war relief; money for the latter, called *imonkin* or *juppeikin*, was earmarked for needy families in Japan who had soldiers engaged in combat or killed in action. Third, the committees sent gift packets to the soldiers on the China front. These packets were called *imonbukuro* filled with nonperishable items like tobacco, razors, dried fruits, soap bars, and candy. Talismans or *senninbari* were often included too. *Senninbari* literally means a thousand stitches. According to folk belief, these talismans protected Japanese soldiers from enemy bullets since each stitch had been knitted, in theory, by a thousand maidens. Last, the committees held periodic patriotic programs to commemorate noteworthy events such as the fall of Hankow and Canton in late 1938.[68]

From the Issei perspective the Sino-Japanese War became an integral part of the Nisei problem because the Nisei generally were ignorant of the war and indifferent to its outcome. Thus the Issei felt compelled to change Nisei attitudes and mold Nisei opinions regarding the war. Japanese-language institutes strove to educate Nisei pupils about the war. In composition exercises Issei teachers required their pupils to write on themes relating to the conflict. Nisei pupils composed two types of compositions: letters of appreciation and essays on the war itself. Letters of appreciation were addressed to Japanese soldiers and forwarded to those fighting on the China front. A typical letter read:

December 15, 1937

To Japanese Soldiers in China:

The year is shortly coming to an end. It's probably cold over there. It's hard for us who live in sunny Southern California to imagine your hardships.

Everyday we learn of your heroic deeds from the newspaper and radio. I believe that people throughout the world will soon acknowledge your efforts of fighting for justice with the Japanese spirit and Bushido. I hope that day will come about quickly.

According to the latest news, we learn that the Imperial Army is launching its final attack on Nanking. We get excited everytime we see the morning newspaper. You will reach your goal soon. The final victory is the most important. I pray that you will be victorious as soon as possible and that you will work towards restoring peace in the Orient.

As we are about to usher in the New Year at this time of crisis, I would like to express our gratitude for your accomplishments so far and to extend our encouragement for the future. I await the day when you will return home as victorious heroes.

Toshiko Nakamura[69]

Issei educators endeavored to counteract the influence of the American press. In their opinion American newspapers were brainwashing the Nisei by publishing news slanted heavily in favor of the Chinese side. Tsutomu Iwamoto, a pupil in the Compton Gakuen, addressed himself to this issue. Under the guidance of his teachers he composed the following essay in 1938:

I worry about how long the Sino-Japanese conflict will continue. Until recently I liked American newspapers, but ever since the beginning of the Sino-Japanese conflict I've grown to dislike them. Why? Because the articles written by Caucasians on the conflict are completely different from the explanations we get from the Japanese language press and our Japanese language teachers. I am upset that only bad things are being written about Japan. Thanks to our teachers, I feel that I understand the true reason for the Sino-Japanese conflict. There is only one reason for Japan sending her troops into China to engage in combat. Most foreigners believe that Japan desires to occupy Chinese territory. They believe such nonsense because they do not know Japanese history or Japan's true intent.

Japan is a very strong nation. Yet she does not cherish warfare. Nor does she, in the least, harbor ambitions to take over another nation's territory. The Sino-Japanese conflict erupted because China killed Japanese soldiers and Japanese residents without any justification and ignored and trampled upon international agreements. China is in chaos, and two or three foreign powers are trying to extend their influence over the country. If China should fall into the hands of another country, Japan will suffer immeasurably.

The current conflict will no doubt come to a conclusion soon. I believe that China will realize Japan's true intent and that the two nations will reconcile with each other.[70]

By teaching their pupils to write this and similar kinds of essays on the Sino-Japanese War, Issei educators taught the Nisei the Japanese interpretation of the underlying causes of the conflict.

The Issei also tried to shape Nisei opinion through the English sections of the Japanese immigrant press. Fujii Sei was the publisher and editor of the *Kashū Mainichi*, one of three Japanese dailies in Southern California. Among Issei leaders, he was one of the most, if not *the* most, ardent supporter of Japan's war efforts in China. To educate Nisei youngsters about the Sino-Japanese War, in September 1937 he started his own English column entitled *Uncle Fujii Speaks*. Written purposely in Fujii's broken English, the column presented "facts" relating to the war. To stimulate the Nisei to study "the facts" themselves, the *Nichibei Shimbun* and *Shin Sekai Asahi* of San Francisco sponsored a joint essay contest in December 1937. The chosen theme was "How I, as a Nisei, can justify Japan's case in China." Larry Tajiri, editor of the *Nichibei Shimbun* English section, summed up the purpose of the essay contest in the following way:

> With the rising flood of anti-Japanese propaganda menacing the interests of American-born Japanese in the United States, one effective means of combating that propaganda is the justification of Japan's objectives in China and the Far East.
>
> It is another case of fighting fire with fire, argument with argument.
>
> For we believe that Japan has a case in China, a case just as strong as any. Just as there is a case for or against foreign intervention in the Far East. And we believe that there is some good to be done in justifying the objectives of Japan's recent military actions.
>
> . . . .
>
> . . . We believe that this can be done and we can still consider ourselves good Americans. In the democracy that is America, there is more than one side to every question. Good Americans are pro-Chinese. We believe good Americans can be pro-Japanese, too.
>
> The first to suffer from anti-Japanese propaganda (and that is the way China's case has been presented) have been, ironically enough, the Americans of Japanese ancestry. We believe it is to be for the interests of these nisei that they be able to justify Japan's objectives.[71]

Written in English with pro-Japan interpretations, the prizewinning essays were published by both newspapers in March and April 1938.[72]

Many Issei tried to instill Japanese patriotism in their children through other cultural institutions. In the late 1930s, branches of the *Butokukai*, or Martial Virtue Society, proliferated within the Japanese immigrant population. The society's aim was to inculcate the "Japanese spirit" in Nisei youngsters by teaching *kendō*, or Japanese swordsmanship. Its titular head was Tsukamoto Matsunosuke, an Issei pioneer; its actual leader was Nakamura Tōkichi, a rabid Japanese nationalist. In 1938 the society opened a special school in Tokyo to accommodate Nisei students. Called the *Hokubei Kōdō Gakuin*, or Imperial Way Institute of North America, this school had Tōyama Mitsuru as an adviser. A right-wing nationalist, Tōyama was the head of the notorious Black Dragon Society in Japan.[73] Also in the late 1930s, Nisei tour groups of Japan invariably included Korea, Manchuria, and North China in their travel itinerary. In 1939, for example, the Southern California Association of Japanese Language Institutes sponsored a summer study tour of Japan that included side trips to Korea, Manchuria, and North China. The purpose of the tour was, in part, to teach its Nisei members "the truth of the present conflict in the Far East."[74]

Issei leaders were disappointed sorely in the older Nisei. Contrary to their high expectation, such Nisei, with few exceptions, failed to act as a bridge of understanding between the United States and Japan. Even more than in the aftermath of the Manchurian Incident, the Issei expected the Nisei to champion Japan's case in China and challenge the anti-Japanese propaganda being spread by Chinese and American publicists. In the face of the anti-Japanese propaganda, however, most older Nisei were paralyzed by confusion, remained aloof from the fray, or, worse yet, added their own voices to the anti-Japanese chorus. In 1938 Yamashita Sōen, a well-known Issei journalist, admitted that the Issei had been "disappointed" in the Nisei's failure to act as a bridge of understanding and now "doubted" the Nisei's ability to fulfill the role. Realistically speaking, he concluded that the Issei "expectation and trust" in the Nisei had been "a fruitless illusion."[75] Similarly, Azumi Suimei, editor of *Nippon to Amerika*, a popular Issei monthly, lamented the failure of the Nisei to defend Japan, which he attributed to their "ignorance" of the historical facts and circumstances surrounding the Sino-Japanese War.[76]

The few Nisei who stood up for Japan naturally drew the praise of Issei leaders. One was Tamotsu Murayama. In 1937 he was a reporter for the Dōmei Tsūshinsha, a quasi-Japanese government news agency. In the fall he went to the China front. In direct dispatches filed to the *Shin Sekai Asahi* of San Francisco, he always defended Japan's cause in China and cited the heroism of the Japanese troops. He also conveyed the gratitude the troops expressed at receiving *imonbukuro* from overseas Japanese, striking responsive chords in the hearts of the Issei who had sent them from the United

States. Subsequent to his China assignment, Murayama embarked on a speaking tour of the Japanese communities on the Pacific Coast in late 1937 and early 1938 and presented firsthand accounts of the Sino-Japanese War to Issei and Nisei audiences. As a Kibei-Nisei, Murayama was no stranger to the Issei. Born in Seattle in 1905, he had received his early education in Japan. On returning to the United States, he attended Lowell High School in San Francisco. During the mid-1930s he had been active in the San Francisco chapter of the Japanese American Citizens League. Consequently, as far as the Issei were concerned, the credibility of Murayama's pro-Japan dispatches and speeches was enhanced considerably by his roots in Japanese immigrant society.[77]

Kazumaro "Buddy" Uno was another war correspondent. A Nisei, he first went to China in the fall of 1937 as a reporter for the *Shin Sekai Asahi* and witnessed the fighting in and around Shanghai. On his second tour of China he covered the siege of Hankow in late 1938 for the *Nichibei Shimbun* and *Rafu Shimpō*. In his English dispatches, Uno was unfailingly enthusiastic about the Japanese army. It seemed to him an efficient and disciplined force, with soldiers who embodied high samurai ideals. While extolling the Japanese troops, Uno denigrated the Chinese at every opportunity. Chinese troops, in his opinion, were "guilty of unimaginable brutality and cruelty," and the Nationalist government was incapable of establishing order and governing China.[78] After each stint as a war correspondent, Uno gave pro-Japan talks before Issei and Nisei groups too. He even debated pro-China speakers in public forums before non-immigrant audiences. To an Issei leader like Abe Toyoji, publisher of the *Shin Sekai Asahi*, it was especially gratifying to see and hear such a rare Nisei like Uno defending Japan before his fellow Nisei and the American public.[79]

Issei leaders also lauded Henry Toshirō Shimanouchi. On behalf of the Japanese Foreign Ministry Shimanouchi undertook a lecture tour of the United States from November 1937 to April 1938. Publicly, he was an official representative of the Foreign Affairs Association of Japan, a semiofficial government body. Broadly speaking, his mission was to stem the tide of adverse publicity Japan was suffering at the hands of the American press. Shimanouchi had an unusual background.[80] Born in 1909 in Japan, he was reared in California since infancy. He grew up in the Japanese settlements of San Francisco, Oakland, Livingston, Fresno, and Los Angeles. His father was a very respected Issei leader associated with the *Nichibei Shimbun* for many years. Educated in American public schools, Shimanouchi was a graduate of Occidental College. By upbringing and schooling, he was closer to being a Nisei than an Issei. In 1933 he returned to Japan where he became a newspaper reporter. Three years later he joined the staff of the *Kokusai Bunka Shinkōkai* and worked alongside Miya Sannomiya as a bilingual staff member. During his American lecture tour, Shimanouchi addressed Issei and Nisei groups throughout the Pacific Coast. Issei leaders took great pride in him, for Shimanouchi had risen from their own ranks. In March 1938 he spoke in Los Angeles at a meeting of the Far East Research Institute, a Nisei study group formed to examine the causes of the Sino-Japanese War. Shimanouchi was a polished bilingual speaker. Fujii Sei thought that his defense of Japan was so masterful that he had nothing but the highest praise for him.[81]

The Sino-Japanese War affected the Foreign Ministry's thinking regarding the Nisei, too. Japanese government officials were dismayed at their own inability to combat pro-Chinese publicity. The American press heavily favored the Chinese side, depicting the Chinese people as underdogs valiantly resisting Japanese military aggression. Men like Murayama, Uno, and Shimanouchi, although few, clearly vindicated the significance and value of the Nisei as spokesmen for the Japanese side. But many more Nisei were needed to counteract the powerful influence of anti-Japanese propaganda. In order to train selected Nisei, the Foreign Ministry established a special school in 1939 called the Heishikan. The idea for this school originated with Kawai Tatsuo, information bureau chief of the Foreign Ministry. Having been once stationed in Vancouver, Canada, Kawai was knowledgeable about the Nisei. He was convinced that they could help to arrest the tide of anti-Japanese publicity if they were picked carefully and properly trained in Japan as press attachés.

The first class was composed of sixteen Nisei recruited from Hawaii, the continental United States, and Canada, all on full scholarships. All of these students were screened by local Japanese consuls. The consuls selected them because they were considered Nisei who were Americanized yet were sympathetic to Japan. As future press attachés to be stationed in the United States, such Nisei, it was believed, would be the most effective in communicating with Americans precisely because they could speak and act exactly like their fellow citizens. All Heishikan students lived and boarded at the school. In a two-year program that commenced on December 1, 1939, they studied the Japanese language and constitution, Japanese history, economics, and politics, and international law. Graduates were scheduled to be assigned to consular offices, the Domei News Agency, and the South Manchurian Railway. The outbreak of the Pacific War with the attack on Pearl Harbor precluded the assignment of the first graduates to consular offices in the United States and Canada. Be that as it may, these Nisei, trained as they were to act as official spokesmen of the Japanese government, represented a real transformation of the concept of the Nisei as a bridge of understanding. Instead of acting as an intermediary between the United States and Japan, they became, in effect, undisguised propagandists or official apologists for Japanese military expansionism in Asia.[82]

The Kibei-Nisei Problem

The so-called Kibei became a part of the Nisei problem in the 1930s. There were two categories of Kibei. Into the first category fell the Nisei in Japan who reached adulthood during the Taisho period, notably in the early 1920s. During the post–World War I years an intellectual climate conducive to new ideas developed in Japan. As a consequence, a wave of new liberal and radical political thought swept across the country, and the Japanese labor movement, suppressed since the late Meiji years, resurfaced with renewed vigor under the influence of the Russian Revolution and left-wing political ideologies. Many of the Nisei educated in this liberal climate were attracted to the prevailing progressive ideas. When such Nisei returned to the United States as the first Kibei in the late 1920s and early 1930s, they clashed with the conservatism of the Issei generation. Some Kibei of this stripe became political radicals, particularly after the onslaught of the Great Depression in 1929. They joined the American labor movement; some joined the American Communist Party. Karl Yoneda is a case in point. Born in 1906 in Glendale, California, he was raised and educated in Japan between 1913 and 1926. During his high school years in the city of Hiroshima, he participated in pro-labor activities. In 1926 he returned to the United States and almost immediately joined the Communist Party and became active in the labor movement.[83]

Although never very numerous, Kibei leftists lent the Nisei problem a distinct ideological dimension. Throughout the 1930s they consistently opposed the Japanese government and its policy in China. In line with their political convictions, they censured the Issei who patriotically rallied behind Japan during the late 1930s and decried the Issei practice of giving political, financial, material, and moral support to the Japanese government. For their part, Issei leaders roundly denounced Kibei radicals as a bunch of traitorous "reds." Local Japanese consuls kept them under close surveillance in an effort to obstruct their anti-Japanese government activities. The consuls feared their possible negative influence over the younger Kibei who returned to the United States during the 1930s. This fear was another reason why the consuls refused to cooperate with the Issei campaign in the mid-1930s to bring back the Nisei in Japan to the United States.

The second Kibei category consisted of the Nisei in Japan who came of age during the 1930s. Beginning with the 1931 Manchurian Incident, the 1930s witnessed the spread of Japanese militarism onto the Asian continent. Domestically, the Japanese government adopted harsh repressive acts, clamping down on all liberals and radicals who criticized government policy. Once the Sino-Japanese War erupted, the government instituted strict thought-control measures to muzzle all dissent and systematically promoted Shinto nationalism to mobilize the country behind the war. Under such circumstances, the Nisei who reached maturity during this decade received a very nationalistic education. Toward the end of the decade many of these Nisei rushed back to the United States. Two factors accounted for this development. The Sino-Japanese War adversely affected United States–Japan relations and cast ominous war clouds over the two nations from 1940. With premonitions of an impending Japanese-American war, those Nisei who did not relish the thought of being stranded in Japan decided to leave the country. Other Nisei men with dual nationality faced a possibility of being conscripted into Japanese military service, a possibility that loomed ever larger with the onset and expansion of the Sino-Japanese War. If they were unwilling to serve, such men came back to the United States as draft evaders. Both of these factors were behind the large number of Nisei who did actually return before the outbreak of the Pacific War.

Besides the ideological dimension, Kibei added other unique sociopsychological features to the Nisei problem. The majority of Kibei were alienated from family, peers, and society. Kibei were strangers to their own Issei parents, with no real emotional ties to them. Because of their long mutual separation, normal family bonds had never developed between the Kibei and their parents. Similarly, Kibei were strangers to their own siblings who were raised in the United States. Rooted in their separate upbringing, the two were divided by a wide, almost unbridgeable, cultural gap. All Kibei were also alienated from their Nisei peers. Many Nisei cruelly ostracized the Kibei for their "Japaneseness" and inability to speak English. To such Nisei, the Kibei represented what they did not want to be in their pathetic but fervent desire to be accepted as Americans. Finally, Kibei were alienated from society as a whole. Along with their Nisei peers, they encountered insurmountable racial barriers in seeking employment. In the case of Kibei, however, their problem was compounded by their inadequate command of English, which further limited their employment prospects. The only work available to them was low-paying, menial jobs, generally as domestic servants, fruit-stand peddlers, or agricultural field hands. And however much the Kibei aspired to study, their language handicap prevented them from enrolling in institutions of higher learning. Estranged from family, peers, and society, the Kibei understandably suffered from acute psychological problems of social isolation, an isolation that heightened their sense of "Kibeiness" just as anti-Japanese agitation reappeared on the eve of Pearl Harbor.[84]

Conclusion

Reflecting the Issei's own shifting perspective over the years, the changing Issei conceptions of the second-generation problem were largely meaningless to the Nisei themselves. Having little or no relationship to their day-to-day life, the conceptions were far too abstract. As mere infants, the Nisei never could of course understand their parents' initial conceptions of the Nisei problem in terms of education and dual nationality. Nor could most Nisei understand the concept of a bridge of understanding. It had no real meaning for the overwhelming majority of Nisei, who were children, or yet teenagers, or working-class adults who were too absorbed in eking out a living. At best, it was applicable to only a handful of middle-class, college-educated Nisei who reached adulthood in the 1920s and early 1930s. As a whole, Japanese-language institutes were unsuccessful in educating Nisei youngsters. They failed miserably to teach the Nisei to speak, read, and write fluent Japanese or to be well-informed of Japan and Far Eastern political affairs. In contrast, American public schools exercised a powerful and lasting influence. They so successfully socialized the Nisei to American values that the Nisei became largely acculturated to American culture and society.

Moreover, the concept of a bridge of understanding became untenable by the late 1930s. At the beginning of the decade men like James Y. Sakamoto, who incorporated the concept into their definition of good American citizenship, could defend Japan's position in China and simultaneously espouse Americanism. In doing so no contradiction existed in their minds. And since American public opinion was not implacably hostile to Japan, it still was possible to stand up in Japan's defense. Such was not the case in the late 1930s. American public opinion one-sidedly blamed Japan for the Sino-Japanese War and allied itself with the beleaguered Chinese Nationalist government of Chiang Kai-shek. As a result the Nisei found themselves in an unenviable position. Issei leaders expected them to champion Japan's case in China and chastised them when they did not. On the other hand, if they stood up in defense of Japan, their loyalty to the United States came under a cloud of suspicion, making any public rationalization of Japan's side in the Sino-Japanese War impossible. In July 1939 the United States government announced that it was unilaterally abrogating the 1911 United States–Japanese Treaty of Commerce and Navigation effective January 1940. From this juncture war clouds began to hover over the two nations, and the FBI and military intelligence agencies coordinated their surveillance of the Japanese immigrant community to monitor the Issei, Kibei, and Nisei suspected of espionage, fifth column activities, and potential sabotage on behalf of the Japanese government.

The Nisei generation's principal organization was the JACL. Small but national, the organization had only five thousand dues-paying members in 1940. Its leaders were mostly men who were urban, college-educated, self-employed professionals. Politically, they tended to be Republicans and hostile to the New Deal and organized labor. As their way of seeking the acceptance of the Nisei by the larger society, these leaders espoused a flag-waving type of 100 percent Americanism. To them the road to acceptance was to demonstrate, by word and deed, that the Nisei truly were as loyal and patriotic as any other American. From 1939 the FBI and military intelligence agents contacted JACL leaders up and down the Pacific Coast to seek information on suspected Issei, Kibei, and Nisei. Caught in the web of their own declaration that they were patriotic, loyal Americans, many JACL leaders actively cooperated with the agents and passed on whatever information they had. Simultaneously, they severed all public contacts with Issei leaders in the hope of dispelling suspicions that the JACL was tainted by alien influences. Under the circumstances, any defense of Japan became untenable. James Y. Sakamoto, an old JACL leader and longtime adherent to the concept of the Nisei as a bridge of understanding, defended Japan throughout the 1930s, but by 1940 he, too, realized that it was no longer possible to do so without reinforcing existing suspicions about Nisei loyalty. Thus from 1940 JACL leaders stressed Americanism above all else and incessantly declared the Nisei to be undivided in their loyalty to their native land. Even Kibei leftists cooperated with American intelligence agents and informed on Issei who engaged in patriotic activities vis-à-vis Japan. Within their ideological framework, such Issei were profascists and promilitarists. The leftists also proclaimed their own loyalty to the United States. Subordinating domestic issues to an international fight against fascism, they urged the JACL to assume the leadership of the Japanese community. In sum, except for the group of alienated Kibei, the Issei and Nisei generations were moving in two diametrically opposite directions on the eve of Pearl Harbor so that the Issei concept of the Nisei as a bridge of understanding lost all meaning and significance.

Notes

1. Satō Tsutau, *Bei-Ka ni Okeru Dai-Nisei no Kyōiku* (Vancouver: Jikyōdō, 1932), 1–2.
2. *Shin Sekai*, May 13, 1908.
3. Mikiko, "Jidō no Kannen ni Tsukite," *Beikoku Bukkyō* 9, no. 9 (Sep. 1, 1908): 15–17.
4. Zaibei Nihonjinkai, *Zaibei Nihonjinkai Hōkokusho* (Annual Report of the Japanese Association of America), no. 1 (San Francisco: Zaibei Nihonjinkai, 1909), 14.
5. *Shin Sekai*, Aug. 12, 28, 1908.
6. *Shin Sekai*, Jan. 13, 1910.
7. Zaibei Nihonjinkai, *Zaibei Nihonjinkai Hōkokusho* (Annual Report of the Japanese Association of America), no. 3 (San Francisco, 1911), 10.
8. For a summary of Nagai's speech see *Shin Tenchi* 1, no. 2 (Aug. 10, 1910): 5–6. This speech was published by the *Nichibei Shimbun* in its entirety under the title "Eijū to Kyōiku Hōshin" on July 26, 1910. Unfortunately, the early years of this newspaper have not been preserved.
9. Tōga Yoichi, "Jidō Kyōiku to Dōhō no Kakugo," *Shin Tenchi* 1, no. 5 (Nov. 10, 1910); Kannansei (pseud.), "Kyōiku Shōgen," *Beikoku Bukkyō* 11, no. 8 (Aug. 1,

1910): 7–9; and *Shin Sekai*, July 27, Aug. 7, 19–21, Sep. 4, 11, 18, 1910. See also Satō, *Bei-Ka ni Okeru Dai-Nisei no Kyōiku*, 18–38, which summarizes the substance of the debate.

10. *Shin Sekai*, July 29, 31, 1910, Aug. 26, 1911.

11. Hokka Nihongo Gakuen Kyōkai, *Beikoku Kashū Nihongo Gakuen Enkakushi* (San Francisco: Hokka Nihongo Gakuen Kyōkai, 1930), 36–37.

12. *Shin Sekai*, April 7, 1912.

13. Hokka Nihongo Gakuen Kyōkai, *Beikoku Kashū Nihongo Gakuen Enkakushi*, 27–28.

14. Ibid., 43.

15. *Shin Sekai*, June 26, 1913.

16. *Shin Sekai*, June 24, 1913.

17. Taiheiyō Engan Nihonjinkai Kyōgikai, "Gijiroku," July 15–16, 1914. The petition was printed in Nihon Imin Kyōkai, *Nihon Imin Kyōkai Hōkokusho*, no. 6 (Feb. 15, 1916): 25–31.

18. "Nijū Kokuseki Mondai no Kaiketsu," *Nihon Imin Kyōkai Hōkokusho*, no. 7 (March 15, 1916): 27–28.

19. Roger Daniels, *The Politics of Prejudice* (New York: Atheneum, 1967), 85.

20. Taiheiyō Engan Nihonjinkai Kyōgikai, "Gijiroku," Feb. 23–25 and June 24–26, 1920.

21. Taiheiyō Engan Nihonjinkai Kyōgikai, "Gijiroku," July 18–21, 1921.

22. Reflecting the youthfulness of the Nisei generation, the members of the American Loyalty League were fifteen years old or older. The majority of the eighty persons who participated in founding the league were in their midteens. *Shin Sekai*, March 29–April 1, 1923.

23. Zaibei Nihonjinkai, *Shussei Todoke Oyobi Kokuseki Ridatsu no Shiori* (San Francisco: Zaibei Nihonjinkai, 1922).

24. Taiheiyō Engan Nihonjinkai Kyōgikai, "Gijiroku," July 18–21, 1921, May 24–26, 1922.

25. Hokka Nihongo Gakuen Kyōkai, *Beikoku Kashū Nihongo Gakuen Enkakushi*, 9–10; and Tamezo Takimoto, "The Japanese Language Schools," March 1923, reel 43 in Japanese American Research Project, Japanese Foreign Ministry Archival Documents (hereafter JARP, JFMAD).

26. Nanka Kyōikukai, *Dai-Nisei no Kyōiku* (Los Angeles: Nanka Kyōikukai, 1926), 14.

27. Hokka Nihongo Gakuen Kyōkai, *Beikoku Kashū Nihongo Gakuen Enkakushi*, 102.

28. S[ukeo] Kitasawa, "Report on the Japanese Language School," ca. 1922, reel 43, JARP, JFMAD.

29. Takimoto Tamezō, "Nihongo Gakuen ni Kansuru Hōkokusho," ca. 1922, reel 42, JARP, JFMAD.

30. *Oakland Tribune*, Oct. 25–31, 1920.

31. Yoshi S. Kuno to Dr. [Benjamin Ide] Wheeler, March 7, 1921, Yoshi S. Kuno Papers (hereafter cited as Kuno Papers), Bancroft Library, University of California, Berkeley.

32. Yoshi S. Kuno to Sam H. Cohn, Oct. 2, 1921, Kuno Papers.

33. Takimoto, "Nihongo Gakuen ni Kansuru Hōkokusho."

34. To be studied at a rate of two volumes per year, this new sixteen-volume series was for an eight-year course of study.

35. *Meyer vs. Nebraska*, 262 U.S. 390 (1923).

36. *Farrington vs. Tokushige*, 273 U.S. 284 (1927). For the background of this case and the litigation process see Hawai Hōchisha, *Hawai no Nihongo Gakkō ni Kansuru Shiso Oyobi Futai Jiken* (Honolulu: Hawai Hōchisha, 1927), and Hawai Hōchisha, *Nihongo Gakkō Shōso Jushūnen Kinenshi* (Honolulu: Hawai Hōchisha, 1937).

37. Abiko Kyūtarō, "Hokubei ni Okeru Nihon Imin Mondai," *Tōkyō Keizai Zasshi* (Dec. 19, 1908), 1113–1115, and (Dec. 26, 1908), 1159–1161; Abiko Kyūtarō, "Hainichi Mondai no Shinsō Oyobi Sono Shōrai," *Taiyō*, 15, no. 5 (May 1909): 60–67.

38. *Nichibei Shimbun*, Jan. 1, 1924.

39. *Nichibei Shimbun*, Sep. 6, 13, 1924. See also *Shin Sekai*, Sep. 13, 1924.

40. *Nichibei Shimbun*, Nov. 1, 1924.

41. Miya Sannomiya, interview, June 1, 1980. See also Miya S. Kikuchi to Robert A. Wilson, Jan. 13, 1968, in Kikuchi Papers, JARP; and Miya Sannomiya, interview, tapes no. 83 and 84, JARP.

42. Shishimoto Hachirō, *Nikkei Shimin wo Kataru* (Tokyo: Shōkasha, 1934), 253–82.

43. Sadako N. Ogata, *Defiance in Manchuria: The Making of Japanese Foreign Policy, 1931–1932* (Berkeley: University of California Press, 1964).

44. Taiheiyō Engan Nihonjinkai Kyōgikai, "Gijiroku," July 14–16, 1927, and *Dai-Sankai Taiheiyō Engan Ryōji Kaigi Gijiroku*, March 12–19, 1928.

45. For Sakamoto's personal background see James Y. Sakamoto Papers, Suzallo Library, University of Washington; Frank S. Miyamoto, "The Seattle JACL and Its Role in Evacuation," n.d., Appendix A, in Japanese Evacuation and Resettlement Study, Bancroft Library, University of California, Berkeley; and Mayumi Tsutakawa, "The Political Conservatism of James Sakamoto's *Japanese American Courier*" (MA thesis, School of Communications, University of Washington, 1976), 20–22.

46. *Japanese American Courier*, Oct. 17, 1931, Jan. 23, Feb. 6, 20, March 19, 26, April 2, June 4, July 2, 16, Aug. 27, 1932.

47. Uchiyama Kiyoshi to Saitō Makoto, May 26, 1932; Uchiyama to Uchida Yasuya, July 22, 1932; and Zai-Shatoru Nihon Ryōjikan, *Zen-Bei Ryōji Kaigi*

Gijiroku ni Kansuru Chōsho, June 1936, Showa Series, Japanese Foreign Ministry, Diplomatic Records Office, Tokyo.

48. *Japanese American Courier*, Jan. 1, 1931.

49. Zai-Beikoku Rafu Nihon Ryōjikan, *Nanka Nihongo Gakuen Seito Ohanashi Taikai Oyobi Sakubun Kyōgi Taikai* (Los Angeles: Rafu Nihon Ryōjikan, 1933), 13–14.

50. Ibid.

51. Hirota Kōki to Tomii Shū et al., Nov. 16, 1934, "Nikkei Gaijin Kankei Zakken," Showa Series, Japanese Foreign Ministry, Diplomatic Records Office, Tokyo.

52. Nakauchi Kenji to Hirota Kōki, Dec. 5, 1934; Hori Kōichi to Hirota, Dec. 28, 1934; Nakamura Toyokazu to Hirota, Feb. 15, 1935; Sawada Kenzō to Hirota, Feb. 28, 1935; Uchiyama Kiyoshi to Hirota, March 7, 1935; Tomii Shū to Hirota, June 18, 1935; and Tamura Teijirō to Hirota, July 9, 1935, "Nikkei Gaijin Kankei Zakken," Showa Series, Japanese Foreign Ministry, Diplomatic Records Office, Tokyo.

53. Compiled from "Nikkei Gaijin Kankei Zakken," Showa Series, Japanese Foreign Ministry, Diplomatic Records Office, Tokyo.

54. Yamashita Sōen, *Nichibei wo Tsunagu Mono* (Tokyo: Bunseisha, 1938), 266.

55. *Rafu Shimpō*, Aug. 17, 1932.

56. Yamashita Sōen, *Nikkei Shimin no Nihon Ryūgaku Jijō* (Tokyo: Bunseisha, 1935), 4–6.

57. Kaigai Kyōiku Kyōkai, *Kaigai Kyōiku Kyōkai Yōran* (Tokyo: Kaigai Kyōiku Kyōkai, 1940).

58. Nihon Beifu Kyōkai, *Nihon Beifu Kyōkai Yōran* (Tokyo: Nihon Beifu Kyōkai, 1937).

59. Nagata Shigeshi, "Waseda Kokusai Gakuin ni Tsuite," *Rikkō Sekai* 375 (March 1936): 28–32.

60. Nagata Shigeshi, "Rikkō Ryūgakusei Ryō no Kaisetsu ni Tsuite," *Rikkō Sekai* 375 (March 1936): 2–6.

61. Nagata Shigeshi, "Tōkyō Kirisutokyō Seinenkai Nichigo Bunka Gakkō Nikkei Gaijinbu," *Rikkō Sekai* 375 (March 1936): 37–40.

62. *Keisen News*, no. 23 (July 1940); and Hana Kawai, interview, April 26, 1974. Hana Kawai was a Nisei instructor at Keisen Girls' School.

63. Yamashita, *Nikkei Shimin no Nihon Ryūgaku Jijō*, 93–99; Yamashita, *Nichibei wo Tsunagu Mono*, 297–300; and Tsunemitsu Kōnen, *Nihon Ryūgaku no Jissai* (Tokyo: Runbini Shuppansha, 1936), 47–53.

64. Fujinami Shōhei to Yamamoto Tatsuo and Hirota Kōki, Dec. 15, 1933, "Nikkei Gaijin Kankei Zakken," Showa Series, Japanese Foreign Ministry, Diplomatic Records Office, Tokyo.

65. Zaibei Nihonjinkai, "Dai-Nisei Kibei no Shiori" (San Francisco: Zaibei Nihonjinkai, 1935). See also Yamashita, *Nikkei Shimin no Nihon Ryūgaku Jijō*, 170–74; Zaibei Nihonjinkai, *Zaibei Nihonjinshi* (San Francisco: Zaibei Nihonjinkai, 1940), 1117–18; and Murayama Tamotsu, *Amerika Nisei—Sono Kunan no Rekishi* (Tokyo: Jiji Tsūshinsha, 1964), 174–88.

66. California Joint Immigration Committee, "Dangers Created by Japanese Dual Citizenship," May 27, 1936.

67. Gaimushō Amerikakyoku, *Hokubei Nikkei Shimin Gaikyō* (Tokyo: Amerikakyoku Daiikka, 1936), 168–80.

68. Yuji Ichioka, "Japanese Immigrant Nationalism: The Issei and the Sino-Japanese War, 1937–1941," unpublished paper, 1981.

69. *Rafu Shimpō*, Jan. 16, 1938.

70. *Rafu Shimpō*, Feb. 27, 1938. The *Rafu Shimpō* published many Nisei essays. See March 27, April 3, 10, May 29, June 19, July 3, Aug. 28, 1938.

71. *Nichibei Shimbun*, Dec. 10, 1937.

72. The essays were published by the *Nichibei Shimbun* from March 14 to April 15, 1938.

73. Momii Ikken, *Hokubei Kendō Taikan* (San Francisco: Hokubei Butokukai, 1939), 561–640.

74. Nanka Nihongo Gakuen Kyōkai, *Kengaku Ryokō Nisshi Kinenchō* (Los Angeles: Nanka Nihongo Gakuen Kyōkai, 1939), 11.

75. Yamashita, *Nichi-Bei wo Tsunagu Mono*, 138.

76. Azumi Suimei, "Shinshun wo Mukaeru Kokoro," *Nippon to Amerika* 7, no. 1 (Jan. 1938): 14–16.

77. Murayama's articles appeared in the *Shin Sekai Asahi* during the months of Sep., Oct., and Nov. 1937. He had published an account of his earlier trips to Latin America and Manchuria in which he discussed the Nisei problem. See Murayama Tamotsu, *Shigosen Nanboku* (Tokyo: Sankōdō, 1936).

78. Uno's initial reportage was in the form of a personal narrative, which he penned after his first tour of the battlefront. This appeared in the *Shin Sekai Asahi* from Dec. 26, 1937, to July 14, 1938. He also published short pieces in the *Rafu Shimpō*, Dec. 27, 28, 1937, and Jan. 3–6, 1938. His dispatches during his second tour appeared in the *Nichibei Shimbun* from Aug. 16 to Dec. 28, 1938. In 1939 he also wrote a series entitled "Let's Face Facts," which appeared in the *Nichibei Shimbun* and *Rafu Shimpō*. It was published in the former from Jan. 12 to June 5, 1939.

79. Shōyōsei, "Toki no Kage," *Shin Sekai Asahi*, Jan. 27, 1938. *Shōyō* was the pen name of Abe Toyoji.

80. Henry Toshirō Shimanouchi, interview, tape no. 67, JARP.

81. *Kashū Mainichi*, March 19, 1938.

82. Hirota Ikurō, "Tatakau 'Nisei Gakkō' Monogatari," *Bungei Shunjū* (April 1956): 262–71; Ikeda Norizane, *Puropaganda Senshi* (Tokyo: Chūō Kōronsha, 1981), 19–28; and Kazuma Ueno, interview, June 27, 1974, Tokyo. A Canadian-born Nisei, Ueno was a member of the first Heishikan class.

83. Karl G. Yoneda, *Ganbatte: Sixty-Year Struggle of a Kibei Worker* (Los Angeles: Asian American Studies Center, University of California, 1983).

84. Zaibei Nihonjinkai, *Zaibei Nihonjinshi*, 1117–22.

THREE

Kengakudan

The Origin of Nisei Study Tours of Japan

The interwar years constitute a distinct period in Japanese American history, particularly from 1924, with the enactment of the 1924 Immigration Act, until the outbreak of the Pacific War. One distinctive feature of this period is the full emergence of the so-called second-generation problem. Japanese immigrants interpreted the enactment of the 1924 Immigration Act, which abruptly terminated all Japanese immigration to the United States, as the culminating event in the string of stunning defeats they suffered at the hands of anti-Japanese exclusionists. The *Nichibei Shimbun* of San Francisco, expressing its reaction to this sequence of defeats, designated 1924 as *yaku-doshi*, or "year of misfortune," for the Japanese people in the United States.[1] From this point in time *Issei* leaders and educators, having failed to stem the tide of Japanese exclusion, advanced the novel ideal that the *Nisei* generation should become a *kakehashi*, or bridge of understanding, between the United States and Japan in order to dispel the misunderstandings that had fueled that movement. Such Issei realized, however, that the Nisei had to be knowledgeable about Japan if they ever hoped to serve as an effective bridge of understanding. So the Issei organized special study tours of Japan called *kengakudan* for the Nisei to give them firsthand exposure to their ancestral land, thereby hoping to promote an ongoing interest in the country among the second generation. The origin of the *kengakudan*, and indeed of the ideal of a bridge of understanding itself, can be traced to the first two *kengakudan* sponsored by the *Nichibei Shimbun* in 1925 and 1926.

The *Nichibei Shimbun* simultaneously mirrored and influenced the

53

changing Issei attitude toward the second generation in the post-1924 years. By the 1920s the *Nichibei Shimbun* had emerged as the undisputed leader among Japanese immigrant dailies published in the United States with the widest circulation and greatest influence. It came out in two editions, one in San Francisco and the other in Los Angeles, with a combined press run of more than twenty-five thousand, and circulated throughout the state of California, the Rocky Mountain region, and even in the Pacific Northwest. Abiko Kyūtarō (1865–1936), one of the original founders and a highly respected Issei leader, was the longtime publisher.[2] From its inception in 1899, the *Nichibei Shimbun* understandably devoted its news coverage to the Issei generation. During the exclusion movement period it ardently exhorted the Issei to cast off their *dekasegi*, or sojourning mentality, and opt for permanent residency in the United States. At the same time, it encouraged the Issei to become productive farmers, to start families, and to adapt themselves to American society. Abiko changed this editorial line in 1924, just as the anti-Japanese exclusion movement was peaking. From January 1924 the *Nichibei Shimbun* began to underscore the growing significance of the Nisei generation in the future of the Japanese in the United States.

According to Abiko's point of view, that future hinged on how the Nisei generation would fare in their own native land.[3] The Issei were so-called aliens ineligible to citizenship without the right of naturalization; the Nisei were American citizens because they were born in America. The Issei were subject to numerous forms of legal discrimination; the Nisei, in theory, had all the rights that all American citizens enjoyed. The Issei were entering old age; the Nisei were about to come of age. The Issei had laid the foundation of Japanese immigrant society, but the Nisei were the ones who were going to construct a lasting edifice on the foundation. Broadly speaking, Abiko perceived the Nisei as extensions of the Yamato race outside of Japan and believed that the ultimate worth of the Japanese people as a whole would be measured by the success or failure of the Nisei generation in the United States.[4] Thus the *Nichibei Shimbun* upheld the view that the Issei had a compelling moral obligation of inspiring, disciplining, and educating the young Nisei to enable them to realize their full potential in American society.

Throughout the stormy anti-Japanese exclusion movement period, Abiko adhered to his belief that the exclusion question could be solved amicably. He never interpreted the question purely in terms of economic competition, political demagoguery, or simple racism, although he acknowledged that all of these factors were involved in one way or another. Some degree of economic competition existed between Japanese immigrants and white Americans, to be sure, but that was not sufficient to explain the anti-Japanese hostility. Occupying different sectors of the labor market, most Japanese were not in direct competition with white workers. Assuming that Chinese immigrants had been, Abiko believed that the Japanese were identified, wrongfully, with the Chinese by white Americans, thereby conjuring up the specter of economic competition. Political demagogues were plentiful enough, but they were offset by other people who were sympathetic to the Japanese. The racial animus toward the Japanese, unlike that toward African Americans, included a white fear that Japanese had superior traits that made them formidable opponents against whom white Americans could not compete successfully. Fundamentally, Abiko viewed the exclusion movement as a problem of ignorance. Americans were ignorant of Japan and Japanese immigrants, and their ignorance was at the bottom of all the misunderstandings that fueled the movement. Abiko had an abiding faith that communication and education could dispel the misunderstandings and clear the way for a solution to the exclusion question.[5]

Accordingly, Abiko placed great stock in the second generation. In order to dispel the ignorance behind the anti-Japanese exclusion movement, he envisioned the Nisei playing a crucial role as a so-called bridge of understanding. In his view the Nisei had a special mission of promoting harmonious relations between Japan and the United States by virtue of their unique background. Being Japanese by blood descent, but American by birth and education, the Nisei were suited ideally to assume the role of dispelling misunderstandings between the two nations. Abiko was aware that the Nisei had to be educated about Japanese affairs if they ever hoped to be an effective bridge of understanding. For Abiko, therefore, the first order of business was to stimulate an interest in Japan among the Nisei. And in order to awaken that interest, Abiko was convinced that the best method was to let the Nisei see the country with their own eyes.

The concept of the Nisei as a bridge of understanding was also tied to another concept: the Pacific era. According to this latter concept the Nisei were coming of age in a new epoch. With the decline of European civilization the Atlantic era was drawing to a close. The center of the world had shifted from the Atlantic to the Pacific, and the United States and Japan had emerged as the two dominant powers at opposite ends of the Pacific basin.

This heralded the beginning of the Pacific era in which the East and West, as represented by Japan and the United States, were meeting each other at long last. The result of this encounter would be a new Pacific culture blending the best elements of Oriental and Occidental cultures. The Nisei had a unique role to play in this historic encounter. By upholding harmonious United States–Japan relations, they were destined to make major contributions toward the peace and stability of the Pacific era. Simultaneously, they were destined to be creators and carriers of the new Pacific culture.

To influence the second generation, the *Nichibei Shimbun* started an English section on April 3, 1925. The newspaper had commenced publication on April 3, 1899, so that April 3 was an auspicious anniversary date. In 1920 it had printed English translations of selected editorials and some articles in English, but these had been aimed primarily at white American readers. Now the English section was directed specifically toward the young Nisei readership. James A. B. Scherer, the first English editor, referred to the onset of the Pacific era by quoting Theodore Roosevelt in his opening editorial: "The Mediterranean era died with the discovery of the Americas. The Atlantic era is now at the height of its development, and must soon exhaust the resources of its command. The Pacific era, destined to be the greatest of all, is just at its dawn."[6]

At the same time, Abiko and the *Nichibei Shimbun* began to espouse what they called *minzoku bunkashugi*, or Japanese ethnic culture. The *Nichibei Shimbun* claimed that past advocates of adaptation had "indiscriminately" and "blindly" promoted "assimilation" among Japanese immigrants in reaction to the allegations of unassimilability leveled by anti-Japanese exclusionists. As a general rule such proponents had been "people closely affiliated with the Christian churches and those overly enamored with Anglo-Americanism," and many of these people had gone to absurd extremes. In the aftermath of the many defeats suffered at the hands of the anti-Japanese forces, however, the proponents of assimilation were "in retreat" and were "scorned" by ordinary Japanese immigrants.[7] Here the *Nichibei Shimbun* was also criticizing itself, albeit indirectly, because it, too, had exhorted Japanese immigrants to assimilate to American ways. In place of its own past advocacy of assimilation the *Nichibei Shimbun* now affirmed the value and uniqueness of Japanese culture derived from the ancient Japanese past, which the Nisei had to study in order to fulfill their own destiny. In Abiko's own words, "the second-generation should . . . make it a point to understand and appreciate

Figure 2. Abiko Kyūtarō (standing to the left of the lifesaver), founder of the first *kengakudan*, greets the 1925 tour group upon their return to San Francisco. His wife, Abiko Yonako, leader of the group, stands next to him, behind the lifesaver. Courtesy of Abiko Family Papers, Special Collections, Charles E. Young Research Library, UCLA.

Japan and the Japanese people. . . . Through knowing the real Japan and its remarkable culture, they can render to the world an inestimable service."[8]

All of this lay behind Abiko's decision to sponsor the first organized Nisei study tours of Japan in 1925 and 1926. These first study tours originated specifically in his belief that the Issei generation, in seeking to inspire, discipline, and educate the Nisei, should afford the Nisei an opportunity to experience directly the culture of their ancestors. In other words, the *Nichibei Shimbun* study tours were organized for the purpose of giving the Nisei firsthand exposure to Japanese society and culture, thereby hoping to stimulate an ongoing interest in Japan among them. In 1925 the *Nichibei Shimbun* described the expected benefits from the first tour:

> After the young Nisei boys and girls see and understand Japan, they will become conscious of their own ethnicity and gain confidence in themselves. Individually, they will be blessed with self-assurance; they will

become essential links in fostering Japanese-American amity, each in their own personal way; and they will naturally realize what they must do as Americans for America. Of course, it is not possible to achieve everything in a short, three-month tour. Yet first impressions have a way of influencing young people for life. We are confident that comparative good results can be achieved in a short time.[9]

Four young Seattle girls had earlier confirmed these high expectations, at least in Abiko's mind. These girls—Taeko Miyagawa, Tokiko Miyagawa, Sumire Okazaki, and Yukiko Otsuki—visited Japan in the spring of 1924 in a tour arranged by the Japanese Women's Christian Temperance Union and learned that their parents' homeland was considerably different from what they had imagined it to be. "[The] real Japan, which I have seen with my eyes," Taeko Miyagawa reported, "was very different from the Japan I had seen in my imagination. I found that the land of my mother's birth was much better than I had expected." Tokiko Miyagawa echoed her cousin's opinion: "Yes, we have seen Japan and we have enjoyed our trip wonderfully. After visiting our parents' country I'm happy that I can say, 'I like Japan very much.'" Tokiko went on to assert that "[the] Japan I knew before I went there and [the] Japan I now know are quite different, and this difference is delightful to mention, because I found it a far better country than what I have known." Sumire Okazaki said, "[T]his trip has brought me very much closer to Japan," making her "realize the great responsibility which rests upon us, the American-born Japanese. In our hands lies the power to bring these two nations into closer relationship and understanding."[10]

Once these four girls returned to Seattle, they gave public lectures before Issei and Nisei audiences on what they had observed and experienced in Japan. The Japanese Association of America, influenced by newspaper accounts of their talks published in the *Hokubei Jiji* and *Taihoku Nippō* of Seattle, invited them to California in the fall. The girls addressed many groups throughout the state, speaking in Japanese before the Issei and in English before the Nisei. The *Nichibei Shimbun* was so impressed that it praised the girls effusively.[11] These events formed the background to Abiko's decision to sponsor the first *kengakudan* of 1925. Not by coincidence, this occurred six months after the enactment of the 1924 Immigration Act marking the triumph of the anti-Japanese exclusion movement.

In November 1924 the *Nichibei Shimbun* announced its intent of sponsoring an all-expense-paid Nisei study group that would tour Japan for three full months in the spring of 1925.[12] The group was to be composed of high school or college students who were to be selected in a kind of popularity contest on a broad geographical basis. Abiko devised a clever selection procedure calculated to increase the circulation of his newspaper. All *Nichibei Shimbun* subscribers were made eligible to cast votes for *kengakudan* members. Any subscriber who renewed his or her subscription for six months was entitled to cast six hundred votes; any subscriber whose renewal was for one year was entitled to fifteen hundred votes. Any new six-month subscriber was entitled to cast eight hundred votes, any new one-year subscriber two thousand. The voting period ran for three months, from November 10, 1924, to February 10, 1925. Nisei who received the highest number of votes became members of the study group.

Eventually, eleven Nisei were selected through this unusual selection process. These Nisei were:[13]

Name	Hometown	Total Votes
Grace Kunie Umezawa	Los Angeles	1,801,704
Yukiko Furuta	Oakland	1,740,313
Margaret Shizuko Tan	San Francisco	1,723,696
Sanae Nakashima	Stockton	1,560,534
Hisako Fujii	Alameda	1,431,345
Clarence Yoneo Arima	Salt Lake City	1,365,190
Shizume Sakamoto	Los Angeles	1,358,918
Thomas Tsutomu Kurihara	Oxnard	1,355,348
Frank Yoneto Kataoka	Los Angeles	1,109,259
George Isaji Okimoto	Denver	789,662
Norman Takashi Kobayashi	Fresno	577,471

The first *kengakudan* members constituted a diverse lot. The girls outnumbered the boys by six to five. All were high school graduates; five were university students. Fluency in the Japanese language varied considerably from individual to individual. Margaret Shizuko Tan, being the most Americanized, knew very little Japanese, while Hisako Fujii and Grace Kunie

Umezawa, who happened to be first cousins, could speak, read, and write Japanese. A Hawaii-born Nisei, George Isaji Okimoto, was the oldest and most capable public speaker, while Sanae Nakashima of Stockton was the youngest. The eleven *kengakudan* members represented various Japanese immigrant communities in California, Utah, and Colorado. Their parents' place of origin in Japan varied greatly—three members traced their origin to Kumamoto Prefecture, two to Fukuoka Prefecture, and one each to Kagoshima, Nagano, Niigata, Hiroshima, and Ehime prefectures. All of the *kengakudan* members were of urban origin, except Thomas Tsutomu Kurihara, who was a son of an Oxnard farmer.[14]

Yukiko Furuta had a very interesting background. Before the well-known incident surrounding John Aiso at Le Conte Junior High in Hollywood, she was at the center of an earlier controversy. In the fall of 1922 Aiso had been elected student body president but was removed from office because of his race. In December 1921 Furuta was selected to be the January 1922 class valedictorian at Oakland High School by the principal and faculty based on her high scholastic achievements. On learning of her selection, a group of disaffected white students petitioned the Oakland superintendent of education and appealed to him to disqualify her as the class valedictorian. The issue of race was central, although the disaffected students denied it. In any event Furuta found herself suddenly at the center of a raging controversy not of her own making.[15]

Much to the credit of the Oakland High School officials, they refused to buckle under the pressure exerted by the disaffected students and permitted Furuta to deliver her valedictorian address. Since this incident generated considerable publicity, Furuta became a cause célèbre and source of immense pride among the Issei in the Oakland–San Francisco area. Indeed, the *Nichibei Shimbun* proudly reported that she delivered her speech, entitled "American Education: An Appreciation," "forcefully" and that she received "a standing ovation" after she finished it.[16] The notoriety Furuta enjoyed no doubt explains in large measure why the East Bay Japanese community cast so many votes in her favor.

The *Nichibei Shimbun* gave wide publicity to the 1925 *kengakudan*:

> Japanese American citizens have the important and lofty mission of contributing to Japanese-American amity by deepening American understanding of Japan and the Japanese. This mission transcends individual lines of

work. Whether called a mission or destiny, it is something with which the Nisei is born. And to fulfill this mission, every Japanese American must have a sound understanding of Japan and the Japanese. Such an understanding can be acquired by seeing Japan at first-hand, by listening to accurate accounts, and by systematic study. In this sense, study tours of Japan are extremely significant.[17]

Mrs. Abiko Yonako (1880–1944), wife of Abiko Kyūtarō, served as the chaperon-leader of the *kengakudan*. She also acted as a surrogate mother figure for the young *kengakudan* members. Mrs. Abiko had a very unusual background. She was a younger sister of Tsuda Umeko, founder of Tsuda College of Tokyo (initially known as Joshi Eigaku Juku), famous for its education in English literature and the English language. As a graduate of a private Methodist mission school, the Peeresses' School, and Tsuda College itself, Mrs. Abiko was a highly educated Issei woman who had a fluent command of English. Indeed, she had achieved fluency well before her marriage to Abiko Kyūtarō in 1909.[18]

Mrs. Abiko was mindful of a negative stereotype of the Nisei in Japan, traceable to a negative stereotype of the Issei generation dating back to the beginning of Japanese emigration in the late nineteenth century. Some Japanese in Japan, prejudiced by class bias and/or outright ignorance, believed that the Issei represented the dregs of Japanese society. And because of this alleged lower-class origin of the Issei generation, such Japanese automatically presumed all Issei to be hopelessly uneducated and uncouth and therefore even blamed them—at least initially—for the emergence of anti-Japanese hostility among white Americans in the belief that the Issei had aroused that hostility through their own misconduct in America. The offspring of the Issei, referred to pejoratively as *imin no ko*, or children of immigrants, were considered no better. Indeed, as an extension of the negative stereotype of the Issei generation, the Nisei were presumed to be equally, if not more, uneducated and uncouth.

To avoid reinforcing this negative image of the Nisei, Mrs. Abiko diligently taught lessons in Japanese social etiquette, Japanese social customs, and Japanese polite language to the *kengakudan* members. Every morning en route to Japan, she held classes aboard ship. According to one member, Mrs. Abiko admonished the *kengakudan* members that they must not come across as *imin no ko* during their stay in Japan.[19] Contrary to the negative stereotype, they had to impress the Japanese people that they were an educated group by speaking polite Japanese, by behaving in a "proper" manner, and by scrupulously observing Japanese social customs. Mrs. Abiko also stressed the paramount importance of strict observance of social hierarchy based on class, age, and gender in interacting with the Japanese people.

In a speech delivered in English during the 1925 tour Mrs. Abiko clearly expressed the purpose of the *kengakudan*:

> The United States and Japan, facing each other across this great ocean, have the important mission of promoting peace and amity among the Pacific countries. I humbly believe that you who have been working for the furtherance of peace will be interested in my party. We are not mere sightseers, we have come with the serious purpose of studying the country of our ancestors. Probably for the first time a group of Japanese students, American born of Japanese descent, is visiting Japan for the express purpose of building themselves into a bridge between the two countries.[20]

Later, in another English speech, Mrs. Abiko recalled what she and her husband had envisioned in organizing the *kengakudan*:

> As my husband and I watched thousands of Japanese children growing up in America and becoming ready to take their places as American citizens, we wondered what their peculiar contribution to American life should be. Naturally, being born and raised in America, they should be able to contribute what every other citizen can contribute, but above that, we felt that they had the God given opportunity of introducing the best parts of their ancient heritage.
>
> Now we realized that these children could not make this best and important contribution because they were so thoroughly Americanized that they no longer knew eastern culture. Thus they were not able to make any worthwhile contribution to American life, or act as bridges of peace and understanding between our two countries as only they could have done. However, with the training of their Japanese fathers and mothers in their homes, we felt that they would quickly understand and appreciate the best in the Orient if only they were given the opportunity of coming into contact with their forefather's [*sic*] culture.[21]

The 1925 *kengakudan* traveled first-class en route to and from Japan and while on tour in the country. In Tokyo they stayed at the Marunouchi

Hotel, near Tokyo Station, then a brand-new, first-class, modern facility. Because Abiko Kyūtarō and his wife had close personal ties with many prominent Japanese, the *kengakudan* had entry into Japanese upper-class society and access to places normally closed to ordinary visitors. Consequently, the *kengakudan* members literally saw Japanese society from the top down. Abiko Kyūtarō had personally asked Viscount Shibusawa Eiichi to assist the *kengakudan*. In a letter to Shibusawa, Abiko noted that "the American-born Nikkei citizens were the key to the solution of future Japanese-American issues and that it was essential to expose these young boys and girls to the culture and scenic beauty of their ancestral land."[22] A leading figure in Japan's financial circle, Shibusawa had worked for better Japanese-American relations during the anti-Japanese exclusion movement period and was personally aware of Japanese immigrants and their American-born children.

Shibusawa himself believed that the Nisei generation should be educated to serve as a bridge of understanding between Japan and the United States. At a reception held in his private residence for the *kengakudan* he reportedly "emphasized especially the responsibility resting on second-generation Japanese in America to bring about a real understanding between the two countries and thus secure permanent peace in the Pacific."[23] And in order to make their tour of Japan as meaningful as possible, Shibusawa assisted in opening many doors for the *kengakudan*. While in Tokyo itself, the members were received by many high Japanese government officials, including Foreign Minister Shidehara Kijūrō, and members of both houses of the Japanese Diet, as well as by the American ambassador to Japan. They were also received by officials of the Yokohama Specie Bank and Sumitomo Bank, by Asano Sōichirō, president of the Oriental Steamship Company, and many other prominent persons. And in addition to making the usual round of various tourist sights in the Tokyo area, they were allowed to see the Imperial Palace and paid calls on the Tokyo metropolitan daily newspapers and other publications. Besides Tokyo, they visited Yokohama, Kamakura, Nikko, Sendai, Nagoya, Kyoto, Nara, Osaka, Okayama, Hiroshima, and Kyushu.[24] Only one unfortunate event marred the study tour. At the beginning Shizume Sakamoto of Los Angeles became ill and had to be sent home early.

In welcoming back the 1925 *kengakudan*, the *Nichibei Shimbun* editorially expressed its expectations of the young returnees:

Born in America, educated in American schools, and raised in an American environment, the Nisei are American citizens who fully understand the United States. At the same time, they have the potential of understanding Japan because they possess an "Oriental sensibility" rooted in their racial background. There is no question that the Nisei can promote understanding of the Orient among Americans and that they have the enormous potential of becoming a great bridge between Japan and the United States. If the returning *kengakudan* members do something in the near future towards the realization of this enormous potential, the main goal of our newspaper will have been attained.[25]

As soon as the *kengakudan* members returned, they immediately embarked on speaking tours of local Japanese communities throughout California and elsewhere. Each member spoke on different topics relating to their experience in Japan, and if their command of the Japanese language was sufficient, they presented their talks in Japanese before the Issei. In San Francisco, on June 27, 1925, Abiko Kyūtarō himself presided over a meeting at which the returnees spoke. Hisako Fujii spoke in Japanese on "A Day in the Nishi-Hongwanji," Margaret Shizuko Tan on "The Religious Movement in Japan," George Isaji Okimoto on "The Ancient Civilization of Japan," Yukiko Furuta on her overall impressions of Japan, and Grace Umezawa on "Thoughts on the Conclusion of the Kengaku Dan Trip."[26]

In writing of his own speaking tour in Idaho and Utah, Clarence Arima wrote:

> I made my first Japanese speech yesterday at a gathering of Japanese people in this district (Burley, Idaho). Talked to them for practically one hour and a half concerning our whole trip to Japan. They were certainly glad to have the information, even if it was delivered in broken Japanese. Many were surprised at my radical improvement in being able to speak so fluently. They marvelled at what the trip had accomplished for me. At Salt Lake City, too, they wish me to speak in Japanese; I have consented, providing they allow me the privilege to speak to the . . . American born in English separately.

Continuing, Arima explained what the tour had personally meant to him:

> This trip has certainly been a great teacher to me, not only in traveling experiences, but socially and psychologically as well. The friends I have

made alone more than doubly repay me for the long, long journey I took. Of course, we all looked forward to a pleasant and joyful voyage, and received it—but, on top of this, I believe there has been a bigger and broader realization awakened in every member's heart. Before going to Japan, what facts did we have in our minds concerning our intimate relations with her? Very few; but now—why, our brains are overflowing with them. A few years ago I realized the fact that it was the duty of the second generation to build up and keep tight the bonds of friendship between America and Japan, but never before has this fact been brought to light more impressively than it has since my journey in the past few months.[27]

The success of the first *kengakudan* prompted the *Nichibei Shimbun* to sponsor a second tour in 1926. In announcing its plans, it said that "the first *kengakudan* had been an unparalleled success, due in no small measure to the enormous support and cooperation it had received from the public."[28] The 1926 *kengakudan* members were to be selected by *Nichibei Shimbun* subscribers under identical rules as those used to pick the 1925 members. The voting period this time extended from September 21, 1925, to January 31, 1926. Any seventeen-to-twenty-five-year-old Nisei was eligible, and in addition this time any Issei, in the same age bracket, who had come to the United States at the age of nine or younger was also eligible.

To promote public interest in the second tour, the *Nichibei Shimbun* carefully orchestrated a publicity campaign. It published accounts, in Japanese, of what the 1925 tour had personally meant for the members of the first *kengakudan*. Such accounts impressed on Issei parents the positive merits of sending the Nisei to Japan. Many parents worried that their children, without a knowledge of Japanese and Japanese culture, would develop an inferiority complex and despise their own Japanese roots. Margaret Shizuko Tan's description of what she had gained from the 1925 tour must have been a source of joy to such parents:

> I have often asked myself why I wasn't born as a Caucasian, but as a yellow-faced Japanese. After touring Japan and associating with the Japanese people, I now realize such thoughts are foolish and childish. I am proud that we [Nisei] are descendants of a race which has a culture fundamentally different from Caucasians. I also now realize acutely that we have the mission of contributing this Japanese culture to American civilization.[29]

In a similar vein Clarence Yoneo Arima said:

> My attitude toward the land of my parents has undergone a radical change. Now I can fully appreciate the civilization and culture of the Japanese people, and I have a keen sense of affinity to them. . . . I was especially impressed by the kindness and cordial treatment accorded to members of the Kengaku Dan by the various business firms and individuals, and also the schools, through their teachers and students. This kindness and courtesy . . . did more than anything else to imbue in me pride in my Japanese origin.[30]

George Isaji Okimoto spoke similarly:

> When I think of my level of understanding of Japan before I toured the country, I get cold chills. I'm embarrassed to say it, but I didn't know anything. I had thought I knew Japan because I had read some English books on Japan and Japanese-American issues. But I learned to my chagrin that Caucasian authors do not understand Japan. It makes me very happy that I learned things one cannot gain from books through my recent trip.[31]

In addition to the personal accounts of the first *kengakudan* members, the *Nichibei Shimbun* also published letters from their parents. These letters informed Issei parents of the beneficial results of study tours and encouraged them to allow their own children to participate. Fujii Matsutarō, father of Hisako Fujii, wrote as follows:

> I sincerely express my gratitude to the *Nichibei Shimbun* for its work on behalf of the second-generation. Based on my personal experience, I state categorically that it is essential to send the American-born Nisei boys and girls on study tours of Japan.
> There is no need for you to worry. I urge you to allow your children to participate. With the support of many people, my own daughter visited Japan as a member of the first *kengakudan*. She learned about Japan's ancient history by visiting old historic sites, Shinto shrines, and Buddhist temples. I'm happy and grateful that she was also able to see Japan's progress in modern industries by visiting schools and factories. My daughter and the entire Fujii family benefitted from the tour, and no doubt our future descendants will, too. I believe that it demonstrates how necessary and valuable it is to send the Nisei, born and educated in the United States with its recent short history of 150 years or so, to tour Japan with her

ancient history of 3,000 years. It also demonstrates that it is our obligation to send them. Whenever we have talked about Japan after dinner in our home, I was until recently always the teacher who taught. After my daughter returned from her trip, however, she has become the teacher who teaches. Just from this simple fact you can imagine what she got out of her trip.

After the tour officially ended in Kumamoto Prefecture, my daughter visited my birthplace in Fukuoka Prefecture where my father of over 80-years-old and my mother of nearly 80-years-old live. My parents wept with joy when they learned that their granddaughter had been sent to Japan under the auspices of the *Nichibei Shimbun* by the Japanese in the United States. My father apparently perceived my "stupid daughter" as his "very smart granddaughter."[32]

Furuta Hamazō, father of Yukiko Furuta, listed what he considered the principal benefits the *kengakudan* members had derived from the first study tour. First, each tour member had made noticeable improvements in speaking Japanese. This in itself spoke well of the *kengakudan*. Second, the members all returned exhibiting "more real Japanese character traits," an even more positive benefit. Third, and here the appeal was directly to the hearts of Issei parents, the *kengakudan* experience had made all members sensitive to the "sufferings and difficulties" their parents had had to endure in the United States, with its "different manners, customs, and language" and consequently made the members realize that they owed a "debt" to their parents. Fourth and last, the members gained something intangible that would help them through the vicissitudes of later life.[33] These presumed benefits no doubt were very appealing to ordinary Issei parents, convincing many of them to support the second *kengakudan* and to cast votes for the Nisei candidate of their choice.

This time the *Nichibei Shimbun* also promoted competition among communities as a part of its publicity campaign. To encourage local communities to support their local candidates, the *Nichibei Shimbun* published daily tallies of the voting results from October 1, 1925. In the early voting tally the Japanese of Sacramento and its vicinity quickly made Flora Yae Tsuda, an exceedingly bright, eighteen-year-old high school senior, the leading vote getter. The people of Oakland, Alameda, and Berkeley rallied behind Makiko Utsumi, reputedly a beautiful vocalist, making her the early second-best vote getter. The Issei of San Diego marshaled their support behind May

Mutsuko Fujito, a high school honor student. In the same manner, the people of the Long Beach area backed Frank Aiji Endo, a recent valedictorian of his graduating class at Long Beach High School. Outside the state of California the Japanese of Portland eventually threw their weight behind the candidacy of Ruth Nomura, a typewriter whiz and employee of the S. Ban Company. The competition among communities also featured special advertisements, with photographs, placed in the *Nichibei Shimbun* by community organizations, describing the qualifications and achievements of their local candidates and listing the local groups endorsing them. The daily tally and advertisements combined to further stimulate popular interest in the 1926 *kengakudan*. All foregoing means were employed by the *Nichibei Shimbun* to publicize the second study tour and indirectly further disseminate Abiko's belief in the necessity of the Nisei generation learning about Japan and Japanese culture.

In the end, ten Nisei were selected as members of the 1926 *kengakudan*:[34]

Name	Hometown	Total Votes
Flora Yae Tsuda	Sacramento	1,285,863
Kimiko Kumamoto	Los Angeles	1,068,035
Kazuko Matsumura	Fresno	981,686
Shigeru Hashii	Moneta	950,098
Makiko Utsumi	Oakland	938,868
May Mutsuko Fujito	San Diego	852,989
Miya Sannomiya	San Francisco	805,011
Yoneko Yamada	Santa Barbara	798,111
Frank Aiji Endo	Long Beach	767,083
Ruth Nomura	Portland	734,451

The 1926 *kengakudan* members were as diverse as the 1925 members. This time there were only two males. Eight were high school graduates; Flora Yae Tsuda of Sacramento and May Mutsuko Fujito of San Diego were the youngest and lone high school students. Of the high school graduates, four were college students. Ruth Nomura of Portland had already graduated from a business school after graduating from high school. The oldest was Miya

Figure 3. The 1926 tour group, with Nakamura Ganjirō, a well-known Japanese Kabuki actor; to his left, Abiko Yonako. Courtesy of Abiko Family Papers, Special Collections, Charles E. Young Research Library, UCLA.

Sannomiya, who was a student at the University of California at Berkeley majoring in German and, by consensus, the maturest and most capable of all the members. Like the 1925 *kengakudan* members, fluency in the Japanese language varied from one member to another; despite her young age, Flora Yae Tsuda was able to speak, read, and write Japanese. Each also represented different Japanese communities in California and Oregon. Their parents' origin in Japan varied widely—two traced their roots to Kumamoto Prefecture; one each to Wakayama, Hiroshima, Yamaguchi, Yamagata, Hyogo, Kagoshima, and Tottori prefectures; and one to the city of Tokyo.[35]

Before the 1926 *kengakudan* set sail, the *Nichibei Shimbun* sponsored a five-day lecture series for the new *kengakudan* members. Delivered by local notables, lectures were on various aspects of Japanese culture, ranging from Japanese painting, architecture, religion, industries, famous tourist sights, and Japanese customs and manners. The *Nichibei Shimbun* noted that these lectures "are being conducted primarily for the purpose of preparing the Nichi-Bei Kengaku-Dan members for their Japanese tour" and that they are "particularly valuable to the young people from the cultural standpoint, as the second-generation are generally ignorant of Japan and Japanese culture, a condition which has done more than any . . . single factor to widen the gap between themselves and the members of the first generation."[36]

Except for minor changes, the itinerary of the 1926 study tour was substantially the same as that of the first tour. The tour members traveled first-class to and from Japan and while on tour in the country. Headed by Mrs. Abiko Kyūtarō again, the three-month trip began on March 2 and ended on May 28. The group visited Tokyo, Kamakura, Nikko, Sendai, Numazu, Nagoya, Kyoto, Nara, Osaka, Kobe, Okayama, Hiroshima, Fukuoka, and Kumamoto. And again, with the help of prominent Japanese and government officials, the *kengakudan* members had access not only to places normally closed to ordinary tourists but to the upper-class elite as well. Everywhere they went, whether they visited historic sites or a modern manufacturing plant, they invariably received red-carpet treatment.

After the 1926 study tour the *kengakudan* members also presented public talks before Issei and Nisei audiences in various Japanese communities throughout California and elsewhere. The first public lecture was held on May 29 in San Francisco at the Golden Gate Institute hall before a gathering of more than a thousand people.[37] Kimiko Kumamoto opened the evening program with an account of how their *kengakudan* had been received in Japan. Ruth Nomura followed with her observations regarding the modernization of Japan. Frank Aiji Endo discussed their visit to a modern paper factory in Kyushu. Flora Yae Tsuda presented what she thought the people of Japan expected of the American-born second generation. Finally, Miya Sannomiya described what she had learned in Japan. Kumamoto, Endo, and Tsuda spoke in Japanese, whereas Nomura and Sannomiya gave their presentations in English. Makiko Utsumi and Yoneko Yamada gave musical presentations.

From Abiko's perspective, Flora Yae Tsuda, perhaps, best validated the worth of study tours. She reported that the people of Japan expected the Nisei to assume the role of a bridge of understanding between Japan and the United States. She was fond of using the Japanese term *chūkaisha*, or intermediary, in speaking of this role.[38] In 1927 she wrote an essay in Japanese. The essay was titled "Natsukashiki Nihon no Omoide" [My Fond Memories of Japan]. She wrote in part:

> I had known that there are beautiful sights in Japan, but I had not realized just how beautiful they are. There was beauty everywhere we went, so

much so that I often wished we had more time to enjoy the sights leisurely. Now when I think of "Matsushima, Oh Beautiful Matsushima," that's exactly how I feel. All of us felt overjoyed that everything was more beautiful than we had ever imagined. And wherever we went, everyone was so cordial, making us feel a great sense of gratitude. We who are American-born Japanese are very fortunate indeed to have this vast America as our mother country and Japan, with her ancient history of thousands of years, as our ancestral land.[39]

All *kengakudan* members unquestionably were heavily influenced by their exposure to Japan. Ruth Nomura traced her lifelong interest in the Japanese arts and her continual participation in the sister-city program between St. Paul and Nagasaki during the post–World War II period to her *kengakudan* experience.[40] Frank Aiji Endo himself decided to embark on a career in architecture precisely because he had seen, in his own words, "so many beautiful temples, castles, and other architectural buildings throughout Japan."[41] Yukiko Furuta was very impressed by Japan but not by everything she experienced. She resented having to board trains after male passengers and rejected what she perceived as the subordinate status of women in Japanese society.[42] Hisako Fujii was struck mostly by the aesthetic aspects of Japanese culture.[43] Miya Sannomiya best exemplifies the profound impact the *kengakudan* experience had on the young Nisei members. In recalling the effect it had on her, she said that "the tour changed my entire life."[44] Indeed, it was behind her decision to study Japanese in Japan in 1931 and her eventual employment in 1934 as an English secretary of the *Kokusai Bunka Shinkōkai* [Society for International Cultural Relations], a Japanese educational society devoted to disseminating information about Japan in various Western languages.

The concept of the Nisei as a bridge of understanding underwent a decisive change in the 1930s. Beginning with the Manchurian Incident of 1931, international political events transformed the significance of the concept. On September 18 a group of junior Japanese army officers contrived an incident and used it as a pretext to occupy Manchuria militarily. The officers took this action in defiance of the high military command. The civilian government, confronted by a fait accompli, defended the action by claiming that the Japanese army had been provoked beyond toleration. And to consolidate political control over Manchuria, the government recognized a political entity called Manchukuo in 1932. Ostensibly an independent state,

Manchukuo in fact was a puppet state created under Japanese government tutelage and maintained under its control. The League of Nations dispatched a fact-finding commission to investigate the events and circumstances that had led up to the establishment of the state of Manchukuo. On completion of its investigation the commission branded Japan a military aggressor, and, based on the recommendation of the commission, the General Assembly of the League of Nations adopted a policy of nonrecognition of Manchukuo. Although not a member of the League of Nations, the United States also branded Japan an aggressor and likewise adopted a policy of nonrecognition. To protest the policy of the international community, Japan withdrew from the League of Nations in February 1933.

These events gave the concept of the bridge of understanding a strong, new political coloration. Until 1931 the Issei mainly had had the Japanese exclusion movement in mind when they applied the concept to the Nisei generation. The Nisei were expected to dispel the misunderstandings behind the exclusion movement by educating Americans about Japanese immigration, thereby removing one of the chief sources of past friction in Japanese-American relations. Now the Nisei were expected to explain larger political events in the Far East and present and justify Japan's side of those events to the American public. In this way the concept of the Nisei as a bridge of understanding was expanded to encompass broader international political issues that adversely affected Japanese-American relations. By 1937 those issues included the Sino-Japanese War, which erupted on July 7, 1937, and continued uninterrupted until the outbreak of the Pacific War.

By 1930 the sending of Nisei study groups to Japan was a firmly established practice within the Japanese community. After the initial 1925 and 1926 *Nichibei Shimbun*–sponsored *kengakudan*, other Japanese immigrant newspapers followed suit and sponsored their own *kengakudan*. Prefectural associations, religious organizations, educational bodies, and other cultural groups also organized their own *kengakudan* and sent them to Japan. And, not surprisingly, these later *kengakudan* of the 1930s invariably included side trips to Korea and Manchuria after 1931 and to North China after 1937. During the course of the 1930s some Nisei endeavored to defend Japan's military actions in China. But as Japanese-American relations progressively deteriorated, such Nisei realized that they could not do so without impugning their own loyalty to the United States. Thus the concept of the Nisei as a bridge of understanding, which appeared viable at its inception with the

1925 and 1926 *kengakudan,* eventually became untenable in the maelstrom of international political events in the late 1930s.

Notes

1. Editorial, *Nichibei Shimbun,* Jan. 1, 1925.
2. For biographical information see Oka Seizō, "Abiko Kyūtarō Den," *Hokubei Mainichi,* May 8–10, 13–16, June 13–14, 17–19, 26–28, July 2–3, 8–9, Aug. 23, 26–29, 1980; Yuji Ichioka, "Abiko Kyūtarō (1865–1936): An Advocate of Permanent Settlement," *Nichi Bei Times,* Jan. 1, 15, 1985; and Yuji Ichioka, *The Issei: The World of the First Generation Japanese Immigrants, 1885–1924* (New York: Free Press, 1988), 20–21, 59–61, 146–50, 174–75, 183–84, 214–15, 217–18, 249, 252.
3. Editorial, *Nichibei Shimbun,* Jan. 1, 1924.
4. Editorial, *Nichibei Shimbun,* Feb. 18, 1925.
5. Abiko Kyūtarō, "Hokubei ni Okeru Nihon Imin Mondai," *Tōkyō Keizai Zasshi* 58, no. 1469 (Dec. 19, 1909): 1113–15, and 58, no. 1470 (Dec. 26, 1908): 1159–61; and Abiko Kyūtarō, "Hainichi Mondai no Shinsō Oyobi Sono Shōrai," *Taiyō* 15, no. 5 (May 1909): 66–67.
6. English Editorial, *Nichibei Shimbun,* April 3, 1925.
7. Editorial, *Nichibei Shimbun,* Feb. 22, 1925.
8. Editorial, *Nichibei Shimbun,* Feb. 16, 1926.
9. Editorial, *Nichibei Shimbun,* Feb. 18, 1925.
10. *Taihoku Nippō,* Jan. 1, 1925.
11. *Nichibei Shimbun,* Sep. 6, 13, 1924.
12. *Nichibei Shimbun,* Nov. 1, 10, 1924.
13. *Nichibei Shimbun,* Feb. 18, 1925.
14. *Nichibei Shimbun,* March 17, 1925.
15. *Oakland Tribune,* Dec. 5–10, 1921.
16. *Nichibei Shimbun,* Feb. 1, 1922. See also *San Francisco Chronicle, San Francisco Call, San Francisco Post,* and *Oakland Tribune,* Jan. 31, 1922.
17. Editorial, *Nichibei Shimbun,* March 16, 1925.
18. Yonako Abiko, "Biographical Statement," June 29, 1943, in Abiko Family Papers, Box 12, Folder 6, Japanese American Research Project Collection (hereafter JARP), UCLA.
19. Ruth Nomura Tambara, interview, Nov. 18, 1990.
20. *Nichibei Shimbun,* May 3, 1925.
21. Yonako Abiko, handwritten text of 1926 speech delivered before the Century Club, Abiko Family Papers, Box 31, Folder 4, JARP.
22. Abiko Kyūtarō to Shibusawa Eiichi, Feb. 27, 1925, in Shibusawa Seien Kinen Zaidan Ryūmonsha, *Shibusawa Eiichi Denki Shiryō* (Tokyo: Shibusawa Eiichi Denki Shiryō Kankōkai, 1961), 39:306.

23. *Nichibei Shimbun*, April 29, 1925.

24. *Nichibei Shimbun*, "Sōkō *Nichibei Shimbun* Shusai Nikkei Beikoku Shimin Nihon Kengakudan Nittei," 1925, in Abiko Family Papers.

25. *Nichibei Shimbun*, June 26, 1925.

26. *Nichibei Shimbun*, June 28, 1925.

27. Clarence Arima to *Japanese American News*, Aug. 17, 1925, in Abiko Family Papers.

28. Editorial, *Nichibei Shimbun*, Sep. 19, 1925.

29. Editorial, *Nichibei Shimbun*, Oct. 20, 1925.

30. Editorial, *Nichibei Shimbun*, Nov. 12, 1925.

31. Ibid.

32. Editorial, *Nichibei Shimbun*, Nov. 1, 1925.

33. Editorial, *Nichibei Shimbun*, Oct. 29, 1925.

34. Editorial, *Nichibei Shimbun*, Feb. 9, 1926.

35. Ibid.; and Nichibei Shimbunsha, *Dai-Nikai Bokoku Kengakudan* (San Francisco: Nichibei Shimbunsha, 1926).

36. *Nichibei Shimbun*, Feb. 16, 1926.

37. *Nichibei Shimbun*, May 31, 1926.

38. Ibid.

39. *Ofu Nippō*, Jan. 1, 1927.

40. Ruth Nomura Tambara, interview by Yuji Ichioka, Nov. 18, 1990. For her autobiography see "Ruth Nomura Tambara," in *Memoirs of Japanese American Women in Minnesota*, ed. John Nobuya Tsuchida (Covina, CA: Pacific Asia Press, 1994), 1–67.

41. Frank Aiji Endo to author, Aug. 31, 1990.

42. Yukiko Furuta, interview by Yuji Ichioka, Jan. 16, 1990.

43. Hisako Fujii Ishii, interview by Yuji Ichioka, Feb. 3, 1990.

44. Miya Sannomiya, interview, June 1, 1980. See also Miya S. Kikuchi to Robert A. Wilson, Jan. 13, 1968, in Kikuchi Papers, JARP; and Miya Sannomiya, interview, Tape nos. 83 and 84, JARP. For a full treatment of her life see Yamamoto, "Miya Sannomiya Kikuchi."

FOUR

Kokugo Gakkō

The Debate over the Role of Japanese-Language Schools

Following the enactment of the 1924 Immigration Act, *Issei* leaders and educators engaged in a renewed, spirited debate over the future of Japanese-
language schools and the need to instill Japanese moral values in the *Nisei*
generation. Two events triggered this debate: the publication of an essay by
Seattle consul Ōhashi Chūichi and the 1928 Fukunaga Incident in Hawaii.
The debate began in the spring of 1925 just as the first *Nichibei Shimbun*–
sponsored *kengakudan* was touring Japan. Seattle consul Ōhashi set it off by
publishing his essay advocating the abolishment of all Japanese-language
schools. Entitled "Dōhō Kokugo Gakkō Hantai-ron" [My Opposition to
Japanese Language Schools], the essay appeared in May in the *Hokubei Jiji*
and *Taihoku Nippō* of Seattle and was subsequently reprinted in the *Shin
Sekai* of San Francisco.[1] During the course of the debate, fundamental
differences about the role of Japanese-language schools in the education of
the second generation were aired.

Consul Ōhashi was unequivocally opposed to Japanese-language schools.
"It will be necessary," he wrote in January 1925, "to educate Nisei children as
complete American citizens." Ōhashi defined a complete American citizen as
"a person who understands American civilization and its political institutions." He claimed that "such a person is imbued with the American concept
of justice and fair play derived from Christian morality, enabling him to contribute to human progress by working harmoniously with others within
American society."[2]

In his May essay Consul Ōhashi started with the ideal that the Nisei should be reared and educated as "one hundred percent Americans." Japanese-language schools were obstructing the realization of this ideal by creating, in his words, "half-baked Americans who are neither American nor Japanese." White Americans "despised" and "discriminated against" such Nisei because they were not versed in American culture, thought, religion, and customs. So, if the Nisei ever hoped to be recognized and accepted as equals by white Americans, they had to become "one hundred percent American." Japanese-language schools, Ōhashi argued, bred "a sense of being half-breed" among Nisei children, thereby artificially setting them apart from American society and hindering their recognition as American citizens.

Moreover, Ōhashi voiced his fear that the Japanese-language schools could become a "rationale" for future anti-Japanese agitation. Aware of past proposals to amend the Fourteenth Amendment to the American Constitution to deny American citizenship to children of "aliens ineligible to citizenship," Ōhashi also expressed his apprehension that such schools might serve as a convenient "pretext" to strip the Nisei of their American citizenship. As long as the Japanese-language schools existed, he felt the Nisei would never be recognized and accepted as Americans. Ōhashi disputed the claim that the Nisei had to learn the Japanese language in order to enhance their chances of future employment because of widespread job discrimination. According to his line of reasoning, the Nisei suffered from such discrimination precisely because they were not recognized as genuine Americans, a view the schools were helping to reinforce and perpetuate by producing "half-baked Americans."

Similarly, Ōhashi rejected the notion that the schools were necessary to facilitate communication between Issei parents and their children and essential to instill feelings of racial pride among the Nisei. As to the first, Ōhashi admonished the Issei for their inability to communicate in English with their children. He contended that if the Issei had taken the trouble to learn English during their initial years in the United States, there would have been no problem of communication. But since they had not, they were the ones who were responsible for the parent-child communication problem. Thus the solution to the problem was for the Issei to learn English, not for the Nisei to learn Japanese. Second, Ōhashi dismissed the argument that without a knowledge of the Japanese language the Nisei would have no "racial pride" and therefore would become "servile." He countered this argument by asserting that "servility" had nothing to do with a lack of knowledge of the Japanese language but developed among some Nisei because they were ashamed of their parents' low socioeconomic status.

If the Japanese language were to be taught at all to Nisei youngsters, Ōhashi believed that it should be taught in American public schools, where the youngsters could study the language alongside their white classmates. Hence he encouraged Issei parents to lobby local school boards to offer classes in Japanese if they really wanted their kids to learn the language in the United States. On the other hand, if Issei parents wanted their children to master Japanese, Ōhashi advised such parents to send their children to Japan for an extended period, giving them an opportunity to study the language intensively within an all-Japanese-speaking environment.

Finally, Consul Ōhashi added a new twist to the ideal that the Nisei generation should be a bridge of understanding between the United States and Japan. He maintained that the ideal of a bridge presupposed the Nisei being recognized and accepted as genuine Americans by white society. In other words, the ideal depended on the Nisei being fully recognized and accepted as Americans. For without such recognition and acceptance, the Nisei would remain pariahs within American society and, consequently, would be unable to influence their fellow Americans about Japan, or anything else for that matter. The inexorable conclusion was that the Issei had to raise and educate the Nisei as "one hundred percent Americans" as a precondition to the realization of the ideal of the Nisei as a bridge of understanding.

With this kind of uncompromising opposition to Japanese-language schools, Ōhashi's essay added fuel to the ongoing debate among Issei leaders and educators regarding the future of the second generation. Its publication coincided with Ōhashi's pending transfer from Seattle to another consular post. But more significant, since it appeared just at the time when a consensus of opinion appeared to be crystallizing regarding the necessity of Japanese-language schools, the essay revived an old debate over the merits and demerits of such schools. In the wake of its publication the immigrant press published many spirited, and often acrimonious, essays and letters by Issei leaders and educators endorsing or denouncing the opinions of Consul Ōhashi.

Supporters of Ōhashi

A small minority of people rallied behind Consul Ōhashi. One supporter attributed the continuing existence of Japanese-language schools to the fact that many Issei still were wavering in their commitment to permanent residency in the United States. Consequently, and regrettably, such Issei wanted their children to learn Japanese in case they decided to return to Japan. This same supporter applied the analogy of a daughter marrying into a wealthy family in Japan to the situation of the Nisei generation in America. Such a marriage required the daughter to sever all ties to her own family. Indeed, she had to adopt and scrupulously follow the rules of her new family and, accordingly, obey her husband and new in-laws. In becoming "good Americans," as dictated by American society, the Nisei were acting like this daughter, and in allowing and encouraging the Nisei to do so, the Issei were analogous to her parents, who had no choice but to urge their daughter to be loyal to her new family. Drawn from the concept of the Japanese family system, any Issei could grasp this simple analogy.[3]

Kanamaru Kenji of San Francisco traced the origins of Japanese-language schools to what he called the "egoism" of the Issei generation.[4] The schools were established because the Issei could not understand the Nisei who were being educated in American schools and being inculcated with Americanism. According to Kanamaru, because of the Issei's poor command of English and ignorance of American society, most Issei could not comprehend the fact that the Nisei could achieve a secure life in America without a knowledge of Japanese or any other foreign language. So he reached the conclusion that the Issei had established Japanese-language schools *for themselves*, to enable them to communicate with the Nisei. To the Nisei such schools were unnecessary and irrelevant to their future in the United States.

Another Issei supporter, who happened to be a young student at Broadway High School in Seattle, based his endorsement of Consul Ōhashi on an optimistic assessment of the Nisei's future in American society. He believed, contrary to the pessimistic forebodings of many Issei leaders and educators, that there were ample future opportunities for the Nisei in American business, industry, and agriculture that would enable the Nisei generation to become an integral part of American society. Those Issei who predicted that the Nisei would end up being treated like "Negroes" were adherents of what this young Issei called *nigegoshi-shugi*, or undue negativism. At the same time, he granted no credence to the view that the education in the Japanese language offered by the Japanese-language schools was essential to enhance the employment prospects of the Nisei. Calling this a *hijōguchi-ron*, or an escape-hatch argument, he rejected it outright because it, too, originated in the same one-sided negative assessment of the Nisei's future in American society.[5]

Fujioka Shirō, a liberal and staff writer of the *Rafu Shimpō* of Los Angeles, indirectly endorsed Ōhashi's essay.[6] He agreed with the consul's observation that the average Issei parents could not communicate with their children in English. This was indeed highly regrettable. He also concurred that if Issei parents really wanted their children to master Japanese, they should send them to Japan, where they could concentrate exclusively on learning the language. A father of nine Nisei children at the time, Fujioka confessed that he had taken his own children out of the Hollywood Japanese Language School once they reached junior high school age because they had the burden of added homework in junior high school. If he insisted that they should continue to attend the Japanese-language school, he feared their work in junior high school would suffer. And if he forced them to attend against their will, he was sure that they would not learn much Japanese.

Critics of Ōhashi

The critics of Consul Ōhashi marshaled an array of counterarguments to rebut his essay. Invariably, most singled out "white racism" as the fundamental reason for the refusal of white Americans to recognize the Nisei as Americans. Yasuda Genshirō of Seattle forcefully put forth this point of view in the *Hokubei Jiji*.[7] In late 1925 he published a novel with the title *Hakujin no Sekai* [The Whiteman's World], in which he railed against the white racism that had victimized the Issei generation.[8] Notwithstanding the fact that the Nisei were American citizens, whites still lumped the Nisei together with the Issei as undesirable aliens. So the issue was not whether or not Japanese-language schools existed, or whether or not the Nisei knew the Japanese language, or even whether or not the Nisei were sufficiently Americanized. Regardless, as long as white prejudice persisted, the Nisei would never fully be accepted by white Americans. Such critics therefore summarily dismissed Ōhashi's argument that Japanese-language schools would be the cause of future anti-Japanese sentiments. They noted that in the past the Japanese side had adopted many measures in the hope of mollifying anti-Japanese exclusionists, including the abolishment of the picture-bride practice in 1920, but such measures had never stopped white racists from championing the cause of Japanese exclusion. In short, white racism was at the bottom of anti-Japanese agitation.

The critics also invariably reaffirmed the view that the Nisei had a special "destiny" or "mission" of acting as "links in blending Eastern and Western cultures."[9] The Nisei had this predetermined destiny by virtue of their racial ancestry being combined with their unique American birth, upbringing, and education. In order to fulfill this destiny, however, it was essential for them to know the Japanese language. Consul Ōhashi, placing foremost value on the complete Americanization of the Nisei, discounted the necessity of studying Japanese and favored abolishing the Japanese-language schools altogether. In effect, his position disregarded the destiny ascribed to the Nisei generation. In the words of two of its harshest detractors, Ōhashi's essay was a "suicidal pronouncement" and tantamount to "the utterance of a conquered person" bowing to the will of his conqueror.[10]

Suzuki Takashi was a prominent critic in California. As the principal of the Golden Gate Institute of San Francisco, he believed that it was essential for the Nisei to commence studying Japanese in childhood. In his opinion, since the value of learning foreign languages was recognized by Americans, the teaching of Japanese should not be treated any differently from teaching any other foreign language. Suzuki cited the decision in the 1923 *Meyers vs. Nebraska* case, through which the United States Supreme Court struck down as unconstitutional a Nebraska state law prohibiting the teaching of German to any youngster who had not completed the eighth grade. By rendering this decision, Suzuki felt the high tribunal acknowledged that the teaching of foreign languages to children was not an obstacle to Americanization and that it was actually protected by the American Constitution. And in agreement with other critics, Suzuki insisted that the cause of anti-Japanese sentiments had nothing to do with the existence of Japanese-language schools but was fundamentally attributable to "white racism."[11]

As a new champion of Japanese ethnic culture, the *Nichibei Shimbun* elected not to reprint Ōhashi's essay. Instead, it simply reaffirmed its support of Japanese-language schools. "We believe," it editorialized, "the teaching of Japanese to the American-born boys and girls will be the foundation of their future understanding of the Orient and ability to introduce the Orient to their fellow Americans. This foundation, in turn, will help contribute to the eventual blending of Oriental and Occidental cultures."[12] Washizu Bunzō, a well-known Issei staff writer of the *Nichibei Shimbun*, ridiculed Ōhashi's essay, saying that it had invited "only my contempt." "Based on a one-sided, pretentious Americanism," he wrote, "it was a fatuous piece divorced from reality."[13] Washizu endorsed the practical utility of Japanese-language schools. By teaching Japanese to Nisei youngsters, they facilitated parent-child communication and enhanced the Nisei's future employment prospects.

Kawamura Masahei, a Japanese-language school teacher at the Watsonville Gakuen, systematically critiqued Consul Ōhashi's essay.[14] Along with other critics, he argued that if Japanese-language schools were eliminated in accordance with Ōhashi's reasoning, the hostility of anti-Japanese agitators would not abate. Previous conciliatory measures, such as the abolishment of the picture-bride practice in 1920, had not mollified such persons. So there was no reason to believe that the elimination of Japanese-language schools would have any different outcome. Kawamura further argued that Ōhashi's notion of having the public schools teach Japanese was completely unrealistic, for no qualified bilingual teachers, acceptable to public school authorities, could be found to teach Japanese.

In his judgment Consul Ōhashi did not understand that the Japanese-language schools were dedicated to producing "good American citizens" who would be "sympathetic to Japan," but "not as half-baked Americans." According to Kawamura there were some Nisei youngsters who were growing up despising their own ancestry, while adopting the worst features of American culture. Disrespectful and even contemptuous of their parents, these youngsters were potential juvenile delinquents. They were the real "half-baked Americans" because they were afflicted with "self-hatred." Issei parents dreaded the thought of their own offspring growing up to be like these youngsters whom Kawamura called "socially deformed children." In order to prevent any further increase in their numbers, Japanese-language schools, he said, were teaching Nisei youngsters to understand and communicate with their parents. They instructed Nisei children to "be filial to your parents as your benefactors who brought you into this world" and to "be loyal to America as your mother country." To be sure, Issei parents were unable to communicate in English with their children, Kawamura admitted, but they were no different from other Japanese—many with much higher education—who could not speak the language.

Kawamura cited the example of a father in Watsonville who had once favored the complete Americanization of his daughter. This father now had serious misgivings about the benefits of Americanization. Kawamura reported that the father recently had been "seized by an indescribable feeling of alienation" as he observed his own eighteen-year-old daughter unable to speak a word of Japanese. So he asked his daughter to start studying Japanese, but she, in a fit of indignation, flatly refused, saying she was "deeply offended by his request." Rhetorically, Kawamura asked how Consul Ōhashi felt about this pathetic but true story.

Ōhashi was eventually transferred to Los Angeles. There he assumed his new post as Japanese consul in November 1925. The Southern California Japanese Educational Society in the following spring invited him to contribute an essay to its inaugural publication devoted to the education of the second generation. In the piece he contributed, Ōhashi explained his motives for writing his 1925 essay.[15] In the aftermath of the 1924 Immigration Act he said that he felt the Issei had become overly pessimistic about the future of the Nisei. In order to counteract this pessimism he had advanced the idea of abolishing Japanese-language schools as a way of gaining the recognition and acceptance of the Nisei as genuine Americans. Now, he declared, he no longer supported such an idea. Because of his public opposition to Japanese-language schools, Ōhashi earned the dubious reputation of being the "Anti-Japanese Language School Consul" within the Japanese immigrant community. The continuing hostility to his controversial stance no doubt explains why Ōhashi decided to reverse himself shortly after he assumed his new consular post in Southern California.

Oka Naoki

Consul Ōhashi's repudiation of his essay did not end the debate over Japanese-language schools. In 1928 Oka Naoki, a Japanese-language school teacher in Isleton, on the Sacramento delta, praised Ōhashi in a long essay on the education of the second generation.[16] In recalling his opposition to Japanese-language schools, Oka wrote that Consul Ōhashi had been "a far-sighted person" who "minced no words" in advocating "the Americanization of the Nisei generation," but the "public" at the time, unwilling to accept his views, had "uniformly opposed him." Oka confessed that in due course he, too, had come to favor the Americanization of the Nisei, even though he was a Japanese-language school teacher himself. In his opinion there was "no need at all for a Japanese language education" for "those Nisei intent on associating exclusively with other Americans."

Oka's views were more extreme than those of Ōhashi. According to Oka it was the height of folly for the Issei generation to try to impose its will on the

Nisei generation. The Issei could not and should not decide what was in the best interest of the Nisei. Nor should the Issei foist on the Nisei generation Japanese concepts of morality and ways of thinking that were "anathema to the American public." Oka admonished those Issei who smugly believed that only the Japanese people had high standards of morality and strict codes of conduct, as exemplified by their frequent "glorification of Bushidō, Japanese social etiquette, and the Japanese spirit." And he chided those Issei who berated the Nisei for their inability to speak "proper" Japanese and to behave according to the norms of Japanese social etiquette. After all, the Nisei were "full-fledged Americans" whose first language was English. Oka believed that Nisei leaders would emerge naturally from the ranks of the second generation and that these leaders, separate and apart from the Issei, would ultimately decide what was best for their own generation.

With such unorthodox views Oka was a "liberal" renegade among Japanese-language school teachers. A native of Kochi Prefecture, he had come to the United States as a student. He had a BA degree from the College of the Pacific and was the younger brother of Oka Shigeki, a well-known Issei socialist who operated a print shop in San Francisco. In 1919 Oka Naoki had supported the Japanese government's decision to cease issuing passports to picture brides. And over the years he had exhorted the Issei to adapt themselves to American society and had even advised them to go along with prohibition, despite the fact that the vast majority of Japanese immigrant males continued to drink various homemade concoctions. Oka resigned from his Isleton teaching post before he published his essay. He realized that his views, if not totally unacceptable to the people of Isleton, would, at a minimum, arouse considerable opposition. In fact, the strong conservative backlash that his essay did arouse left no doubt that, by 1928, an orthodoxy regarding the education of the second generation had fully emerged within the Japanese immigrant community, allowing for little or no tolerance of dissenting opinions. Oka returned to Japan in 1929. In the ensuing decade no other "liberal" renegade in his mold dared to voice similar opinions.

The 1928 Fukunaga Incident

Besides Consul Ōhashi's call for the abolishment of Japanese-language schools, another event caused Issei leaders and educators to reemphasize the overriding importance of providing "moral education" to the Nisei generation. More than anything else, the 1928 Fukunaga Incident concretely illustrated the urgency of Japanese-style moral education. On September 18, 1928, in the city of Honolulu, a nineteen-year-old Nisei youth by the name of Myles Yutaka Fukunaga kidnapped Gill Jamieson, the ten-year-old son of Frederick W. Jamieson, vice president of the Hawaiian Trust Company.[17] The kidnapping took place at the Punahou School, where the white elite of Honolulu sent their children to school. In exchange for the safe return of the boy, Fukunaga demanded a ransom of $10,000. Because this case involved the son of a prominent white family, it attracted wide public attention. The press gave it extensive coverage, and the Honolulu police launched an immediate and unprecedented manhunt. Two days after the kidnapping, on September 20, the body of Gill Jamieson was uncovered in a dense thicket in the Waikiki area. The boy had been bludgeoned and choked to death. On September 22 the police arrested Fukunaga and charged him with kidnapping and first-degree premeditated homicide. His trial commenced on October 1 and ended on October 4. The jury found the defendant guilty as charged, and on October 8 the judge sentenced the young man to death by hanging. A mere three weeks elapsed from the date of kidnapping to the date of sentencing.

Fukunaga was not a deranged Nisei youth. He was born in 1909 on the island of Kauai. His parents—Fukunaga Jūsuke and Ide—were natives of Yamaguchi Prefecture. His father had arrived in Hawaii in 1896 as a contract laborer. Like most Nisei youngsters in Hawaii, Fukunaga grew up under impoverished conditions on a sugar plantation. As a young boy he did very well in school, attending public schools as well as the local Japanese-language school. Many people regarded him as a "model youth" who behaved well and earned good grades. Indeed, his Japanese-language school teacher went so far as to describe him as a *tensaiji*, or precocious young lad. Because of his family's poverty, however, Fukunaga was forced to quit school at the age of fourteen. Thus his formal education ended abruptly at the eighth-grade level. Subsequently, he worked at various menial jobs. In 1928 he was working as a janitor in a hospital. Personality-wise, he was an introverted loner, alienated from his peers. In social isolation he spent much of his time immersing himself in reading literature and mysteries.[18]

Under police interrogation Fukunaga freely confessed that he had planned everything in advance. In terms of his motives he said that revenge had been foremost in his mind. In 1928 his parents had been unable to meet monthly rental payments. The Hawaiian Trust Company served as the collecting agent for their landlord and had sent a rent collector to the Fukunaga family to demand full payment of back rent. Humiliated and ashamed, Fukunaga bitterly resented the bank's action and, on learning that Vice President Frederick W. Jamieson had a son, he decided to seek revenge against the Hawaiian Trust Company by kidnapping and murdering the boy. Fukunaga also confessed to another motive. As the eldest son of seven children, Fukunaga stated that he had felt a filial obligation to help his poor parents. According to his confession, both his father and mother had been homesick and continually told him that one day they wished to return to their native village in Yamaguchi Prefecture. So Fukunaga decided that the best thing he could do was to send them back to Japan with enough money to enable them to live out the remainder of their lives in relative comfort. He said that he had hoped to accomplish this filial act with the ransom money that he anticipated receiving from Frederick W. Jamieson.

Fukunaga executed his plan in a cold and calculated manner. In his confession he cited the famous 1924 Leopold-Loeb case of Chicago and the 1927 Hickman case of Los Angeles, which, he said, had served as models for him in planning the kidnapping and murder of Gill Jamieson. Both cases involved young men who, after deliberate and careful planning, had kidnapped and executed their victims in cold blood. Both cases had received national publicity and provoked a loud public outcry against the crime of kidnapping. Fukunaga never once attempted to deny, rationalize, or minimize his crime. He even maintained that he was perfectly sane when he committed it and was prepared to accept whatever punishment the court may decide to mete out.

The Fukunaga Incident sent shock waves through every Japanese community, not only in Hawaii but on the mainland as well. News of the incident reached the Pacific Coast just as mainland Issei leaders and educators were engaged in a discussion of the rise of Nisei juvenile gangs and the need for moral education. Every mainland Japanese immigrant daily carried articles and ran editorials on the Fukunaga Incident. From the beginning of its coverage, the *Rafu Shimpō* referred to the incident as a "Second Hickman Affair," which was not surprising in view of the fact that the first Hickman affair had occurred in Los Angeles in 1927. This well-publicized earlier case involved a young bank clerk by the name of Edward Hickman who kidnapped and murdered the twelve-year-old daughter of a prominent Los Angeles banker.[19]

Fukunaga had patterned his own kidnapping and murder more on the

Hickman case than on the Leopold-Loeb case. Hickman had kidnapped his victim at her junior high school on the pretext that he was taking her to see her father, who had gotten ill. Fukunaga kidnapped Gill Jamieson at the Punahou School on the pretext that he was taking him to see his mother, who, he said, also had been stricken ill. Hickman, after murdering his victim in cold blood, had demanded ransom through a series of threatening letters. Fukunaga did the same thing. Hickman was arrested, tried, and found guilty, and on October 19, 1928, eleven days after Fukunaga himself was sentenced to death, he was executed at San Quentin Prison.

The *Rafu Shimpō*'s first editorial caption read, "Horrifying!—A Japanese Suspect in a Second Hickman Affair." "We are genuinely horrified," the editorial read, "since we felt that it would be a stigma on our race if any Japanese name were to be implicated in any way as a suspect in this incident." This was "a very dangerous development," it went on to say, "because a hot-headed Nisei youngster was motivated to seek revenge against Caucasians as a result of racial insults and economic hardships."[20] A day later the *Rafu Shimpō* editorialized that "the incident was a matter of deep concern, not just for American society, but for the Japanese immigrant community as well."[21] Right after the end of Fukunaga's trial the newspaper published his full confession.[22]

The *Nichibei Shimbun* likewise called the Fukunaga Incident "a second Hickman Affair" and reported that all Issei were "stunned because the criminal was a bright Nisei."[23] It immediately polled the reactions and opinions of prominent Issei educators and church leaders of San Francisco, such as Suzuki Takashi, principal of the Golden Gate Institute; Sano Kazō, principal of the Nippon Gakuin; Ichio Hatsuko, principal of the Kyōwa Gakuen; the Reverend Takahashi Kakue of the San Francisco Buddhist Church; and the Reverend Sō Shōkichi, head of the Northern California Federation of Japanese Christian Churches. Everyone agreed that the Fukunaga case underscored the urgent need to develop, in cooperation with the family, church, and school, "personal character" in Nisei youngsters through "moral education." The *Nichibei Shimbun* warned its readers that "it would be foolhardy to think that the Fukunaga Incident could never have happened in California."[24] And like the *Rafu Shimpō*, the *Nichibei Shimbun* reprinted Fukunaga's full confession.

After the Honolulu jury handed down its guilty verdict, the *Nichibei Shimbun* also published Fukunaga's parents' public apology. In it they expressed sincere remorse for "the heinous crime of murder" committed by "our son," which had "caused such a public outrage, aroused feelings of anxiety among the Issei, and damaged irreparably the face and honor of the Japanese people as a whole." All of this was "the result of insufficient family education" within the Fukunaga home, for which, Mr. and Mrs. Fukunaga said, they assumed complete responsibility with "deep and utter shame."[25] The *Nichibei Shimbun*, in editorializing on this public apology, declared that "it could not but feel deep sympathy for the parents of the criminal." The Fukunaga Incident had caused "all Issei parents to reflect upon ourselves." It warned them that they "must give much more serious attention to the education and discipline of [their] own children."[26]

As the head of the Japanese Salvation Army, Kobayashi Masasuke took up the issue of parental responsibility. He passed moral judgment on Mr. and Mrs. Fukunaga by referring to their son's self-confessed motives of revenge and filial piety. Kobayashi traced both motives back to the parents. On the one hand, he reasoned that if the parents had been able to meet their monthly rental payments, their son would not have felt so humiliated and ashamed as to seek revenge. On the other hand, if they had firmly resolved to settle down permanently in Hawaii, they would not have voiced a desire to return to Japan and hence would not have made their son feel obligated to send them back to Japan with money. In this way Kobayashi shifted the burden of responsibility for Fukunaga's crime onto the shoulders of his parents. His message to other Issei parents was clear. To avoid the ignominious fate of Fukunaga's parents, they had to improve their own economic condition and unequivocally commit themselves to living out their lives in the United States.[27]

Others stressed the central role played by Fukunaga's social environment. He had shown great promise as a bright, well-behaved young student but had not been able to realize his full potential because of poverty and racial barriers, as evidenced by his inability to attend high school. As a result he became alienated from both the Japanese community and American society. He was "a victim of hapless circumstances" and "an unlucky young man" who had had to "shoulder the burden of societal shortcomings."[28] In commenting on the Fukunaga Incident, the *Taihoku Nippō* observed that "there are always family and social causes behind the appearance of juvenile delinquents" and "that studies of the causes of juvenile delinquency are now being conducted by some Issei under the influence of Fukunaga's heinous crime."[29]

Kawamura Masahei, formerly of the Watsonville Gakuen and now a Japanese-language school teacher in Isleton, came to Fukunaga's defense in his own idiosyncratic way. From his perspective Fukunaga had committed his crime in an "American way with American models." In sharp contrast, he had admitted his guilt in a "Japanese way." Kawamura likened Fukunaga's confession to the "moral integrity of a Japanese samurai warrior." Edward Hickman had resorted to all sorts of subterfuge during his trial to evade responsibility for his crime. Fukunaga, on the other hand, recognizing the gravity of his own crime, had freely confessed as soon as he was arrested. If Kawamura had been asked to defend Fukunaga in court, he said he would have adopted a simple twofold strategy. First, he would have argued that the fundamental cause of Fukunaga's crime was to be found in the "American obsession with materialism," of which he was highly critical. Second, he would have extolled "Japanese moral virtues," which Fukunaga had exhibited, in part, by his instant and open admission of guilt. To Kawamura, Fukunaga was not a depraved or deranged criminal. He was at bottom "a decent young man" who had gone astray because of his social isolation, obsession with literature, and family poverty.[30]

In the end the Fukunaga Incident had the effect of underlining the urgency, already keenly felt by Issei educators, of teaching "moral education" to the second generation through the Japanese-language schools. Issei educators always made the standard Japanese distinction between intellectual, physical, and moral education. American public schools were adequate at imparting basic knowledge and skills and at promoting physical fitness but were wanting in instilling moral principles or teaching what the educators called *tokuiku*, or moral education. The *Yuta Nippō* of Salt Lake City editorialized that Fukunaga was "Hawaii's Japanese Hickman" but one who still had "a moral conscience." His case "clearly illustrates the value of instilling in Nisei youngsters, so susceptible as they are to environmental influences, the strength of Oriental morality."[31] Similarly, the *Shin Sekai* editorialized that the case made "tokuiku" imperative for "Nisei youngster."[32] In sum, the Fukunaga Incident strongly reinforced the rationale for teaching Japanese-style moral education through the Japanese-language schools.

Conclusion

Coincident with the ongoing Issei debate over the role of Japanese-language schools, a 1927 United States Supreme Court decision insured not only the continued existence of such schools but their ability to operate without government constraints. In the *Farrington vs. Tokushige* case, the Supreme Court struck down as unconstitutional a 1920 Hawaiian Territorial Act regulating private foreign-language schools.[33] That enactment had regulated the operation of such schools, the certification of teachers, and the content of instructional material. All Japanese-language schools in Hawaii were under its stringent provisions until the 1927 ruling by the high court. The Court's decision simultaneously nullified an almost identical California state law enacted in 1921.[34] The debate among Issei leaders and educators over the role of Japanese-language schools more or less settled the question of the need for such schools and of their crucial importance in inculcating Japanese moral values in the second generation. The Court's decision meant that Japanese immigrants, whether in Hawaii or California, were now free to operate their Japanese-language schools without having to satisfy any government regulations, which strengthened the hands of those who stressed their necessity and advocated their continued existence.

Notes

1. For the entire run of the essay see Ōhashi Chūichi, "Dōhō Kokugo Gakkō Hantai Ron," *Shin Sekai*, May 24–28, 1925.

2. Ōhashi Chūichi, "Zaibei Shijo ni Taisuru Nihongo Kyōiku Mondai," *Taihoku Nippō*, Jan. 1–7, 1925.

3. Hoshi Kōshichi, "Ryōji ni Dōkan," *Taihoku Nippō*, June 1–3, 1925.

4. Kanamaru Kenji, "Mazu Dai-Issei no Rikoshugi," *Shin Sekai*, June 7–8, 1925.

5. Murakami Futoshi, "Kokkō Haishi Sansei," *Taihoku Nippō*, June 20, 22–27, 1926.

6. Fujioka Shirō, "Sono Hi, Sono Hi," *Rafu Shimpō*, June 11, 1925. See also Fujioka Shirō, *Minzoku Hatten no Senkusha* (Tokyo: Dōbunsha, 1927), 427–29.

7. For references to Yasuda's commentary see Maruyama Shingo, "Yasuda-shi no Bun wo yomite," *Taihoku Nippō*, June 11, 1925; and Murakami Futoshi, "Kokkō Haishi Sansei," *Taihoku Nippō*, June 20, 24–26, 1925. Yasuda's original is not available, for the *Hokubei Jiji* newspaper for this period is not available.

8. Yasuda Genshirō, *Hakujin no Sekai* (Tokyo: Seikyōsha, 1925).

9. See, e.g., Maruyama Shingo, "Hihan to Kokuhaku," *Taihoku Nippō*, June 2, 1925.

10. Fujii Ryūichi, "Ōhashi Ryōji no Ronshi wa Jisatsuteki Shosetsu nari," *Shin Sekai*, June 3–5, 1925; and Maruyama Shingo, "Hihan to Kokuhaku," *Taihoku*

Nippō, June 1–3, 1925. Fujii was an instructor in the Japanese-language school attached to the Fresno Japanese Buddhist Church.

11. Suzuki Takashi, "Ōhashi Shatoru Ryōji no Nihongo Gakkō Hantai Ron wo Yomite," *Shin Sekai*, May 29–June 2, 1925.

12. Editorial, *Nichibei Shimbun*, June 1, 1925. See also Endō Kōshirō, *Kanputon Ryōgakuen Enpō* (Tokyo: Nara Naoichi, 1936), 220–23.

13. Washizu Shakuma, "Nichigo Gakkō ni Kansuru Zaibei Hōjin no Sho-Kanten," *Nichibei Shimbun*, June 22–27, 1925. See also Washizu Shakuma, *Zaibei Nihonjin Shikan* (Los Angeles: Rafu Shimpōsha, 1930), 114–25. *Shakuma* was the pen name of Washizu Bunzō.

14. Kawamura Yūsen, "Shūfū Rakujitsu Hainichi no Kōya ni Shitei wo Sodateru Oya—Ōhashi Ryōji ni Tou," *Shin Sekai*, June 15–21, 1925. Kawamura had earlier published a short essay justifying the need to teach Japanese to Nisei youngsters. See Kason Yūsensei, "Naze Nihongo wa Hitsuyō Ka," *Shin Sekai*, March 21–22, 1925. See also Kawamura Yūsen, *Hainichi Sensen wo Toppa Shitsutsu* (Isleton, CA: Kawamura Yūsen, 1930), 305–20. *Yūsen* was Kawamura's pen name. *Kason* means "Watsonville," where Kawamura was teaching at this time.

15. Ōhashi Chūichi, "Kokugo Gakkō Undō to Dai-Nisei," in *Dai-Nisei no Kyōiku*, by Nanka Kyōiku Kai (Los Angeles: Nanka Kyōiku Kai, 1926), 4–7.

16. Oka Naoki, "Nao Imada Sakan ni Rongichū no Dai-Nisei no Kyōiku Mondai," *Shin Sekai*, July 29–Aug. 14, 1928.

17. For this incident see Miwa Haruie, *Tensaiji Fukunaga Yutaka* (Honolulu: Matsuzakaya Shoten, 1929); Kihara Ryūkichi, *Hawai Nihonjin Shi* (Tokyo: Bunseisha, 1935), 770–75; Sōga Yasutarō, *Gojūnenkan no Hawai Kaiko* (Honolulu: Gojūnenkan no Hawaii Kaiko Kankōkai, 1953), 431–38; Makino Kinzaburō Den Hensan Iinkai, *Makino Kinzaburō Den* (Honolulu: Makino Michie, 1965), 65–67; Ozawa Gijō, ed., *Hawai Nihongo Gakkō Kyōiku Shi* (Honolulu: Hawai Kyōiku Kai, 1972), 153–54; Dennis M. Ogawa, *JAN KEN PO: The World of Hawaii's Japanese Americans* (Honolulu: Japanese American Research Center, 1973), 112–49; Ronald Kotani, *The Japanese in Hawaii: A Century of Struggle* (Honolulu: Hawaii Hochi, 1985), 71–76; and Tamura, *Americanization, Acculturation, and Ethnic Identity*, 81–83, 168.

18. For Fukunaga's early background see Miwa, *Tensaiji Fukunaga Yutaka*, 60–67.

19. See Charles Williams, *The Story of Hickman's Crime* (Los Angeles: Williams, 1928); and Edward Dean Sullivan, *The Snatch Racket* (New York: Vanguard Press, 1932), 178–81.

20. Editorial, *Rafu Shimpō*, Sep. 23, 1928.

21. Editorial, *Rafu Shimpō*, Sep. 24, 1928.

22. "Fukunaga Yutaka no Jihaku," *Rafu Shimpō*, Oct. 4–9, 1928.

23. Editorial, *Nichibei Shimbun*, Sep. 24, 1928.

24. Editorial, *Nichibei Shimbun*, Sep. 25, 1928.

25. Editorial, *Nichibei Shimbun*, Oct. 6, 1928.

26. Editorials, *Nichibei Shimbun*, Oct. 6–7, 1928.

27. Kobayashi Masasuke, "Dai-Nisei no Tokuiku ni Taisuru Dai-Issei no Sekinin Kannen," *Nichibei Shimbun*, Oct. 8, 1928. See also Kobayashi Masasuke, "Kanashimubeki Jiken," *Nichibei Shimbun*, Sep. 24, 1928; "Shōnen Zansatsu Hannin ga Nihonjin Furyō Seinen da to no Hō wo Yomite," *Shin Sekai*, Sep. 24–25, 1928; and Ibuka Seiko, ed., *Nihon Minzoku no Sekaiteki Bōchō: Kobayashi Masasuke Ronbunshū* (Tokyo: Keigansha, 1933), 378–86.

28. Shimizu Sekizan, "Shakai no Tsumi, Fuun na Seinen Datta," *Nichibei Shimbun*, Oct. 8, 1928.

29. Editorials, *Taihoku Nippō*, Sep. 24, Oct. 17, 1928.

30. Kawamura Yūsen, "Fukunaga Jiken no Hihan," *Nichibei Shimbun*, Oct. 22–26, 1928. See also Kawamura, *Hainichi Sensen wo Toppa Shitsutsu*, 293–304.

31. Editorial, *Yuta Nippō*, Sep. 24, 1928.

32. Editorial, *Shin Sekai*, Sep. 23, 1928.

33. See Tamura, *Americanization, Acculturation, and Ethnic Identity*, 146–51.

34. Yuji Ichioka, *The Issei: The World of the First Generation Japanese Immigrants, 1885–1924* (New York: Free Press, 1988), 207–10.

A Study in Dualism

James Yoshinori Sakamoto and the Japanese American Courier, *1928–1942*

"The dastardly and treacherous attack on the United States . . . last Sunday absolutely absolves the resident Japanese in this country and their American-born children from any consideration they may ever have owed the Japanese Empire." This blunt editorial statement, completely repudiating Japan, appeared in the *Japanese American Courier* immediately after the attack on Pearl Harbor.[1] Historically, the *Courier* was an unusual newspaper within the prewar Japanese immigrant press. Founded on January 1, 1928, it was an English-language weekly published in Seattle, Washington, exclusively for the *Nisei* generation. Its founder and publisher was James Yoshinori Sakamoto (1903–55). A Nisei himself, Sakamoto launched the *Courier* to guide his much younger fellow Nisei in their quest for full acceptance into American life and to educate them about local, national, and international affairs. It consisted of four pages, one devoted to national and international news, one to editorials and features, and one each to the Japanese community and sports. At the outset Sakamoto and his wife, Misao, single-handedly issued the *Courier,* but over the years they had the help of a number of aspiring young Nisei journalists. And notwithstanding great difficulties, they managed to publish it continuously until 1942.[2]

The *Courier*'s total repudiation of Japan in the wake of Pearl Harbor was a sharp departure from Sakamoto's established editorial policy. Over the life of the weekly, he espoused a kind of dualism consisting of two complementary components. On the one hand, he preached "Americanism" as the path the Nisei should take in order to gain full acceptance. On the other hand, he adhered to the concept of the Nisei as a bridge of understanding between Japan and the United States. Sakamoto's espousal of Americanism did not mean the Nisei had to repudiate Japan. Quite the contrary, the Nisei had to be knowledgeable about Japanese affairs, Sakamoto believed, because they had the civic duty of educating their fellow Americans about their parents' homeland. Sakamoto's dualism represented a conservative response to the so-called second-generation Japanese American problem prior to World War II. This chapter will trace the origin and content of this dualism and show how it became untenable in the maelstrom of international and national events that overwhelmed the Nisei in the late 1930s.

Personal Background

A native of Seattle, Sakamoto was born in 1903. His parents were originally from Yamaguchi Prefecture. Arriving in 1894, his father initially worked as a farmhand and sawmill laborer. Eventually, his parents engaged in small business, operating at different times a restaurant, hotel, and used-furniture shop in Seattle. Sakamoto was educated in the public schools of the city. He attended Pacific Grammar School and Franklin High. During his high school years he established a reputation as "an athletic immortal" by his prowess in sports, especially in the "manly" American sport of football. Although he weighed only 128 pounds, he was a scrappy player who played halfback on the Franklin High team. In 1920 his team beat archrival Broadway High for the first time. Sakamoto was also proficient in baseball, judo, and boxing. Before graduating from Franklin High, he moved to the East Coast, where he attended a school in Princeton, New Jersey. Subsequently, he became an English editor for the *Japanese American News*, a Japanese immigrant newspaper published in New York City. Sakamoto held this position for three years, and it proved to be his initiation into the field of journalism. As he worked as an English editor, Sakamoto tried his hand at professional boxing. After a number of fights, including a few at Madison Square Garden, he was injured seriously in 1926. He sustained a detached retina in both eyes, forcing him to retire from the ring and causing his eventual blindness.[3]

Sakamoto was among the handful of older Nisei who attained adulthood right after World War I. The war and its aftermath undoubtedly shaped his conservative political outlook. During the 1916 presidential election campaign, President Woodrow Wilson assailed German Americans for supporting their German homeland in the war and accused them of being hyphenated Americans with divided loyalties. In 1917 Wilson led the nation into the war. With great fanfare American troops were sent off to the European battlefront under a wave of patriotism that swept across the United States. After the war the nation retreated into isolationism. Despite Wilson's personal crusade, the Senate rejected the League of Nations Covenant and refused to commit the United States in any way to the new international body. Simultaneously, the country fell into the grip of xenophobia and a so-called Red Scare. Political radicalism, associated allegedly with foreigners, came under severe repression with the infamous Palmer Raids, and a national Americanization campaign, dedicated to the goal of eradicating all alien elements within American society, arose. The Americanization campaign placed all new immigrants and their descendants in a defensive posture, subjecting them to a coercive form of assimilation. As a condition of acceptance into American society, immigrant groups were compelled to shed their old-world languages, traits, and customs. If they refused, they were deemed and damned as undesirable aliens with no hope of being accepted. All new immigrants were expected to recast themselves in the mold of old-stock white Anglo-Saxon Protestant Americans.[4]

The post–World War I years also witnessed a resurgence of anti-Japanese agitation.[5] The Japanese exclusion movement originated in California at the turn of the century but had subsided with the outbreak of World War I. Once the war ended, however, it resurfaced with renewed vigor and rapidly spread throughout the western states, including the state of Washington. By the early 1920s, as the movement gained popular support, it developed into a national campaign to terminate all Japanese immigration. Sakamoto turned fourteen when the United States entered World War I and attended high school during the postwar years. As an impressionable youth, he witnessed the intense wartime patriotism, experienced the postwar national Americanization campaign, and reached adulthood as the anti-Japanese agitation peaked. Sakamoto tried to enlist in the U.S. Army shortly after the United States entered the war but was rejected because of his age. In 1920 he testified before the House Committee on Immigration and Naturalization.[6] His brief testimony revealed a Japanese American youth striving to project himself as an American. Given the climate of the time, Sakamoto undoubtedly felt overwhelming social pressures to adopt and conform to American ways.

Americanism

Sakamoto's espousal of "Americanism" formed one side of his dualism. He started the *Courier* as significant demographic changes were occurring within Japanese immigrant society during the late 1920s. The Nisei population was increasing so much that it was on the verge of numerically surpassing the *Issei* population. The Issei generation was aging, while the Nisei generation was about to come of age. Sakamoto anticipated that the Nisei would have to take their "rightful place" in American society and discharge their "obligations and duties," which they had "inherited" as "natural born American" citizens.[7] Wary of the Nisei being identified as foreigners, Sakamoto never used the term *Nisei* because it was of Japanese origin. He preferred to use "American born Japanese" or "American citizens of Japanese ancestry" in referring to the Nisei in order to underscore the fact that they were Americans. According to Sakamoto, because of "the wholly American education" and "training, the mode of thought and custom, and . . . the totally American perspective" the Nisei possessed, America was their natural "homeland."[8] In this sense the Nisei were "pioneers" in their own right. They were the "first-generation to be born in America," which placed a special burden on their shoulders.

The long-term goal of the Nisei was the "amalgamation" of the Japanese into the general American population. Yet such a goal was not attainable by the Nisei themselves. Requiring more than a span of a single generation, it would have to await the third generation. In Sakamoto's thinking, assimilation preceded amalgamation. As pioneers, the Nisei were obliged to take the first step toward amalgamation by assimilating themselves into American life. They had a "sacrificial" role of seeking "the proper recognition of themselves as genuine American citizens" by assimilating into American society, thereby facilitating the eventual "amalgamation of the third generation into American life" and assuring "future generations of Americans of Japanese ancestry . . . the fortunes of a better existence." This would not be an easy task, however. The responsibility was "heavy" and would "take the entire second generation era to discharge."[9]

To use Sakamoto's metaphor, the Nisei had to "lower the anchor" into American life.[10] To integrate themselves into society, the Nisei first had to demonstrate, in words as well as deeds, that they were truly loyal American citizens. They had to identify themselves fully with American political traditions, American ideals, and American institutions. "Only if the second generation as a whole works to inculcate in all its members the true spirit of American patriotism," Sakamoto believed, "can the group escape the unhappy fate of being a clan apart from the rest of American life." If they did not, they were doomed to be racial outcasts. In exhorting the Nisei to become patriotic Americans, Sakamoto loved to use platitudes such as "undivided allegiance" and "full-blooded Americanism." He defined "full-blooded Americanism" as "the healthy, well-rounded political, social and economic development of the individual so that he may be a loyal citizen."[11] In this way Sakamoto placed the onus of integrating into American life onto the shoulders of the Nisei themselves. The Nisei were to solve their racial problem by proving that they were exactly like other loyal Americans.

Sakamoto had a rather benign view of white racism. He never related the Nisei's racial problem to that of other racial minorities or formulated a concept of social change as a solution to racism. Nor did he embrace a historical concept of racism or of the ideology of white supremacy with which to interpret the Nisei's racial plight. "Race prejudice" was but an extension of "group prejudice." It occurred whenever "the lines of group prejudice coincide with those of race." It was "secondary and incidental to other prejudice and is thrust to the fore by idiotic sensationalists" and "aggravated by pseudo-patriots." It was "a relic of the past, a form of provincialism which, unless kept alive by jingo agitation, would tend to disappear in the light of knowledge and increased understanding between races." In a word, race prejudice was simply a "bugaboo."[12] With this kind of benign interpretation of racism, Sakamoto argued that education would suffice to dispel it.

As a result, Sakamoto had a sanguine view of the Nisei's future. He assumed that, once the Nisei proved themselves to be worthy American citizens, they would be readily accepted into society. Still, they had to be patient. They had to prepare themselves adequately to become full participants in society to work alongside their fellow citizens. Sakamoto cautioned the Nisei that they "should display no tendency to push themselves unduly" but "should not hang back when the opportunity presents itself to share in the wider life of the American community." From his perspective, there was "nothing inherent" in the Nisei "which would automatically bar them from acceptance by their fellows." Nor was there "anything about them which would make them lovable for their own sakes by . . . white Americans." The Nisei simply had to "be able to act and to talk like their fellow Americans. If they can do that, there will be no question of their being accepted by their fellows."[13] In short, the problem was reduced to educating white Americans about the Nisei.

Sakamoto questioned the efficacy of public protests against racism. In 1939 Afro-American leaders protested the refusal of the Daughters of the American Revolution to provide the usage of its Constitution Hall in Washington, DC, for a concert recital by Marian Anderson, the noted black contralto. In Sakamoto's judgment this protest did not serve to advance the black man's cause. Admittedly, "the cultivated white people of this country have not accepted the Negro on the basis of full social equality." Nevertheless, "those who stir up strife between the Negro and the white . . . do the cause of the Negro an injury." "It should be remembered," Sakamoto cautioned, "that the members of the D.A.R. are extremely proud of their background." And in conclusion he said that the Anderson affair "affords the opportunity to observe that in racial matters it behooves the leaders of all groups to use the utmost caution and forbearance."[14] Sakamoto's interpretation of this episode revealed his inbred conservatism on racial issues. In his opinion Afro-American leaders had exacerbated racial tensions by protesting the action of the D.A.R. They had not exercised "utmost caution and forbearance." Black people were better off forgoing such protests because they antagonized groups like the D.A.R., with its "proud" members.

The Japanese American Citizens League (JACL) was the principal vehicle by which the Nisei would assimilate themselves into American life. The JACL was a national civic organization established by a small group of older Nisei in 1930.[15] Sakamoto was a founding father. Throughout the 1930s he was an active leader and a national president from 1936 to 1938. He equated the establishment of the league with "a citizens' movement" launched to prepare the Nisei to exercise the franchise. Such a movement was designed to "assure and pledge the loyalty and devotion of Americans of Japanese ancestry" to the United States and to strengthen "the fabric and ideals of democratic government." The objective of the league was to educate the young Nisei about American politics on a nonpartisan basis, so that they would realize what their civic responsibilities were and be able to "discharge their public duties" when they reached actual voting age. In so educating the Nisei generation, the JACL would play an indispensable role and "blaze the trail into American life."[16]

Sakamoto deplored anything antithetical to his brand of Americanism.

Communism fell into this category. In 1934 the JACL adopted a resolution that endorsed the deportation of "undesirable alien communists who are found guilty of subversive acts." Sakamoto interpreted this resolution as "one more splendid example of how the League is proving in every way that it is a very real part of American life and of how the members . . . realize their duties as citizens of this country." And he emphasized that the league favored the deportation of undesirable alien Communists "regardless of race"[17] (coincidentally, seventeen Issei Communists were actually deported from the United States between 1931 and 1934). The Communist Party of the United States was "an alien organization" with "un-American principles." Inasmuch as it was "foreign and foreign-dominated" in taking "orders from Moscow," Sakamoto wanted to ban the party from participation in American elections, and he advocated the adoption of measures to see that "the un-American principles of Communism do not obtain . . . a strangle hold on our political life."[18] In 1938 the House of Representatives Special Committee on Un-American Activities (HUAC) was formed under the chairmanship of Congressman Martin Dies of Texas, a rabid anti-Communist. Sakamoto welcomed the Dies Committee's probe of subversives, especially of members of the Communist Party. It was a most effective instrument to investigate their subversive activities in the United States.[19]

Next to the Communist Party, Sakamoto distrusted the Congress of Industrial Organizations (CIO). In 1935 the CIO was established within the American Federation of Labor (AFL) as the Committee for Industrial Organizations. Headed by John L. Lewis, president of the United Mine Workers of America, its purpose was to promote industrial unions in the new mass-production industries. This committee achieved spectacular success in a short span of time. In 1936 and 1937 the nation witnessed the greatest upsurge of labor organizing in American history. With initial dramatic results in the steel and automobile industries, the CIO quickly organized workers in the rubber, electric, aluminum, textile, maritime, and other industries. Many Communists were active as dedicated organizers in the CIO organizing drives. From the outset the CIO aroused the enmity of old-guard AFL leaders who rigidly adhered to craft unionism. John L. Lewis and William Green, AFL president, clashed openly, and as the two men hardened their positions, a parting of ways became inevitable. In August 1936 the AFL Executive Council suspended all CIO unions, and the AFL annual convention, held in late 1936, upheld the council's action, thereby splitting the labor movement into two hostile, competing camps. In 1938 the CIO was redesignated officially as the Congress of Industrial Organizations.[20]

In the AFL-CIO conflict Sakamoto always sided with the AFL. He identified William Green as a conservative labor leader who pursued a policy of being "non-partisan in politics." To Green's credit he was willing to support Republican and Democratic candidates, depending on their position in any given labor issue. On the other hand, John L. Lewis was too partisan. In 1936 he lined up the CIO solidly behind the Democratic Party and contributed close to five hundred thousand dollars to Franklin D. Roosevelt's reelection campaign. From Sakamoto's point of view, cooperation between labor and capital was necessary if the nation hoped to pull out of the Great Depression. "Business men and conservative labor leaders are agreed," he wrote, "that one of the essential points for business recovery is peace between labor and industry."[21] As a new labor federation, he felt, the CIO fomented discord.

Part of the problem was the Wagner Act, which, in Sakamoto's opinion, unduly favored labor. Enacted in 1935, the act recognized the right of workers to join unions of their own choice and upheld their right to collective bargaining. The CIO had achieved its phenomenal success in organizing workers under the protective shield of this act, often resorting to sit-down strikes in which workers seized and occupied plants. Sakamoto believed that it was necessary to amend the act to rectify its one-sided prolabor bias.[22] The Wagner Act also created a National Labor Relations Board, entrusted with the job of mediating labor disputes. Sakamoto believed that the composition and policy of this board had to be changed as well, because it always appeared to favor the CIO in jurisdictional fights between the CIO and AFL. Reflecting his dislike of the CIO, in 1939 Sakamoto hailed the United States Supreme Court decision outlawing sit-down strikes and interpreted the ruling as "a start . . . toward labor peace."[23]

The CIO arrived on the West Coast in 1937. During the 1934 San Francisco maritime strike, Harry Bridges had emerged as the leader of the West Coast longshoremen. Under his leadership the International Longshoremen's and Warehousemen's Union (ILWU) switched its affiliation from the AFL to the CIO in August 1937, and Bridges himself was appointed as the CIO director on the West Coast. Sakamoto was always critical of Bridges. He saw "a subversive element" in the leadership of the 1934 maritime strike, which of course included Bridges. Sakamoto asserted that the strike leaders had seized "the opportunities offered . . . by the strike" and used them as "expedients to further their own causes."[24] The Dies Committee eventually accused Bridges of being a Communist. Sakamoto favored his deportation on grounds that he was an undesirable alien. To justify his stand, he quoted American Legion officials who declared that Bridges was "a menace to American institutions."[25] In 1937 the Alaska Cannery Workers Union, Local 5 of San Francisco, affiliated with the CIO, and in the next year Local 7 of Seattle followed suit. Both locals had a sizable Japanese membership; local 5 was tied closely to the ILWU. Although Sakamoto avoided taking a public position on these two unions switching their affiliation to the CIO, he no doubt believed that they should have remained affiliated with the AFL. In this he stood in opposition to the young Nisei progressives who emerged in the late 1930s and who saw in industrial unionism and the CIO the hope of the Japanese American working class.[26]

Throughout the 1930s Sakamoto never deviated from espousing Americanism as his fundamental solution to the problem of the Nisei. It was the way to break down the various political, economic, social, and racial barriers that the Nisei faced. It was the way to disprove the negative stereotypes of the Nisei as unassimilable and forever foreign. It was the way for the Nisei to get out of their narrow ethnic enclave and join the American mainstream. In short, Americanism was the key to the full acceptance of the Nisei into American life. Nothing in Sakamoto's Americanism called for changes in society. He neither questioned nor doubted the worth of the American traditions, ideals, and institutions to which he asked the Nisei to be faithful and loyal. He accepted them as sacred cows, and in so doing he planted the seeds of the superpatriotism that he would espouse from 1940.

Bridge of Understanding

The second side of Sakamoto's dualism was his espousal of the Nisei as a so-called bridge of understanding. Sakamoto was a firm believer and ardent supporter of the concept of the Nisei as a bridge of understanding. To popularize it among his fellow Nisei, he frequently published the opinions of high Japanese government officials who endorsed the concept. In 1931 he cited Japanese ambassador Debuchi Katsumi, who expressed his expectation of the Nisei in the following way:

Being of Japanese descent, you are naturally expected to know more about the native country of your parents than does the average American. I urge you to live up to that expectation. You should study about Japan, about things Japanese, about the national spirit and ideals which are back of the marvelous progress achieved by that island nation in the last half century.

You are expected to be the most effective of the connecting links between Japan and America. You can live up to this expectation only by knowing and understanding Japan as you know and understand America.[27]

In interpreting Ambassador Debuchi's expectation, Sakamoto asserted that the Nisei "have a natural love for the country of their birth as they have . . . a natural love for [that of] their parents." It was "only reasonable that they should become a strong and determined factor in bringing about better and friendly relationships between the Japanese and American nations."[28] In 1935 Sakamoto published the opinion of Foreign Minister Hirota Kōki. In his message to the Nisei Hirota stated that the Nisei made Japan and America "truly kindred nations, reinforcing with indestructible ties of blood the economic and cultural bond that unites the countries."[29]

Sakamoto cited prominent Japanese and American educators as well. In an interview with the *Courier* Nitobe Inazō, a well-known Japanese scholar, addressed the Nisei generation. He said that he had "heard on occasions . . . that the second generation feels that they are between two walls, floating in the breach, so to say, and that they feel handicapped. This I believe to be a foolish attitude. They must assume a proper pride in their citizenship as well as in the high heritage of their race and transform what they believe to be their handicap into an advantage." That advantage was to be found in the unique position of the Nisei: "You are placed in a special position to interpret the East to the West and the West to the East," Nitobe said, so "that they may meet on common grounds to effect the principles of peace and mutual welfare."[30] Stanford president Ray L. Wilbur echoed Nitobe's opinion. He emphatically stated, "I think that one of the great responsibilities of our American-born Japanese is to interpret Japan to all of our citizens."[31] Bruno Lasker, associate editor of *Pacific Affairs*, declared that the Nisei must "serve as interpreters between two civilizations and two cultures."[32]

Sakamoto likewise cited prominent Nisei leaders like Clarence Arai. Like Sakamoto, Arai was among the first-born Nisei. He fully subscribed to the concept of the Nisei as a bridge of understanding in the so-called Pacific era.

As the president of the Seattle Progressive Citizens' League, an early Nisei organization, Arai said:

> . . . I like to think of the second generation as a diplomat of good-will, whose duty is to bring about a better understanding between the East and the West, thereby eradicating the evil of prejudice from the minds of the people. We are all participating in a wonderful era, the Pacific Era. The Mediterranean had long passed away, which in turn gave away to the Atlantic. But now the Atlantic Era is about to become a thing of "yesterday," for today the East is facing the West and the West the East. It is around the Pacific that things are now happening and where news originate[s]. Japan has become a world power, China is awakening. Even India is restless. It is here where the future lies. The second generation should consecrate their lives to this special task so that the Pacific Era will be an era characterized with everlasting peace.[33]

Sakamoto himself firmly believed that a Pacific era had dawned. In convoluted prose he predicted that "the cradle of future world events" would be in the Pacific:

> . . . It is . . . in the Pacific where the future historians will lay eyes upon a civilization which will seek to tie the strands of human relations in a knot of friendship and understanding between races and peoples. It is . . . in the Pacific where they will see the first bridge of understanding and a common interest in a united culture which should span the gulf of racial differences and prejudices.
>
>   It is evident that the Pacific is the coming center of gravitation for all cultural interests, commercial enterprises and human activities. The world trend is toward this basin; what will transpire on the Pacific Rim will be vitally interesting to the human race.[34]

"The two great nations" of Japan and the United States stood "on opposite rims of the Pacific basin," and "the responsibility of the coming era" rested "upon the shoulders of these two nations." The Nisei had a crucial role to play in this Pacific era as "the linking chain of understanding" between the two countries.[35]

Sakamoto was aware that the Nisei had to be knowledgeable about Japanese affairs if they ever hoped to be an effective bridge of understanding. As a first step in advancing their knowledge, Sakamoto urged the Nisei to study the Japanese language. He disagreed with those who held that the Nisei should forget their parents' native tongue. "The notion that a second generation must show his ignorance of the Japanese language . . . in order to be recognized as an American," he said, "is not only idiotic but indicates the grossest hypocrisy. Any American with common sense knows that a knowledge of any language . . . would be an asset, not a liability." "Americans of Japanese ancestry should not forget their position of being the linking chain of two cultures and peoples," he added, "and a better knowledge of their parents' tongue would hurt them none the whit."[36] By learning the language, the Nisei could "increase their own sphere of knowledge" and "make themselves better fitted to maintain understanding between two great nations in the world."[37] In other words, a knowledge of Japanese equipped them to assume the role of a bridge of understanding between the United States and Japan.

To stimulate the study of Japanese among the Nisei, Sakamoto ran a weekly column on the Japanese language in the *Courier*. The columnist was Henry S. Tatsumi, a Nisei lecturer in Japanese at the University of Washington. Offering simple lessons, his column was titled *Japanese Language* and appeared from November 1932 to December 1933. At the beginning of January 1934 the column was retitled *Nipponology* and featured lessons on Japanese conversation, as well as articles on Japanese civilization. Sakamoto also advocated the teaching of Japanese and Chinese at the secondary-school level as substitutes for Greek, Latin, and modern European languages. In the Pacific era it was anomalous not to offer high school students the choice of learning Oriental languages in place of European ones.[38]

Sakamoto endorsed the *kengakudan* practice established by the Issei as a way of stimulating an interest in Japan among young Nisei. In 1928 the Seattle Federation of Japanese Christian Churches organized their own *kengakudan*. Sakamoto believed that this tour group would provide the Nisei with "a more substantial and thorough knowledge of the customs and . . . mannerisms of the Japanese people." Moreover, "it would bring them into a real and tangible contact with another civilization of a different type as to give them a broader perspective of things in general."[39] As a rule, travel to Japan would enable young Nisei "to acquire an understanding of the problems which exist in that country, and [to] approach them in a more sympathetic manner. This, however, is not the only point to be considered. The idea, as we see it, is that our young folk upon their return would be in a position better to fulfill the duties of citizenship in the United States."[40]

Sakamoto singled out the Nisei who gained firsthand knowledge of Japan and its people through excursion tours. In 1929 he cited the case of David Suzuki, whom he quoted:

> There is something . . . in the cultural and historical background of Japan which has made the Empire a truly great one. In order to appreciate its value in making one's life valuable and in the forming of character, there is a useful need for the second generation to visit the island Kingdom and come into contact with the daily life of Japan and her people and gain the essence, at least, of what has made Japan a great nation.[41]

In 1934 Sakamoto cited the case of Henry Tsuchiya, a junior at the University of Washington. Tsuchiya visited Tokyo as a member of the American delegation to the first Japan-America Student Conference, held in 1934. This first and subsequent annual conference brought together students of both countries—always including a number of Nisei—for roundtable discussions of issues affecting Japanese-American relations. After his trip to Tokyo Tsuchiya concluded that "one cannot understand or become accustomed to Japan, or the Japanese people, merely by reading or hearing of them." "He must actually see the country and her inhabitants first hand," he said, "to acquire an understanding of them."[42] By publicizing the value of visiting Japan, Sakamoto encouraged the Nisei to visit the country.

Sakamoto linked a knowledge of Japanese culture with the Nisei's being good American citizens. He ascribed the "greatness" of Japan to the "ethical culture" of the country. If the Nisei could "truly appreciate" this culture, Sakamoto argued, it would help them "become good American citizens." Conversely, if the Nisei forgot it, they "will not be able to qualify as good American citizens."[43] In 1931 Sakamoto visited Japan to seek treatment for his worsening blindness. He wrote of his own experience in Japan:

> I have learned of the deep respect that the Japanese people hold for their ancestors to whom they believe they owe their present lot, however fortunate that may be. I have learned that they feel their present duty to fulfill the obligations of daily existence in a worthy manner for the sake of paving the proper groundwork for their children and posterity. The most impressive thing I learned was their sincere love for their children and their far-sighted thought for the well-being of posterity.

That in a nutshell, in my opinion, is the root of Japan's present day greatness with a firm pillar of loyalty personifying Japan's spirit expressed in the love for their Emperor.

Sakamoto believed that a particular Japanese concept of loyalty would make the Nisei better American citizens. In speaking of himself, he said, "I feel that I have been made a much better American in setting foot upon the soil of my ancestors," who "knew only one master and one loyalty."[44] Here Sakamoto had in mind an old Japanese proverb that taught that a faithful retainer could have only one lord (*chūshin wa nikun ni tsukaezu*). Being American-born citizens, the Nisei, by analogy, had only their native land, the United States, to which they owed undivided allegiance.

Sakamoto himself strove to be a bridge of understanding, especially after the Manchurian Incident. In his capacity as a Nisei leader, publisher, and editor he actively promoted the Japanese case in China among his fellow Nisei and the local American public. Sakamoto was instrumental in organizing the Committee on Pacific Information in early 1932. Composed of a handful of Nisei and Ashley E. Holden, executive secretary of the Japan Society of Seattle, this committee disseminated information favorable to the Japanese side on the Manchurian question. Sakamoto staunchly defended the Japanese government in frequent editorials. In October 1931 he interpreted the movement of Japanese troops beyond the South Manchurian Railway zone as necessary "to establish law and order to ensure protection to life and property." This movement was not "an aggression nor an invasion."[45] Later he wrote:

Japan is only desirous of fair treatment accorded to her nationals and her interests in China. This has not been accorded her. Irritated beyond the limits of any nation's patience, she is now determined to teach China the meaning of a responsible government. She is determined to teach China that treaty rights must be respected.

Were Japan's motives any other than these, the course of her actions in China would have been entirely different. Everyone realizes that if she desired to, Japan could over-whelm China within a few days. The fact that she has not done so, but has sent her forces only to those regions where her interests and the lives and the property of her nationals are jeopardized, proves the sincerity of her only desire for justice.[46]

In addition to supporting Japan's case in editorials, Sakamoto published many extensive pro-Japan articles. He published speeches on the Manchurian Incident by Seattle consul Uchiyama Kiyoshi, Japanese ambassador Saitō Hiroshi, Foreign Minister Shidehara Kijūrō, and other high Japanese government officials. He also published the complete text of Japanese Foreign Ministry press releases.[47] The issues of the *Courier* that carried such speeches and press releases were distributed to prominent local Americans in an effort to influence their opinion. At Consul Uchiyama's suggestion, Sakamoto gave Ashley E. Holden space in the *Courier*. Utilizing the allotted space as a news outlet for the Japan Society, Holden wrote a column titled "Notes of Japan Society."[48] Members of the society were advised to subscribe to the *Courier* to keep abreast of the society's activities. Consul Uchiyama hoped that Holden's column would induce Americans in the Pacific Northwest who were interested in Far Eastern affairs to actually subscribe to the *Courier*, thereby increasing the newspaper's circulation and influence. From 1934 Sakamoto had a weekly thirty-minute radio program on local station KXA. In five-minute news spots he also broadcast news favorable to Japan. In his reports to Tokyo, Consul Uchiyama praised Sakamoto for being cooperative. Uchiyama noted with regret that most American newspapers ignored Japanese government press releases. In light of this fact Sakamoto was performing an invaluable service in publishing and broadcasting pro-Japan news. Indeed, Consul Uchiyama valued Sakamoto's service so highly that he donated money in support of the *Courier*.[49]

To Sakamoto there was no contradiction in his adhering to the concept of a bridge of understanding and in his being an American citizen. Sakamoto identified the role of a bridge with being a loyal American by incorporating it into his definition of good American citizenship. To be a responsible, worthwhile American citizen, the Nisei had to assume the role. Otherwise, they would be shirking their duty. In other words, a good American of Japanese ancestry was a person who assumed the role of a bridge of understanding. In enlightening their fellow Americans about the Japanese side of Far Eastern affairs, the Nisei were promoting better relations between the United States and Japan. Consequently, Sakamoto never saw himself as a propagandist for the Japanese government. In his own mind he was being a loyal American citizen whenever he disseminated pro-Japan information. In Consul Uchiyama's opinion Sakamoto vindicated the worth of the concept of the Nisei as a bridge of understanding to the Japanese government.

Even after the outbreak of the Sino-Japanese War, Sakamoto continued to defend Japan. In August 1937 he asserted that "Japanese troops are in North China by right, and have been acting only to protect the interests of their people." He claimed that "the Japanese army is not making war on the Chinese people, nor even on the Chinese army. It has no program except to preserve law and order, but this unfortunately has been difficult on account of a combination of Chinese war lords and Communist agents."[50] A month later he stressed the growing menace of Communism. "Machinations of Red Russia become more and more apparent with every lifting of the war clouds over Asia," he declared, "and every glimpse makes more apparent the red hand of Communism." Only Japan stood as a "bulwark" against this menace:

> As the stabilizing influence in eastern Asia, and the only great power there to so stand, Japan fights for security and peace. She is the bulwark between Communism and all it stands for, and those in the rest of the world who seek good government for the people generally. If Japan falls, good government falls. Communism has no more place in the capitals of countries that wish peace and safety than has the Cossack heel in the Imperial Palace of the Mings.[51]

In striving to establish law and order in China, Japan was "the real underdog."[52] Boycotts of Japanese-made goods in protest against Japan's military actions in China were unconscionable to Sakamoto. From his point of view they accomplished no purpose and were patently unfair to Issei merchants who retailed such goods.[53] Public demonstrations against the shipment of scrap iron and metal to Japan were also unfair. "If a foreign nation is allowed to purchase an article in this country," Sakamoto wrote, "then fairness would seem to indicate that this government should protect the purchaser in consummating the deal." Since the United States had not classified scrap iron and metal as "contraband" material, Japan was legally allowed to buy them. Thus until such materials "have been declared contraband . . . the protection of the federal arm should be extended to those who in good faith have made their purchase here."[54]

As the conflict expanded beyond North China, Sakamoto's defense of Japan did not diminish. In late 1938 after the fall of Hankow, Sakamoto editorialized that "Japan deserves support." "A new epoch in China" had commenced "with the fall of Hankow." The past had been characterized by internal chaos, with "the western powers" having "failed to establish law and order in China." According to Sakamoto, "Japan has now undertaken the task at enormous cost of blood and treasure," so he concluded that "the western powers should support her, passively, if not actively."[55] In October 1939 Sakamoto marked the twenty-eighth anniversary of the toppling of the Ch'ing dynasty with an editorial entitled "28th Years of Misery." Seeing a sad spectacle, he observed:

> This 28th anniversary of the overthrow of the Manchu dynasty must be a sad occasion for those who looked for regeneration of the Chinese government. In contrast with the chaotic conditions, the misery and suffering prevailing there, they can look across the sea and behold in Japan an established government where law and order prevail, and where life and property are safe. They might listen to Dr. Wang [Ching-wei] instead of trying to kill him. With the sordid history of Chiang and his regime before them, they might well consider whether it is not time to end the government that has continued through 28 years of misery.[56]

Sakamoto clung to the slim hope that Wang Ching-wei could somehow insure peace and security. Consequently, Sakamoto recognized the existence of a new Nanking government established in March 1940 by Wang with the support of the Japanese government. In China there had been "no peace, law, order or security of life or property." This having been the case, Sakamoto reasoned, "the world might let Wang Ching-wei have a try, at least."[57]

Following Sakamoto's lead, Henry S. Tatsumi transformed his column into a weekly defense of Japan's cause in China. He asked the rhetorical question, "What must American-Japanese do in the face of the Far Eastern crisis?" Tatsumi's answer was that the Nisei had to educate the American public. He started with the premise that the Nisei, although sympathetic to their parents' country, must remain loyal to the United States, their native land. "Every American citizen of Japanese ancestry," he said, "must remain loyal to the United States and strive to uphold the ideals for which she stands in the face of the Far Eastern crisis." In his opinion "Soviet Russia, China, England and France" were "spreading wanton propaganda in their effort to involve the United States in the face of Japan's determined effort to check the anti-Japanese policy the Chinese leaders have been imposing upon the peace-loving masses of China." This propaganda was designed to draw the United States unwittingly into the conflict. Given this dangerous possibility, it was the duty of the Nisei "to counteract this vicious foreign propaganda" to prevent the country from becoming involved unnecessarily. If the Nisei failed to do so, according to Tatsumi, the "ideals and privileges which have been preserved by the sacrifices of the American people since the founding of the nation" would be destroyed.[58] As loyal American citizens, therefore, the Nisei had the duty of educating their fellow citizens about the Sino-Japanese War. Tatsumi himself fulfilled this duty by presenting in his column information that justified Japan's actions in China.

In 1940 Sakamoto published a series of articles by Bill Hosokawa, a young Nisei journalist who had worked on the *Courier*. After the outbreak of the Sino-Japanese War, Hosokawa worked for the Japanese Consulate of Seattle as an English secretary. Subsequently, he worked in Singapore, putting out the *Singapore Herald*, ostensibly an independent English-language newspaper but in fact under control of the Japanese government. Thereafter he was employed by the *Shanghai Times*. In 1940 Hosokawa toured North China, Manchuria, and Korea and devoted a series of articles to what he considered to be the beneficial influence of the Japanese presence on the Asian continent. "The books say that Korea was just about as hopeless a place as was to be found when the Japanese incorporated the country" in 1910, he said, but "today there is hope and life, and the people say with pride that Korea is not a 'colony,' but a detached 'prefecture' of Japan."[59] Hosokawa highlighted developments in Manchuria, seeing Mukden as "the center of a growing nation in a land of almost limitless possibilities."[60] He never alluded to, nor discussed, Japanese military aggression or colonialism but rather emphasized the economic progress that had been achieved under Japanese influence and the need for peace and capital in the future economic development of Manchukuo and North China. The publication of Hosokawa's series was Sakamoto's last stab at trying to present Japan in a favorable light.

The Dualism Becomes Untenable

The maelstrom of international and national events from 1939 made Sakamoto's dualism untenable in the end. Throughout the course of the 1930s Sakamoto earnestly endeavored to strike a balance between the two sides of his dualism, but by the eve of Pearl Harbor he did not even pretend to act as a bridge of understanding. Because of the turn of political events, he was no longer able to defend Japan, so he ceased writing and publishing pro-Japan editorials and news altogether. Instead, he began to espouse Americanism exclusively and refashioned his original Americanism into a flag-waving form of 200 percent patriotism. This radical shift in emphasis to what can only be called an exaggerated, one-dimensional superpatriotism occurred in 1940 and conditioned Sakamoto's eventual response to Pearl Harbor.

International political events cast ominous war clouds over Japanese-American relations from late 1939. In July the United States government announced that it was going to abrogate unilaterally the existing 1911 Treaty of Commerce and Navigation between the United States and Japan. Requiring six-month advance notice, the abrogation became effective January 26, 1940. In September 1939 Germany invaded Poland, an event that marked the beginning of World War II in Europe. By early 1940 Germany had occupied the low countries and France, leaving England alone resisting German military advances. In the summer of 1940 the United States set restrictions on the export of strategic material abroad and in September imposed an embargo on the shipment of scrap iron and metal to Japan specifically. This embargo coincided with the signing of the Tripartite Pact by Germany, Italy, and Japan, by which Japan recognized Germany's right to establish a new order in Europe, and Germany and Italy, in turn, recognized Japan's right to establish a so-called new order in Asia.

All of these events had a far-reaching impact on American national life. The European war set off an intense national debate between those who favored intervention in the war and those who favored neutrality and isolationism. At the same time, the war generated a public hysteria concerning fifth columnists. Fifth columnists, identified with aliens and radicals, were alleged to be fomenting domestic strife to undermine American society, as well as engaging in espionage and sabotage. As a result of this hysteria Congress enacted the Smith Act of June 1940, requiring all aliens to be registered and fingerprinted with the federal government. In terms of the Sino-Japanese War, American public opinion grew implacably hostile to Japan. It identified the beleaguered Chinese Nationalist government and Chiang Kai-shek as the underdog valiantly fighting for survival.

Given this turn of political events, the Nisei found themselves in a terrible quandary. Many people perceived them as fifth columnists. Saburo Kido, a prominent JACL leader, described the situation of the Nisei: "A Nisei is in constant fear of being suspected as a 'fifth columnist' if he should speak his mind. A dark cloud is hovering over us which may break forth into mob violence. There are groups in this country who are so steeped in racial animosity that they are willing to go to any extent to make life unbearable for the race they despise and hate."[61] The American public was unable to draw a distinction between the Japanese in Japan and the Japanese here. To make matters worse, it also was unable to distinguish between the Issei and the Nisei. If the Nisei dared to stand up in defense of Japan, their loyalty to the United States was impugned, making any public rationalization of Japan's actions in China virtually impossible. And whether the Nisei defended Japan or not, they still were associated with Japan in the public mind. The term *Nisei-baiting* came into vogue in 1940 to denote the practice of linking the Nisei to Japan and holding them accountable for her military conduct. Because of this fearful and dangerous tendency, Sakamoto pleaded for understanding and tolerance. Mindful of what had happened to German Americans during World War I, he feared the same thing might happen to Japanese Americans. Sakamoto insisted that it was possible to separate "loyal" persons from "disloyal" ones and asked the public not to fall prey to "impetuous 'patriots.'"[62]

In his plea for tolerance Sakamoto was influenced strongly by Louis Adamic, a Slovenian immigrant writer. Adamic rejected the old notion of an American melting pot that required all new immigrant groups to discard their old-world traits and to recast themselves in the mold of Anglo-Saxon Americans. He believed that every immigrant group had something valuable to contribute to American society. "Americanism" was not the monopoly of old-stock Americans but "an expanding concept" that embraced all Americans, old and new, who still were in the process of "becoming" by contributing toward the creation of "a universal or pan-human culture." "Anti-alienism" and "racism" had bred intolerance and hatred among Americans, putting new immigrants and racial minorities "on the defensive" and crippling their capacity to function as full human beings. Americanism involved the "acceptance" of cultural and racial differences, and the future of America, to Adamic, lay in a "unity within diversity."[63] The world was engulfed in war. America had yet to solve its own festering racial problem, not to mention its economic and social ills. With profound unrest at home, how could the country ever create unity if it decided to enter the war? How could it champion democracy against fascism without tackling its own problems? This crisis of 1940 represented, to Adamic, an opportunity to forge a new vision of what America could be around which all Americans might rally.

Adamic had an abiding faith in education. Acceptance of diversity was to be fostered by educating Americans about each other. Thus he published *From Many Lands* in late 1940. This book was a collection of portraits of various immigrant groups designed to promote understanding of Americans who had different backgrounds. Among the portraits, Adamic included one of an alienated Nisei.[64] Adamic wanted his readers to understand that the Nisei shared common problems with second-generation Americans of European descent. The Nisei also were suspended between two worlds, between that of their parents and the larger society. They, too, dreamed of participating fully in a democratic society but were rebuffed by ignorant elements. They, too, were frustrated and insecure about the future, living an ambiguous existence without much hope of achieving a sense of wholeness. Adamic also wanted his readers to understand that the Nisei's predicament was compounded by white racism.

Sakamoto enthusiastically embraced Adamic's ideas. In early 1940 Adamic spoke to many Nisei groups on the Pacific Coast and appealed to the Nisei for their cooperation in his projected publication of *From Many Lands*. Sakamoto welcomed Adamic with open arms and published the complete text of one of his standard lectures.[65] In addition, he reprinted an essay entitled "This Crisis Is an Opportunity," in which Adamic pleaded for tolerance and appealed for "unity within diversity."[66] This essay originally appeared in *Common Ground*, a quarterly journal Adamic launched to disseminate knowledge about different immigrant groups in order to promote mutual understanding and acceptance. Sakamoto reported very favorably on *From Many Lands* when it actually came out and sold it at a discount rate through the *Courier*. Aware of the dire predicament in which the Nisei found themselves in 1940, Sakamoto latched on to the ideas of Louis Adamic in his own plea for tolerance.

While he appealed for tolerance, Sakamoto affirmed, again and again, the undivided allegiance of the Nisei. In 1940 the JACL national convention was held in Portland, Oregon, and became a platform from which JACLers proclaimed their patriotism to the American public. Sakamoto covered the proceedings closely. National president Walter T. Tsukamoto set the patriotic tone of the convention in his opening address. "It is the duty of every American," he avowed, "to be prepared to protect, defend, and to perpetuate our American form of government and our way of life." Tsukamoto went out of his way to identify the Nisei solely with America:

The Americans of Japanese ancestry have a duty to the country . . . and this . . . duty does not and must not be colored by any thought of foreign ties. . . . I am happy and proud to be able to tell you and the millions of fellow Americans of other racial extractions that . . . coursing through the veins of the Nisei is a fervent love for the country of their birth equalling that of any American and certainly surpassed by no American of whatever racial origin.

"We stand ready at all times," he asserted, "to contribute to the progress of our American principles of democracy, and . . . whenever the need should arise we will be among the first to fight for the preservation of [our] ideals." Sakamoto hailed Tsukamoto's opening address because it left "no doubt where we stand." "All that the second-generation asks," he insisted, "is that their fellow Americans shall believe in them, and accept them as a part of the national life." The Nisei were "ready to contribute their talents and their efforts to the preservation and the upbuilding of America."[67] In Sakamoto's judgment no JACL convention had ever come out "more emphatically for citizenship and the defense of citizenship than did the Portland convention."[68]

In an attempt to forestall and diffuse anti-Nisei hostility, Sakamoto favored all local JACL chapters holding "Americanism Day" programs. Toyo Suyemoto, a student at the University of California, solicited his advice in October 1940. She informed him that "there have been serious concern[s] and talk among the students and some faculty" at her school "as to the welfare of the nisei in case of definite hostilities between the United States and Japan." Suyemoto asked Sakamoto about the "protective measures" the Nisei might adopt to protect themselves "against indiscriminate prejudice among the general public."[69] Sakamoto advised her that the best measure was for the Nisei to "reaffirm their loyalty to America." The Nisei should invite "well-known Americans" to patriotic meetings convened by local JACL chapters, hold flag ceremonies, and proclaim their loyalty. Sakamoto reasoned that if the Nisei "can show the American public that we are part and parcel of the nation and that we intend to remain so despite the ill-advised actions of some ignorant groups, I am sure" that this "will be the best protective measure."[70]

By 1941 Americanism dominated the pages of the *Courier*. A New Year's editorial entitled "Our Way of Life" sounded the increasingly shrill note of patriotism. "The most vital duty that confronts the American people in 1941," it said, "is to protect, defend, assure and continue our way of life."[71] A typical editorial stated "We believe in America!"

This government of the people, by the people, for the people must not perish, as Lincoln said. It is the greatest government the world has ever seen for safeguarding the freedom of its citizens, and it casts its beneficent rays of hope over a weary world today.

Under such a beneficient [*sic*] form of government our people will not fail. They will translate their words into deeds to prove to the world that we indeed believe in America, that we will cherish and uphold her traditions and will not cease in our efforts until peace shall return to our land and others, and democracy shall be enthroned.[72]

In late August the JACL Northwest District Council met. The United States had frozen all Japanese assets in July, and a sense of acute crisis pervaded the Japanese community. Sakamoto attached great significance to the council meeting because it was planned as a forum at which JACL leaders were going to pledge publicly their loyalty to the United States. President Thomas Iseri delivered a fervent patriotic speech. "The time has now come upon us," he said, "when we must prove ourselves as Americans," and "this proof must be based upon substantial reasons and not upon empty utterances for a temporary period." "If America is worth living for," Iseri proclaimed, "then America is worth dying for."[73] Sakamoto lavishly praised this speech as representing the patriotic sentiments of the entire Nisei generation.

This patriotic rhetoric had an important consequence in terms of the JACL leadership's relationship to the Issei generation. The overwhelming majority of Issei rallied behind Japan during the Sino-Japanese War and engaged in various activities to provide political, financial, material, and moral support to their homeland. Some JACL leaders looked askance at the Issei's nationalistic identification with Japan. In the words of Togo Tanaka, unofficial historian of the JACL, "out of the habit of defining loyalty, talking about loyalty, interpreting it for both the Japanese and Caucasian communities, a segment of J.A.C.L. leadership in 1939 and 1940 began to arrogate to itself the authority to judge and evaluate the loyalty of members of the Japanese community." Asked to cooperate in "guarding against sabotage and espionage" by federal agents, "the J.A.C.L. representatives for the most part . . . responded with a patriotic zeal exceeded only by their public expressions of American loyalty."[74] Except for national vice president Ken Matsumoto, Tanaka does not name those leaders who engaged in this practice.

A longtime JACL leader, Mike Masaoka explained the JACL's connection with intelligence agencies:

JACL did cooperate with the Federal Bureau of Investigation, Naval Intelligence, and other agencies by furnishing them with all the information which we might have had at our disposal regarding the suspects the agencies questioned us about. This is the duty of every American. But, since we of the JACL are not, and were not then, trained investigators in counter-espionage, we were not able to furnish them with more than what was general community knowledge. . . . In summary, JACL did not institute a witch-hunt; neither did we evade our duty as patriotic Americans interested, as are other Americans, in protecting our nation from espionage and sabotage.[75]

In other words, some JACL leaders cooperated or collaborated, depending on one's interpretation, with federal agents to vindicate themselves as self-proclaimed loyal Americans. As captives of their own patriotic rhetoric, they felt compelled to act as informants and passed on information they had on persons under investigation. "From the standpoint . . . within the Japanese community," according to Tanaka, such JACL leaders were perceived as "spies and stooges for the F.B.I."[76]

National vice president Ken Matsumoto had a very close relationship with Lieutenant Commander Kenneth Ringle, intelligence officer of the Eleventh Naval District of Southern California. Indeed, it was Matsumoto who persuaded JACL leaders that they should cooperate with Ringle and other federal operatives. In concert with Matsumoto, Ringle invited members of the JACL Southern California District Council for a meeting at the University of Southern California in the spring of 1941. Ringle then arranged for JACL leaders in other locales to meet other federal agents. In this connection national president Saburo Kido reported to Sakamoto:

When I visited Los Angeles during the latter part of March, Ken Matsumoto took me down to San Pedro to see Lieutenant Commander Ringle, who was instrumental in inviting the Southern California District Council members to a discussion group. During the course of our conversation the matter of holding similar meetings in the various districts came up. Commander Ringle has written to Seattle and San Francisco and ascertained the officers in charge of the Intelligence Bureau. Lieutenant Commander Liebenow of Seattle replied favorably, stating that he would be delighted to cooperate with the JACL in the Northwest if he receives an invitation. I would suggest that either you or Tom Iseri . . . or the Northwest District Council contact him and arrange for a meeting.[77]

Matsumoto informed Sakamoto that he had communicated with Kido "about the arrangements that Lt. Comm. Ringle has made for the JACL of your area to meet with the Head of the Naval Intelligence of your district, the 13th." Matsumoto assured Sakamoto that "their office is ready to meet the JACL leaders at any time they wish, and I believe that it ought to be done at once."[78]

There is no evidence that Sakamoto met with naval intelligence officers in the Pacific Northwest, but Sakamoto unquestionably believed that the Nisei should cooperate with federal agencies. In 1940 he said so in so many words: "Every loyal American citizen . . . will lend all possible support to the constituted authorities to see that subversive activities are promptly put down."[79] After the arrest of a Japanese spy in June 1941 he warned that "every officer and every member of the [JACL] must be on the alert."[80] On December 12, 1941, five days after Pearl Harbor, Sakamoto established the JACL Emergency Defense Council of Seattle, with himself as its chairman. Within this council a special committee was formed "to cooperate with the F.B.I." and to report "subversive activities in the Community."[81] Sakamoto notified the FBI that the Emergency Defense Council was prepared to "co-operate in any way with your office" and "to do our share in the prosecution of the war to a victorious end."[82]

Sakamoto testified before the Tolan Committee in February 1942. Under questioning, Sakamoto was badgered by Congressman Carl T. Curtis of Nebraska about the policy of the JACL regarding "disloyal Japanese." Sakamoto stated that "I know definitely that our organization, both locally and nationally, has, let us say, 'turned in' people whom we thought should be checked into." When questioned about what he meant by "turned in," Sakamoto replied that "Japanese" had been turned in. And he added parenthetically: "Of course, we will turn in Germans and Italians, too, and even good English American citizens, if we know that they are subversive. We have been working chiefly among the Japanese, and we have repeatedly stated at our meetings that it is our loyal duty to ferret out those among us who are disloyal, because our interests must be first for America, and, secondly, for ourselves."[83] In sum, Sakamoto's Americanism required the Nisei "to ferret out" the "disloyal" element among the Japanese. Any Nisei who claimed to be a loyal American had this duty, and the duty was a logical extension of the superpatriotic posture Sakamoto had assumed on the eve of Pearl Harbor.

Sakamoto's superpatriotism conditioned his response to Pearl Harbor and the ensuing mass internment of Japanese Americans. It was behind his immediate and total repudiation of Japan. Japan had committed a "dastardly and treacherous" act in attacking the United States. That act had "cut the last thin thread that may have existed between the Japanese people of all groups in this country and the Japanese Government."[84] Once "evacuation" became imminent, Sakamoto urged everyone to obey the American government. "A basic tenet of loyalty," he wrote, "is to obey the orders of the government to which one owes his allegiance. . . . When the final evacuation order comes, it will be for us to remember it was not Uncle Sam in the first place who brought that to pass." By a tortured logic Sakamoto reasoned that the American government had been "compelled to take the step of evacuation by the ruthless and treacherous course of the Tokio military clique." So he advised everyone, "Let's obey the order loyally," and "cheerfully" at that.[85] The final issue of the *Courier* appeared on April 24, 1942. On that day Sakamoto stated in his farewell editorial: "We contribute now by our cooperation with the government," accepting what he called evacuation "as a patriotic contribution" by Japanese Americans to the ultimate defeat of Japan. And he closed his editorial with the words, "And so, until we meet again . . . may God Bless America, our beloved country!"[86] With Americanism in complete ascendancy, Sakamoto's original dualism disappeared altogether without a trace of the concept of the Nisei as a bridge of understanding.

Conclusion

Sakamoto and the *Courier* had a very limited appeal to the Nisei generation as a whole. Before World War II the majority of Nisei were still children or teenagers. They were much too young to be interested in international and national affairs. If they read the *Courier* at all, it was because the newspaper had an entire page devoted to Nisei sports activities. On the other hand, most adult Nisei were working-class people who had little interest or time to devote to international and national affairs. They were too busy eking out a living in the middle of the Great Depression. To such adult Nisei the concept of a bridge of understanding had no meaning. It was an abstract ideal that had no bearing on their daily lives. Young progressive working-class Nisei were highly critical of Sakamoto. They were dismayed at his anti-CIO bias and characterized his espousal of Americanism as a "hat-in-hand" approach to better race relations. Moreover, the influence of the *Courier*, whatever its extent, was geographically restricted to the Pacific Northwest. In 1940 the *Courier* had a circulation of only thirteen hundred, with 75 percent of its subscribers in Seattle and adjacent towns.

Sakamoto's editorial writing itself detracted from the appeal of the *Courier*. Sakamoto had a pedantic, very convoluted style of writing that made his editorials less than readable. His editorial topics covered a wide range of topics. Besides issues directly involving the Nisei, he wrote about Far Eastern and European politics, business and labor problems, tariff rates and banking policy, and other broad subjects. To the average Nisei reader these editorial topics were beyond their ken of knowledge and interest. Indeed, many of the young Nisei journalists who helped Sakamoto put out the *Courier* recommended a more popular level of writing, but Sakamoto refused to change his writing style and editorial format.

The limited appeal of the *Courier* was mainly to a small group of college-bound and college-educated Nisei. These Nisei tended to be middle-class, urban, and active JACLers. Molly Oyama is a case in point. A product of the Sacramento area, she attended the University of Southern California in the mid-1930s. Sakamoto published many of her speeches and articles, which echoed his own editorials.[87] Oyama urged her fellow Nisei to study as much as possible about Japan. She was active in the JACL and supported its program to educate the Nisei as to their civic responsibilities. And she adhered to the concept of the Nisei as a bridge of understanding and to the idea of the Pacific era with its emerging new Pacific culture, which would combine the best elements of Oriental and Occidental civilization. As a young college-educated Nisei, she found Sakamoto's dualism applicable to her own personal situation.

Before World War II, white racism relegated the Nisei to a subordinate position in virtually every sphere of American life. Politically, the Nisei were identified with Japan as foreigners; economically, they faced severe job discrimination; socially, they were barred from certain neighborhoods, public facilities, and social institutions; and racially, they were considered inferior, unassimilable, and undesirable. To solve the plight of the Nisei, Sakamoto placed the burden of responsibility onto the shoulders of the Nisei themselves. He made the victims of racism rather than its perpetrators the key to his solution. To gain full acceptance into American life, the Nisei had to demonstrate their acceptability by proving that they were loyal Americans.

Neither side of Sakamoto's dualism called for social changes in American society to eliminate white racism to enable the Nisei to rise above their subordinate status to full equality. In this fundamental sense his dualism was a conservative response to racial subordination.

In the final analysis Sakamoto's dualism was untenable because the Nisei, by themselves, had no influence over crucial political developments, either in Japan or in the United States. Regardless of whether they publicly pledged their loyalty or endeavored to act as a bridge of understanding, the Nisei were still subject to political forces and events over which they had no control and which eventually sealed their fate. From 1940 those uncontrollable forces and events overtook Sakamoto and explain why he transformed his original Americanism into superpatriotism, marking the end of his adherence to the concept of the Nisei as a bridge of understanding. One-dimensional superpatriotism, then, became Sakamoto's rationale for "cooperating" with federal intelligence agencies and exhorting the Nisei to loyally obey the American government's decision to imprison them in 1942. From today's perspective it serves no useful purpose to excoriate Sakamoto for the position he adopted. It is better to place him within the context of the racism that prevailed during his time. That racism victimized the Nisei in many different ways, to such an insidious extent, indeed, that some like Sakamoto felt they had no choice but to cooperate in their own victimization.

Notes

1. *Japanese American Courier*, Dec. 12, 1941.

2. To date, the only study of the *Japanese American Courier* has been Mayumi Tsutakawa, "The Political Conservatism of James Sakamoto's *Japanese American Courier*" (MA thesis, School of Communications, University of Washington, 1976). For Sakamoto's organization of a Nisei baseball league see Samuel O. Regalado, "'Play Ball!' Baseball and Seattle's Japanese-American Courier League, 1928–1941," *Pacific Northwest Quarterly* 87, no. 1 (winter 1995/96): 29–37.

3. I have based my summary account of Sakamoto's family and personal background primarily on the James Y. Sakamoto Papers, Suzallo Library, University of Washington (hereafter Sakamoto Papers); Misao Sakamoto, interview, Nov. 20, 1984; Frank Miyamoto, "The Seattle JACL and Its Role in Evacuation," n.d., appendix A, in Japanese American Evacuation and Resettlement Study Collection, Bancroft Library, University of California, Berkeley (hereafter JERS); and Tsutakawa, "Political Conservatism," 20–22. I also consulted Matsuda Motosuke, *Gotaiten Kinen: Bōchō Jinshi Hatten Kagami* (Yamaguchi-shi: Santobō, 1932), 65;

Pacific Citizen, Dec. 9, 16, 23, 1955; Hosokawa, *Nisei*, 195–97; Hosokawa, *JACL*, 26; and Komori Yoshihisa, *Haruka na Nippon* (Tokyo: Mainichi Shimbunsha, 1984), 23–51.

4. For the foregoing see such works as Louis L. Gerson, *The Hyphenate in Recent American Politics and Diplomacy* (Lawrence: University of Kansas Press, 1964), esp. 3–108; Frederick Luebke, *Bonds of Loyalty: German-Americans and World War I* (Dekalb: Northern Illinois University Press, 1974); Robert K. Murray, *Red Scare: A Study in National Hysteria, 1919–1920* (Minneapolis: University of Minnesota Press, 1955); William Preston Jr., *Aliens and Dissenters: Federal Suppression of Radicals, 1903–1933* (Cambridge, MA: Harvard University Press, 1963); Edward G. Hartmann, *The Movement to Americanize the Immigrant* (New York: Columbia University Press, 1948); John Higham, *Strangers in the Land: Patterns of American Nativism, 1860–1925* (New York: Atheneum, 1963), esp. 234–63; and John F. McClymer, "The Federal Government and the Americanization Movement, 1915–1924," *Prologue: Journal of the National Archives* 10, no. 1 (1978): 22–41.

5. Roger Daniels, *The Politics of Prejudice* (Berkeley: University of California Press, 1962).

6. U.S. Congress, House Committee on Immigration and Naturalization, *Japanese Immigration: Hearings Before the Committee on Immigration and Naturalization*, Part 4 (Washington, DC: GPO, 1921), 1198–1201.

7. *Japanese American Courier*, Jan. 1, 1928.

8. *Japanese American Courier*, May 11, 1929.

9. *Japanese American Courier*, July 12, 1930.

10. *Japanese American Courier*, Aug. 31, 1929.

11. *Japanese American Courier*, July 1, 1933.

12. *Japanese American Courier*, March 24, 1928.

13. *Japanese American Courier*, Oct. 10, 1936.

14. *Japanese American Courier*, April 15, 1939.

15. For an in-house history of the JACL see Hosokawa, *JACL*. For a somewhat critical appraisal of the JACL see Daniels, "The Japanese"; and Spickard, "The Nisei Assume Power."

16. *Japanese American Courier*, Sep. 13, 1930. See also ibid., Aug. 30, Sep. 6, 20, and Oct. 4, 1930.

17. *Japanese American Courier*, Sep. 22, 29, 1934.

18. *Japanese American Courier*, July 9, Aug. 20, 1938.

19. *Japanese American Courier*, Aug. 27, 1938, Oct. 28, 1939, Jan. 27, 1940. Martin Dies's anti-Communism was detailed in Martin Dies, *The Trojan Horse in America* (New York: Dodd, Mead, 1940). For a study of the man and his ideas see William Gellermann, *Martin Dies* (New York: John Day, 1944). For a study of the

Dies Committee itself see August R. Ogden, *The Dies Committee: A Study of the Special House Committee for the Investigation of Un-American Activities, 1938–1944* (Washington, DC: Catholic University of America Press, 1945).

20. Walter Galenson, *The CIO Challenge to the AFL; A History of the American Labor Movement, 1935–1941* (Cambridge, MA: Harvard University Press, 1960). See also Melvin Dubofsky and Warren Van Tine, *John L. Lewis: A Biography* (New York: Quadrangle, 1977).

21. *Japanese American Courier*, March 4, 1939.

22. *Japanese American Courier*, Aug. 27, 1938, March 4, Dec. 2, 1939.

23. *Japanese American Courier*, March 4, 1939.

24. *Japanese American Courier*, July 21, 1934.

25. *Japanese American Courier*, Jan. 6, 1940. See also April 1, 29, 1939.

26. Takahashi, "Japanese American Responses."

27. *Japanese American Courier*, Jan. 1, 1931.

28. Ibid.

29. *Japanese American Courier*, Jan. 1, 1935.

30. *Japanese American Courier*, June 3, 1933.

31. *Japanese American Courier*, Jan. 1, 1935.

32. *Japanese American Courier*, Jan. 12, 1935.

33. *Japanese American Courier*, April 7, 1928.

34. *Japanese American Courier*, Dec. 8, 1929. See also Oct. 4, Dec. 15, 1928, and May 4, 1929.

35. *Japanese American Courier*, May 24, 1930.

36. *Japanese American Courier*, May 10, 1930.

37. *Japanese American Courier*, July 1, 1933.

38. *Japanese American Courier*, Sep. 16, 1933.

39. *Japanese American Courier*, Feb. 11, 1928.

40. *Japanese American Courier*, Jan. 9, 1937.

41. *Japanese American Courier*, May 11, 1929.

42. *Japanese American Courier*, Oct. 6, 1934.

43. Sakamoto to George Okuzaki, Feb. 21, 1931, Sakamoto Papers.

44. Sakamoto to Captain Fukuda, Feb. 15, 1932, Sakamoto Papers.

45. *Japanese American Courier*, Oct. 3, 1931.

46. *Japanese American Courier*, Nov. 24, 1931.

47. *Japanese American Courier*, Oct. 17, 1931, Jan. 23, Feb. 6, 20, March 19, 26, April 2, June 4, July 2, 16, Aug. 27, 1932.

48. Holden's column began on June 18, 1932.

49. Uchiyama Kiyoshi to Saitō Makoto, May 26, 1932; Uchiyama to Uchida Yasuya, July 22, 1932; and Zai-Shatoru Nihon Ryōjikan, "Zen-Bei Ryōji Kaigi Gijiroku ni Kansuru Chōsho," June 1936, Japanese Foreign Ministry, Diplomatic

Records Office, Tokyo. In 1942 the FBI investigated Sakamoto. It suspected him of having been a paid agent of the Japanese government and explored the possibility of prosecuting him for failing to register with the United States government as required by law. Under questioning, Sakamoto admitted receiving regular cash payments of twenty-five to fifty dollars from Consul Uchiyama Kiyoshi and Consul Okamoto Issaku. He also admitted receiving an average of about $150 per month from Consul Satō Yuki between 1938 and 1940. Sakamoto denied, however, that the consuls controlled or influenced, in any way, the *Courier*'s editorial policy through these cash payments. The Justice Department never instituted legal action against Sakamoto. See Reports of Special Agent, Nov. 20, Dec. 8, 1942, and Wendell Berge, Assistant Attorney General, to Director, FBI, memorandum, July 1, 1943, all obtained through the Freedom of Information/Privacy Acts.

50. *Japanese American Courier*, Aug. 28, 1937.

51. *Japanese American Courier*, Sep. 18, 1937.

52. *Japanese American Courier*, Oct. 2, 1937.

53. *Japanese American Courier*, Oct. 23, 1937.

54. *Japanese American Courier*, March 18, 1939.

55. *Japanese American Courier*, Oct. 29, 1938.

56. *Japanese American Courier*, Oct. 14, 1939.

57. *Japanese American Courier*, April 6, 1940.

58. *Japanese American Courier*, Sep. 11, 1937.

59. *Japanese American Courier*, Aug. 31, 1940.

60. *Japanese American Courier*, Sep. 7, 1940. See also Sep. 14, 21, 28, Oct. 5, 12, 1940. These articles were published simultaneously by the *Japan Times* in Tokyo under the title *Here and There in New East Asia*. See *Japan Times*, Sep. 1, 9, 16, 23, 29, Oct. 7, 14, 1940.

61. *Japanese American Courier*, Jan. 1, 1941.

62. *Japanese American Courier*, June 1, 15, 1940.

63. Louis Adamic, "This Crisis Is an Opportunity," *Common Ground* 1 (1940): 62–73. See also Louis Adamic, "Thirty Million New Americans," *Harper's Magazine*, Nov. 1934, 684–94; Louis Adamic, *My America* (New York: Harper and Brothers, 1938), esp. the chapter entitled "Ellis Island and Plymouth Rock," 187–259; Louis Adamic, *A Nation of Nations* (New York: Harper, 1945); and Louis Adamic, "On Tolerance," in Bradford Smith, *Americans from Japan* (Philadelphia, PA: Lippincott, 1948), vii–xii. For different interpretations of Adamic's ideas on ethnicity see Henry A. Christian, "Louis Adamic and the American Dream," *Journal of General Education* 27 (1975): 113–23; Rudolph Vecoli, "Louis Adamic and the Contemporary Search for Roots," *Ethnic Studies* (Monash University, Australia) 2 (1978): 29–35; Richard Weiss, "Ethnicity and Reform: Minorities and the Ambience of the Depression Years," *Journal of American History* 66 (1979):

566–85; Deborah Ann Overmyer, "Common Ground and America's Minorities, 1940–1949: A Study in the Changing Climate of Opinion" (PhD diss., University of Cincinnati, 1984), 53–83; and Robert F. Harney, "E Pluribus Unum: Louis Adamic and the Meaning of Ethnic History," *Journal of Ethnic Studies* 14, no. 1 (1986): 29–46. Sakamoto believed that Adamic's ideas coincided with his belief.

64. Adamic, "A Young American with a Japanese Face." This portrait was based on the life of Charles Kikuchi, a real but unusual Nisei because he was raised in an orphanage. See also Modell, *The Kikuchi Diary*, 1–39.

65. *Japanese American Courier*, March 16, April 6, 13, 20, 27, May 4, 1940. The lecture was entitled "Ellis Island and Plymouth Rock," which Adamic delivered before many European immigrants and their American-born descendants in 1938 and 1939.

66. *Japanese American Courier*, Oct. 26, Nov. 2, 9, 16, 23, 30, 1940.

67. *Japanese American Courier*, Aug. 31, 1940.

68. *Japanese American Courier*, Sep. 7, 1940.

69. Toyo Suyemoto to Sakamoto, Oct. 10, 1940, Sakamoto Papers.

70. Sakamoto to Suyemoto, Oct. 14, 1940, Sakamoto Papers.

71. *Japanese American Courier*, Jan. 1, 1941.

72. *Japanese American Courier*, June 28, 1941.

73. *Japanese American Courier*, Sep. 5, 1941.

74. Togo Tanaka, "History of J.A.C.L.," n.d., JERS.

75. Mike Masaoka, "Final Report," April 22, 1944, 43–44, JERS.

76. Tanaka, "History of J.A.C.L."

77. Saburo Kido to Sakamoto, April 25, 1941, Sakamoto Papers.

78. Ken Matsumoto to Sakamoto, June 13, 1941, Sakamoto Papers. In August 1941 former national president Walter T. Tsukamoto wrote to Sakamoto regarding his own contact with FBI agents: "I have had an interesting two hour conversation with the agents of the FBI today and during the course of our conversation, it was brought out that the nisei by their past actions have given the impression to the bureau that they are personally withholding vital information and that they are in other ways wilfully uncooperative. I assured them that such was not the case, that the League had hoped the FBI would contact its leaders in an effort to work out some sort of program which would help the bureau and also convince them of the loyalty and sincerity of the nisei" (Walter T. Tsukamoto to Sakamoto, Aug. 27, 1941, Sakamoto Papers).

79. *Japanese American Courier*, June 1, 1940.

80. *Japanese American Courier*, June 21, 1941. The spy was Lieutenant Commander Tachibana Itaru, who was arrested in Los Angeles on June 7, 1941. For more on Tachibana see Chapter 9 of this volume.

81. Emergency Defense Council, Minutes of Dec. 12, 1941, Friday, Meeting,

Sakamoto Papers. Clarence Arai was appointed the chairman of this special committee. The names of committee members were never disclosed.

82. Sakamoto to B. Gordon, Feb. 3, 1942, Sakamoto Papers.

83. U.S. Congress, House, Select Committee Investigating National Defense Migration, *National Defense Migration*, Part 30, *Portland and Seattle Hearings*, Feb. 26 and 28, March 2, 1942 (Washington, DC: GPO, 1942), 11475.

84. *Japanese American Courier*, Jan. 9, 1942.

85. *Japanese American Courier*, March 6, 1942.

86. *Japanese American Courier*, April 24, 1942. Sakamoto dubbed the so-called Puyallup Assembly Center "Camp Harmony." For his subsequent cooperative role in the mass internment of Japanese Americans see Miyamoto, "The Seattle JACL," JERS.

87. *Japanese American Courier*, Sep. 9, 1933, Jan. 13, 20, March 17, 31, April 7, Oct. 20, 1934.

PART TWO

SIX

"Unity Within Diversity"

Louis Adamic and Japanese Americans

Introduction

Race and ethnicity, depending on how they are defined, can be mutually exclusive or overlapping concepts. During the 1930s and 1940s, Louis Adamic, based on his own conception of ethnicity, with no clear concept of racism, projected his own vision of a pluralistic society, envisioning the day when ethnic and racial diversity would be accepted as a fact of everyday American life. To express his ideal of cultural pluralism, he coined the phrase "unity within diversity." As a European immigrant, Adamic was concerned with the well-being of the new European immigrants of his day and with the sociopsychological adjustment problems of their American-born descendants. Because of a Eurocentric orientation, neither Asian immigrants nor their American-born descendants figured in his initial thinking, even though Japanese, Korean, East Indian, and Filipino immigration to the United States occurred concurrently with the new immigration from Europe. The American-born generation of the new European immigrants and that of Japanese immigrants appeared simultaneously, with the first-born of each generation coming of age in the 1930s. As members of an ethnic and racial minority, the *Nisei*, or Japanese American second generation, faced the problem of defining their own ethnicity in the face of white racism. In 1940 Adamic incorporated the Nisei into his vision of a pluralistic society with a flawed understanding of the racial and ethnic problems of Japanese Americans.

Personal Background

Born in 1898 in Slovenia, Adamic landed in America in 1913. He was the eldest son in a fairly well-off peasant family. Since his childhood days in his native village of Blato, Adamic had acquired a knowledge of America. He avidly read anything about America he could lay his hands on, including the *Narodni Glas*, a New York City newspaper devoted to Slovenian immigrant life in the United States. He also heard directly about the country from fellow villagers who had immigrated to America but had returned to Blato. Everything he learned fired his imagination and fueled his desire to see and experience the United States for himself. In 1913 he was expelled from a gymnasium he was attending in the city of Lublyana for participating in illegal political activities. His expulsion became the reason for his decision to emigrate from Slovenia and embark on a new life in the United States at the age of fifteen.

Adamic established himself as a writer in the 1920s. During his initial years in the United States, he worked at various jobs. He began as an assistant in the mail and editorial room of the *Narodni Glas*; later he worked as a manual laborer briefly. In 1916 he enlisted in the United States Army and served in Panama, Louisiana, and Hawaii. While stationed in Louisiana, he became a naturalized American citizen in 1918. After World War I he completed his term of enlistment at Fort MacArthur, located in San Pedro, California. Iconoclastic in nature, Adamic's first writings appeared in the mid-1920s, most prominently in several Haldeman-Julius publications; and a series of articles in the *American Mercury*, published in the late 1920s, catapulted him to national fame. In 1931 he published the first of his many books, *Dynamite*, which dealt with the violent clashes between labor and capital during the industrialization of the United States from the nineteenth century down through the 1920s. In 1932 Adamic published *Laughing in the Jungle*, in part an autobiography and in part an account of his fellow "Bohunk" immigrants' life in the United States. And in 1933 he published *The Native's Return*, an autobiographical account of his triumphant return to his native land as a recognized American writer.[1]

One of Adamic's enduring concerns was the question of ethnicity for the American-born descendants of the new European immigrants. In 1934 Adamic estimated that there were thirty million people who fell into this category. Of predominantly eastern and southern European ancestry, he labeled these people the "New Americans" to distinguish them from old-stock, Anglo-Saxon Americans. Adamic observed that these new Americans suffered from crippling "feelings of inferiority" in relation to old-stock, Anglo-Saxon Americans. The immigrant parents of the new Americans also suffered from feelings of inferiority, but their awareness of where they had come from and of who they were mitigated the effects of such feelings. That was not so with the new Americans, however, for they had "no consciousness or instinctive feeling of any racial or cultural background."[2] Rootless, they were like Martians who had been dropped off on Earth with no knowledge at all of Mars.

The new Americans were caught between two worlds. They faced the choice of living isolated lives in separate ethnic enclaves or of trying to carve out a place for themselves in the larger society. In opting for the second choice, many new Americans felt compelled to repudiate their immigrant parents and deny their own ethnicity in order to be accepted by old-stock Americans. Because of their sense of inferiority, such new Americans became, in Adamic's words, "chauvinistically patriotic," yet "their chauvinism" had "no basis in any vital feeling."[3] Or they engaged in various types of antisocial behavior. Both were forms of psychological compensation. From Adamic's point of view the "new Americans of this type . . . were . . . hollow, absurd, objectionable persons" who, having been cut off from their own cultural past, had no real understanding of themselves.[4] Adamic believed that all new Americans should be encouraged to "become real men and women on the pattern of their own natural cultures" rather than pressured into transforming themselves into hollow replicas of old-stock, Anglo-Saxon Americans.[5]

The new European immigration had changed the composition of the American population, which called for a new definition of American culture. Old-stock, Anglo-Saxon Americans were no longer the dominant majority. Adamic rejected the old notion of a melting pot that required all new immigrant groups to discard their old-world traits and to recast themselves in the mold of old-stock, Anglo-Saxon Americans. He believed that every immigrant group had something valuable to contribute to American society. "Americanism" was not the monopoly of old-stock Americans but "an expanding concept" that embraced all Americans, old and new, who still were in the process of "becoming" by contributing toward the creation of "a universal or pan-human culture." "Anti-alienism" and "racism" had bred intolerance and hatred among Americans, putting new immigrants and racial minorities "on the defensive" and crippling their capacity to function as full human beings. Americanism involved the "acceptance" of cultural and racial differences, and the future of America, to Adamic, lay in a "unity within diversity."[6] In long-run terms Adamic foresaw the eventual emergence of a new melting pot in which all of the diverse cultural and racial elements in American society would fuse together to form his ideal of "a universal or pan-human culture." This would involve "the gradual, organic merging of all . . . groups into a nation that culturally and spiritually will be a fusion of all the races and nations now in the United States."[7]

Adamic advocated the establishment of an organization that would educate the new Americans and old-stock Americans about each other. Such an organization would strive "to give . . . millions of New Americans a knowledge of, and pride in, their own heritage," which "would operate to counteract their feelings of inferiority." At the same time, it would strive "to create a sympathetic understanding toward them on the part of older Americans, so that the latter's anti-'foreign' prejudice . . . would tend to lessen and ultimately be reduced to a minimum."[8] In 1938 Adamic published *My America*, a sequel to *Laughing in the Jungle*, in which he outlined his ideas in a chapter entitled "Ellis Island and Plymouth Rock," the former symbolizing the new European immigrants and their descendants and the latter old-stock Americans. Subsequently, Adamic set out to write a series of books, under the general title of A Nation of Nations, through which he planned to narrate the full story of those who had passed through Ellis Island.

To amass firsthand information, Adamic distributed a broadside questionnaire, beginning in 1939, to new European immigrants as well as old-stock Americans. The broadside declared that a new conception of America was in order:

> What is now needed is a new consciousness of America, of ourselves as a people made up of over fifty races and nationalities. What is needed is a new Americanization idea which will recognize and accept, not merely tolerate, the various national and racial groupings as such; which will see the desirability of diversity in our population; which will take a firm stand against alien-baiting and insist that the immigrant citizens and their American-born children belong here as much as the old-stock Americans because this is their America as much as anybody's; which will help all citizens to identify themselves with the U.S.; and which will, thus, work

toward national unity—against fear in our national life—toward gradual assimilation or racial-cultural fusion that will operate naturally, not only one way, but in many directions. . . . Anglo-Saxons will have to become partly assimilated or fused into the various new immigrant groups just as the latter will have to become partly assimilated into the Anglo-Saxon group and into one another.[9]

The broadside broached many questions. Of the new European immigrants, it asked about their native land, their history in the United States, their achievements and outstanding leaders, and their problems of adjustment. It also asked about their "cultural gifts and talents" and their evaluation of this country and old-stock Americans. In terms of the "New Americans," the broadside asked about their "feelings of inferiority in relation to old-stock Americans," how these feelings "manifested themselves," and how some had managed to "overcome" them. Of old-stock Americans, the broadside asked about their opinion of and experience with the new immigrants. Adamic mailed copies of the broadside to thousands of immigrants and their American-born descendants, as well as to many organizations and institutions dealing with them. The replies to the broadside were to serve as source material for his projected Nation of Nations series.

Adamic recognized that Afro-Americans could not be placed into the same category as European immigrants and their American-born descendants. "The Negroes are the only major element in the American population," he wrote, "whose ancestors did not come to the New World of their own free will as emigrants getting away from unsatisfactory conditions in the Old World." They had been "brought over forcibly to be sold into permanent servitude," and white racism had "made the Negroes a more sharply defined group than any other in the United States."[10] Nevertheless, Adamic insisted that the " 'Negro Problem' is not something apart from the country's general cultural-social-economic set up." Its solution depended upon "whether or not the American people as a whole can rid themselves of their fears, especially racial fears" and "on the country's ability to discard the idea that it is exclusively White, Protestant and Anglo-Saxon."[11] Adamic recognized that "many immigrant Americans are anti-Negro," but he explained their prejudice as a "psychological compensation for their own inferior status under the White-Protestant-Anglo-Saxon concept."[12] Thus he implied that the elimination of the WASP concept would dispel the racial prejudice toward Afro-Americans held by many new European immigrants and their American-born descendants.

Initially, Adamic's treatment of ethnicity did not include Asian immigrants or their American-born descendants. Significantly, his broadside was entitled "Plymouth Rock and Ellis Island," a title that conspicuously omitted Angel Island. Adamic had had some exposure to Asian immigrants. During his term of military service he was stationed for a while in Hawaii, where many Asian immigrants resided. During the 1920s he lived in San Pedro, California, where a thriving Japanese immigrant fishing community existed on Terminal Island just opposite the city. Notwithstanding these contacts, Adamic failed to incorporate Asian immigrants and their American-born children into his initial concern with the problem of the ethnicity of European immigrants and their American-born descendants.

On the eve of Pearl Harbor the second-generation Japanese American made up two-thirds of the Japanese population on the continental United States. Numbering 79,642 out of the 1940 Japanese population of 126,947, the Nisei were very young. The majority were in their early teens or younger; only a few Nisei were adults. In contrast, the *Issei* generation was much older. In 1942 the median age of the Nisei was seventeen, while that of male Issei was fifty-five and female Issei forty-seven.[13] As with other second-generation groups, the Nisei were products of two worlds. On the one hand, they were raised in the Japanese immigrant family and community and hence exposed to Japanese cultural values. On the other hand, they were educated in American public schools, which had a powerful Americanizing influence on them. Consequently, many Nisei experienced cultural conflicts, and some were in direct conflict with the Issei generation. A minority of Nisei were so-called *Kibei*, Nisei who had been educated partially or entirely in Japan.

During the late 1930s the outlook for the Nisei was very bleak. Like the Issei, the Nisei were subject to numerous forms of social discrimination, including residential segregation. Economically, due to severe job discrimination, the Nisei had virtually no hope of obtaining employment outside of the Japanese immigrant community. Even college graduates faced the dismal prospect of having to work as fruit and vegetable stand peddlers. Politically, the Nisei were considered aliens by most Americans, even though they were American citizens. Indeed, many people identified the Nisei with Japan, some even holding the Nisei accountable for Japan's military conduct in

China. Racially, the Nisei were considered undesirable and unassimilable. In sum, second-generation Japanese Americans were consigned to a racially subordinate position in American society.

The Nisei's principal organization was the Japanese American Citizens League (JACL), a civic body founded in 1930.[14] The objective of the league was to educate the Nisei generation about American politics on a nonpartisan basis. From its inception, the JACL adopted Americanism as its guiding principle. Its leadership was composed of a handful of older Nisei who were urban, college-educated, self-employed professionals and conservative Republicans. In order to promote the acceptance of the Nisei by the larger society, this leadership projected the Nisei as loyal Americans who were undivided in their allegiance to the United States. Written in 1940, the JACL Creed fully expressed this patriotic posture of the JACL:

I am proud that I am an American citizen of Japanese ancestry, for my very background makes me appreciate more fully the wonderful advantages of this nation. I believe in her institutions, ideals, and traditions; I glory in her heritage; I boast of her history; I trust in her future. She has granted me liberties and opportunities such as no individual enjoys in this world today. She has given me an education befitting kings. She has permitted me to build a home, to earn a livelihood, to worship, think, speak, and act as I please—as a free man equal to every other man.

Although some individuals may discriminate against me, I shall never become bitter or lose faith, for I know that such persons are not representative of the majority of the American people. True, I shall do all in my power to discourage such practices, but I shall do it in the American way: above-board, in the open, through courts of law, by education, by proving myself to be worthy of equal treatment and consideration. I am firm in my belief that American sportsmanship and attitude of fair play will judge citizenship and patriotism on the basis of action and achievement, and not on the basis of physical characteristics.

Because I believe in America, and I trust she believes in me, and because I have received innumerable benefits from her, I pledge myself to do honor to her at all times and in all places; to support her constitution; to obey her laws; to respect her flag; to defend her against all enemies, foreign or domestic; to actively assume my duties and obligations as a citizen, cheerfully and without any reservations whatsoever, in the hope that I may become a better American in a greater America.[15]

In late 1939 Adamic contacted some Japanese Americans because he decided to include Japanese Americans in his projected Nation of Nations series. More than any other Nisei, Mary Oyama played the most pivotal role in introducing Adamic to many Nisei. An aspiring writer, she admired Adamic greatly. She had met him and his wife, Stella, around 1938 through mutual friends in Los Angeles. Their mutual friends included Carey McWilliams, Ross Wills, and John Fante. On learning that Adamic was interested in devoting a chapter to Japanese Americans in his Nation of Nations series, she enthusiastically supported his project.[16] She supplied him with the names and addresses of prominent Nisei, among them James Y. Sakamoto, publisher of the *Japanese American Courier*, and Larry Tajiri, English editor of the *Japanese American News*. Obtaining copies of Adamic's broadside questionnaire, she distributed them to many Nisei, urging them to mail their answers to Adamic directly. And she wrote articles about his project in the Japanese immigrant press, characterizing Adamic as "one of America's foremost writers" who "will write of, for, and about the nisei."[17] "All Nisei are invited by the author," she said, "to write their . . . personal case history . . . , or to answer the thought-provoking . . . broadside, or to write freely on any particular phase of this subject which most interests the Nisei themselves."[18]

Adamic solicited the help of Shuji Fujii, editor of the *Dōhō*, a Japanese American leftist weekly published in Los Angeles. He had learned of this publication through his friend Carey McWilliams. "In my forthcoming book, 'A Nation of Nations,'" Adamic wrote to Fujii, "I plan to have one or more chapters on the Japanese. I should like your putting me in touch with other people who are qualified to tell me something of the Japanese story in California."[19] Fujii thought "highly of Adamic," not only because he "is the famous author of such outstanding works as 'The Native's Return,' 'Dynamite,' and 'My America'" but because "he frankly paints the picture of America as a chaotic maelstrom of mu[l]tifarious humanity, yet holds out a hope for those who come here from other lands, a vision of a homogeneous America, molded out of the various divergent racial and cultural elements."[20] Consequently, Fujii pledged to cooperate. "You can count on me as one of your most enthusiastic supporters," he said; I "shall be more than glad to co-operate with you [in] any way possible."[21]

As the publisher and editor of the *Japanese American Courier*, James Y. Sakamoto gave Adamic wide publicity. Sakamoto described the Nation of Nations series as "one of the most important, interesting and far-reaching surveys," and he reprinted portions of Adamic's broadside questionnaire in his paper. He concurred with Adamic's assessment of the importance of the non-Anglo-Saxon element in the American population and believed that this element "affords an opportunity to create on this continent an extraordinarily rich culture and civilization."[22] "Personally," he wrote to Adamic, "I have been stating from some years back that no one racial group has a corner on the spirit of Americanism and all of us must be contributing elements to the national life stream of Full-Blooded Americanism." "I believe that this idea somewhat coincides with yours," he added, "in that each group can retain the best in their culture and which in turn can become the contribution to a new and national pattern of American culture."[23] Sakamoto even submitted his own life history to Adamic.

Other Nisei either wrote to Adamic directly or met him in person. A former regent of the University of California, Yori Wada was a senior at the University of California when he met Adamic in October 1939 at the University YMCA. Wada had read his essay "Thirty Million New Americans" and *My America* and believed that, to Adamic, "there is no Young Negro, no Young Japanese, no Young Chinese, no Young Germans, no Young Armenians—they are all Young Americans." Echoing Adamic's view, he insisted that "there must be acceptance of all groups" separate and apart from "the political aspects of the mother countries." Wada interpreted this to mean that "Americans must accept the others who will come with the culture and the characteristics of their forefathers." Adamic impressed Wada as "dynamic, thoughtful, [and] capable of deep convictions," an impression that led him to conclude, "I'm glad I met Louis Adamic."[24]

Other Nisei, like Franklin Chino of Chicago, Sam Hohri of Los Angeles, Kimi Gengo of New York City, Hideo Hashimoto of Philadelphia, and others corresponded with Adamic and offered their opinions regarding the condition of Japanese immigrants and their American-born descendants.[25] In the fall of 1940 Adamic met with Nisei in Seattle, Portland, San Francisco, and Los Angeles, many of whom were leaders of the JACL. In all of his meetings he had an opportunity to exchange opinions with those Nisei who gathered to listen to him.[26] In San Francisco he told JACL leaders that "each foreign group should hang on to their own culture and add it to the sum total of the new American culture." He reported what to him was a case of a misguided Nisei who "came to see me yesterday and seemed to be proud of the fact that he did not know much Japanese." Adamic told his audience, "I bawled him out."[27]

"A Young American with a Japanese Face"

Ultimately, Adamic picked Charles Kikuchi as a model for his portrait of a Japanese American youth that he published under the title "A Young American with a Japanese Face" in *From Many Lands* in 1940. Kikuchi met Adamic around October 1939. Alfred G. Fisk, a professor at San Francisco State College, who had Kikuchi as a student in one of his philosophy classes, introduced him to Adamic. Fisk was aware of Adamic's interest in the second generation and recommended Kikuchi as "a very interesting case of a second-generation Japanese-American."[28] Kikuchi had heard of Adamic through another San Francisco State College professor who had shown him Adamic's broadside questionnaire. With his curiosity aroused, Adamic contacted Kikuchi and interviewed him. Intrigued by his account of his life, Adamic then asked the young man to put his life history into writing. Kikuchi submitted several versions of a life history he had written for a sociology class in the spring of 1939.[29]

Kikuchi was an unusual Nisei because he had been raised in an orphanage. For the most part Adamic remained faithful to the factual details of Kikuchi's early life but rewrote his life history into his own style, embellishing it in places and adding his own interpretation and plea for understanding. Told in the first-person narrative form, the portrait that emerged was of a Nisei who fits the classic mold of a marginal man. Without any roots in his own cultural past, this Nisei has no positive self-identity. He is so riddled with conflicts that he is incapable of identifying with any group or institution. He is alienated from his own family, his Nisei peers, the Japanese community, and white society.

As the eldest son in a poor Japanese immigrant family, he is sadistically beaten by his father during his childhood. At the age of eight he is placed into an orphanage, where, despite initial difficulties, he manages to survive. Eventually he attends a local high school near the orphanage. Active in sports and attaining good scholastic marks, he enjoys a short period of happiness during which, he recalls, "I was never anything but an American." Yet moments of doubt lingered, as "when my Japanese body was conspicuous among the white bodies," intimating that he was not altogether sure of his identity. After graduation he leaves the haven of the orphanage, and he first realizes the consequences of having "a Japanese face." As his initial encounter with racial discrimination, in San Francisco he is denied a haircut, has trou-

ble finding a room, and is unable to obtain a job. At the same time, he realizes, ironically, how American he is. Visiting the Japanese settlement of San
Francisco, he feels "a foreigner," for he has forgotten what little Japanese he
had known and is ignorant of Japanese customs. He also realizes that he is a
stranger to his own family. When he visits his family, he discovers that he
cannot communicate with his parents and that he does not know his own
siblings. He even dislikes his mother's Japanese cooking; it "nearly gagged"
him.

With no sense of belonging, he decides to remain independent of his family. In order to support himself, he becomes a houseboy in a white household
in San Francisco but hates the job because it is demeaning to him. He also
decides to enroll in college and begins attending San Francisco State College,
where he is a loner who is tormented by fear, distrust, and self-hatred.
Feeling estranged from his fellow students, he shuns his Japanese, Chinese,
and white classmates. Eventually, Adamic has this alienated Nisei come to
the realization that "the only reason I felt ashamed . . . , and therefore, afraid
and resentful, was that I had been trying to conceal what I could not conceal," that is, "my Japanese face." Once he accepts this fact, he comes out of
his shell. To learn about his own background, he starts to study about Japan
and Japanese Americans. He educates his white boss about what it means to
be an American-born Japanese. He renews ties with his family and becomes
attached to his siblings. He becomes active in student affairs and mixes with
Japanese and Chinese students. He explores the inside of the Japanese community and learns that the problems of many Nisei parallel his own. He also
joins the International Club on campus, composed of students from diverse
backgrounds. In all of these activities he tries to establish links that might
give him a meaningful self-identity.

But, alas, that identity eludes him. Once he graduates from college, he
runs squarely into the most unsettling of problems: he cannot find a job. No
matter where he applies, he is turned down. Out of desperation he tries to
enlist in the armed forces but is denied admission because he is a "Jap," symbolizing his rejection by American society on racial grounds. In the end
Adamic describes this youth's distraught state of mind in terms of the dis-
cordant sounds made by San Francisco cable cars. As the portrait closes,
Adamic has the Nisei riding a cable car, which "groaned and jangled,"
metaphorically alluding to the unresolved turmoil raging within him.

Adamic had an abiding faith in education. Acceptance of diversity was to be promoted by educating Americans about each other. Adamic wanted his readers to understand that the Nisei shared common problems with many new Americans. The Nisei, too, were suspended between two worlds, between that of their immigrant parents and the larger society. They, too, dreamed of participating fully in a democratic society but were rebuffed by ignorant elements. They, too, were crippled by feelings of inferiority and frustrated and insecure about the future, living an ambiguous existence without much hope of ever achieving a sense of wholeness. Adamic also wanted his readers to understand that the Nisei's problems were compounded by their yellow faces and white racism, but he never analyzed how racism qualitatively set apart the problems of the Nisei from those of white ethnic groups.

The overall Nisei reception to Adamic's portrait of a Nisei was positive. Everyone noted that it was not of a "typical" Nisei but that it still touched on the major adjustment problems of the Nisei. A reviewer in the *Shin Sekai* of San Francisco observed that the portrait was "a little exaggerated in places." Nevertheless, "Mr. Adamic has rendered the Nisei a great service because he has enabled the American public to have some idea of what obstacles confront" the Nisei. "Many of the readers may not have known that the Nisei are American citizens. It presents a picture which is bound to arouse a sympathetic attitude."[30] Another reviewer in the *Kashū Mainichi* wrote that Adamic was "a voice in the wilderness" who had "written, and written well," this "story of a nisei" who was not "typical."[31] Yori Wada believed that Adamic had captured the conflicts of the Nisei "with vividness, with force, [and] with earnestness."[32] Mary Oyama wrote that "the story sustains interest at a high pitch and key from the very beginning to the end because of it's [*sic*] intensely personal nature and subjective viewpoint." She believed that "you get the 'feel' and the correct presentation of the Japanese-American or nisei psychology." Oyama mistakenly attributed this to the fact that Adamic himself was a Nisei.[33]

Sakamoto had a Maryknoll Church priest of Seattle, L. H. Tibesar, review *From Many Lands*. In Father Tibesar's opinion, "Mr. Adamic has placed us all in his debt by giving us this book. It is at once thoughtful and thought-provoking. It may mirror any or all of us." Tibesar added that "many . . . Nisei will try to read the story of their lives and imagined struggles" into the chapter on a Japanese American youth.[34] Sam Hohri was a typical Nisei. He was born in Japan but raised as a Nisei in California. After reading *From*

Many Lands, he reached the conclusion that "the problems of the nisei are not unique." Since other new Americans shared those problems, Hohri believed that the solution to everyone's problems "lies in appreciating the contributions" of each new American and "accepting each other as fellow Americans."[35]

Adamic offered no panacea for the plight of the Nisei. He only reiterated the need for reassessing the meaning of Americanism by having his alienated Nisei reflect:

> Isn't Americanism, perhaps, an attitude of one's mind and feelings that issues out of an inner harmony which is respected by one's environment and should endure anywhere? I haven't that harmony. Nor has most of the second generation of Oriental descent. We are all orphans psychologically, confused; cluttered up with our past, with the past of our immigrant parents; afflicted with our faces—all of which, of course, involves also America, which, cluttered up with her own past, thinks she is still the America of a hundred or fifty years ago, when the great majority of people here were Anglo-Saxon Americans.[36]

Here, too, Adamic implied that the elimination of the WASP concept would solve the ethnic and racial problems of the Nisei, just as it would solve the problems of European ethnic groups and Afro-Americans.

Adamic never specified what he considered valuable in Japanese culture that the Nisei should retain and what they could contribute to the leavening of American culture. Indeed, there was nothing redeeming about the Japanese immigrant family and community, at least as Adamic characterized them in his portrait of an alienated Japanese American youth. The family and community exerted negative influences on the Nisei because they socialized the Nisei to Japanese values, which impeded their Americanization. In fact, the father in his portrait is a sadistic man who cruelly beats his son in fits of drunken anger. At best, Adamic alluded to a Japanese sense of visual esthetics as a possible contribution that Nisei might make to American culture.

American Cultural Hegemony

Adamic's negative characterization of the Japanese immigrant family and community was in line with academic studies of Japanese Americans. Robert

E. Park of the University of Chicago conducted the first sociological survey of the Japanese immigrants and their American-born children. Known as the Survey of Race Relations, this survey commenced in January 1924 with the purpose of improving race relations as the anti-Japanese agitation was peaking on the Pacific Coast. The survey explored the racial conflict on the Pacific Coast within the framework of Park's so-called race-relations cycle. In Park's broad overview two separate and distinct civilizations, the Orient and the Occident, had come into contact on the Pacific Coast as a result of immigration from Asia. Consequently, the white and yellow races confronted each other directly in a manner characterized initially by competition and conflict, followed by accommodation, and eventually leading to the assimilation of Asians in an irreversible process. Within this cyclical scheme, Park juxtaposed a static, traditional East with a progressive, dynamic West presumed to be superior. For the Nisei the overriding problem was their racial features, which they could not obliterate. Whites always identified them as Asian rather than American because of race. Even though the Nisei had become "culturally an Occidental," they remained "racially an Oriental." Neither a child wholly of the East nor of the West, the Nisei were destined to live out a marginal existence straddling two worlds, culturally as well as psychologically. Their marginality was the burden of what Park called the Nisei's "racial mask."[37]

William C. Smith, one of Park's assistants, authored the survey's preliminary report on the "second-generation Oriental" in 1927, which he expanded into a book in 1937.[38] Smith traced the cultural conflicts of the Nisei to the Japanese immigrant family, in which Japanese and American cultural values collided. The immigrant family exercised "autocratic control" over its members and was the repository of "traditional" Japanese values relating to subordinate roles, preference for males, separation of sexes, and arranged marriages. These values clashed with American values of individualism, spontaneity, sex equality, and romantic love. The assimilation of the Nisei was to be measured by the degree to which they discarded Japanese family values in favor of American ones. Here Smith, like Park, contrasted a static East with a dynamic West, with no doubt as to which was superior. Smith dwelt at great length on the marginal status of the Nisei. In his words, the Nisei "are oriental in appearance, but not in reality. . . . They belong to both groups and yet to neither; they are neither fully oriental nor yet fully occidental." This marginality of the Nisei was magnified by white racism because it severely limited employment opportunities.

During the 1930s Emory S. Bogardus and Forrest E. La Violette studied the Nisei under the influence of Robert E. Park. Both men began with four crucial assumptions: that Japanese and American values were incompatible; that the latter were superior to the former; that cultural conflicts resulted from this incompatibility; and that the Nisei's assimilation was to be gauged by the extent to which they adopted American values. Bogardus expanded Park's original race-relations cycle into seven stages and formulated his own "second-generation race-relations cycle" with which he studied the Nisei.[39] La Violette's central concern was the question of how far the Nisei had become Americanized. He set out to ascertain the extent by looking at their socialization in the Japanese immigrant family and community. The Japanese immigrant family socialized the Nisei to accept and defer to parental authority, to assume subordinate roles, and to uphold the family integrity within the Japanese community. Japanese community institutions socialized the Nisei to an elaborate "deferential authority" and "traditional obligations" that governed the affairs of the Japanese immigrant world outside of the family. The socialization in the family and community constituted the essential Japanese "cultural heritage" of the Nisei, a heritage that clashed with American individualism, spontaneity, creativity, sex equality, and romantic love. As a result, the Nisei experienced acute cultural and psychological conflicts. Social and economic discrimination against the Nisei exacerbated their marginality and retarded their Americanization.[40]

Outside of academic circles, liberals like Carey McWilliams shared the same negative assessment of the Japanese immigrant family and community. A close friend of Adamic, in 1944 McWilliams published *Prejudice; Japanese-Americans: Symbol of Racial Intolerance*, which discussed the wartime internment of Japanese Americans. McWilliams saw the mass internment of Japanese Americans as an opportunity to draw public attention to the entire race issue in the United States. His book was a policy-oriented study that advocated federal management of race relations. McWilliams was looking ahead to the postwar period. He believed that "the kind of world that emerges from this war will have a great deal to do with the future of racial minorities in the United States." "A sound postwar foreign policy" presupposed "a comprehensive national policy on racial minorities," including Japanese Americans.[41]

McWilliams argued that mass internment had had an unexpected "salutary" effect on most Nisei, in spite of the undemocratic manner in which it had been carried out. In his view the Japanese immigrant family and community, in addition to racial discrimination, had retarded the prewar assimilation of the Nisei. When the attack on Pearl Harbor occurred, the Nisei were just starting to reach out beyond the insular confines of their family and community. "Without realizing why," in McWilliams's words, "the nisei were seeking a larger world; they were suffocating in Little Tokyo," which "was essentially a petty world."[42] He agreed with La Violette's evaluation that the Japanese family was the seat of "reactionary" Japanese values and that the community pressured the Nisei to conform to Japanese patterns of behavior. Mass internment had "an unintended democratic potential" because it had taken the Nisei out of "Little Tokyo" and freed them from the conservative hold of the Japanese family and community.

Common Council for American Unity

The Common Council for American Unity (CCAU) was the organization through which Adamic sought to educate the new Americans and old-stock Americans about each other. Its predecessor was the Foreign Language Information Service (FLIS), organized in 1918 as a part of the Committee of Public Information, which President Woodrow Wilson had founded in 1917 to explain America's entry into World War I. After World War I the FLIS became an independent agency, promoting the welfare of the foreign-born population in the United States.[43] With redefined goals, the FLIS was reorganized as the CCAU in November 1939. Consonant with Adamic's concept of Americanism, the CCAU had four fundamental goals:

> To help create among the American people the unity and mutual understanding resulting from a common citizenship, a common belief in democracy and the ideals of liberty, the placing of the common good before the interests of any group, and the acceptance, in fact as well as in law, of all citizens, whatever their national or racial origins, as equal partners in American society.
> To further an appreciation of what each group has contributed to America, to uphold the freedom to be different, and to encourage the growth of an American culture which will be truly representative of all the elements that make up the American people.

To overcome intolerance and discrimination because of foreign birth or descent, race or nationality.

To help the foreign-born and their children solve their special problems of adjustment, know and value their particular cultural heritage, and share fully and constructively in American life.[44]

With Adamic as its initial editor, the CCAU published *Common Ground*, a quarterly journal, from September 1940.

During the life of *Common Ground*, from 1940 to 1949, many articles by and on Japanese Americans appeared in the journal, initially under the editorship of Adamic and later under his successor, Margaret Anderson. Collectively these articles undoubtedly contributed toward a wider public awareness of the Nisei and the wartime internment of Japanese Americans. The articles shared several themes. First, they always projected the Nisei as assimilated Americans who were free of Japanese cultural traits. In 1941 *Common Ground* editorialized that "the Nisei are and want to be Americans— a fact as yet inadequately appreciated by Americans of other races and strains."[45] In the winter of 1941 it published a short story entitled "Lil' Yokohama" by Toshio Mori, a young Nisei writer. His story depicted a small rural Japanese community coming together to play baseball on a weekend. Except for the usage of Japanese names, the story could have been about any rural American community. "Lil' Yokohama" essentially emphasized that Japanese Americans were no different from other Americans.[46]

After Pearl Harbor *Common Ground* featured articles upholding the Americanism of the Nisei. It reprinted the JACL Creed in full and published essays that exuded optimism. In the interval between Pearl Harbor and internment Mary Oyama wrote, "After this stressful period of inevitably intensified prejudice, intolerance, and discrimination, we hope for—and we fight for—a new era wherein we Nisei will be accepted as full-fledged Americans. By that time we will have proved our loyalty; our Nisei soldiers will have died to preserve the ideals of the only country we know. Somehow we will see this hard interlude through."[47] Another Nisei in New York City wrote, "We are all engaged in this war for democracy. We believe in it. We want to see it stamp out prejudice and discrimination which are symptoms of the very thing we are fighting—fascism. And when the war is finally over, we know it will be found that we Japanese-Americans have acquitted ourselves creditably and honorably in the defense of our country."[48] An American-born but Japan-reared Nisei described her upbringing in "feudal" Japan in a story entitled "I Am Alive." Regarding her attachment to her native land, she wrote, "We must not make the mistake we made after the first world war. We must go all the way this time, with our American spirit—fair, intelligent, co-operative, scientific, thoughtful—accepting all people as people—to bring the better world of tomorrow. America can do this. America can serve to unite and build a higher, wider, happier world for common people, as she has done on her own new continent."[49]

In 1942 *Common Ground* sponsored a writing contest and awarded the first-place prize to a Nisei. In the prizewinning essay, entitled "Strangers' Rice," the author wrote that she preferred "to dwell on the wonderful kindness men and women of another color, race, and creed have shown me; how they imbued in me a still deeper love of my America." This attachment to her native land was unshakeable, she said, even though "the seed of my birth originated in a nation" that had "become my country's treacherous enemy." And she naively concluded, "Personally my daily life has not been marred since the outbreak of war, even though my skin is yellow. Even strangers smile and start conversations on street cars, something that has not happened often before. This continued kindly courtesy cements my belief in the broader scope of an American's mind."[50]

Common Ground articles also covered the wartime internment of Japanese Americans and the so-called resettlement policy of the War Relocation Authority (WRA). Based on a loyalty registration, administered in early 1943, the WRA divided the interned Japanese American population into so-called loyal and disloyal categories. From the summer of 1943 it then granted clearance to "loyal" Japanese Americans to leave the internment camps and "resettle" elsewhere, principally in the Midwest, for work or study. The official WRA interpretation of this policy was that it enabled "loyal" Nisei to enter the mainstream of American life.[51] In the summer of 1943 Margaret Anderson rallied *Common Ground* behind the WRA policy of resettlement and dispersal with the cry, "Get the Evacuees Out!" and published special articles on the problems of resettlement.[52] She even published essays by Dillon Myer, the WRA director. In 1944 Larry Tajiri, editor of the *Pacific Citizen*, official organ of the JACL, contributed an article entitled "Farewell to Little Tokyo," in which he parroted the WRA interpretation. A "great paradox" or "amazing contradiction" marked "the wartime treatment of Americans of Japanese descent," he said, because "in losing a part of America" the Nisei "are having opened to them the whole of it," creating a situation "auspicious for the integration of Japanese Americans into the main stream of American life."[53] In sum, *Common Ground* articles by and on Japanese Americans all stressed the Americanism and assimilation of the Nisei, saying nothing about any aspect of Japanese culture with which the Nisei might affirm their ethnicity.

Toward a New Ethnic History

Besides the CCAU and *Common Ground,* Adamic used history to popularize his concept of "unity within diversity." He authored four books as a part of his Nation of Nations series. The first three were *From Many Lands* (1940), *Two-Way Passage* (1941), and *What's Your Name?* (1942). The fourth volume was actually entitled *A Nation of Nations* (1945), in which Adamic presented brief histories of Afro-Americans and twelve European ethnic groups. He insisted "that the pattern of the United States is not essentially Anglo-Saxon" but "a blend of cultures from many lands, woven of threads from many corners of the world."[54] Although "diversity" was the essential pattern, this historical fact, Adamic warned, "will remain a rather chilly formula until we become aware of the abundant details which give it life, until we know more about the experiences and qualities, hopes and achievements of the many kinds of people who have made America."[55] The Nation of Nations series was Adamic's first effort to furnish some of the "abundant details."

The main problem was the "discrepancy" between "history as a record and history as a process." According to Adamic, "American history as it is written is not the same as American history as it happened." Written from an Anglo-Saxon point of view, it left out non-Anglo-Saxons and portrayed "the United States . . . as a white-Protestant-Anglo-Saxon country with a white-Anglo-Saxon civilization patched here and there with pieces of alien civilizations." Consequently, non-Anglo-Saxons had difficulty identifying with such an American past. They certainly had no emotional attachment to it. So the WASP interpretation of history had to be discarded and replaced with a new ethnic history that would include all elements of the American population. Only then would non-Anglo-Saxons "have a sense of belonging to an America whose continuity and whose essential strength includes all the people who helped make her."[56]

In 1943 the J. B. Lippincott Company, a Philadelphia-based publishing house, planned a new multivolume series entitled The Peoples of America under the general editorship of Louis Adamic. The idea was to publish a separate volume on every ethnic and racial group in the United States. According to Adamic, the plan "was to tell the story of the United States . . . around the various elements in the population stemming from countries and regions in Europe, Africa and Asia, and from lands north and south of us in the Western Hemisphere." The general aim of the series was "to influence" each ethnic and racial group and "the population as a whole in the direction of a sound American culture drawing eagerly on all its roots and sources."[57] The first volume came out in 1947 under the title *Americans from Holland*; four others later appeared: *Americans from Hungary* (1948), *Americans from Japan* (1948), *Americans from Sweden* (1950), and *Americans from Norway* (1950). Each was written by a separate author.

The author of *Americans from Japan* was Bradford Smith. Like Adamic's portrait of an alienated Japanese American youth and *Common Ground* articles, Smith's volume served to educate the public about Japanese Americans in order to promote their acceptance into society. Indeed, Adamic wrote the preface, in which he made a crucial distinction between "tolerance" and "acceptance." The former was not synonymous with the latter; one could tolerate people without accepting them. Acceptance required a positive act, an active embracing of others. Adamic appealed for the acceptance of ethnic groups and racial minorities in this sense. In *Americans from Japan* Smith described the background of the Nisei and the adversity they faced before and during World War II and then told how they, battling against enormous odds, rose to the challenge. The Nisei vindicated themselves of imputations of disloyalty. They served valiantly in the armed forces and in the European theater compiled a record of heroism unprecedented in the annals of the American army. Unconstitutionally imprisoned in internment camps at the beginning of the war, the Nisei never lost faith in America, endured bitter disappointment, and eventually entered the mainstream of American life through the WRA resettlement program.

In recounting this saga of struggle, Smith offered a novel explanation as to why the Nisei had persevered. He acknowledged Park's concept of the Nisei as marginal men but rejected his assumption that American values were superior to Japanese values. Park and his followers had imputed negative influences to Japanese values. Smith attributed the Nisei's triumph over adversity to Japanese values that the Nisei had inherited from their parents—specifically to the Japanese cultural values of duty, gratitude, integrity, and loyalty. Smith turned the cultural argument around. These Japanese values were positive and were "a stimulus rather than a deterrent to Americanization."[58] The Nisei applied them to their American life, and it was their application that enabled them to triumph. Smith concluded his book with the following words:

> It is still hard for many Americans to look at an Oriental and see a man—to know that he is moved by the same impulses, basically, and cherishes the same desires. Yet until this happens, America cannot become a leader the whole world can accept. In many places in the world today America is no longer the beacon of equal opportunity that once shed the light of its promise across the earth. Men, particularly of the colored races, are turning to communism in disappointment over what seems to them our failure. Yet the solutions are in our hands: we have the human and natural resources to make a civilization to guide the world. Our impediments are personal greed, pampered individualism, and spiritual starvation. The Oriental virtues and the Oriental view of life as aesthetic experience have much to suggest. Unlike most nations, we have the carriers of that culture within our own borders. Our strength, if we but knew it, is in our minorities. It is a strength we have scarcely tapped.[59]

Adamic never specified what was worthwhile in the Japanese cultural heritage of the Nisei. *Common Ground* focused almost exclusively on the Americanism and assimilation of the Nisei. Smith upheld the worth of Japanese values and, within the context of the beginning of the cold war, argued that the Nisei's inherited values were essential antidotes to American individualism, materialism, competitiveness, and self-indulgence. Here, at last, Adamic, through Smith, affirmed specific aspects of the Nisei's cultural heritage.

Conclusions

Some academic historians downgrade the significance of Adamic, focusing on his lapses into filiopietism and ethnic stereotyping.[60] Such a one-sided judgment, I believe, is unduly harsh, at least from a Japanese American perspective. Admittedly, Adamic had erroneous notions about the Japanese immigrant family and community and tended mistakenly to equate the racial problems of the Nisei with the ethnic problems of European ethnic groups. Yet for all that, Adamic was, as a Nisei reviewer of *From Many Lands* wrote in 1940, a welcome "voice in the wilderness." For however flawed his discussion of the Nisei might have been, Adamic had a genuine interest in Japanese Americans. He sought in all earnestness to educate the public about the Nisei at a time when the public was almost wholly ignorant of and hostile to Japanese Americans.

Most Nisei felt that they had no choice but to conform to Anglo-Saxon standards if they ever hoped to rise above the racially subordinate status to which they were consigned. Unlike European ethnic groups, however, they were under much greater pressure because of their race and identification with the "treacherous" Japanese enemy during World War II. Indeed, most Americanized Japanese Americans repudiated Japan altogether and even disassociated themselves from their parents' generation. The WRA policy of resettlement and dispersal accelerated this dual process of cultural severance. During the immediate postwar years, the Nisei went about the business of reconstructing their lives and quietly assimilating into American society. When Bradford Smith upheld the worth of Japanese values in 1948, the Nisei were in no position to affirm such values. In 1948 the sensational "Tokyo Rose" trial began in San Francisco.[61] The defendant was Iva Toguri, a Los Angeles–born and educated Nisei, who went on trial for treason. She had been a radio announcer for NHK Radio, or the Japan Broadcasting Corporation, during World War II. Given the climate of the time, the overwhelming majority of Nisei still felt compelled to distance themselves from the likes of Iva Toguri and, by extension, anything identified with Japan.

The civil rights movement of the 1960s had a profound impact on all ethnic and racial minorities. Under the influence of the movement Japanese Americans began to reexamine their own history in a new light and to reassess specifically what had happened to them during the Second World War. This in turn led them to explore their own ethnicity without being defensive or apologetic and to affirm what they considered valuable in their own cultural heritage. What had been merely an ideal with Louis Adamic (and Bradford Smith) in the 1930s and 1940s became a reality in the 1960s and 1970s. Today we have a much better understanding of race and ethnicity in American life as a direct consequence of the civil rights movement.

Despite Adamic's flawed treatment of Japanese Americans, he should be acknowledged as a forerunner of the 1960s and duly credited for popularizing the idea of accepting ethnic and racial diversity within our society. "Unity within diversity" embodied Adamic's conception of a new America in which, in the words of Rudolph Vecoli, a leading historian of ethnicity in American history, "a pluralism of equality among groups as well as individuals" ideally would be realized.[62] We have yet to witness the realization of such an ideal form of pluralism.

Notes

1. For Adamic's early life and career see Louis Adamic, *Laughing in the Jungle* (New York: Harper and Brothers, 1932); Carey McWilliams, *Louis Adamic and Shadow America* (Los Angeles: A. Whipple, 1935); Henry A. Christian, *Louis Adamic: A Checklist* (Kent, OH: Kent State University Press, 1971), xix–xlvii; Henry A. Christian, "Louis Adamic and the American Dream," *Journal of General Education* 27 (1975): 113–23; Janez Stanonik, ed., *Louis Adamic: Symposium* (Ljubljana Univerza Edvarda Kardelja v Ljubljani, 1981); and Deborah A. Overmyer, "'Common Ground' and America's Minorities, 1940–1949: A Study in the Changing Climate of Opinion" (PhD diss., University of Cincinnati, 1984), 53–83.

2. Louis Adamic, "Thirty Million New Americans," *Harper's Magazine*, Nov. 1934, 686.

3. Ibid., 687.

4. Louis Adamic, *My America* (New York: Harper and Brothers, 1938), 213.

5. Ibid., 218.

6. Louis Adamic, "This Crisis Is an Opportunity," *Common Ground* 1 (autumn 1940): 62–73.

7. Adamic, *My America*, 207. Two scholars have emphasized this aspect of Adamic's thinking. See Richard Weiss, "Ethnicity and Reform: Minorities and the Ambience of the Depression Years," *Journal of American History* 66 (1979): 566–85; and Robert F. Harney, "E Pluribus Unum: Louis Adamic and the Meaning of Ethnic History," *Journal of Ethnic Studies* 14, no. 1 (1986): 29–46.

8. Adamic, *My America*, 219.

9. "The Broadside," in *From Many Lands*, by Louis Adamic (New York: Harper, 1940), 308.

10. Louis Adamic, *A Nation of Nations* (New York: Harper, 1945), 196.

11. Ibid., 217.

12. Ibid., 219.

13. Thomas, *The Salvage*, 19.

14. For an in-house history of the JACL see Hosokawa, *JACL*; and Masaoka,

They Call Me Moses Masaoka. For a somewhat critical appraisal of the JACL
see Daniels, "The Japanese"; Takahashi, "Japanese American Responses"; and
Spickard, "The Nisei Assume Power." For a scathing criticism of the JACL see
Drinnon, *Keeper of Concentration Camps.*

15. Hosokawa, *JACL*, 279–80. The JACL Creed was authored by Mike
Masaoka, a young JACL leader who became the field secretary of the organization
in 1941.

16. Mary Oyama, interview by Yuji Ichioka, Dec. 17, 1985; Mary Oyama to
Adamic, Dec. 19, 1939; and Oyama to Adamic, Dec. 28, 1939, Louis Adamic
Papers, Princeton University Library (hereafter, unless otherwise noted, all letters
cited below are from the Adamic Papers).

17. Mary Oyama, "A Spokesman for the Nisei," *Rafu Shimpō*, March 10, 1940.

18. Mary Oyama, "Inviting Diversity," *Rafu Shimpō*, March 24, 1940. See also
Mary Oyama, "Louis Adamic's Nation of Nations," *Rafu Shimpō*, March 3, 1940;
and Mary Oyama, "Informal Portraits: The Adamics," *Current Life*, Dec. 1940.

19. Adamic to [Shuji] Fujii, n.d., repr. in *Dōhō*, Dec. 1, 1939.

20. *Dōhō*, Dec. 1, 1939.

21. Shuji Fujii to Adamic, Dec. 20, 1939.

22. Editorial, *Japanese American Courier*, March 16, 1940.

23. James Y. Sakamoto to Adamic, Oct. 15, 1940, James Y. Sakamoto Papers,
Suzallo Library, University of Washington.

24. Yori Wada, "I'm Glad I Met Louis Adamic, " *Rafu Shimpō*, June 2, 1940.
This article appeared originally in the *Daily Californian* (a student newspaper at
the University of California), Oct. 27, 1939.

25. Franklin Chino to Adamic, n.d., Apr. 11, 1940, and May 25, 1940; Sam
Hohri to Adamic, March 15, 1940; Kimi Gengo to Adamic, March 19, 1939; and
Hideo Hashimoto to Adamic, Dec. 5, 1939.

26. *Shin Sekai*, Sep. 14, 1940, and *Nichibei Shimbun*, Sep. 14, 1940.

27. *Nichibei Shimbun*, Sep. 14, 1940.

28. Alfred G. Fisk to Adamic, Oct. 27, 1939.

29. Charles Kikuchi to author, Dec. 17, 1985, in author's personal
correspondence file. See also the introduction to John Modell, ed., *The Kikuchi
Diary: Chronicle From an American Concentration Camp* (Urbana: University of
Illinois Press, 1973), 1–39. An undated, twenty-one-page typed version of
Kikuchi's life history is in the Adamic Papers.

30. "Timely Topic," *Shin Sekai*, Dec. 15, 1940.

31. Tomomasa Yamazaki, "Book Review," *Kashū Mainichi*, Oct. 27, 1940.

32. Yori Wada, "I'm Glad I Met Louis Adamic," *Rafu Shimpō*, Dec. 22, 1940.

33. Mary Oyama to Adamic, Aug. 14, 1940.

34. L. H. Tibesar, review of *From Many Lands, Japanese American Courier*, Oct. 19, 1940.

35. Sam Hohri, *Rafu Shimpō*, Dec. 29, 1940.

36. Adamic, "A Young American," 232–33.

37. For Park's ideas on race relations see Robert E. Park, "Behind Our Masks" and "Our Racial Frontier on the Pacific," *Survey Graphic*, May 1, 1926, 135–39 and 192–96; see also his collected essays in Robert E. Park, *Race and Culture: Essays in the Sociology of Contemporary Man* (New York: Free Press, 1950). See also Stanford M. Lyman, "The Race Relations Cycle of Robert E. Park," *Pacific Sociological Review* 11 (1968): 16–21; and Winifred Raushenbush, *Robert E. Park: Biography of a Sociologist* (Durham, NC: Duke University Press, 1979), 107–18.

38. William C. Smith, *The Second Generation Oriental in America* (Honolulu: Institute of Pacific Relations, 1927); and William C. Smith, *Americans in Process: A Study of Our Citizens of Oriental Ancestry* (Ann Arbor, MI: Edwards Brothers, 1937). See also William C. Smith, "Born American, But—," *Survey Graphic*, May 1, 1926, 167–68; and William C. Smith, "Changing Personality Traits of Second Generation Orientals in America," *American Journal of Sociology* 33 (1928): 922–29.

39. Emory S. Bogardus, "A Race-Relations Cycle," *American Journal of Sociology* 35 (1930): 612–17; Robert H. Ross and Emory S. Bogardus, "The Second-Generation Race Relations Cycle," *Sociology and Social Research* 24 (1940): 357–63; and Robert H. Ross and Emory S. Bogardus, "Four Types of Nisei Marriage Patterns," *Sociology and Social Research* 25 (1940): 63–66.

40. La Violette, *Americans of Japanese Ancestry*. Although this study was published in 1945, it was conducted before the war in the Pacific Northwest. See also La Violette, "American-Born Japanese."

41. Carey McWilliams, *Prejudice: Japanese-Americans: Symbol of Racial Intolerance* (Boston: Little, Brown, 1944), 279.

42. Ibid., 104–5.

43. Daniel E. Weinberg, "The Foreign Language Information Service and the Foreign Born, 1918–1939" (PhD diss., University of Minnesota, 1973).

44. *Common Ground* 1 (autumn 1940): 69–70.

45. *Common Ground* 1 (winter 1941): 79.

46. Toshio Mori, "Lil' Yokohama," *Common Ground* 1 (winter 1941): 54–56.

47. Mary Oyama, "After Pearl Harbor: Los Angeles," *Common Ground* 2 (spring 1942): 13.

48. Tooru Kanazawa, "After Pearl Harbor: New York," *Common Ground* 2 (spring 1942): 14.

49. Satoko Murakami, "I Am Alive," *Common Ground* 2 (spring 1942): 18.

50. Asami Kawachi, "Strangers' Rice," *Common Ground* 2 (summer 1942): 73–76.

51. War Relocation Authority, *WRA: A Story of Human Conservation*; and Myer, *Uprooted Americans.*

52. M. Margaret Anderson, "Get The Evacuees Out!" *Common Ground* 3 (summer 1943): 65–66; Robert W. Frase, "Relocating a People," ibid., 67–72; and Robert W. O'Brien, "Student Relocation," ibid., 73–78.

53. Larry Tajiri, "Farewell to Little Tokyo," *Common Ground* 4 (winter 1944): 90–95. For a more detailed discussion of Louis Adamic, *Common Ground*, and *Common Ground's* treatment of Japanese Americans and other ethnic and racial minorities, see William C. Beyer, "Louis Adamic and *Common Ground*, 1940–1949," in Stanonik, *Louis Adamic: Symposium*, 223–39; John L. Modic, "Louis Adamic and the Story of *Common Ground*," in Stanonik, *Louis Adamic: Symposium*, 241–53; and Overmyer, "'Common Ground' and America's Minorities."

54. Adamic, *A Nation of Nations*, 6.

55. Ibid., 11.

56. Louis Adamic, "American History as a Record and a Process," *Common Ground* 8 (summer 1948): 20–23. See also Harney, "E Pluribus Unum."

57. Louis Adamic, "The Peoples of America Series," in Arnold Mulder, *Americans from Holland* (Philadelphia, PA: Lippincott, 1947), 5.

58. Bradford Smith, *Americans from Japan* (Philadelphia, PA: Lippincott, 1948), 382.

59. Ibid., 384.

60. Edward N. Saveth, *American Historians and European Immigrants, 1875–1925* (New York: Columbia University Press, 1948), 216–17. See also Harney, "E Pluribus Unum."

61. Duus, *Tokyo Rose*, 150–223.

62. Rudolph Vecoli, "Louis Adamic and the Contemporary Search for Roots," *Ethnic Studies* (Monash University, Australia) 2 (1978): 35.

SEVEN

The Meaning of Loyalty

The Case of Kazumaro Buddy Uno

Introduction

A central theme in Japanese American history has been the question of loyalty of the American-born second generation. Before the Second World War the Nisei were never recognized as genuine Americans. Anti-Japanese racists alleged that they constituted an unassimilable, dangerous alien element within American society. In response to this negative characterization, the Nisei endeavored to convince the American public, by frequent public declarations, that they were, like all other Americans, equally loyal to the United States. The military necessity rationale, advanced by the War Department to justify the wartime internment of Japanese Americans, was based on the racial assumption that there were no means to distinguish loyal Japanese Americans from disloyal ones. Japanese Americans who protested internment, resisted military service, or renounced their American citizenship were all branded as disloyal persons. Much of Japanese American history written during the postwar period one-sidedly stresses the wartime heroism of Nisei soldiers and the overall loyalty of Japanese Americans during and after the Pacific War.

Kazumaro Buddy Uno (1913–1954), also known as George K. Uno, was a well-known Nisei in the prewar Japanese American community. Throughout the 1930s he was active as a journalist writing in English for the Japanese

Figure 4. Kazamuro Buddy Uno, in front of *Shin Sekai Asahi*, San Francisco, 1935. Yuji Ichioka Papers.

American vernacular press. Because of his pro-Japan reporting before Pearl Harbor and his wartime work for the Japanese army, Uno became and remains a controversial figure. Consequently, he is conspicuously absent from histories of Japanese Americans. When Uno is mentioned at all, it is primarily in connection with the postwar trials of Iva Toguri and Charles H. Cousens, both of whom were tried for treason for participating in Japanese wartime propaganda radio programs.[1] Or he is cited in books on Japan's psychological warfare or in a recent autobiographical account of captivity by a former Japanese American POW.[2] The fundamental reason for Uno's absence from Japanese American history is that he was on the Japanese side during the Pacific War and therefore, by definition, a so-called disloyal Nisei. Through a reconsideration of his case this chapter will explore the complex meaning of loyalty in Japanese American history.

Interpretations

Past views of Uno are at sharp variance. On the one hand, to those Japanese Americans on the left Uno was ideologically "a lackey of Japanese militarists" and "a pro-Japan fascist."[3] On the other hand, Issei leaders like Abe Shōyō of the *Shin Sekai Asahi* of San Francisco and Terazawa Uneo of the *Yuta Nippō* of Salt Lake City praised Uno as a courageous Nisei who had the guts to stand up and defend Japan before white Americans.[4] To the late Howard Imazeki, his former colleague at the *Shin Sekai Asahi*, Uno was simply "an opportunist."[5] Former Allied POWs have testified that Uno was guilty of psychologically tormenting them during the war.[6] In contrast, Carl Mydans, famed photojournalist for *Life* magazine, sympathetically portrays Uno as "a lost American," while Bob Collins, another American reporter, believes that he was "a forgiving and compassionate person" who actually aided Allied POWs.[7] Togo Tanaka remembers him as "a typical Nisei."[8] These varied and conflicting views of Uno, however partially accurate they may be, do not offer a complete picture of the man.

In 1984 John J. Stephan of the University of Hawaii published a book entitled *Hawaii Under the Rising Sun: Japan's Plans for Conquest After Pearl Harbor*. Until the publication of this book, conventional wisdom had it that the Japanese military had never had a plan for the invasion and occupation of the Hawaiian Islands. The Japanese navy, it was believed, had the sole objective of destroying the American Pacific fleet based in Honolulu. Stephan demonstrated the fallacy of this conventional wisdom by presenting evidence of a Japanese military plan to actually invade and occupy the islands. In connection with Kazumaro Buddy Uno, the details of this plan are not important. What is significant is the fact that a few Japanese Americans played a role in drafting it up.

According to Stephan there have been two stereotypes of the Nisei, both of which obstruct historical understanding of the Nisei generation. One stereotype, predating the Second World War, depicts the Nisei "as a cohesive, unassimilated minority with questionable loyalty to the United States." The second stresses the overriding "'100 percent American' character" of the Nisei.[9] In the postwar period, the latter supplanted the former as the dominant stereotype as a result of the wide publicity given to the heroic wartime exploits of Nisei soldiers. In Stephan's opinion both stereotypes grossly oversimplify the complexities within the Nisei generation.

During the prewar period the question of loyalty was never black and white. Stephan writes:

> It is hard to believe that any Japanese-American . . . felt 100 percent loyalty to Japan or to the United States in the 1930s if such loyalty meant the exclusion of emotional feelings and respect toward one or the other country. Available evidence and common sense suggest that a majority felt an attachment to both countries. . . . The nisei could hardly be expected to reject their ancestral land, the birthplace of their parents, and the home of their grandparents, uncles, aunts, and cousins.[10]

The Nisei who provided Japanese military planners with information about the Hawaiian Islands "went beyond sympathy and collaborated with the Japanese authorities." "Yet their actions," Stephan insists, "need to be understood within the turbulent and complex conditions" in which these Nisei found themselves.[11] Those conditions included, among other things, the prewar experience of racial discrimination, dual nationality, conflicting identities, and multiple loyalties. Accordingly, Stephan refuses to interpret the Hawaii Nisei as traitors or disloyal Americans. Granting historical legitimacy to their behavior, he argues that we should not judge their actions in terms of the simplistic wartime categories of loyalty versus disloyalty.

Wartime Activities

Kazumaro Buddy Uno also was in the service of the Japanese government but in a different capacity. From January 1940 he was attached to the Press Bureau of the Japanese army in Shanghai as a civilian journalist serving as a liaison between the army and foreign correspondents. At the same time, he monitored the *East Asia Review*, a fortnightly English news magazine published unofficially by the Press Bureau. In June 1941 Uno assumed the editorship of a new publication called *Asiana*. Ostensibly independent, but also published by the Press Bureau, it was a monthly news magazine patterned after *Time* magazine, the American weekly. As editor-in-chief, Uno used the alias of Brian O'Hara to conceal his identity until November 1942, after which he used his real name.[12]

Shortly after Pearl Harbor the Japanese army established stringent regulations governing the activities of all foreigners living in the International Settlement of Shanghai. The Press Bureau banned certain publications, while allowing others to continue publication but only under strict censorship. In the case of the *Shanghai Evening Post and Mercury*, an American-owned daily that had been very anti-Japanese, the Press Bureau assumed direct control over its operation by appointing Uno as editor-in-chief in January 1942. Three months later Uno went to the Philippines, where he covered the siege of Corregidor in early May and witnessed the actual surrender of the American forces. Based in part on interviews with captured American soldiers and civilians, Uno wrote a series of articles on the fall of Corregidor for the *Shanghai Evening Post and Mercury*. This series was later published in book form under the title *Corregidor, Isle of Delusion*.[13] In addition to all of these activities, in 1942 Uno also edited an illustrated magazine called *Freedom*. Modeled after *Life* magazine, it featured photographs and brief articles on the Japanese "liberation" of Asia from Euro-American colonialism and racism.

In April 1943 Uno left Shanghai and returned to Tokyo. The Japanese military brought Allied POWs to Tokyo and forced them to participate in propaganda radio programs. Uno was assigned to the Bunka Camp in Surugadai, where such POWs were confined, and placed in charge of supervising them in the writing of radio scripts.[14] Then in October 1944 he was reassigned again, this time to Manila in the Philippines. There he was in charge of English radio broadcasting that featured the Filipino counterpart of Tokyo Rose, known as "Manila Rose," who was an announcer in a special propaganda program called *Melody Lane*.[15] For all of these prewar and wartime activities Uno became a so-called disloyal Nisei, thereby disqualifying himself from the pantheon of loyal Japanese Americans.

Personal Background

It is time to reconsider Uno's place in Japanese American history. Just as Stephan insists on placing those Nisei who assisted Japanese military planners in their precise historical context, we should begin by locating Uno firmly within *his* historical context and see him, first and foremost, as a Nisei who grew up in a racist America. Uno was born in 1913, the eldest child of Mr. and Mrs. George Kumemaro Uno in Oakland, California. His father, a native of

Sendai, grew up in the city of Kanazawa in Ishikawa Prefecture, the home-town of his parents. Mr. Uno immigrated to the United States in 1905 at the age of nineteen. In 1912 he married Kita Riki, a native of the town of Mattō, south of Kanazawa, with whom he eventually had a total of ten children.

In 1916 the Uno family moved from the San Francisco Bay Area to Salt Lake City, Utah. By upbringing in his native Japan, Mr. Uno was a Christian, and in 1918 he became one of the lay Issei founders of the Japanese Church of Christ of Salt Lake City. Thus Kazumaro Buddy Uno grew up in a Japanese Christian immigrant family and received his elementary school education in Salt Lake City. In 1926 the Uno family moved back to California and settled down in Los Angeles. Uno attended Stevenson Junior High School in Boyle Heights and graduated from this school in 1929. Between 1929 and 1931 he attended Jefferson High School but eventually graduated from Compton High School in 1932. Throughout his years in the public schools of Southern California, Uno was a self-supporting student who worked at various odd jobs, including being a stock boy in small grocery stores.[16]

Uno's career as a journalist commenced in 1931 with the *Rafu Shimpō* of Los Angeles, when he was a senior at Compton High School. In the fall of that year he began to contribute an occasional short column titled "Echoes from the Tartar Campus" under the byline "Y.K." or "You Know." This was followed by another column under the same byline called "Finger-Points" in the summer of 1932. From June 1933 to March 1934 he wrote a regular weekly column under his own name devoted to Hollywood movies called *Just a Moment Please*. His most widely read and most lasting column was his *A Nisei Melodrama* weekly, which he published from July 1934 until August 1937. It first appeared in the *Rafu Shimpō* but also later in the *Shin Sekai*, *Hokubei Asahi*, *Japanese American Courier*, and *Shin Sekai Asahi*. Hence *A Nisei Melodrama*, published simultaneously in Los Angeles, San Francisco, and Seattle, had a sizable readership, making Uno a very well-known writer among Nisei readers up and down the Pacific Coast.

After the outbreak of the Sino-Japanese War Uno went to China twice as a war correspondent, once in 1937 and again in 1938. His first tour of the China warfront was not prearranged. In August 1937, in the hope of covering the war, Uno sailed from San Francisco for Japan as a cabin boy aboard a Danish freighter. As soon as he arrived in Japan, he contacted his maternal uncle, Doi Ihachi, and asked him for help in obtaining permission to go to China as a reporter. His uncle obliged by introducing him to the minister of communications, Nagai Ryūtarō. Doi and Nagai knew each other as natives of Ishikawa Prefecture. Nagai, in turn, introduced Uno to Kawai Tatsuo, chief of the Information Bureau of the Foreign Ministry. Kawai, then, introduced Uno to the army and navy ministries, which granted him authorization to go to China with other foreign correspondents as an officially recognized reporter.[17]

After his tours of the battlefront Uno published extensive pro-Japanese accounts of the war, first in a series in the *Shin Sekai Asahi* from December 1937 to January 1938 and second in another series in the *Rafu Shimpō* and *Nichibei Shimbun* from August 1938 to December 1938. Besides publishing these accounts, Uno lectured widely on the Sino-Japanese War, both within and without the Japanese American community. His lectures were often sponsored by local chapters of the Japanese American Citizens League (JACL), the principal organization of the second generation. Uno also debated pro-China proponents in open forums. In 1939 he published a series on Nisei life in America as he saw it under the title *Let's Face Facts* in both the *Nichibei Shimbun* and *Rafu Shimpō*.[18]

Nisei Experience

Uno's early writings are those of an Americanized but naive and marginal Nisei youth who wrote bad English. In his "Echoes from the Tartar Campus" column, written as a senior at Compton High School, he mostly gossiped about his Nisei classmates, while writing about social dancing and Nisei athletes. Apart from chatty items about the Nisei, "Echoes" was devoid of any substantive campus news. An unedited sample of the column reads:

INTRODUCING:

Mary Ito, the supposed friend of us, is no relation to handsome Ken Ito, to bad Mary. Here's a break for us. Our new friend Rioko Kinoshita is an excellent dancer and an ace at grammar.

The on-coming Senior and Junior prom at—I think—Surf and Sand club of Santa Monica looks pretty good to us.

We know already Ben Izumida is the "C" track honor man, but did you know he is also a physics "A" man?

Young Kurashige deserves lots of applause for his track accomplishments, while on the Junior college track team. Fred Odanaka has won many honors.

Figure 5. *Rafu Shimpō* dinner/reception, after a 1938 lecture before the Far East Research Institute. Pictured from left to right: Togo Tanaka, H. T. Komai, Henry Mori, John T. Saito, unidentified, Fumi Tanaka, Buddy Uno (standing), Maki Ichiyasu, Laura Horii, Eiji Tanabe, Yone Sugahara, Kay Sugahara, Michael Horii, and Tad Uyeno. Yuji Ichioka Papers.

A little bird told us the other day that a certain femme in chemistry by the name of Asaka sure knows her formulas and compositions.

Here's news for the boys. The best of Japanese Tartarnettes can be seen after school on hockey teams.

Who's the big "shot" with the loud new pants? Looks like "INAKA" Takeuchi is getting all the breaks lately. Can't fool me, old man—we know our dates too.

Well, when we get lonesome out in "the land that God almost forgot" give us a little introduction.[19]

Compton High School was predominantly a white school. As a member of a racial minority, Uno was on the margin of the white student body. He did not serve in any elected student office nor work on the school newspaper or annual. His extracurricular activities consisted of membership in the International Club, the Men's Chorus, the Spanish-speaking club called Los Amigos, and the tennis team. Uno's marginality is clearly evidenced by his views regarding the 1932 Compton High School production of *The Mikado*. "Take my advice," he warned his Nisei classmates, "if you don't want to be ridiculed, don't see this imitation Japanese operetta." Uno was supposed to participate as a member of the men's chorus, but he declined to do so "because it all looked too silly."[20]

Long before he started his *Just a Moment Please* column, Uno was capti-
vated by Hollywood movies. Indeed, he had been a film fan since early
childhood. He saw his first American film at the age of nine. It was "Tom
Mix in 'Three Jumps Ahead' with his famous horse, Tony," he recalled. "I
was so enthusied [*sic*] with his picture," he continued, "that I never missed
any for years after that. I remember his 'Mile-a-Minute Ro[d]eo,' 'Riders of
the Purple Sage,' 'Rainbow Trail,' and many others."[21] Reflecting Uno's own
identification with Hollywood stars, he enjoyed matching the names of individual Nisei with famous Hollywood actors and actresses. For example, he
matched Lily Oyama with Janet Gaynor, Sam Minami with Leslie Howard,
Margaret Uchiyamada with Jean Harlow, Larry Tajiri with Lee Tracy, and
Frank Kamada with Clark Gable.[22]

In his weekly *Nisei Melodrama* column Uno narrated stories of ordinary
Nisei boys and girls trying to make their way in the uncertain world in
which they lived. Originating in firsthand accounts of actual Nisei, his stories invariably had a basis in real Nisei life. Whenever Uno heard what he
considered an interesting Nisei story, he changed the names of the people
involved, altered a few factual details, and then retold the story in fictional
form. All of his stories had a strong moralistic quality with a didactic purpose. Through them he advised young Nisei men not to gamble or drink
excessively, not to become infatuated with blond girls, and not to fall victim
to anger, pessimism, or indolence. On the one hand, he urged everyone to
study hard, to be ambitious but realistic about the future, to improve their
personal habits and character, and, yes, to join the JACL to ameliorate the
lot of the Nisei generation. He himself was an active member of the San
Francisco chapter from 1935. On the other hand, he warned young Nisei
girls of the pitfalls of adolescent love, of becoming obsessed with Hollywood
movies, and of overindulging in frivolous social activities. On the positive
side, he counseled them to be realistic about the future, too. Uno believed
that they should think primarily of getting married and raising children.

Uno was ever mindful of the racism facing his generation. At the age of
twelve he himself had had a humiliating experience of racial rejection as a
Boy Scout in Utah. As a member of a white Presbyterian scout troop, he was
denied admission to a summer jamboree camp. Along with his fellow Nisei
in Utah, Uno was also denied access to public swimming facilities and
restricted to the segregated section for nonwhites in movie theaters.
According to Uno, white employment discrimination and white refusal to
recognize the Nisei as Americans were the two crucial impediments to the

socioeconomic advancement of the Nisei. "We are living in a distasteful era of discrimination," he said, "particularly in California." "Insofar as we are trying to be worthy and loyal Americans," he asserted, "no effort" or "sacrifice" should be spared "in fighting this social evil." But what will become of the Nisei, he asked rhetorically, "if in the process of becoming Good Americans[,] we are objects of unjustifiable and humiliating racial prejudice and discrimination?"[23]

Uno had his own simple answer to this dilemma. He accepted the then prevailing idea, which originated with Issei leaders in the 1920s, that the Nisei had a special mission as American citizens to act as intermediaries between Japan and America.[24] This civic duty entailed educating Americans about Japan in order to dispel misconceptions and misunderstandings Americans had about the Nisei's ancestral land. Uno believed that if the Nisei fulfilled this civic duty, whites would ultimately recognize them as genuine Americans. After all, by serving as effective go-betweens, the Nisei would be contributing to the preservation of harmonious Japanese American relations as so-called American citizens of Japanese ancestry.

Yet the Nisei, at least as Uno perceived them in his time, labored under the "greatest handicap" of being ignorant of their own Japanese cultural heritage. In his view the Nisei "did not know himself" and "does not have an appreciation of the advantages of his ancestry."[25] To truly fulfill their civic duty of educating Americans, therefore, the Nisei first had to educate themselves about Japan. So Uno exhorted the Nisei to "seriously study the history and culture" of Japan and, "if the opportunity afforded, to see Japan, at least once."[26] "In this way," he said, "we will be preparing ourselves to fulfill a lofty duty which is expected of us as American citizens of Japanese ancestry."[27]

Uno's advice to study Japan stemmed in part, no doubt, from his own background. He himself had a poor command of the Japanese language. He never attended a Japanese-language school because his father had not been in favor of such schools. According to Louise Suski, the former English editor of the *Rafu Shimpō*, Uno's Japanese was very poor when he first began contributing articles to her newspaper in 1931.[28] Uno wrote of the positive benefits of learning Japanese as early as 1934 and regularly praised any Nisei who exhibited a good command of the language. In keeping with the idea of the Nisei serving as intermediaries between Japan and America, Uno consistently urged all Nisei to study Japan and learn the Japanese language. And if the opportunity afforded itself, he recommended that everyone visit Japan to experience firsthand their ancestral land.[29]

The Sino-Japanese War vastly complicated the idea of the Nisei as intermediaries by adding a crucial political dimension. This came in the form of an additional responsibility imposed on the Nisei generation to explain and justify Japan's military actions in China. On his two stints as a war correspondent to the China front, in 1937 and 1938, Uno was thoroughly taken in by the Japanese army. It seemed to him an efficient and disciplined fighting force, with soldiers who embodied high samurai virtues of honor, sacrifice, and courage. In 1938 he went on a bombing mission on a Japanese bomber. He was impressed by the modern aircraft and the efficiency of the Japanese crew. "All in all," he wrote, "this was a thrilling experience and one that will never be forgotten."[30] While extolling the Japanese military, Uno denigrated the Chinese at every opportunity. The soldiers of the Chinese army, in his opinion, were "guilty of unimaginable brutality and cruelty," and the Nationalist government was incapable of establishing order and governing China.[31] According to Uno, "every patriotic American of Japanese ancestry" faced the "challenge" of "presenting facts concerning the vital Far East issue, thereby fostering better understanding between the peoples of our father's country, Japan, and our country, the United States."[32] In a sense, Uno himself had risen to the challenge, but the facts, as he marshaled and presented them, were all in favor of the Japanese side.

In June 1939, after completing a long lecture tour of California, Utah, and Idaho, Uno embarked for Japan again, this time, he said, for a three-year period of study. In 1940 he was in Shanghai, already in the service of the Japanese army as a civilian journalist. From there he wrote a revealing piece assessing the status of the Nisei in the United States and Japan.

> Generally speaking, the Nisei is grateful for his Nippon heritage, but he realizes also that he is constitutionally and psychologically an American. Let there be no doubts about this. . . . They are loyal citizens of the United States to whom they pledge their allegiance and to whom they feel more obligated than the country from which their parents came. Frankly, the Nisei cannot be blamed for this attitude. Nipponese should appreciate and admire this trait in the Nisei character.
>
> Ironically, in spite of their disposition in the United States and in Nippon, the Nisei is an important contributor to both Nippon and the United States—politically and socially. Though not subjects of Nippon,

Figure 6. Uno with wife Tomoko, Jessfield Park, Shanghai, May 1941. Yuji Ichioka Papers.

they are faithful and useful benefactors in matters relating [to] the two Pacific countries.

Whatever failures the Nisei may have experienced at home and abroad, it has been the responsibility of the individual. In the United States, fighting numerous racial handicaps, the Nisei are winning a place in the American community. In Nippon, likewise combating many handicaps, the Nisei are gradually winning the respect and recognition of the people.[33]

This assessment of the Nisei applies to Uno himself and can be read as an autobiographical description of his own situation. Inasmuch as he was born, raised, and educated in the United States, Uno identified himself as a loyal American, but white racism made him marginal to American society. He did not feel recognized, much less accepted, as an American. Indeed, aware of the seemingly insurmountable racial barriers confronting his generation, he reached the conclusion that his future lay not in America but in Japan or with Japan in Asia, especially after his trips to the Orient. Despite being of Japanese ancestry and making strides in studying Japan and learning the Japanese language, however, Uno did not feel at home in Japan either. The Japanese, he knew from personal experience, did not fully understand and accept him as he was, that is, "constitutionally and psychologically an American." Being in Japan made him realize more than ever that he was a Nisei and not a Japanese.

Marginality

Uno was the classic case of a marginal man. Regardless of where he was, whether in the United States or Japan, he was a quintessential Nisei with complex, ambivalent sentiments and attitudes toward both societies. Given his marginality, Uno had multiple and often conflicting loyalties that shifted over time and with changing circumstances. But at any given time, he never fit neatly into either of John J. Stephan's two stereotypes of the Nisei. He was never a 100 percent loyal American nor a completely unassimilated disloyal Nisei. He was always emotionally attached to America but at the same time felt alienated from American society because of racial prejudice and discrimination. Indignant at the racial subordination of his generation, Uno resented white presumptions of superiority and understandably harbored antiwhite feelings. His dual nationality no doubt reinforced his marginality.

In 1940 a crucial event occurred in Uno's life. While employed by the Press Bureau of the Japanese army, he was conscripted into the Japanese military, but his service time amounted to only one day. Since the Press Bureau considered him invaluable, if not indispensable, as a publicist, the army discharged him promptly and allowed him to resume his job as a civilian journalist. As a result of his one-day military service, however, Uno lost his American citizenship. According to American law, any American who served in a foreign army automatically lost his or her American citizenship. By his own admission, Uno, from this point in time, began to consider himself a Japanese citizen and to shift his loyalty more in favor of Japan.[34]

His awareness of his samurai family background also influenced his shifting self-identity. All through the Tokugawa period, the Uno family had served the Maeda fiefdom as specialists in falconry. His grandfather, Uno Tomiyoshi, was a graduate of the Japanese Military Academy and a wounded and decorated officer during the suppression of the Satsuma Rebellion. Uno spent his preschool childhood in Japan. In 1915 his mother had taken him and his younger brother, Howard Yasumaro, to Kanazawa to celebrate the Golden Wedding Anniversary of their paternal grandparents. In 1916 the mother returned alone to the United States, leaving her two sons in the care of paternal relatives. Uno himself returned in 1920 with a paternal uncle.[35] His childhood knowledge of his family background was deepened with renewed contacts with his relatives in 1937 and 1938 when he revisited Japan as a war correspondent. All of this combined to undergird his shifting self-identity. And his marriage to a Japanese woman in 1941 no doubt further reinforced it.[36]

Multiple Aspects of Racism

Because of his own racial experience in the United States, the racial ideology of Japan had a special appeal to Uno.[37] During the war Japan claimed that it was fighting to "liberate" Asia from Anglo-American colonialism and white racial domination. Uno was convinced that white Americans had always had "a Janus, two-faced attitude of superiority" toward nonwhite people.[38] Of his own sense of racial rejection, he recalled bitterly to a white American correspondent, "I was treated like a yellow skibby and not an American citizen. . . . So I decided, the hell with the United States. I'd go to Japan where my knowledge of the States would be appreciated."[39] According to a dictionary of slang in the American West, *skibby* has the meaning of a Japanese prostitute. In using this term to describe his racial experience, Uno was saying essentially that he had been treated like a yellow whore by white men.

By returning to Japan in 1939 and gaining employment in Shanghai, Uno found what to him was meaningful and satisfying work with the Japanese army Press Bureau. For that work enabled him to ply his journalistic skills, giving him social recognition and status with considerable authority, something he had never enjoyed in his own native country. Indeed, he became the editor-in-chief of the *Shanghai Evening Post and Mercury*, an American-owned daily newspaper. Furthermore, working as a journalist with the Press Bureau entitled Uno to wear a special army uniform and to carry a sword, giving him an added aura of military authority that he relished. At the time when Uno was first hired, the head of the Press Bureau in Shanghai was Lieutenant Colonel Saitō Jirō. Saitō had spent his childhood and early youth in Hawaii as the son of Saitō Miki, the Japanese consul stationed in Honolulu at the turn of the century. In fact, he had attended McKinley High School with many Nisei.[40] Uno described Saitō as "a Yankeefied Japanese officer" who was "jovial" and "humorous." He was "popular among the foreign correspondents as a 'good time Charlie,'"[41] and knew the value of English as a language of propaganda in the Shanghai International Settlement.

Uno glorified Japan's ideological goal of "liberating" Asia in the *Asiana* and *Freedom*. In editorial after editorial he boasted of the superiority, and hence invincibility, of the Japanese army and navy, and he reveled in the sweeping Japanese military victories of 1941–42. He interpreted the swift and decisive victories over the American and British forces at Wake, Guam, Hong Kong, Shanghai, Malaya, Singapore, and the Philippines as sounding the death knell of Anglo-American colonialism and white racial dominance in Asia. Moreover, the victories heralded the beginning of a "Greater East Asia" under the leadership of Japan in which Asia, at long last, would become a region for "Asiatics" rather than a place dominated and exploited by Euro-Americans. In short, Uno's own racial experience led him to subscribe readily to the antiwhite wartime ideology of Japan.

According to a 1942 *Asiana* editorial, the goals of Anglo-Americans and of the Japanese were at fundamental odds with each other in a "now or never, do or die" war situation: "The goal of the Allies is victory over Japan, re-establishment of Anglo-American imperialism in East Asia and perpetuation of Anglo-Saxon prestige over the colored races. The goal of Japan is emancipation of the Asiatics from Anglo-American economic and physical domination, rejuvenating the spiritual philosophy of the Orient and establishment of economic, political and social independence for the peoples of East Asia."[42] In looking back at the "glorious" events of 1942, the 1943 New Year editorial in *Asiana* triumphantly proclaimed:

> The year 1942 will be remembered as a year of emancipation for the peoples of East Asia[,] for during the brief 12 months, through the consistent victories of the Imperial Nipponese Armed Forces, millions have been released from the shackles of Anglo-American imperialism.
>
> In one year Nippon has liberated her neighboring brothers from 100 years of bondage and exploitation in the hands of ruthless British, American and Dutch tyrants. Freedom has been obtained through Nippon's military superiority over the Anglo-Americans. Millions of liberated people, including Malaians [*sic*], Filipinos, Djawanese, Burmese and Indians, today know the true meaning of racial equality and freedom in pursuit of happiness. Truly 1942 has been a kind year for the peoples of East Asia, thanks to Nippon's sweeping victories.[43]

Uno's hostility toward whites is revealed in his attitude and treatment of the Allied POWs who came under his supervision at the Bunka Camp in Tokyo. Almost to a man, these POWs have testified that Uno abused them as he directed them in the writing of radio scripts. George H. Henshaw described him as "a treacherous, deceitful, sadistic brute" who "didn't like any white man" and that he "threatened us almost daily with removal to the Kempei for execution if we didn't do as he said."[44] After a fellow POW refused to participate in propaganda programs, Henshaw recorded in his diary, "He [Uno] threatened us with everything from a firing squad to the tortures of a gestapo dungeon if any ever dares to question an order in this camp again."[45] Another former POW, Frederick M. Hoblitt, remembered Uno in a similar way. He testified that "on numerous occasions I heard Uno threaten different Prisoners of War with death if they didn't comply with his requests."[46] Still another POW, Charles Cousens, described Uno as "a cold-blooded, treacherous savage."[47] Other POWs gave similar testimonies. Uno's superior was Lieutenant Colonel Tsuneishi Shigetsugu, who headed the Japanese army's psychological warfare program. Under postwar interrogation by American occupation forces, Tsuneishi denied that any POW under his charge had been mistreated. He admitted, however, that, because of Uno's "hostility towards whites," Uno was at times "somewhat heavy-handed" in his dealings with them.[48] On one occasion, Tsuneishi recalled, Uno tore off the insignia of a POW, which prompted him to have Uno transferred to the Philippines.[49]

Uno arrived in Manila on October 24, 1944, four days after General Douglas MacArthur had landed on Leyte. Some of his associates warned him that if he ever went to the Philippines, he would never be able to return alive. Seven months later, in May 1945, he was taken prisoner by Filipino guerrillas. With scattered remnants of the Japanese army, Uno had fled Manila on February 4, the day after American forces entered the outskirts of the city. His group first escaped into the mountains east of Manila via Antipolo and Boso Boso to Santa Inez and the San Angelo gold mine. From there they wandered through a dense jungle for seven weeks and eventually reached the east coast of Luzon. In the end, on the verge of starvation, stricken with malaria and beriberi, and utterly exhausted, Uno, along with four Japanese soldiers, surrendered to Filipino guerrillas. The guerrillas killed the Japanese soldiers on the spot but mercifully spared Uno's life because they thought, on hearing his fluent English, that he was a Japanese officer in possession of possible valuable intelligence.[50]

Uno was turned over to American military authorities and imprisoned at the New Bilibid Prison with other Japanese POWs. His physical condition had deteriorated badly. Almost totally emaciated, he weighed slightly over a hundred pounds, down sharply from his normal weight of 160 pounds. He still had malaria and acute diarrhea and suffered from severe bouts of delirium. He realized that he was a POW but insisted that he was not "a traitor" to the United States. His fellow Japanese POWs kept him at a distance. They suspected him of being "an American spy" because of his outbursts of English, with which he tried to explain his position as a Nisei. Uno also suffered from delusions that he had been transferred to "an American POW camp in San Francisco" and that his sister Hana, with whom he was the closest among his siblings, had come to visit him.[51] Even in captivity Uno remained a marginal Nisei.

Conclusion

Under the influence of the redress movement, scholars have reevaluated many aspects of the Japanese American wartime internment experience. For example, they have reinterpreted the meaning of camp protest activities, the War Relocation Authority classification of disloyalty, the renunciation of American citizenship, the draft resistance movement, and the JACL and its wartime role. But Uno and other Nisei like him have yet to receive similar scholarly consideration. It is a truism to say that the Nisei, regardless of where they stood on the wartime political spectrum, were all victims of racism. That racism imposed on them a very narrow range of options and underlay all of the excruciating choices the Nisei were forced to make before and during the Second World War. Whether the Nisei sought a future in Japan, decided to volunteer for military service or resist the draft, answered yes/yes or otherwise to the loyalty registration questions, or engaged in protest activities and renounced their citizenship, they chose to do so under racist conditions and circumstances.

Uno was no exception. Because of racism he chose to go to Japan and ended up on the Japanese side during the Pacific War. He cannot be faulted for having felt alienated from American society and resentful of white attitudes and practices of racial superiority. Uno was not unique among his Nisei peers. He was not some kind of mutation or aberration. Many other Nisei went to Japan in the 1930s. They were just as marginal to American society as Uno was, sharing his ambivalent sentiments and attitudes toward America and Japan. Some also defended Japan's military actions in China during the Sino-Japanese War and served in the Japanese government in different capacities before and during the Second World War. Such Nisei like Tamotsu Murayama, George Nakamoto, Kenneth Oki, Charles Yoshii, Kay Tateishi, and many others come to mind.

Uno can be faulted for many things. As a journalist he was, to put it mildly, deficient in the fundamentals of good writing. In fact, when he contributed to the vernacular press in the 1930s, he wrote horrid English, ungrammatically and frequently with crude and clumsy modes of expression. During his two tours of the China front, in 1937 and 1938, he accepted Japanese military press releases on their face value. His first series of articles on the Sino-Japanese War consisted essentially of such press releases with a few words and sentences altered here and there. During the wartime years his writing style improved considerably, reflecting his maturation as a journalist. Uno was also very naive and gullible about Japan and the Japanese military. His championing of the racial ideology of Japan, while understandable in the light of his racial experience in America, was extremely naive to say the least, especially when placed alongside Japan's actual racial policies and practices in Asia.

Uno's gullibility is most unabashedly manifest in his view of the Korean people. He wrote:

> The people of Korea today enjoy the economic, industrial, and political
> conditions as improved by the Japanese. . . . The younger generation enjoy
> spiritual happiness . . . as they now have the same education system
> throughout Korea as in Japan[,] and they are given opportunity to
> volunteer for service in the Army. [In Japan], they prefer to be called
> Japanese rather than Koreans. And in Korea, they call themselves
> "Hantojin" meaning peninsulaeso and not Koreans.[52]

With smug arrogance Uno here repeated the official Japanese government cant about the "beneficent" effects of Japanese colonial rule in Korea. His disparagement of the Chinese people is equally revolting and unforgivable. Still, finding fault with Uno is not the same as branding him with the label of disloyalty.

Since he was on the Japanese side during the Pacific War, Uno has been banished into historical oblivion as a persona non grata. His case raises a fundamental historical question. What is the meaning of loyalty in a racist society? Speaking specifically in terms of Japanese Americans, how can white

America justifiably classify any Nisei as disloyal when it itself refused to accept the Nisei as Americans? Rephrased in another way, how can the category of a disloyal Nisei have any meaning in a society that overwhelmingly rejected the Nisei on racial grounds? If we place Uno, with all of his faults, within the framework of these questions, there is no justification for treating him as a disloyal Nisei and keeping him beyond the pale of Japanese American history. That history cannot and must not be an exclusive one of so-called loyal Japanese Americans. In order to fully comprehend the Nisei generation in all its *complexities*, it must become *inclusive*. And that entails bringing Kazumaro Buddy Uno back within the pale and granting him— and other Nisei like him—a rightful place in Japanese American history.[53]

Notes

1. Masayo Duus, *Tokyo Rose: Orphan of the Pacific* (Tokyo: Kodansha, 1979); Russell W. Howe, *The Hunt for "Tokyo Rose"* (New York: Madison Books, 1990); and Ivan Chapman, *Tokyo Calling: The Charles Cousens Case* (Sydney: Hale and Iremonger, 1990).

2. Tsuneishi Shigetsugu, *Shinri Sakusen no Kaisō* (Tokyo: Tōsen Shuppan, 1978), 208, 227; Ikeda Norizane, *Hinomaru Awā: Tai-Bei Bōryaku Hōsō Monogatari* (Tokyo: Chūō Kōronsha, 1979), 61–62, 100; Kaigai Hōsō Kenkyū Gurūpu, *NHK Senji Kaigai Hōsō* (Tokyo: Genshobō, 1982); and Stanley L. Falk, *Foo, a Japanese-American Prisoner of the Rising Sun: The Secret Prison Diary of Frank 'Foo' Fujita* (Denton: University of North Texas Press, 1993).

3. *Dōhō*, Dec. 5, 1938, April 25, 1939. See also Karl Yoneda, *Ganbatte: Sixty-Year Struggle of a Kibei Worker* (Los Angeles: Asian American Studies Center, UCLA, 1983), 106.

4. "Toki no Kage," *Shin Sekai Asahi*, Jan. 27, 1938; and *Yuta Nippō*, April 18, 20, 1938. Terazawa Uneo took special pride in the fact that Uno had been raised in Utah. He remembered him as a "mischievous boy" but claimed him as a native son of Salt Lake City. Terazawa praised him as a Nisei who had become a first-rate journalist, marveling at his ability to speak convincingly in defense of Japan, especially before white Americans.

5. Howard Imazeki, interview by Yuji Ichioka, Sep. 16, 1988.

6. A handful of Allied POWs were brought to Tokyo and confined at the Bunka Camp, Surugadai, Kanda District, where they were compelled to participate in NHK Radio programs for Japanese propaganda purposes. These POWs came into direct contact with Uno.

7. Carl Mydans, *More Than Meets the Eye* (New York: Harper and Brothers, 1959), 104–7; and Bob Collins, "I Knew Buddy Uno," *Pacific Citizen*, Nov. 1,

1968. See also *Nichibei Times*, Nov. 3, 1968. Carl Mydans has not changed his opinion of Uno over the years. Carl Mydans, interview by Yuji Ichioka, Jan. 5, 1996.

8. Togo Tanaka, interview by Yuji Ichioka, Oct. 17, 1994.

9. John J. Stephan, *Hawaii Under the Rising Sun: Japan's Plans for Conquest After Pearl Harbor* (Honolulu: University of Hawaii Press, 1984), 6.

10. Ibid.

11. Ibid., 7.

12. The unidentified editor of the *East Asia Review* was an Englishman by the name of Edward Dunn, who edited the fortnightly from its inception in 1938 to its demise in 1941. Uno had a very low opinion of the man. As he monitored the publication for the Press Bureau, Uno grew to dislike Dunn intensely because, in his opinion, Dunn acted purely out of his own self-interest and was not editing an effective news magazine. No bylines appeared in the *East Asia Review*, except when it reprinted articles from the Western press. Besides monitoring the magazine, Uno appears to have occasionally contributed articles, at least in 1941. For example, an article titled "Whither Democracy?—United States Joins World War II When 'Aid to Democracies' Signed" appeared in the January 1941 issue of the fortnightly without a byline. See *East Asia Review* 5, no. 6 (Jan. 25, 1941): 13–23. A Japanese translation of this article subsequently appeared in a Tokyo journal under Uno's name. See Uno Kazumaro, "Dai-Nisei no Mita Amerika: Beikoku ni Demokurashi Ariya," *Yōsukō*, 4, no. 5 (May 1941): 44–50. In any event Uno considered the *East Asia Review* an ineffective news magazine. Accordingly, he persuaded his superiors to discontinue publication of the fortnightly and to replace it with the *Asiana* under his own editorship in June 1941.

13. Kazumaro Uno, *Corregidor, Isle of Delusion* (Shanghai: Mercury Press, 1942). A laudatory review appeared in *Asiana*, no. 19 (Dec. 1942): 56. A very inaccurate Japanese translation was published in 1944. See Shibata Kenjirō and Mochizuki Motoo, trans., *Korehidoru: Saigo no Hi* (Tokyo: Seitoku Shoin, 1944). The original English version was sold in Shanghai bookstores. See Edgar D. Whitcomb, *Escape from Corregidor* (London: Allan Wingate, 1959), 231. In 1942 the Japanese daily published in Shanghai carried an extended Japanese version of Uno's account of the fall of Corregidor and the surrender of Lt. General Jonathan Wainwright. See *Tairiku Shimpō*, May 22, 1942.

14. Tsuneishi, *Shinri Sakusen no Kaisō*, 195–208, Ikeda, *Hinomaru Awā*, 58–62.

15. Tsuneishi, *Shinri Sakusen no Kaisō*, 208. For Uno's detailed autobiographical account of all his wartime activities, see Statement, George Kazumaro Uno, New Bilibid Prison, Manila, [Sep. 19, 1945]; and Special Agent 2851, "Memorandum for the Officer in Charge, Subject: George K. Uno," Oct. 4, 1945, Headquarters, Counter Intelligence Corps, Area no. 2, United States Army Forces,

Pacific, U.S. Army Intelligence and Security Command, Ft. George G. Meade, obtained through the Freedom of Information Act.

16. I have pieced together Uno's biographical profile from various sources: George K. Uno to Tom C. Clark, "Appeal for Release," May 1, 1946, in Edison Uno Papers, Japanese American Research Project Collection (hereafter cited as Edison Papers), UCLA, Box 37, Folder 9; Edison Uno, "Brief Uno Family Biography—NBC News," April 19, 1972, Edison Papers, Box 76, Folder 5; JACP, Inc., *Japanese American Journey: The Story of a People* (San Mateo: Japanese American Curriculum Project, 1985), 141–48; Ted Nagata, ed., *The Japanese Church of Christ* ([Salt Lake City]: n.p., n.d.); Genevieve Lim, "Edison Uno, "Nisei Civil Rights Advocate," *Bridge* 5, no. 1 (April 1977): 22–24; Amy Uno Ishii, interview, July 9, 18, 1973, Betty E. Mitson and Kristin Mitchell, California State University, Fullerton, Oral History Program, 1978; Buddy Uno, "It All Began—A Nisei Melodrama," *Rafu Shimpō*, April 21, 1935; Compton Junior College, *Dar-U-Gar*, Compton yearbook, 1932; Joy Nozaki Gee, ed., *Crystal City Internment Camp: 50th Anniversary Reunion Album, October 8–10, 1993* (Monterey, CA: Crystal City Association, 1993), 23–25, 102; Records Relating to Japanese Civilian Internees During World War II, 1942–1946, Provost Marshall General, George Kumemaro Uno File, Box 107, RG 389, NA; Immigration and Naturalization Service, World War II Internment Files, George Kumemaro Uno File, Box 190, RG 85, NA Branch Depository, Crystal City, TX; Statement, George Kazumaro Uno, New Bilibid Prison, Manila, [Sep. 19, 1945]; Deposition of George Kazumaro Uno, April 15, 1949, Records of the District Courts of the United States, Northern District of California, San Francisco, Criminal Case Files, 1936–49, "Tokyo Rose," Box 264, File 31712R, RG 21, NA Branch Depository, San Bruno, CA; and George K[umemaro] Uno, comp., "Comprehensive Genealogy of Uno Family" (1959), Yuji Ichioka Papers, Special Collections, Charles E. Young Research Library, UCLA.

17. For accounts of this episode see George Kazumaro Uno, Statement, New Bilibid Prison, Manila, [Sep. 19, 1945]; *Hawai Hōchi*, Dec. 16, 1937; Uno Kazumaro, "Tatakau Sokoku wo Mite Nippon Seishin ni Mezameru: Beikoku Umare Dai-Nisei no Shuki," *Hanashi* 7, no. 2 (Feb. 1, 1939): 166–72; and *Tairiku Shimpō*, Jan. 14, 1942.

18. *Let's Face Facts* appeared in the *Nichibei Shimbun*, Jan. 12–June 5, 1939. In addition to this series Uno published a travel account of a 1937 TWA flight to the East Coast and back. See "A Flying Vacation with Buddy Uno via TWA, the Lindbergh Line," *Shin Sekai Asahi*, July 7–Aug. 22, 1937.

19. *Rafu Shimpō*, April 10, 1932.

20. *Rafu Shimpō*, April 3, 1932.

21. *Rafu Shimpō*, Dec. 3, 1933.

22. *Rafu Shimpō*, Oct. 8, 1933.

23. *Nichibei Shimbun*, April 23, 1939.

24. *Nichibei Shimbun*, Jan. 11, 1939. For the Issei origin of the idea see Yuji Ichioka, "*Kengakudan*: The Origin of Nisei Study Tours of Japan," *California History* 73, no. 1 (1994): 30–43, 87–88. See also Jere Takahashi, "Japanese American Responses to Race Relations: The Formation of Nisei Perspectives," *Amerasia Journal* 9, no. 1 (1982): 29–57; and Yuji Ichioka, "A Study in Dualism: James Yoshinori Sakamoto and the *Japanese American Courier*, 1928–1941," *Amerasia Journal* 13, no. 2 (1986–87): 49–81.

25. *Nichibei Shimbun*, Jan. 11, 1939.

26. Ibid.

27. *Nichibei Shimbun*, Jan. 16, 1939.

28. Louise Suski, telephone interview by Yuji Ichioka, Feb. 23, 1995. Even after his extensive experience in Japan and Asia, Uno's command of Japanese remained very halting and heavily accented. Kay K. Tateishi, interview by Yuji Ichioka, Aug. 16, 1995; and Kazuma Uyeno, interview by Yuji Ichioka, Aug. 18, 1995. His eldest son and daughter recall that their father did not even have a rudimentary reading knowledge of Japanese. He could only read the Japanese syllabary. His knowledge of Chinese characters amounted to no more than being able to write his full name. Uno Katsumaro and Ishidate Emiko, interview by Yuji Ichioka, Aug. 22, 1995.

29. *Nichibei Shimbun*, April 10, 1939.

30. *Nichibei Shimbun*, Oct. 24, 1938.

31. *Shin Sekai Asahi*, Feb. 10, 1938.

32. *Nichibei Shimbun*, June 8, 1939.

33. *Nichibei Shimbun*, May 11, 1940.

34. Deposition of George Kazumaro Uno, April 15, 1949.

35. Uno, "Comprehensive Genealogy."

36. Uno married Tomoko in Tokyo. Because of the Pacific War and Uno's early death in 1954, Tomoko was unable to visit the United States until 1987. After her trip she wrote a touching account. See Uno Tomoko, "Rokujūgosai, Amerika wo Yuku," *Kakurenbō*, no. 4 (Feb. 1988): 59–62; no. 5 (May 1988): 44–46; no. 6 (Aug. 1988): 72–77; no. 7 (Nov. 1988): 59–63; and no. 8 (Feb. 1989): 64–69.

37. For the racial aspect of World War II from the Japanese side see John W. Dower, *War Without Mercy: Race and Power in the Pacific War* (New York: Pantheon, 1986), 203–90.

38. Uno, *Corregidor, Isle of Delusion*, 50.

39. Royal Arch Gunnison, *So Sorry, No Peace* (New York: Viking, 1944), 114.

40. For Lt. Col. Saitō Jirō's background see *Hawai Hōchi*, June 8, 1938; and *Nippu Jiji*, Nov. 26, 1940.

41. Statement, George Kazumaro Uno, New Bilibid Prison, Manila [1945].

42. Editorial, *Asiana*, Dec. 1942, 5.

43. Editorial, *Asiana*, Jan. 1943, 5.

44. Diary of Lt. George H. Henshaw, Dec. 6, 1943, entry, in Department of Army, U.S. Army Intelligence and Security Command, Ft. Meade, Maryland, *George K. Uno File*, obtained through the Freedom of Information Act.

45. George Herbert Henshaw, Testimony, Central Police Court, Sydney, Oct. 1, 1946, Supreme Commander for the Allied Powers, Legal Section, Investigation Division, Investigation Reports, 1945–49, Box 1807, File 1181, RG 331, NA.

46. Frederick M. Hoblitt, Sworn Statement, Oct. 8, 1947, Supreme Commander for the Allied Powers, Legal Section, Investigation Division, Investigation Reports, 1945–49, Box 1807, File 1181, RG 331, NA.

47. Chapman, *Tokyo Calling*, 278.

48. Tsuneishi, *Shinri Sakusen no Kaisō*, 227.

49. Shigetsugu Tsuneishi, Affidavit, Oct. 27, 1947, in RG 331, NA (see note 45).

50. The foregoing account of Uno's flight from Manila and capture by Filipino guerrillas is taken from Statement, George Kazumaro Uno, New Bilibid Prison, Manila [1945]; and Deposition of George Kazumaro Uno, April 15, 1949.

51. Kazumaro George Uno, "Notebook," May 24, 1945. Uno jotted down notes during his captivity in a small notebook in the possession of his son, Uno Katsumaro. In a twist of history Uno's younger brother, Howard Yasumaro, visited him at the New Bilibid Prison in July 1945. Howard landed in Manila on July 4 as a member of the Allied Translator and Interpreter Section of G-2 in General Douglas MacArthur's headquarters. Along with his brother Stanley, he had volunteered for Military Intelligence Service. At the beginning of the Pacific War he was unaware of his brother's wartime activities. While stationed at Brisbane, Australia, in 1943, however, he unexpectedly heard a special Radio Tokyo program marking the first anniversary of the fall of Corregidor. Howard immediately recognized the broadcaster's voice as that of his brother, who identified himself as "George K. Uno" at the end of the program. The text of Uno's radio presentation was printed in the *Nippon Times*. See Kazumaro Uno, "I Saw Wainwright Surrender: America's Last Outpost Was Isle of Delusion," *Nippon Times*, April 25–28, 1943. Howard had a two-hour visit with his brother. Uno appeared to be regaining his health. Howard saw his brother only once. On July 18 he suffered a severe back injury that required him to be hospitalized for a year. Howard Yasumaro Uno, interview by Yuji Ichioka, June 22, 1995. George Kanegai, a fellow Nisei from Los Angeles, also visited Uno at the New Bilibid Prison. He had landed in Manila in May, also as a member of the Allied Translator and Interpreter Section. Since he had known Uno and his siblings in Southern California before the war, Kanegai went to visit

him as soon as he learned that he was imprisoned. Kanegai recognized him immediately. George Kanegai, interview by Yuji Ichioka, May 2, 1995. Uno was repatriated to Japan in May 1946 and died on December 10, 1954, in Kobe.

52. *Nichibei Shimbun*, Feb. 9, 1939.

53. The members of Uno's family were all interned during the war. Uno had nine younger siblings. Their names and years of birth are as follows: Howard Yasumaro, 1914; Hanna Hanako, 1918; Mae Akiko, 1919; Amy Emiko, 1920; Stanley Toshimaro, 1922; Ernest Nobumaro, 1925; Robert Akimaro, 1927; Edison Tomimaro, 1929; and Kay Keiko, 1932. His mother and siblings were interned, first at the Santa Anita Assembly Center and then at the Amache Relocation Center at Granada, Colorado. The exception was Amy, who was interned at Heart Mountain, Wyoming. She married Alfred T. Tanaka of Honolulu in August 1942 at Santa Anita and accompanied her new husband to Wyoming. Three brothers— Howard, Stanley, and Ernest—served in the U.S. Army during the war. Howard and Stanley were among the earliest Nisei volunteers to sign up for the Military Intelligence Service.

George Kumemaro Uno was arrested by the FBI in February 1942 and detained at first as "a potentially dangerous enemy alien." Subsequently, he was reclassified and interned as "a dangerous enemy alien." Under the separate custody of the Justice Department, he was confined successively at Ft. Lincoln, North Dakota; Lordsburg and Santa Fe, New Mexico; and Crystal City, Texas. In November 1945 the Justice Department served notice on George Kumemaro Uno that he was going to be repatriated to Japan because he was still considered a dangerous enemy alien. Mr. Uno successfully appealed this notice of repatriation, which enabled him to avoid deportation, but he was not officially released until September 1947. His prolonged internment was related directly to his son's wartime activities.

In early 1944 the *Pacific Citizen*, the JACL weekly, ran a short front-page story under the caption "Three Nisei Soldiers Vow Death of Brother in Japan." The story was on Royal Arch Gunnison, a North American Newspaper Alliance foreign correspondent, who had been in POW camps in Manila and Shanghai and had been interviewed by Kazumaro Buddy Uno. Once he returned to the United States aboard the exchange ship *Gripsholm*, he publicized the "traitorous" behavior of Uno. Erroneously identifying him as a Japanese officer, he quoted Uno as saying, "My family, my brothers are dumb Americans. They are stupid enough to believe there is such a thing as equality for race or creed in the United States." Gunnison then published a letter that he said he had received from Uno's three brothers serving in the U.S. Army. The letter, in part, read, "We wish to inform you that the Jap officer—our brother—is a traitor to the American way of life under which he has enjoyed the benefits of education and freedom. We have pledged the destruction of him and all those like him" (*Pacific Citizen*, April 1,

1944). Unbeknown to either Howard or Ernest, Stanley had actually written this
letter on his own. Howard Yasumaro Uno, interview by Yuji Ichioka, June 22, 1995.

The *Heart Mountain Sentinel* repeated this story under the caption, "World
War I Veteran's Nephews Pledge Destruction of Brother." The World War I
veteran was none other than Clarence Hachiro Uno, younger brother of George
Kumemaro Uno and hence uncle to Buddy and his siblings, who had served in
the U.S. Army in France in 1918–19. "There was little doubt here last week," the
story line read, "that Clarence Uno, were he alive today, would add the fire of his
wrath to that of his three nephews who condemned the statement of their brother
and pledged his destruction" (*Heart Mountain Sentinel*, April 8, 1944). Clarence
Uno had died on January 20, 1943, at Heart Mountain. For his obituary see *Heart
Mountain Sentinel*, Jan. 23, 1943, and *Pacific Citizen*, Jan. 21, 1943.

In 1939 Stanley had accompanied his brother to Shanghai in order to work as
an apprentice for maternal relatives engaged in business in the city. Stanley
returned to the United States before Pearl Harbor, despite his brother's efforts to
persuade him to remain in Shanghai. He actually returned in October 1941 aboard
the last ship sailing from Shanghai to San Francisco. At this time the American
consul had asked Buddy if he would be interested in returning to the United
States with Stanley. Buddy answered no. He told the consul that "I had a better
job [in Shanghai] than if I were to go back to America and apply for another job."
Stanley strongly opposed his older brother's pro-Japan activities. In his parting
words Stanley, in apparent anticipation of a war between the United States and
Japan, told his brother, according to Buddy, "if you see me first you had better
shoot, because if I see you, I will sure shoot." See Deposition of George Kazumaro
Uno, April 15, 1949.

In October 1944 Royal Arch Gunnison published a book recounting his own
story of captivity and repatriation. While in Shanghai, Gunnison had been interrogated by Uno. Of his impressions of Uno, he wrote:

> Uno spoke perfect American. In fact he had trouble with his Japanese, which he
> spoke with an American accent. This made him suspect among the Japanese. But
> there was little need for that. He was, and still is, a loyal Japanese subject; also bit-
> terly anti-American because he says, "I was treated like a yellow skibby and not an
> American citizen, although my education was as good as any other American's. So I
> decided, the hell with the United States. I'd go to Japan where my knowledge of the
> States would be appreciated." And it was. Uno was obviously a privileged character
> in the Japanese army Press Bureau. From those of his stories which I read I think he
> was a more factually accurate reporter than most Japanese, probably because of his
> American training. However, he could be just as screwy as all the rest when it came
> to the hay-wire type of propaganda they try to peddle as emotional come-on.
> (Gunnison, *So Sorry, No Peace*, 113–14)

These impressions of Uno, in shorter form, appeared in Royal Arch Gunnison, "Surrender at Corregidor," *Collier's*, March 18, 1944, 13.

The *Pacific Citizen* article upset sixteen-year-old Robert Uno, who was confined at Crystal City, Texas, at the time. Along with his mother, Edison, and Kay, he had been transferred from Amache to Crystal City at the end of February 1944 to join his father. Stanley's letter upset Robert so much that he dashed off a letter of protest to Stanley, which prompted Stanley, in turn, to write a quick reply. Stanley said that he had written to Gunnison because "his article" had been "harmful" to "we Nisei in the Army" and asked him to refrain from writing any further articles. At the same time, Stanley told Robert "I love this country" and "am unashamed of my love." Interestingly, he never mentioned Buddy but closed his letter by pleading with Robert to understand the patriotic motives of his brothers in the U.S. Army. See Stanley [Uno] to Robert [Uno], April 26, 1944; E. D. McAlexander, Chief Internal Security Officer, to J. L. O'Rourke, Officer in Charge, memorandum, May 2, 1944; J. L. O'Rourke, Officer in Charge, to W. F. Kelly, Assistant Commissioner for Alien Control, Central Office, memorandum, May 3, 1944, Immigration and Naturalization Service, World War II Internment Files, Box 190, RG 85, NA Branch Depository, Crystal City, TX.

In May 1945 at the age of eighteen, Robert answered the loyalty registration questions required of all Japanese Americans eligible for conscription. He answered "no" to Question 27, that is, that he was not willing to serve in the armed forces of the United States wherever ordered. A few months later he altered his answer to "yes" and requested that his draft status be changed from 4C to 1A. To explain his change of heart, he informed his local draft board that "since last May, I have been very unhappy, I've become grouchy and cranky because my conscience has been bothering me." "When I signed the papers," he explained, "I was under a great deal of pressure which was brought on me by the Issei . . . of this camp but . . . I have received letters from my brothers . . . wanting to know why I did such a thing." But now, he concluded, "I have finally realized after many letters from them that they are fighting for me and my place . . . in this country" (Robert Uno to Selective Service, Local Board No. 1, Crystal City, August 1, 1945, Immigration and Naturalization Service, World War II Internment Files, Box 190, RG 85, NA Branch Depository, Crystal City, TX).

The Office of the Provost Marshall in the War Department maintained an investigative card file on Japanese American military personnel. In November 1943 the card entry on Howard Yasumaro Uno reads as follows: "Subj's fathr considrd very pro-Jap by many neighbrs; subj's brothr apprntly Lt in Jap Army. Subj mad statmnt to effect tht he hd left hs hom frm time to time because of argumnts with his fathr, who ws opposed to subj's pro-Americanism. Thes argmnts or periods of absence from his home could nt be verified. Inv found subj to be industrious, polite, quiet, resrvd, & Americanzd as to habits & customs. No recommendatn made pending inv of undev leads. Pending in MID," Pvt. Howard Yasumaro Uno, ASN 17145569, Records of the Office Provost Marshall General, Records of the Internal Security Division, Records of the Japanese-American Branch, Japanese-American Personal Data Cards, Box 8, Tayama, Harry M. to Yamasaki, Tsunio Francis, RG 389, NA. The investigation of Howard Uno was closed in January 1944.

Michio Uno was the first cousin of Buddy and Howard. His investigative card entry reads, "Inter. Of. Memo 10/3/42 frm Strateg. Serv. states that one, KAZU-MARO UNO, alleg. to be responsi. for cert. Eng. lang. publica. entit. 'Freedom' & 'Photoplay' brought out by the Jap. for propa. purposes in Shanghai. Mr. KAZUMARO UNO is abt. 25 yrs. old, born in Los Angeles; educat. at Salt Lake City, and is said to have a broth; (bel. to be subj.) in the Amer. Army or AAF" (Michio Uno, ASN 19066191, Records of the Office Provost Marshall General, Records of the Internal Security Division, Records of the Japanese-American Branch, Japanese-American Personal Data Cards, Box 8, RG 389, NA).

Japanese Immigrant Nationalism

The Issei and the Sino-Japanese War, 1937–1941

Prior to the so-called mass evacuation of all Japanese Americans from the Pacific Coast, many *Issei* were arrested and detained by the Justice Department. In doing this, the Justice Department did not act in a random manner. During the decade of the 1930s, the FBI and army and navy intelligence had the Japanese immigrant community under close surveillance. Based on information amassed from this surveillance, the FBI had classified certain Issei as "dangerous enemy aliens" and proceeded to systematically arrest and detain such Issei as soon as Pearl Harbor was attacked. To fully understand this early FBI roundup, it is essential to examine the prewar Issei nationalism that developed after the outbreak of the Sino-Japanese War in 1937 and continued unabated until 1941. This nationalism involved an intense patriotic identification with Japan on the part of the Issei, as evidenced by their various activities to lend political, financial, material, and moral support to Japan's war effort in China.[1]

The undeclared war between Japan and China broke out with the Marco Polo Bridge Incident of July 7, 1937. During the ensuing crisis Issei leaders in every Japanese community in the western United States established emergency committees, the majority of them in the fall as it became apparent that no quick resolution was imminent. Set up usually within preexisting Japanese associations, these committees served four purposes.[2] First, they disseminated pro-Japanese propaganda to counteract local publicity that blamed Japan for the war. Toward this end the committees issued political pamphlets in English, sponsored public lectures, and promoted special radio programs.

Figure 7. *Imonbukuro* (care packages for Japanese soldiers), ready to be shipped to Tokyo, in front of the Japanese Association of San Francisco building, ca. 1937. Reproduced from Zaibei Nihonjinkai, *Zaibei Nihonjinshi* (1940).

Second, they collected money and goods, which they sent to Japan. Funds were raised for national defense and war relief; money for the latter, called *imonkin* and *juppeikin*, were earmarked for needy families who had soldiers engaged in combat or killed in action. Third, the committees sent gift packets to the Japanese soldiers on the China front. These packets were called *imonbukuro* and were filled with nonperishable items like tobacco, razors, dried fruits, soap bars, and candy. *Senninbari*, or talismans, were often forwarded, too. Literally meaning "a thousand stitches," these talismans, it was believed, protected Japanese soldiers from the Chinese enemy because each stitch, in theory, had been knitted by one thousand maidens. Fourth and last, the committees sponsored periodic patriotic meetings to commemorate historic events such as the fall of Canton and Hankow in 1938.

The Japanese associations and Japanese chambers of commerce of San Francisco, Seattle, Portland, Los Angeles, Chicago, and New York City assumed the task of issuing political pamphlets. In San Francisco, for example, the Japanese Association of America and the Japanese chamber of commerce published eleven separate pamphlets as of December 1937. Some fifty thousand to sixty thousand copies of these pamphlets were printed under such titles as "What Is Japan Fighting For?" and "Facts of the China Trouble" and "What Is The Fighting About?" Based on Japanese Foreign Ministry material, they were underwritten by the San Francisco Japanese Consulate and distributed as widely as possible by the Japanese chamber of commerce and the Japanese Association of America and its affiliated local associations. In Portland the Japanese Association of Oregon printed and distributed twenty thousand copies of a pamphlet entitled "The North China Incident, 1937," and in Seattle the Japanese Association of North America and the Japanese chamber of commerce jointly printed and distributed twenty thousand copies of two pamphlets entitled "The Undeclared Sino-Japanese War" and "The Oriental Conflagration; Who Struck the Spark That Started It?" In Los Angeles the Japanese chamber of commerce printed and distributed twenty thousand copies of a pamphlet entitled "Japan's Position in the Shanghai and North China Hostilities." In Chicago and New York City similar pamphlets were issued by the corresponding organizations in these two cities. All of the pamphlets presented the Japanese justifications for military action undertaken in China.[3]

Two rural Japanese communities typify the patriotic activities in which ordinary Issei participated. The first is Yakima, Washington, located on an American Indian reservation. In August 1937 Issei leaders of this farming settlement organized an emergency committee within the local Japanese association. Between that date and March 1939 the committee raised $5,774.70 for national defense, a sizable sum of money for this small community, which, in 1940, had a population of only 814. During the same period of time, the committee collected 1,714 *imonbukuro* and sent them to the Japanese soldiers on the China front via the Japanese Consulate in Seattle.[4]

The second community is Walnut Grove, California, situated in the Sacramento delta region. In this small farming settlement, too, an emergency committee was organized by the local Japanese association to collect national defense funds and *imonbukuro* and to distribute locally the pamphlets published in San Francisco and other cities. In addition to these activities, the committee held a "war victory celebration" on November 3, 1938, to commemorate the fall of Canton and Hankow. The entire community of five hundred people attended the program, which included the latest war-related newsreels from Japan. And the coincidence of the celebration with the Meiji emperor's birthday infused it with added nationalistic meaning. This event was followed by another commemoration on February 11, 1939, a day on which the Issei celebrated *Kigensetsu.* The Japanese of Walnut Grove had never observed this Japanese national holiday. February 11 was the date on which Jimmu, the first Japanese emperor, was said to have ascended the imperial throne in 660 BC, marking the beginning of the imperial line that Shinto nationalists claimed had been unbroken through the ages. In the same month and year, a local branch of the *Heimushakai* was formed, an organization comprising men who still were of draftable age according to Japanese law. Since such men enjoyed draft deferments by virtue of living abroad, they established the local *Heimushakai* branch to remit money in lieu of military service. Local members pledged to donate fifty cents per month and also solicited additional donations from nonmembers.[5]

What transpired in Yakima and Walnut Grove was repeated in every Japanese settlement up and down the Pacific Coast and in the adjacent western states. As of June 1939 the Japanese of Seattle donated 59,152 yen for national defense, 23,700 yen for medical supplies, and 12,600 yen for war relief (in the late 1930s the yen-dollar exchange rate fluctuated between four to five yen per dollar). They also donated 5,184 *imonbukuro* and an unspecified amount of *imonhin* or war relief goods. And, as their Walnut Grove compatriots did, they observed the fall of Canton and Hankow with a victory celebration and sent congratulatory telegrams to the Japanese army and navy ministries.[6] The Japanese of Tacoma forwarded 5,326 *imonbukuro* between August 1937 and February 1939. On October 10, 1937, they donated $3,345.75 for national defense; and the local Japanese association, in August 1938, urged all local residents to contribute a dollar or more per person every month for the duration of the war. Three months later the association contributed $938 for war relief.[7] The *Heimushakai*, originally organized in San Francisco in August 1937, had branches in numerous Japanese settlements in California, Nevada, Idaho, and Utah, and as of June 1940 it claimed to have raised over five hundred thousand yen.[8] In San Francisco the Issei commemorated the first anniversary of the Marco Polo Bridge Incident with a memorial rite. Fifteen hundred persons assembled at the Scottish Rite Hall to honor the Japanese war dead on July 7, 1938. San Francisco consul general Shiozaki Kanzō delivered an address and proposed that every Issei contribute a dollar to families in Japan who had lost loved ones in combat.[9]

In Southern California Issei patriotism was especially intense. In September

1937 an emergency committee was organized by the Central Japanese Association of Southern California, the Japanese Association of Los Angeles, and the Japanese chamber of commerce. On September 29 this committee forwarded 255,660 yen to the Japanese military, divided equally between the army and the navy.[10] In October another special committee, spearheaded by the Japanese Association of Pasadena and composed of various community organizations, was formed to raise funds specifically for two military aircraft. In January 1938 this second committee donated $8,775 to the army for a liaison aircraft; seven months later it donated $15,724 to the navy for a carrier-based fighter bomber.[11] In April 1938 a Los Angeles branch of the Nihon Aikoku Fujinkai, or Women's Patriotic Society of Japan, was established by prominent Issei women.[12]

By July 1938 Los Angeles consul Ōta Ichirō felt that matters had gotten out of control. In his opinion groups were competing wildly with each other to see who could raise the most money. They solicited openly in public and publicized the results of fund-raising drives in the local Japanese-language press. Ōta singled out the *Heimushakai* and *Hōkokukai*, yet another patriotic body, for using strong-arm tactics to coerce people into making donations. Engaging so conspicuously in pro-Japanese activities, he feared, would alarm the American public. Mindful of possible adverse repercussions, Ōta warned the Issei leaders of the dangers involved, but much to his dismay zealous individuals and groups refused to heed his words of admonition.[13]

Thus Ōta advised the Foreign Ministry to take measures to curb or dampen the "excessive patriotic ardor" of the Issei.[14] In a revealing report, dated July 10, he recommended to Tokyo that the prime minister or foreign minister should issue a statement to the effect that, while it was laudable for overseas Japanese to contribute money to Japan's war efforts, it was by far better for them to use such funds to educate the citizens of the country in which they resided about Japan's policy. If such a statement were aired over shortwave radio or released through the Dōmei News Agency, Ōta believed that it would have a salutary effect. He assumed that the Issei who had refused to heed his words would abide by the words of the prime minister or foreign minister. Consul Shiozaki of San Francisco reported that overzealous patriotism had also emerged in his jurisdiction, so he endorsed Ōta's recommendation.[15] Inasmuch as Shiozaki's endorsement came right after he had proposed that every Issei donate a dollar to families who had lost men in combat, this was somewhat ironic, an irony which did not escape the attention of later critics of Consul Shiozaki and Consul Ōta. Ōta did not receive an instant reply from Tokyo. Less than a month later he reiterated his recommendation because of continuing excesses in Southern California.[16]

The Foreign Ministry ultimately released a statement on August 9 through the Dōmei News Agency.[17] Instead of the prime minister or foreign minister, it was issued in the name of Kawai Tatsuo, the information section chief of the Foreign Ministry. Kawai began by cautioning overseas Japanese about excessive and competitive fund-raising campaigns. Raising national defense and war relief funds was commendable, but it was not the only way of being patriotic. Overseas Japanese were in a position to educate foreigners about the Japanese side of the Sino-Japanese conflict. The Japanese in America in particular were situated to inform Americans about the war. If the Issei dedicated themselves to this educational task, Kawai asserted, they would be acting as "true patriots." Indeed, they would be contributing toward the preservation of good Japanese-American relations, which was more important than the remission of national defense and war relief funds. Interestingly enough, the Foreign Ministry released Kawai's opinions as "informal remarks" rather than as an official statement of policy. Tokyo, in all likelihood, adopted this low-keyed, tactful approach in order to avoid unduly antagonizing overseas Japanese.

As soon as the statement was released, many people assailed it as an affront to all overseas Japanese. The *Nichibei Shimbun* of San Francisco ran a series of protest letters from its readers. One reader stated that every Issei who had read the statement "felt a sense of indignation" and urged everyone to "disregard" Kawai's advice.[18] Yusa Keizō of Guadalupe, a noted Issei poet, pointed out with barbed sarcasm the irony of Kawai's statement in the light of Consul Shiozaki's appeal to the Issei to contribute war relief funds.[19] The harshest and most vocal critic was Fujii Sei, publisher and editor of the *Kashū Mainichi* of Los Angeles. Fujii was enraged by the statement, and he minced no words in lashing out at it and at Consul Ōta. Cantankerous and opinionated by nature, he had championed the patriotic activities of the Issei from the very beginning, and he had been critical of Consul Hori Kōichi, Ōta's predecessor, who, in his opinion, had given only lukewarm support to the drive to collect funds for military aircraft.[20] Fujii correctly surmised that Ōta had filed a report to Tokyo in which he recommended that the statement be issued. In bitter diatribes in his daily column, Fujii heaped abuse on Ōta, calling him an arrogant, ignorant, and insensitive elitist who was incapable of fathoming the motives of the common Issei. And he sternly rebuked him for having insulted them in an unforgivable manner.[21] According to Fujii the Issei donated money and collected *imonbukuro* out of a sincerity of feeling above all else. Self-considerations played no role. The Issei were profoundly grateful for the sacrifices the Japanese soldiers were making on the battlefield. They truly grieved for the families who had lost loved ones, and they possessed an undying love of their mother country. Fujii was fond of referring to his newspaper as "a country newspaper edited by a country editor for country folk." His subscribers, who lived for the most part in small farming communities, doubtless nodded in approval at his scathing indictment of Consul Ōta, for Fujii appealed to the sensibilities of ordinary Issei.

There were many cultural expressions of Issei nationalism. The Issei regularly expressed their patriotic sentiments through poetry. Every Japanese immigrant daily published patriotic poems. The *Rafu Shimpō* of Los Angeles, for example, sponsored annual poetry contests on war-related themes and published the results in its special New Year's edition. In January 1938 the theme was the so-called "China Incident"; in January 1939 it was "War Victory" to commemorate the fall of Canton and Hankow; and in January 1940 it was the coming "New Order" in Asia.[22] Simple verses described Issei patriotic activities:

> Sennin-bari
> Sewn to deflect
> Chinese bullets;
> Overtime
> Homefront contributions
> Increase even more
> Imonhin
> My younger sister
> Includes talismans.

Other poems expressed Japanese patriotism from an immigrant perspective:

> War victory
> Celebration in an alien land
> Swelling with pride

War victory
Hands outstretched
Towards the motherland
The flag of the Rising Sun
Bowing in silence
An old immigrant

And still others expressed keen interest in the progress of the Sino-Japanese War:

The China Incident
Ears upturned
The radio news
War victory
Radio news
Until daybreak

The Japanese government-designated *Aikoku Kōshin-kyoku*, or Patriotic Marching Song, became an overnight hit among Japanese immigrants in early 1938. Soon after, another patriotic march, composed and written by Nozaki Kiyoshi of Arroyo Grande, became the unofficial patriotic song of the Issei in Southern California. This second tune was an American version of the official Japanese patriotic march. The Issei sang both at patriotic gatherings.[23]

Many Issei endeavored to instill Japanese patriotism in their children through cultural institutions. In the late 1930s, branches of the *Butokukai*, or Martial Virtue Society, proliferated within Japanese immigrant society. Under the leadership of Nakamura Tōkichi, a rabid nationalist, the aim of the society was to inculcate the "Japanese spirit" in *Nisei* youngsters through the teaching of Japanese swordsmanship. The society even established a special institute in Tokyo in 1938 to accommodate Nisei students. Called the *Hokubei Kōdō Gakuin*, or Imperial Way Institute of North America, the school listed Tōyama Mitsuru, a notorious right-wing nationalist, as an adviser.[24] Japanese-language school teachers promoted Japanese patriotism among Nisei youngsters by teaching them to compose essays in Japanese with themes relating to the Sino-Japanese War. Many teachers also taught their pupils to write letters of appreciation to Japanese soldiers and forwarded them to the China front. Here is how a typical letter read:

December 15, 1937

To Japanese soldiers in China:

The year is fast coming to an end. It's probably cold over there. It's hard for us who live in sunny Southern California to imagine your hardships.

Everyday we learn of your heroic deeds from the newspaper and radio. I believe that people throughout the world will soon acknowledge your efforts in fighting for justice with the Japanese spirit and Bushido. I hope that day will come quickly.

According to the latest news, we learn that the Imperial Army is launching its final attack on Nanking. We get excited everytime we see the morning newspaper. You will reach your goal soon. The final victory is the most important. I pray that you will be victorious as soon as possible and that you will work towards restoring peace in the Orient.

As we are about to usher in the New Year in this time of crisis, I would like to express our gratitude for your accomplishments thus far and to extend our encouragement for the future. I await the day when you will return home as victorious heroes.

Toshiko Nakamura[25]

Various institutions and individuals shaped Issei opinion regarding the Sino-Japanese War. The Japanese immigrant press was by far the most influential. All daily newspapers relied heavily on Dōmei News Agency dispatches from Japan for day-to-day coverage of the war. This agency was established in 1936 with a monopoly over the release of news abroad.[26] Ostensibly an independent agency, it was in fact under the control of the Japanese government, so its coverage of the Sino-Japanese War was always heavily biased in favor of the Japanese side. For the average Issei the daily Dōmei dispatches, which the immigrant press carried, were the main source of information about the war. In addition, each newspaper had its own correspondent in Tokyo who reported on the war in supplemental articles slanted toward the Issei. In every case these correspondents were men with whom the Issei were familiar because they had worked for the immigrant press at one time or another. For example, the *Rafu Shimpō* of Los Angeles had Mutō Shōgo, the *Nichibei Shimbun* of San Francisco had Sagitani Seiichi, and the *Kashū Mainichi* of Los Angeles had Komatsu Yoshimoto.

Three newspapers had their own war correspondents who also molded opinion. The *Shin Sekai Asahi* had three men at different times. The most prolific was Tamotsu Murayama, who was a Dōmei reporter at the outbreak of the Sino-Japanese War. In the fall of 1937 he went to the China front, from where he filed dispatches to the *Shin Sekai Asahi*. Murayama unfailingly cited the heroism of Japanese soldiers in reporting on the fighting. He also conveyed the gratitude the soldiers expressed at receiving *imonbukuro* from overseas Japanese, striking undoubtedly responsive chords in the hearts of the Issei who sent them. After his China assignment Murayama embarked on an extensive speaking tour of the Japanese communities on the Pacific Coast. In late 1937 and early 1938 he gave firsthand accounts of the war before Issei and Nisei audiences. Murayama was no stranger to the Issei. He was a *Kibei-Nisei*. Born in Seattle in 1905, he had received his early education in Japan. On returning to the United States, he attended Lowell High School in San Francisco. During the early 1930s he had been very active in the San Francisco chapter of the Japanese American Citizens League. Thus, among the Issei, the credibility of Murayama's pro-Japan dispatches and speeches was enhanced considerably by his personal roots in Japanese immigrant society.[27]

Ebina Kazuo and Suzuki Kamenosuke were the other two war correspondents for the *Shin Sekai Asahi*. Both followed Murayama to the China front toward the end of 1937. An Issei, Ebina had been a newspaperman in California for more than twenty years. He contributed a regular column to the *Shin Sekai Asahi* in which his war reportage appeared.[28] Suzuki was the Tokyo-based correspondent of the *Shin Sekai Asahi*. Both men reported glowingly on the Japanese army in action. Like Murayama, Suzuki came to the United States and spoke to Issei groups. Under the sponsorship of his newspaper, he presented fifty-nine talks in all in a two-month speaking tour.[29]

The *Nichibei Shimbun* and the *Rafu Shimpō* had Kazumaro "Buddy" Uno. A Nisei, Uno was the only war correspondent who reported in English. He first went to the China front as a reporter for the *Shin Sekai Asahi* in the fall of 1937 and witnessed the fighting in and around Shanghai. It was on his second tour of the battlefield that he reported for the *Nichibei Shimbun* and the *Rafu Shimpō*, covering the siege of Hankow in late 1938. Uno was thoroughly taken in by the Japanese army. It seemed to him an efficient and disciplined fighting force with soldiers who embodied high samurai virtues. While extolling the Japanese, Uno denigrated the Chinese at every opportunity. The soldiers of the Chinese army, in his opinion, were "guilty of unimaginable brutality and cruelty," and the Nationalist government was incapable of establishing order and governing China.[30] After each stint as a war correspondent, Uno gave pro-Japan talks before Issei and Nisei groups, too. He even debated pro-China speakers in public forums before nonimmigrant audiences.

Understandably, Uno drew high praise from Issei leaders. Ever since the outbreak of hostilities, the adult Nisei on the whole had not stood up in defense of Japan. They either were simply indifferent or adopted a neutral stance. Or they were critical of Japan. The Issei expected the Nisei to act as a so-called bridge of understanding between Japan and the United States and present Japan's side in the Sino-Japanese conflict to the American public. Yet the Nisei, save for a few notable exceptions, did not fulfill this expectation. In 1938 Yamashita Sōen, Tokyo-based correspondent of the *Nippu Jiji* of Honolulu, wrote a book on the Nisei in which he asserted that Issei leaders were all "shocked" at the failure of the Nisei to champion Japan's case.[31] Similarly, Azumi Suimei, editor of the popular monthly *Nippon to Amerika*, lamented the Nisei's failure, which he attributed to "a lack of knowledge" of the historical circumstances surrounding the conflict.[32] Recognizing the ignorance of the Nisei, the *Nichibei Shimbun* and *Shin Sekai Asahi* sponsored a joint essay contest in December 1937 in order to encourage the Nisei to study "the facts." The chosen theme was "How I, as a Nisei, can justify Japan's case in China."[33] In September 1937 Fujii Sei started his own English column, *Uncle Fujii Speaks*, in the *Kashū Mainichi* expressly for the purpose of educating Nisei youngsters about the Sino-Japanese conflict.[34] To an Issei leader like Abe Toyoji, publisher of the *Shin Sekai Asahi*, therefore, it was especially gratifying to see and hear a Nisei like Uno standing up for Japan before his fellow Nisei and the American public.[35]

The Foreign Ministry sent unofficial spokesmen to speak to the Issei about the Sino-Japanese War. They, too, influenced opinion. Shishimoto Hachirō was handpicked to take a speaking tour of Japanese settlements. Having been a newspaperman with the immigrant press from 1915 to 1931, he was a well-known figure within Japanese immigrant society. In 1932 he had returned to Japan. In late 1937 the Foreign Ministry first dispatched Shishimoto to North China to enable him to prepare for his tour. There he observed the fighting firsthand and obtained fresh information. He arrived in the United States at the beginning of 1938, and he spoke in almost every Japanese community, including rural ones like Walnut Grove. The Foreign Ministry selected Shishimoto as an unofficial spokesman precisely because he had connections with Japanese immigrant society. His old ties, it was assumed, would accrue to his effectiveness among the Issei.[36]

Henry Toshirō Shimanouchi was another unofficial spokesman. He undertook a nationwide lecture tour of the United States on behalf of the Foreign Ministry from November 1937 to April 1938. He also visited North China in preparation for his tour. Publicly he was an official representative of the Foreign Affairs Association of Japan, a semiofficial government body. His mission, broadly speaking, was to stem the tide of adverse publicity Japan was suffering at the hands of the American press. Shimanouchi had an unusual background.[37] Born in 1909 in Japan, he was reared in California from the age of one, growing up in the Japanese settlements of San Francisco, Oakland, Livingston, Fresno, and Los Angeles. His father was a respected Issei leader who was associated with the *Nichibei Shimbun* for many years.[38] Educated in American public schools, Shimanouchi was a graduate of Occidental College. By upbringing and schooling, therefore, he was closer to being a Nisei than an Issei. In 1933 he returned to Japan, where he found employment as a reporter for an English newspaper, and in 1936 he joined the staff of the *Kokusai Bunka Shinkōkai*, an organization that disseminated knowledge of Japan in Western languages. During his American lecture tour Shimanouchi addressed Issei and Nisei groups throughout the Pacific Coast. Issei leaders took great pride in him, for he had risen from the ranks of the Nisei. In March 1938 he spoke in Los Angeles at a meeting of the Far East Research Institute, a Nisei group formed to study the Sino-Japanese conflict. A polished bilingual speaker, Shimanouchi's defense of Japan was so masterful in the opinion of Fujii Sei that he had nothing but the highest words of praise for him.[39] As a staunch defender of Japan to the Issei, Shimanouchi's credibility was also enhanced by his own personal background in Japanese immigrant society.

Miya Sannomiya and Nakamura Kaju were two additional persons sent by the Foreign Ministry. Sannomiya was a Nisei. Born in 1902 in Hawaii, she was raised in California. Her father was a longtime farmer in the Stockton area. A product of American public schools, she was a graduate of the University of California. In 1926 she toured Japan with the second Nisei *kengakudan* sponsored by the *Nichibei Shimbun*. That trip stimulated her lifelong interest in Japan. In 1931 she had gone to Japan to master the Japanese language. When the *Kokusai Bunka Shinkōkai* was organized in 1934, she joined the staff as an English secretary.[40] She arrived with Shimanouchi in November 1937. Frequently sharing the same platform with him, she talked principally about cultural affairs rather than politics. Nakamura, a former member of the Japanese Diet, was head of a private institute in Tokyo that offered special classes on Japan and the Far East to foreign students. Since he recruited Nisei to enroll in his school, the Issei were acquainted with him. Nakamura arrived with Shishimoto Hachirō in January 1938. He also presented pro-Japan talks before Issei groups during his own lecture itinerary.[41]

Other people who were not affiliated with the Japanese government also shaped Issei opinion. Many persons representing private groups paraded across the Pacific to address immigrant audiences. The most influential ones were those who had some kind of personal links to the Issei. Frank Takizō Matsumoto was among them. In 1937 he happened to be on the East Coast studying at the Harvard Business School. Like Shimanouchi, Matsumoto was born in Japan but raised in California. In 1921 he had returned to Japan and had become a professor at Meiji University. During the summer of 1937 Matsumoto, on his own initiative, defended Japan before the Issei and took the Nisei to task for failing to take up Japan's cause.[42] Yamada Waka appealed specifically to Issei women. She arrived in October 1937 as a member of a private delegation. She represented *Shufu no Tomo*, a popular women's monthly and the most widely read Japanese magazine among Issei women. Her reputation as a writer-critic rested on her regular contributions to this monthly. Yamada herself had very old ties to Japanese immigrant society. In 1902 she had been a prostitute in Seattle; later she lived in the San Francisco Japanese settlement. Most Issei women probably were unaware of her past until Oka Shigeki, an Issei newspaperman, publicized it in his San Francisco weekly after her arrival.[43] With backing of Mrs. Abiko Kyūtarō, publisher of the *Nichibei Shimbun*, Yamada toured Japanese communities and appealed to the patriotic sentiments of ordinary Issei women.[44] Kiyosawa Kiyoshi, a leading political commentator, made his own personal appeal. He had been a newspaperman with the immigrant press in his youth. He arrived in San Francisco in October 1937. Learning of the pro-China activities of Chinese Americans, Kiyosawa challenged the Nisei to come out in defense of Japan to combat the anti-Japanese propaganda their Chinese counterparts were spreading. Issei leaders hailed his appeal to the Nisei.[45] All of these private individuals, together with many others who had no ties to the Issei, also helped to foster pro-Japan sentiments and attitudes among the Issei.

Finally, there was a small group of influential Issei. Many large communities, at one time or another, sent representatives to the China front. These

Issei were known as *imonshi* who delivered *imonbukuro* and national defense and war relief funds to Japanese military authorities. Stopping off normally in Japan, Korea, and Manchuria en route to North China, they toured the battlefront to console Japanese troops, visited the wounded in military hospitals, and participated in special ceremonies. To name a few specific individuals, in 1938 the following Issei went to China in this capacity: Miyazawa Yasutarō of Seattle, Yamazaki Masato of Tacoma, Iseda Gōsuke of Riverside, Nishimura Sueji of Pasadena, Furusawa Sachiko of Los Angeles, and Fukuda Yoshiaki of San Francisco. Nishimura represented the Southern California committee that raised funds for military aircraft. He attended the ceremony held at Haneda Airfield in October 1938 at which a naval fighter bomber, the second aircraft paid for by the committee, was christened as the "Japanese Patriots of Southern California." Mrs. Furusawa represented the Federated Japanese Women's Associations of Southern California. *Imonshi* were significant for a simple reason. They were all Issei leaders who returned to give eyewitness accounts of the war to their compatriots. After a grand tour of five and a half months, Fukuda Yoshiaki, for example, addressed Issei audiences throughout California in 1939. Fukuda was the bishop of the Konkōkyō Church, a Shinto sect. As a part of his presentation he reported that the Japanese troops at the front looked forward to receiving *imonbukuro* almost as much as letters from home, generating immense satisfaction among the Issei who had taken the trouble to collect and forward them.[46]

Shortwave radio broadcasts from Japan had some influence. The Japan Broadcasting Corporation or NHK Radio, a Japanese government controlled enterprise, commenced shortwave overseas broadcasting in June 1935. Broadcasting to the Pacific Coast initially consisted of daily one-hour programs with two five-minute news spots, one in Japanese and one in English.[47] After the Marco Polo Bridge Incident the daily program was increased by half an hour, and in August 1938 a special weekly *Nisei Hour*, mostly in English, was added. NHK shortwave radio programs provided the Issei with another source of Japanese government controlled news about the Sino-Japanese War. Yet the effectiveness of the broadcasts was limited. Most Issei did not have shortwave radio receivers. In addition, reception was not always clear. Static periodically interfered so much that programs on many days were all but unintelligible or inaudible. Thus NHK Radio influenced only those Issei who had access to receivers and only on those days reception was intelligible.

Issei patriotism reached its zenith at the first conference of overseas Japanese. Sponsored by the Japanese government, this conference was held in Tokyo in November 1940. Delegates from Manchuria, Southeast Asia, the Americas, and elsewhere met together for the first time; some came from as far as Brazil and Argentina. Nearly every Japanese settlement in the United States was represented. The American delegation was composed of sixty-two delegates who were chosen by local Japanese consulates. Tsukamoto Matsunosuke of San Francisco, a venerable eighty-three-year-old pioneer, headed the delegation. He had resided in the United States since 1887. Minami Yaemon, a successful Guadalupe farmer, was the senior delegate from Southern California. More than four hundred unofficial delegates from the United States, many of whom were members of special tour groups organized to take in the conference, augmented the American delegation. The conference had four basic purposes: to formalize relations between overseas and domestic organizations; to study the educational problems of overseas Japanese children; to learn about conditions abroad from overseas Japanese; and to introduce conditions in Japan to overseas Japanese and through them to publicize those conditions abroad.[48]

Two factors gave the conference an ultranationalistic character. First, it was convened in conjunction with the observance of the so-called birth of Japan. The first emperor, Jimmu, according to Shinto ideologues, ascended the imperial throne in 660 BC, an event they used to date the genesis not only of the imperial line but the Japanese nation as well. The year 1940 was the twenty-sixth centennial of that mythical event in antiquity, so Shinto nationalism permeated the conference. Second, political chauvinism characterized the proceedings. Less than two months prior to the conference, Japan had entered the Tripartite Pact by which Germany and Italy recognized Japan's right to establish a new order in Asia. That order, as it was formulated by Japan, was embodied in the concept of a Greater East Asia Co-Prosperity Sphere under which Japan was destined to rule Asia. Political slogans and speakers at the conference heralded the coming new order and Japanese expansionism abroad.

The conference opened with a grand procession. The fifteen hundred official delegates marched to the first assembly site located in Hibiya Park. As the oldest delegate, Tsukamoto occupied a place of honor at the head of the procession. Behind him came Minami Kunitarō, another elderly Issei who hailed from Oakland, California. Every delegation marched behind these two men in an order that corresponded to the historical sequence of emigration from Japan. The American (Hawaii included) and Canadian contingents led the procession because Japanese immigrants had first immigrated to North America in the nineteenth century. The Issei delegates from North America were honored in this way as the forerunners of all those who later immigrated abroad, including the Japanese who went to colonize Manchuria in the 1930s. As such they were considered, symbolically speaking, the harbingers of Japanese expansionism onto the Asian continent.

The conference featured sundry activities. Each delegation presented reports on the Japanese settlements in its country or territory. Government speakers delivered lectures on the political, economic, and social conditions in Japan and the state of military affairs in the Sino-Japanese War. Delegates engaged in roundtable discussions, inspected military installations, and enjoyed nightly social functions. The few Nisei who were in attendance participated in an open forum held for their benefit. Simultaneously, the Takashimaya Department Store hosted an exhibition of photographs and materials depicting the life of overseas Japanese. Among the display of printed matter were Japanese-language newspapers, magazines, and books published abroad and even essays written in Japanese by Nisei youngsters. The opening addresses, delivered by no less than Foreign Minister Matsuoka Yōsuke and other high government officials, were aired live over NHK Radio.

Concurrent with all of these activities in Japan, most Japanese communities in the United States held special commemorative programs. In Southern California the Japanese Association of Los Angeles sponsored a day-long affair of political and cultural events, featuring Shinto rites in observance of the twenty-six hundredth anniversary of the so-called birth of Japan.[49] Japanese-language school teachers taught Nisei pupils to write nationalistic essays in commemoration of the twenty-six hundredth anniversary.[50] In conjunction with the Tokyo conference, the *Heimushakai* contributed nearly fifteen thousand dollars for the erection of an ablution station within the Yasukuni Shrine, the national Shinto shrine in Tokyo dedicated to Japanese soldiers killed in action since the first Sino-Japanese War of 1894–95.[51]

The Japanese government granted awards to each delegate from North America and to a few other Issei who did not attend the conference. Three men received highly coveted medals. Everyone else received written commendations. These awards were presented by Foreign Minister Matsuoka

Yōsuke, who had negotiated the Tripartite Pact. His presence at the conference had special meaning for the Issei in the United States. Matsuoka was
not just another high government official to them. Quite the contrary, he
was a man with whom the Issei identified in a personal way. Matsuoka lived
in America from 1893 to 1902.[52] As a young lad of thirteen years old he had
come to this country to obtain an education. He started his studies in
Portland, Oregon, subsequently attended high school in Oakland, and eventually graduated from the University of Oregon in 1901. He always worked
to support himself, often at menial jobs as a domestic servant and restaurant
worker.

In 1902 Matsuoka returned to Japan and launched his career with the
Foreign Ministry. In 1933 he attracted global attention as the Japanese
ambassador to the League of Nations when he withdrew Japan from that
international body to protest its policy of nonrecognition of the puppet state
of Manchukuo. En route back to Tokyo from Geneva, Matsuoka stopped
over in San Francisco and Portland and renewed his ties to the Issei.[53] The
Issei in general felt an affinity to Matsuoka because of his background in
early immigrant society. They identified him as a person who had shared
their American experience, with all its attendant hardships, and who had
risen from their own midst to the lofty position of foreign minister. This personal identification added extra significance to Matsuoka's presentation of
the awards, heightening the Issei recipients' sense of deep gratitude for the
high honor accorded to them.

The awards themselves had a symbolic meaning. The term *kimin* appears
in the writings of the Issei. Meaning an abandoned people, this term tersely
expresses the Issei feeling of having been rejected by their homeland. It refers
specifically to the failure of the Japanese government to come to their aid in
times of need. During the anti-Japanese exclusion movement, Japanese
diplomats usually sacrificed the immigrants' welfare for the sake of what they
perceived as diplomatic necessity. Prejudiced by class and bureaucratic bias,
many officials and prominent persons in Japan indeed looked down with
arrogant contempt on their uprooted countrymen as an uneducated lot and
blamed them for the hostility of white Americans. Such people believed that
the Issei, by their own ignorant misconduct in America, had aroused the
exclusion movement. The 1940 conference symbolized a reversal of attitude
toward the Issei, at least as it was interpreted by them. By convening the conference, the Japanese government had finally extended its hand of recogni-

tion to all overseas Japanese; and by bestowing awards on the delegates from North America, it had acknowledged the specific contributions the Japanese immigrants in the United States and Canada had made ever since the nineteenth century. In sum, Issei patriotism reached its peak at this first conference of overseas Japanese just a short year before that fateful Sunday morning of December 7, 1941.

Conclusion

Issei nationalism had many grave consequences. First, it was behind the so-called preevacuation roundup of Issei leaders on December 7, 1941, and after. During the 1930s, American intelligence agencies kept close surveillance over the Japanese immigrant community but in an uncoordinated manner. This changed in the summer of 1939, when President Franklin D. Roosevelt ordered army and navy intelligence to coordinate surveillance activities under the direction of FBI chief J. Edgar Hoover.[54] American intelligence agencies classified almost every single Issei leader who engaged in patriotic activities as a "dangerous enemy alien," and the FBI arrested and detained these leaders on Pearl Harbor Day or shortly after. Second, Issei nationalism drove a deep wedge between the Issei generation and the leaders of the JACL. From 1939 the FBI and army and naval intelligence agents began to approach JACL officers about Issei leaders who were suspected of being disloyal. Some JACL leaders looked askance at the Issei's nationalistic identification with Japan. In the words of Togo Tanaka, unofficial historian of the JACL, "out of the habit of defining loyalty, talking about loyalty, interpreting it for both the Japanese and Caucasian communities, a segment of J.A.C.L. leadership in 1939 and 1940 began to arrogate to itself the authority to judge and evaluate the loyalty of members of the Japanese community." Asked to cooperate in "guarding against sabotage and espionage" by federal agents, "the J.A.C.L. representatives for the most part . . . responded with a patriotic zeal exceeded only by their public expressions of American loyalty. From the standpoint . . . within the Japanese community," according to Tanaka, such JACL leaders were perceived as "spies and stooges for the F.B.I."[55] Issei nationalism also drove a wedge between the Issei generation and the handful of Japanese American leftists and progressives who unequivocally condemned Japanese military aggression in Asia. In short, Issei nationalism of the 1930s formed a crucial but heretofore neglected background to the wartime internment of Japanese Americans.

In one sense Issei patriotism was not at all out of the ordinary. It did not entail fifth column activities to subvert the sociopolitical fabric of American society nor espionage or sabotage on behalf of the Japanese government. The Issei had rallied behind Japan in three previous wars: the first Sino-Japanese War of 1894–95, the Russo-Japanese War of 1904–5, and the First World War. In all three conflicts they gave the same kind of moral, financial, and material backing to the homeland as they did after the Marco Polo Bridge Incident. The difference was only a matter of degree. Every immigrant group in America, whether of Asian or European origin, has rendered patriotic assistance to its native land in times of crisis. In the twentieth century, Chinese immigrant aid to Sun Yat-sen played an important role in the toppling of the Ch'ing dynasty and the establishment of the Republic of China. Korean immigrants engaged in nationalistic activities to promote an independent Korea free from Japanese colonial domination. Irish, Polish, and Jewish immigrants actively sought the establishment of independent homelands, too. During the First World War, German immigrants supported their mother country, while Greek immigrants joined their compatriots in struggle against Turkish Ottoman rule. In patriotically identifying with Japan, the Japanese were no different from these other immigrant groups.

In another sense, however, Issei patriotism had a unique basis in the Japanese immigrant experience in America.[56] The Issei were so-called aliens ineligible to citizenship. Denied the right of naturalization, they were unable to participate in the American political process. Numerous legal and social barriers, moreover, confined them to narrow niches within society. Economically, the Issei were limited to certain occupations; socially, they were residentially segregated and barred from many public and private facilities. The anti-Japanese exclusion movement climaxed with the passage of the 1924 Immigration Act, which terminated all Japanese immigration. From the Issei point of view the enactment of the 1924 Immigration Act, based on the assumption of racial inferiority and hence undesirability of the Japanese, signified that America had rejected them on racial grounds.

The Issei experience in America left a legacy of disillusionment and bitter resentment. After July 1, 1924, the effective date of the 1924 Immigration Act, the Issei no longer saw any future for themselves in this country. Their only conceivable future was that of their American-born children, who were American citizens. Japan entered the world political arena in the aftermath of the Manchurian Incident in 1931. During the ensuing decade the Issei progressively identified with the political fortunes of Japan in the Far East, culminating in their patriotic support of the homeland during the Sino-Japanese War. Underlying that process was the preceding American rejection of the Issei. The Issei had never been a part of the American body politic and knew that they never could be. As political pariahs they had nothing here with which to politically identify, a void that necessarily strengthened their patriotic identification with their homeland. The majority of Issei did not believe, or refused to believe, in the possibility of war between Japan and the United States, at least until the freezing of all Japanese assets in the summer of 1941. Hence their patriotic support of Japan, in their own minds, never contradicted their residency in this country. Anti-Japanese agitators often ascribed sinister motives and aims to Issei patriotic activities. American intelligence agents often equated the activities wrongfully with subversion, sabotage, and espionage. Victims of racial oppression can repudiate their oppressors in different ways. Patriotic identification with Japan was a way by which the Issei psychologically turned away from the America that had rejected them.

Notes

1. Two studies examine aspects of Issei nationalism: Brian Masaru Hayashi, *"For the Sake of Our Japanese Brethren": Assimilation, Nationalism, and Protestantism Among the Japanese of Los Angeles, 1895–1942* (Stanford, CA: Stanford University Press, 1995), with reference to Issei Christians in Southern California; and, Stephan, *Hawaii Under the Rising Sun*, which examines Issei in Hawaii. A few studies examine the Nisei reaction to the Sino-Japanese conflict. For example, see La Violette, "American-Born Japanese"; La Violette, *Americans of Japanese Ancestry*, 143–47; and O'Brien, "Reaction of the College Nisei." John Modell, *The Economics and Politics of Racial Accommodation: The Japanese of Los Angeles, 1900–1942* (Urbana: University of Illinois Press, 1977), 175–76, briefly treats the same topic. Most historical writings on the 1930s concentrate on the Japanese American Citizens League (JACL), the principal organization of the Nisei generation. In-house accounts of the JACL are most numerous: Hosokawa, *Nisei*, 190–219; Hosokawa, *JACL*, 33–108; and Masaoka, *They Call Me Moses Masaoka*, 37–54. A few studies look at the JACL critically: Daniels, "The Japanese"; and Ichioka, "A Study in Dualism." Kumamoto, "The Search for Spies," examines the American

government surveillance of the Japanese community. Takahashi, "Japanese American Responses," analyzes various Nisei prewar responses to racial subordination. Valerie Matsumoto's two essays "Desperately Seeking 'Deirdre'" and "Redefining Expectations" examine Nisei women in the 1930s.

2. For the early background to the Japanese associations see Yuji Ichioka, "Japanese Associations and the Japanese Government: A Special Relationship, 1909–1926," *Pacific Historical Review* 46 (1977): 409–37.

3. Gaimushō Jōhōbu, "Shōwa Jūninen Shitsumu Hōkoku," Dec. 1937, 105–23. Unless otherwise noted, all Japanese Foreign Ministry documents used in this study are deposited at the Diplomatic Records Office (DRO), Tokyo, Japan.

4. Satō Yuki to Arita Hachirō, June 15, 1939, DRO.

5. Kawashimo Nihonjinkai, "Kiroku," v. 7, Japanese American Research Project Collection, Department of Special Collections, University Research Library, UCLA (hereafter JARP). This source contains the records of the Walnut Grove Japanese Association.

6. Satō to Arita (see note 4).

7. Takoma Shūhōsha, *Takoma-shi Oyobi Chihō Nihonjinshi* (Tacoma, WA: Takoma Shūhōsha: 1941), 115–17.

8. Yusa Keizō, *Hanboku Zenshū* (Santa Maria, CA: Yusa Keizō, 1940), 10. *Hanboku* was the pen name of Yusa Keizō.

9. *Nichibei Shimbun*, July 9, 1938.

10. Fujioka Shirō, *Beikoku Chūō Nihonjinkaishi* (Los Angeles: Beikoku Chūō Nihonjinkai, 1940), 332–33.

11. Yusa, *Hanboku Zenshū*, 26–29.

12. *Rafu Shimpō*, April 4, 1938.

13. Ōta Ichirō to Ugaki Kazushige, July 10, 1938, DRO.

14. Ibid.

15. Shiozaki Kanzō to Ugaki, July 14, 1938, DRO.

16. Ōta Ichirō to Ugaki Kazushige, Aug. 6, 1938, DRO.

17. *Nichibei Shimbun*, Aug. 11, 1938.

18. *Nichibei Shimbun*, Aug. 18, 1938. For other critical comments see *Nichibei Shimbun*, Aug. 19–20, 23–25, 30, 1938; *Kashū Mainichi*, Aug. 19–20, 1938; *Ōfu Nippō*, Aug. 19, 1938; and *Kakushū Jiji*, Aug. 20, 1938.

19. *Kashū Mainichi*, Aug. 22, 1938.

20. Editorials, *Kashū Mainichi*, July 31, Aug. 24, 1937.

21. Editorials, *Kashū Mainichi*, Aug. 22–Sep. 29, 1938. Fujii's five-week editorial tirade was titled *Ōta Ryōji no Hansei wo Unagasu*. For two uncritical biographies of Fujii Sei see Satō Kenichi, *Rafu Gigyū Ondo* (Tokyo: Zenponsha, 1983); and Ōno Kaoru, *Rafu ni Taoru* (Tokyo: Ushio Shuppansha, 1984). For a more critical study see Sakata Yasuo, "'*Kashū Mainichi Shimbun*' to Fujii Sei no

Shūhen," in *Seigi wa Ware ni Ari*, ed. Tamura Norio (Tokyo: Shakai Hyōronsha, 1995), 121–43.

22. *Rafu Shimpō*, Jan. 1, 1938, Jan. 1, 1939, and Jan. 1, 1940.

23. Yusa, *Hanboku Zenshū*, 38–40.

24. Momii Ikken, *Hokubei Kendō Taikan* (San Francisco: Hokubei Butokukai, 1939), 635–40.

25. *Rafu Shimpō*, Jan. 16, 1938.

26. Gaimushō Jōhōbu, "Shōwa Jūichinen Shitsumu Hōkoku," Dec. 1936, 20–28, DRO. See also Tomiko Kakegawa, "The Press and Public Opinion in Japan, 1931–1941," in *Pearl Harbor as History*, ed. Dorothy Borg and Shumpei Okamoto (New York: Columbia University Press, 1973), 533–49.

27. Murayama's articles appeared in the *Shin Sekai Asahi* during the months of September, October, and November 1937.

28. Ebina's column was titled *Nozoki Megane* under his byline, Shunjūrō.

29. Suzuki Kamenosuke, *Jihen to Zaibei Dōhō* (Tokyo: Shinsekai Asahi Shimbunsha Tokyo Shisha, 1938).

30. Uno's initial reportage was in the form of a personal narrative, which he wrote after his first tour of the battlefront. It appeared in the *Shin Sekai Asahi* from December 26, 1937, to July 14, 1938. His dispatches during his second tour appeared in the *Nichibei Shimbun* from August 16, 1938, to December 28, 1938. In 1939 he also wrote a series, *Let's Face Facts*, which appeared in the *Nichibei Shimbun* and *Rafu Shimpō*. It was published in the former from January 12 to June 5, 1939.

31. Yamashita Sōen, *Nichibei wo Tsunagu Mono* (Tokyo: Bunseisha, 1938), 138.

32. Azumi Suimei, "Shinshun wo Mukaeru Kokoro," *Nippon to Amerika*, Jan. 1938, 14–16.

33. *Nichibei Shimbun*, Dec. 10, 1937. The prizewinning essays were published by both newspapers in March and April 1938.

34. Fujii Sei purposely used his unedited "Japanesy" English in the belief that it would appeal to Nisei youngsters.

35. Shōyōsei, "Toki no Kage," *Shin Sekai Asahi*, Jan. 27, 1938. *Shōyō* was the pen name of Abe Toyoji.

36. Gaimushō Jōhōbu, "Shōwa Jūninen Shitsumu Hōkoku," Dec. 1937, 66–77, DRO. While on his speaking tour, Shishimoto contributed to the *Nichibei Shimbun*. See Shishimoto Hachirō, "Shina Jihen ni Tsuite Beikokujin ni Uttau," *Nichibei Shimbun*, Jan. 26–Feb. 5, 1938; and "Zenbei Kōen Angya wo Oe," *Nichibei Shimbun*, Apr. 30–May 5, 1938. Shishimoto also published a book about his American tour. See Shishimoto Hachirō, *Amerika Ijō Ari* (Tokyo: Seinen shobō, 1938). Issei readers were familiar with three previous books he had authored: *Kore Demo Beikoku Ka* (Tokyo: Shinkōsha, 1932), in which he recounted the key events in the anti-Japanese exclusion movement; *Nichibei wa Dōnaru Ka*

(Tokyo: Jitsugyōno Nihonsha, 1936), in which he examined future prospects in Japanese-American relations, including possible revisions in the 1924 Immigration Act; and *Nikkei Shimin wo Kataru* (Tokyo: Shōkasha, 1936), in which he presented the problems of the Nisei generation, among whom he included his own son, Ichirō.

37. Henry Toshirō Shimanouchi, interview, Tape no. 67, JARP.

38. His father was Shimanouchi Yoshinobu. He was the managing editor of the Los Angeles edition of the *Nichibei Shimbun* published from 1922 to 1931.

39. *Kashū Mainichi*, March 19, 1938. See also *Rafu Shimpō*, March 19, 1938.

40. Miya S. Kikuchi to Robert A. Wilson, Jan. 13, 1968, in Kikuchi Papers, JARP; Miya Sannomiya, interview, Tapes no. 83 and 84, JARP; and interview by author, June 1, 1980.

41. Nakamura Kaju, "Shita no Angya wo Owatte," *Nichibei Shimbun*, May 19–20, 22–26, 1938. See also Nakamura Kaju, *Hokubei Shita no Seisen* (Tokyo: Tamagawa Gakuen Shuppanbu, 1940).

42. For Matsumoto's background see *Shin Sekai Asahi*, Sep. 26, 1937; and Bill Hosokawa, "Disquisitions," *Shin Sekai Asahi*, July 10, 1938.

43. Oka Shigeki, "Arabya Oyae Shusse Monogatari," *Amerika Shimbun*, Feb. 12, 26, March 5, 1938.

44. Yamada Waka, "Taiheiyōjō no Kokumin Shisetsu Dai-Zadankai," *Shufu no Tomo*, Dec. 1937, 264–71; "Beikoku Ware wo Ryōdo Shinryaku to Yobi," *Shufu no Tomo*, Jan. 1938, 210–17; "Beikoku Daitōryō Fujin to Kenkai Suru Ki," *Shufu no Tomo*, Feb. 1938, 84–89. See also *Nichibei Shimbun*, Oct. 30–31, 1938.

45. Tengaisei, "Toki no Mondai," *Nichibei Shimbun*, Oct. 18–19, 1938. *Tengai* was the pen name of Kawashima Isamu.

46. Fukuda Yoshiaki, "Kōgun Imon no Tabi Yori Kaerite," *Nichibei Shimbun*, Feb. 27–March 2, 4–14, 1939.

47. Gaimushō Jōhōbu, "Shōwa Jūichinen Shitsumu Hōkoku," Dec. 1936, 81–87, DRO; and "Shōwa Jūninen Shitsumu Hōkoku," Dec. 1937, 55–65, DRO. See also Kitayama Setsurō, *Rajio Tōkyō* (Tokyo: Tahata Shoten, 1987), 1:108–34.

48. Yamashita Sōen, *Hōshuku Kigen Nisen Roppyakunen to Kaigai Dōhō* (Tokyo: Hōshuku Kigen Nisen Roppyakunen to Kaigai Dōhō Kankōkai, 1941); Nihon Takushoku Kyōkai, *Kōki Nisen Roppyakunen Zaigai Dōhō Daihyō wo Mukaete* (Tokyo: Nihon Takushoku Kyōkai, 1941); Gaimushō Takumushō, *Kigen Nisei Roppyakunen Hōshuku Zaigai Dōhō Daihyōsha Kaigi Gijiroku Dai-Ikkai* (Tokyo: Gaimushō and Takumushō, 1941); and Kaigai Dōhō Chūōkai, *Kigen Nisen Roppyakunen Hōshuku Kaigai Dōhō Tōkyō Taikai Hōkokusho* (Tokyo: Kaigai Dōhō Chūō Kai, 1941).

49. *Rafu Shimpō*, Nov. 10–11, 1940; and *Kashū Mainichi*, Nov. 10–11, 1940.

50. For examples of such essays see Rafu Shimpōsha, *Kigen Nisen Roppyakunen Hōshuku Kinen Taikan* (Los Angeles: Rafu Shimpōsha, 1940), 29–56.

51. Yusa, *Hanboku Zenshū*, 10–20.

52. For Matsuoka's early life in the United States see Miwa Kimitada, *Matsuoka Yōsuke: Sono Hito to Gaikō* (Tokyo: Chūō Kōronsha, 1971), 20–37; and Matsuoka Yōsuke Denki Kankōkai, *Matsuoka Yōsuke: Sono Hito to Shōgai* (Tokyo: Kōdansha, 1974), 31–52.

53. On April 10, 1933, Matsuoka addressed five thousand Issei in San Francisco at a special welcoming rally. The immigrant press interpreted his appearance as the return of a native son. See *Shin Sekai*, April 12–13, 1933.

54. See Kumamoto, "The Search for Spies."

55. Togo Tanaka, "History of J.A.C.L.," n.d., Japanese American Evacuation and Resettlement Study Collection, Bancroft Library, University of California, Berkeley.

56. Yuji Ichioka, *The Issei: The World of the First-Generation Japanese Immigrants, 1885–1924* (New York: Free Press, 1988).

NINE

National Security on the Eve of Pearl Harbor

The 1941 Tachibana Espionage Case and Implicated Issei Leaders

Introduction

Immediately after the attack on Pearl Harbor on December 7, 1941, the U.S. Justice Department issued warrants for the arrest and detention of Japanese immigrants classified as so-called dangerous enemy aliens. One of the unquestioned assumptions of the Japanese American redress movement was that the United States government had no justification, whatsoever, in arresting and detaining such *Issei*. Accordingly, they—like all other Japanese Americans—are judged to have been innocent victims of an American government policy rooted in anti-Japanese racism. Exactly six months before Pearl Harbor, on June 7, 1941, Tachibana Itaru, a Japanese naval lieutenant commander, was arrested by the FBI in Los Angeles, California, and subsequently arraigned on the charge of espionage.[1] The FBI investigation revealed that certain Japanese immigrants had very close connections with him. This chapter examines the Tachibana case and questions the assumption that each and every Issei arrested as a dangerous enemy alien was an innocent victim of anti-Japanese racism. Specifically, it delves into the national security issue raised by the case on the eve of Pearl Harbor and the justification the Justice Department had in arresting and interning those Issei who were implicated with Tachibana.

Tachibana Itaru

A graduate of the Japanese Naval Academy and Naval War College, Lieutenant Commander Tachibana arrived in Los Angeles in February 1940 as a naval language officer ostensibly to study English at the University of Southern California. He had the status of a naval attaché reporting to the head of the Japanese Office of Naval Attachés in Washington, DC. While based in Los Angeles, Tachibana resided at the Olympic Hotel, located at 117 N. San Pedro Street in the heart of Little Tokyo. He had arrived earlier in the United States, in July 1939, and spent his initial time in Philadelphia, where he took classes at the University of Pennsylvania. His arrival in Southern California coincided with the return to Japan of his language officer predecessor stationed in Los Angeles.

Tachibana was arrested by the FBI as a result of a joint ONI and FBI sting operation.[2] Kōno Toraichi, an Issei accomplice, was also arrested. The operation involved an ONI informant by the name of Al Blake, who served as a conduit between Tachibana and Kōno, on the one hand, and a fictitious yeoman in the U.S. Navy, on the other. At the beginning of the operation Blake led Kōno to believe that he had a friend in the U.S. Navy stationed in Honolulu who was willing to supply confidential information. As a former private secretary and chauffeur of Charlie Chaplin, the internationally famous Hollywood actor, Kōno was on familiar terms with many Hollywood actors and actresses, including Blake, an actor-turned-would-be-ONI informant. The ONI and FBI had both Tachibana and Kōno under close surveillance on suspicion of espionage. In order to entrap Tachibana, they cleverly used Blake.

Kōno introduced Blake to Tachibana. When informed of the possibility of securing intelligence information through Blake, Tachibana agreed to pay Blake for any valuable information. Blake promptly informed ONI of Tachibana's offer of money, and ONI decided to retain Blake as an undercover informant. Then, on two separate occasions, Tachibana paid Blake six hundred dollars to go to Honolulu to obtain confidential information. And on one occasion he actually accepted information that had been furnished to Blake in Honolulu by the ONI by design.[3] The FBI investigation disclosed that Tachibana had traveled to Washington, DC, to discuss these matters with the chief of the Japanese Office of Naval Attachés. Indeed, the chief had approved the second payment of six hundred dollars and had given Tachibana the green light to dispatch Blake to Honolulu the second time.[4]

A search of Tachibana's Olympic Hotel room subsequent to his arrest revealed that he had amassed a considerable amount of information pertaining to the U.S. Navy, national defense, and maritime affairs in general. This material consisted of notes, photographs, newspaper clippings, and other printed data of a public nature. It also included documents relating to naval facilities and plans for the defense of Boeing plants in the Pacific Northwest. This latter material had been delivered to Tachibana by Lt. Commander Okada Sadatomo, another Japanese naval language officer who was stationed in Seattle.[5] The arrest of Tachibana and Kōno occurred less than seven weeks before the American government froze all Japanese assets in the United States. Since war clouds already hovered over Japanese-American relations, their arrest resulted in sensational local headlines, arousing public fear across the country of widespread Japanese espionage.[6] Bail was set at fifty thousand dollars for Tachibana and twenty-five thousand dollars for Kōno. Tachibana was released on June 9 once the Japanese government posted his bail after his arraignment, but Kōno had to languish in jail since no one posted bail on his behalf.

Furusawa Takashi and Sachiko

Among all Japanese immigrants, Dr. Furusawa Takashi and his wife, Sachiko, had the closest ties to Tachibana. A native of Okayama Prefecture, Dr. Furusawa (1875–1953) was an old-time Issei who had arrived in the United States in 1901. By profession he was a medical doctor, whose office and residence were located at 117 1/2 Weller Street in Little Tokyo. As a practicing physician and elder in the Okayama Prefectural Association, he was a respected leader within the Japanese immigrant community. His wife, Sachiko (1884–1959), was a native of Ehime Prefecture. She had arrived in the United States in 1908 and had married Dr. Furusawa in 1913. Like her husband, she was a very prominent person in the Japanese community as president of the Southern California Women's Federation and vice president of the Los Angeles branch of the *Aikoku Fujinkai*, a patriotic women's group. In the former capacity she served as the chief hostess for periodic receptions given in honor of the officers and crew of Japanese naval vessels and training

Figure 8. Dr. Furusawa Takashi and wife Sachiko, 1920s.
Yuji Ichioka Papers.

squadrons whenever they visited Los Angeles. Indeed, because of her unceasing devotion to the Japanese navy throughout the 1920s and 1930s, she earned the nickname of "Mother of the Japanese Navy." As a result, Mrs. Furusawa was often addressed by this honorific appellation, which bestowed high social status on her within the Japanese community.[7]

Dr. Furusawa and his wife were founders of the Los Angeles branch of the Japanese Navy Association.[8] Headquartered in Tokyo, the Japanese Navy Association was a quasi-civilian organization dedicated to the strengthening of the Japanese navy and Japan as a maritime power. The association maintained branches throughout Japan and in parts of her colonial possessions.

Figure 9. Mrs. Furusawa (front row, fourth from right) and members of the Southern California Women's Federation, 1940. Yuji Ichioka Papers.

Using their own home address, the Furusawas opened a temporary office on November 3, 1938.[9] As an initial step toward the recruitment of members, this office published and distributed a prospectus explaining the purpose of the Japanese Navy Association.[10] By early 1939 the Furusawas had recruited sixty members, and in the following year they changed the office to the Los Angeles branch of the Japanese Navy Association with the official blessing of Tokyo. And in keeping with the goal of strengthening the Japanese navy, the Los Angeles branch had a research section devoted to the study of domestic and foreign navies and all other matters relating to maritime affairs. Regular members paid dues of twenty-five dollars; supporting members paid dues of fifty dollars. All members were entitled to wear special membership badges and to receive copies of *Umi no Nippon*, the official organ of the Japanese Navy Association. In addition they were granted the privilege of inspecting Japanese naval vessels whenever they docked in Los Angeles harbor.[11]

Imonshi

Mrs. Furusawa had been encouraged by high Japanese navy officials to form a branch of the Japanese Navy Association in Los Angeles. In the spring of 1938 she visited Japan as a so-called *imonshi*, or special emissary, representing women's societies of Southern California to console Japanese military personnel who had been wounded in the Sino-Japanese War. Accompanying her were three other women: Murase Akiko, an Issei and president of the Kōyasan Women's Society, and Mitsuyo Kuriki and Teruko Kiyomura, two young *Nisei* girls.[12] As soon as their party landed in Yokohama on April 1, Mrs. Furusawa and her group were met by Japanese navy officials who escorted them to Tokyo in a limousine provided by the Navy Ministry so that they could first pay respects to Admiral Yonai Mitsumasa, the navy minister. On April 7 Admiral Yonai held a formal reception in their honor at his official residence. To welcome Mrs. Furusawa and her group, he invited officers who had visited Los Angeles and who remembered the warm welcome they had received by Japanese immigrants with Mrs. Furusawa acting as the official hostess. For Admiral Yonai to hold such a reception for four women was unprecedented. All of the Tokyo dailies carried noteworthy accounts of their arrival and initial reception by Admiral Yonai, and in so doing they invariably referred to Mrs. Furusawa as the "Mother of the Japanese Navy Abroad." The *Kokumin Shimbun* even featured her in a column devoted to people in the spotlight.[13]

Mrs. Furusawa and her group toured military hospitals throughout Japan and China. From Tokyo they successively visited Shizuoka, Nagoya, Kyoto, Osaka, Kobe, Okayama, Hiroshima, Fukuoka, Kumamoto, and Sasebo. At each stop along the way they called at local military hospitals to console the sick and wounded, and local newspapers invariably carried patriotic accounts of their visits to such hospitals.[14] At a Japanese military airbase in Fukuoka City, they boarded a specially provided naval aircraft that flew them to Shanghai and Nanking and back, enabling them to visit field hospitals there. During their almost two-month-long tour of Japan and China, Mrs. Furusawa was impressed deeply with the branches of the Japanese Navy Association at the local level. Consequently, she expressed an interest in forming a branch in the United States to Vice Admiral Iida Hisatsune, vice president of the Japanese Navy Association. Before Mrs. Furusawa left Japan, Admiral Iida encouraged her to do so, and to expedite the formation of a North American branch, he presented her with a special work of calligraphy signed by eight high-ranking admirals, including Admiral Yonai, inscribed with the slogan "loyalty and filial piety [chūko]."[15] Admiral Iida also supplied her with navy badges to be handed out to new members of the Japanese Navy Association. In sum, the origins of the Los Angeles branch

Figure 10. *Imonshi*, special emissaries to Japan, including Furusawa Sachiko (second from left), Murase Akiko, Mitsuyo Kuriki, and Teruko Kiyomura, 1938. Yuji Ichioka Papers.

can be traced back directly to Mrs. Furusawa's 1938 trip to Japan and the close relationships she established with high-level Japanese navy officials.

Mrs. Furusawa's successful tour of Japan and China gave her immense prestige within the Japanese community and had the effect of generating considerable patriotic feeling and pride among Japanese immigrants, especially among Issei women. Mrs. Furusawa returned safely to Los Angeles on July 31. A welcoming party of local community members met her at the San Pedro pier.[16] Members of the local community were well aware of her reception and activities in Japan as a result of the extensive press coverage given to her. For example, Mutō Shōgo, the Tokyo correspondent of the *Rafu Shimpō*, acclaimed the "unprecedented reception" accorded to her by Admiral Yonai and reported laudably on her tour of Japan and China.[17] One article carried an impressive photograph of Admiral Yonai presenting Japanese dolls as his personal present to Mrs. Furusawa and her group. The *Rafu Shimpō* even serialized Mrs. Furusawa's personal account of her successful trip.[18] On August 17,

Figure 11. *Imonshi* at the Japanese Navy Ministry; Furusawa Sachiko (fourth from left) is sitting next to Admiral Yonai Mitsumasa, the navy minister. Yuji Ichioka Papers.

under the sponsorship of various women's societies and other organizations, Mrs. Furusawa presented a report on her trip before a jam-packed audience at a patriotic meeting held at the Yamato Hall in Little Tokyo. The program of formal speeches was interspersed with patriotic songs and dances, with the back of the stage draped with the imposing flags of the Japanese navy and the Rising Sun.[19] Subsequently, Mrs. Furusawa went on a speaking tour of the outlying rural Japanese communities of Southern California, spreading her message about the great sacrifices being made by Japanese soldiers and sailors and the formidable strength of the Japanese navy.

Los Angeles Branch

According to an FBI report on the Los Angeles branch of the Japanese Navy Association, the branch had a total membership of 217 persons as of August

1941.[20] This membership included many well-known Issei leaders throughout Southern California. Publicly, in both 1939 and 1940, the Los Angeles branch celebrated Japanese Navy Day on May 27, a date coinciding with the Japanese naval defeat of the Russian fleet during the 1904–5 Russo-Japanese War.[21] The 1940 celebration was especially auspicious because it took place aboard the *Erimo*, a special duty vessel visiting San Pedro at the time. Five hundred Issei attended this commemorative event, which climaxed with boisterous toasts of "Banzai" to the Japanese navy. Privately, over and beyond membership dues, the Los Angeles branch solicited special donations to the Tokyo headquarters of the Japanese Navy Association. Issei were exhorted to contribute the equivalent of one thousand yen, a not-inconsiderable sum of money. The *Umi no Nippon* published the names of such donors, giving them the coveted recognition of the Tokyo headquarters and high status in the eyes of the general public. One of the first to do so was Tanaka Kakuo, a close friend of Dr. Furusawa from Okayama Prefecture. Minami Yaemon and Aratani Setsuo of Guadalupe and Hasuike Susumu of Los Angeles followed suit and donated one thousand yen in early 1939. All of these donors received special awards granted to them by the Japanese Navy Association for their generous donations. According to Dr. Furusawa, the Los Angeles branch forwarded a total of twenty-five thousand dollars in donations to Tokyo.

That Dr. Furusawa Takashi and Sachiko had close ties to the Japanese navy goes without saying. All of the material seized by the FBI in Tachibana's hotel room provided irrefutable evidence of this fact. The membership roster and ledgers of the Los Angeles branch of the Japanese Navy Association, a file of letters exchanged between Wada Jun, the Tokyo executive director of the Japanese Navy Association, and Dr. Furusawa, and the incoming miscellaneous correspondence file of Dr. and Mrs. Furusawa were among the seized material. Of the letters exchanged between Wada and Dr. Furusawa, many related directly to matters concerning the establishment of the initial Los Angeles office and eventual branch of the Japanese Navy Association. Some were in connection with the earlier formation of the Sakura Kai, a group that preceded the Los Angeles branch of the Japanese Navy Association. The Sakura Kai was a "social club" of prominent Issei leaders, formed in August 1938 around Commander Nagasawa Hiroshi, the then Japanese naval language officer stationed in Los Angeles. Besides Dr. and Mrs. Furusawa, prominent Issei leaders such as Nakamura Gongorō, Kumamoto Shunten, Amano Ajika, and Aratani Setsuo were members. In

Figure 12. Furusawa Takashi and Sachiko, late 1940s. Yuji
Ichioka Papers.

January 1939 Wada instructed Dr. Furusawa that, in all matters relating to
the Japanese navy, he should first consult with Commander Nagasawa,
clearly indicating that Dr. Furusawa already had close ties with one of
Tachibana's predecessors. As of November 1938 the Sakura Kai had fifteen
members led by Dr. and Mrs. Furusawa. Within the Sakura Kai there was a
research committee with Dr. and Mrs. Furusawa, again, playing the leading
role. Last, the couple were also leaders in the Suikō Sha, a fraternal organization of Japanese naval reserve officers.[22]

An ONI report on Japanese intelligence and propaganda activities in 1941
summarized the connection between these various organizations with
Tachibana in the following way:

Prominent among the organizations which were apparently furnishing information to the Japanese Government through Tachibana were the NIPPON KAIGUN KYOKAI (Japanese Navy Association), the SAKURA KAI (Cherry Association) and the SUIKO SHA (Reserve Officers Club).

The many ramifications of Tachibana's activities were disclosed by translating into English numerous Japanese papers, documents, and reports which were seized by the F.B.I. at the time of his arrest at the Olympic Hotel in Los Angeles.

Part of the material seized consisted of the records of the North American branch of the JAPANESE NAVY ASSOCIATION (Nippon Kaigun Kyokai). With headquarters in Tokyo, this organization has as its chief objectives the dissemination of information about navies of other countries and the development of Japanese Naval strength. To this end, it has established investigating agencies to study domestic and foreign navies, maritime transportation and other maritime matters. Investigation disclosed that members of the Japanese Navy Association had been working in collaboration with rank officers of the Imperial Japanese Navy stationed in Los Angeles, and it appears that Tachibana, who was collecting intelligence for the benefit of the Japanese navy, was assisted by the investigating branch of that association.

Among Tachibana's effects was found considerable correspondence from Dr. Takishi [*sic*] Furusawa, director of the Los Angeles Suiko Sha, which is an organization composed of officers and reserve officers of the Imperial Japanese Navy. He and his wife, Mrs. Sachiko Furusawa, appear to be the directive force behind this organization. Both of them are exceedingly prominent in Japanese community affairs.

The names of Dr. Kijima [*sic*] Amano, secretary of the Sakura Kai, Shunten Kumamoto, president of the Los Angeles Japanese Association[,] and Gongoro Nakamura, president of the Central Japanese Association of California, also appear among Tachibana's papers and it is interesting to note that all of them, including the Furusawas, are on the research committee of the Sakura Kai.[23]

This ONI report did not assert flatly that the Japanese Navy Association, Sakura Kai, and Suikō Sha supplied information to Tachibana. In more tentative language it said instead that these three organizations "apparently furnished information to the Japanese government through Tachibana." The qualifying adverb *apparently* was inserted, in all probability, because no evidence of a conclusive nature had turned up pinpointing specific Issei members of these groups as the actual sources of the material seized in Tachibana's hotel room.

The close connection between Tachibana and Dr. and Mrs. Furusawa is confirmed by a non-FBI source. A *Kibei-Nisei*, Nobuo Tsuboi was a live-in student in the Furusawa home prior to the Second World War. Dr. Furusawa knew his parents because they had originated from Okayama Prefecture, so he had accepted Tsuboi as a live-in student on his return from Japan in 1938. According to Tsuboi, Tachibana was a constant visitor in the Furusawa home, so much so that Tachibana, as Tsuboi remembered him, felt free to drop in unannounced at any time. Indeed, the Olympic Hotel where Tachibana resided was but two short blocks from Weller Street, where Dr. Furusawa maintained his office and residence. Moreover, Tsuboi recalls delivering many things to Tachibana at the request of Dr. Furusawa on numerous occasions, including the membership roster of the Los Angeles branch of the Japanese Navy Association.[24]

Impact of the Tachibana Case

The Tachibana case had a tremendous impact on American intelligence agencies, the Japanese immigrant community, and Japanese-American relations. It convinced the intelligence community that Japan was engaged in widespread espionage requiring more vigilance and more effective counterintelligence measures and raised legitimate concern about the overall national security of the United States. As a direct result of the Tachibana case, in July 1941 the ONI in the Fourteenth Naval District in Honolulu began a serious effort to recruit undercover agents among the Nisei in order to improve its surveillance of the Japanese immigrant community.[25] Lt. Commander Kenneth Ringle of the Eleventh Naval District of Southern California had already adopted this policy, reporting that "many . . . Nisei voluntarily contributed valuable anti-subversive information."[26] A November 1941 FBI memorandum on "Japanese Espionage," in highlighting the Tachibana case, noted the dangers posed specifically by Japanese naval language officers. It said that such

language officers, men in this country for the obvious purpose of studying English but who are known from past experience to have engaged in espionage, come under the direct supervision of the Naval Attache. It has been stated that previous to being ordered to the United States for language duty, these officers are assigned to temporary duty with the Japanese Naval Intelligence for a period of approximately four months. Upon their arrival in this country, they report immediately to the Naval Attache and are assigned to temporary duty in Washington, D.C., for a brief time after which they arrange for a technical course at one of the universities or are sent to the West Coast. Those who attend school travel extensively during the summer throughout the United States and Canada. It is also noted that these officers are generally stationed in cities like Seattle, Los Angeles, San Francisco, Washington, Philadelphia and Boston where their observations would be most productive.[27]

The FBI had had Dr. and Mrs. Furusawa under surveillance since September 1939. Immediately after the arrest of Tachibana Itaru, the FBI conducted further investigations of Dr. and Mrs. Furusawa and their affiliated organizations, resulting in a comprehensive report by Agent A. P. LeGrand dated July 9, 1941. The FBI followed up this report with another one, dated August 26, 1941, by Agent F. H. Holmes, on the background of all 217 members of the Los Angeles branch of the Japanese Navy Association. And on October 8, 1941, two months before Pearl Harbor Day, the FBI conducted a search of the Furusawa home based on a written voluntary consent by Dr. Furusawa.

The Tachibana case sent tremors of fear through the Japanese community. Before the Second World War the Nisei were never recognized as genuine Americans by American society. In efforts to solve this fundamental problem, they endeavored to convince the general public, by frequent public declarations, that they were, like all other Americans, equally loyal and patriotic to the United States. The arrest of Tachibana and Kōno, however, cast grave doubts on such declarations, causing an acute sense of crisis, bordering on panic, among the Nisei. In breaking the news of the Tachibana case, the *Rafu Shimpō* said that a "nightmare" had "descended over [the] Los Angeles Japanese population . . . with the disclosure of [the] alleged espionage" case.[28] "Irreparable damage" had been done to the "reputation" of the Issei and Nisei "as loyal and law-abiding" people.[29]

A month before the Tachibana case, on May 10, the Los Angeles chapter of the Japanese American Citizens League had sponsored "a patriotic rally" at the American Legion Hall in Hollywood. The purpose of the rally was to affirm the loyalty of Japanese Americans before the American public. Togo

Tanaka, English editor of the *Rafu Shimpō*, was the key Nisei speaker. His speech was titled "United We Stand." In it he declared that Japanese Americans "have all been given an American and democratic privilege to set an example for faithful, enduring, and courageous loyalty to our country—THE UNITED STATES OF AMERICA."[30] Other speakers included Deputy Mayor Frank Petersen, Dr. John R. Lechner, County Supervisor John Anson Ford, American Legion County Commander Irving R. Snyder, and Nakamura Gongorō.

In his weekly *Rafu Shimpō* column Tad Uyeno voiced his sense of deep alarm. "The impression that Americans now have . . . is that there are spies among our midst," he wrote, "and no matter how much we have denied" it, "facts alone [now] stand out glaringly that spies are on the loose."[31] In the previous week Uyeno had summarily dismissed an article alleging Japanese espionage activities that appeared in a sensational local magazine. But he now feared, even though Tachibana and Kōno were Japanese nationals, that Americans would identify all Japanese Americans with the two men. In his opinion the Tachibana case negated much or all of the public relations efforts exerted to convince the general public of the loyalty of Japanese Americans.

Community organizations quickly issued declarations of loyalty. Organized by the Japanese American Citizens League, the Coordinating Committee of the Citizens League for Southern California Defense declared that "loyalty and patriotism to America by the resident Japanese face a test in these headline-breaking incidents. Every loyal American knows his duty. The issei and nisei here must be no different."[32] Thus it alerted loyal Japanese Americans to be on guard against disloyal elements within their own midst and ferret them out immediately. Mutō Kichitarō, vice president of the Central Japanese Association, the main political organization of the Issei generation, affirmed the loyalty of the Issei in a special radio broadcast, claiming that his "association is preparing to launch a program under which it may place its facilities and personnel to more effectively cooperate with local and federal authorities to stamp out 'espionage' among the Japanese population here."[33]

The Welfare Committee of the Central Japanese Association issued "a public report," entitled "The American's Creed," to reaffirm the loyalty of the entire Japanese population. A thinly disguised, plagiarized version of the "Japanese American Creed" authored by Mike Masaoka, this creed read:

I believe in the United States of America as a Government of the people, by the people, for the people; whose just powers are derived from the consent of the governed; a democracy in a republic; a sovereign nation, one and inseparable; established upon those principles of freedom, equality, justice and humanity for which American patriots sacrificed their lives and fortunes. I therefore believe it is my duty to my country to love it; to support its Constitution; to obey its laws; to respect its flag; and to defend it against all enemies.[34]

The supreme irony of this reaffirmation of loyalty by the Central Japanese Association was that its president, Nakamura Gongorō, and four of its vice presidents—Mutō Kichitarō, Hashimoto Kazuichi, Sasaki Masami, and Otoi Masanosuke—were all members of the Los Angeles branch of the Japanese Navy Association.

The Tachibana case had an adverse impact on Japanese-American relations as well. Before undertaking to arrest Tachibana, the Justice Department had asked the State Department if it had any objection to his arrest. The State Department replied that it had no objection, provided it was assured that the FBI and ONI were certain of the facts, that conviction could be obtained, and that the apprehension of Tachibana was considered important. A week after his arrest, on June 14, Japanese ambassador Nomura Kichisaburō called on the State Department to lodge a protest and requested that the department intervene on Tachibana's behalf so that he would not be subject to prosecution. The ambassador said he made this special request in order to preserve cordial relations between Japan and the United States.

In the end the State Department acceded to Ambassador Nomura's request.[35] Relations between the United States and Japan had already deteriorated by the time of the arrest of Tachibana. If he were tried in public for espionage, the department anticipated that such a proceeding would have unpredictable, dire consequences and therefore would inevitably worsen tensions in Japanese-American relations. So it reached the conclusion that, for the sake of diplomacy, deportation was the best course of action to take. Consequently, it asked the Justice Department to forgo criminal proceedings against Tachibana. The Justice Department, for its part, reluctantly complied with the State Department's request. The ONI of the Eleventh Naval District in Southern California had initiated the surveillance of Tachibana. Accordingly, Secretary of Navy Frank Knox informed Rear Admiral Charles A. Blakely, commandant of the Eleventh Naval District, of the Justice Department's decision not to prosecute Tachibana, saying that it had been made "on grounds of high policy." He advised him to accept this decision "whole-heartedly" but warned that it must not "diminish the zeal of your intelligence service."[36] Tachibana left San Francisco on June 21 for Japan aboard the *Nitta Maru*.

Unlike Tachibana, Kōno Toraichi was not deported. He had been a long-time Issei resident but not a member of the Los Angeles branch of the Japanese Navy Association. A native of Hiroshima Prefecture, Kōno had arrived in the United States in 1900. From 1916 to 1934 he served as the private secretary and chauffeur to Charlie Chaplin. During this time he lived on the Chaplin estate with his own wife and two children, separate and apart from the Japanese immigrant community. In 1932 he accompanied Chaplin on his tour of Japan. Idolized by Japanese movie fans, Chaplin received a roaring reception in Kobe, where he landed, and later in Tokyo itself. By virtue of his close association with Chaplin, Kōno enjoyed secondary celebrity status in Japan.[37] During the 1930s many prominent Japanese, including Japanese military personnel, called on his home in Hollywood to pay their respects, no doubt hoping to hear firsthand accounts of his life with Chaplin.

Kōno was released from jail on June 25, a few days after Tachibana sailed for Japan.[38] The deportation of Tachibana had forced the Justice Department to alter its legal handling of the case against Kōno. Initially, it fully intended to try him as a co-conspirator. But once the department had agreed to allow Tachibana to leave the country without prosecution, it became no longer feasible to pursue its case against Kōno. For how could Kōno be tried as an accomplice in espionage without the presence of the chief conspirator? Using this identical line of legal logic, the Justice Department decided to forgo criminal prosecution of Dr. and Mrs. Furusawa, too, even after the FBI had completed its comprehensive reports on the couple and the Japanese Navy Association. On December 7, 1941, Pearl Harbor Day, however, the FBI did not hesitate to arrest and intern Kōno and Dr. and Mrs. Furusawa, along with every member of the Los Angeles branch of the Japanese Navy Association, as dangerous enemy aliens.

Conclusion

So the question remains: was the Justice Department justified in arresting and interning Kōno and the Furusawas? The ONI and FBI unquestionably had a legitimate national security interest in pursuing their investigation of

Lieutenant Commander Tachibana Itaru. All military attachés, regardless of nationality, collect information on foreign military forces, but in the case of Tachibana the ONI caught him red-handed in their sting operation paying for information from Blake. The seized material in his hotel room provided incontrovertible proof that he had been collecting information on the American navy, national defense, and other maritime affairs. The ONI and FBI investigation into Dr. and Mrs. Furusawa revealed that they had close ties to Tachibana. Although the investigation could not pinpoint the couple as the source of specific material found in Tachibana's possession, it is safe to assume that they cooperated with him in the collection of information. Kōno served as the intermediary between Blake and Tachibana, so he was an obvious accomplice to Tachibana. In the light of these connections to Tachibana, one cannot but conclude that the Justice Department had sufficient national security reasons to arrest and detain Dr. and Mrs. Furusawa[39] and Kōno Toraichi (but not to deny them due process of law).

It is difficult to reach the same conclusion regarding other Issei who were close to Dr. and Mrs. Furusawa. If we take the example of Nakamura Gongorō, who was also arrested on Pearl Harbor Day, he was not arrested solely on the basis of his membership in the Japanese Navy Association and Sakura Kai. Nakamura was one of the most visible Issei leaders active in numerous community organizations. First and foremost, he was the president of the Central Japanese Association and former president of the Japanese Association of Los Angeles. He was the director of the Japanese Cultural Center and served as an adviser to the Okinawan Overseas Association and to various Buddhist and Shinto religious bodies. Unlike the case of Dr. and Mrs. Furusawa, no FBI report linked Nakamura directly to Tachibana. As with many of the Issei classified as dangerous enemy aliens, Nakamura's arrest and internment were related fundamentally to his leadership role in the Japanese community, plus his membership in the Japanese Navy Association and Sakura Kai.

Less publicly visible members of the Japanese Navy Association joined the organization out of social obligation, for social status, and/or out of patriotic sentiments. Since dues were not cheap, membership was limited to people who were relatively well off. Like Dr. Furusawa, many members were physicians or natives of Okayama Prefecture. Others were businessmen or professionals. And still others were successful in agriculture, like Minami Yaemon and Aratani Setsuo in Guadalupe. But regardless of what their backgrounds were, the majority of these people were personal acquaintances of Dr. and Mrs. Furusawa. They did not join the Japanese Navy Association to engage in espionage activities on behalf of the Japanese government. They joined because of Dr. and Mrs. Furusawa's personal appeal to them to support the Japanese navy and Japan's side in the Sino-Japanese War. In this sense their membership was an expression of their immigrant nationalism in the United States and their patriotic identification with their homeland's cause in China.[40] From today's historical perspective, that membership, in and of itself, cannot and should not be seen as having posed any threat to the internal security of the United States. Consequently, one must conclude that the Justice Department did not have any probable cause in arresting and interning every member of the Japanese Navy Association.[41]

Notes

1. For the most recent scholarly treatment of the case see Pedro Loureiro, "The Imperial Japanese Navy and Espionage: The Itaru Tachibana Case," *International Journal of Intelligence and Counterintelligence* 3, no. 1 (1989): 105–21; and Pedro Loureiro, "Japanese Espionage and American Countermeasures in Pre-Pearl Harbor California," *Journal of American-East Asian Relations* 3, no. 3 (1994): 197–210. See also Kumamoto, "Search for Spies." Kumamoto, in analyzing the reason for the continual surveillance of the Japanese community by U.S. intelligence agencies during the 1930s, presents the dubious thesis that the "federal government" was motivated primarily "by a desire . . . to eliminate Japanese culture from American society" for racial reasons (46). Refusing to acknowledge that the government had legitimate national security reasons right up to Pearl Harbor Day, he implies that all the Issei who were arrested as dangerous enemy aliens by the FBI were innocent victims of racism. Some studies relating to the attack on Pearl Harbor cite the Tachibana case. For example, see Layton, *"And I Was There,"* 106–9; Prange, *At Dawn We Slept*, 149–51; and Prange, *Pearl Harbor*, 108. For a sensational wartime account see Hynd, *Betrayal from the East*.

2. The following summary account of the Tachibana case is pieced together from the Tachibana Itaru files in General Records of the Department of State, Decimal File, 1940–44, 894.20211, Box 5903, Record Group 59, National Archives (hereafter cited as RG 59, NA). These files contain original FBI reports and memoranda exchanged between the Justice Department and State Department relating to the Tachibana case, as well as communications exchanged between the State Department and the Japanese Embassy. The Justice Department submitted copies of FBI reports to the State Department in order to assure the latter that it had sufficient evidence to try and convict Tachibana on espionage charges. Lt.

Commander Kenneth D. Ringle of ONI, Eleventh Naval District of Southern California, played a leading role in the investigation of Tachibana, which included an initial midnight break-in into the offices of the Los Angeles Japanese Consulate. That break-in apparently turned up evidence that Tachibana had handed over intelligence information to the consulate to be forwarded to Tokyo. Unfortunately, I have been unable thus far to locate any of Ringle's ONI reports to confirm this break-in. His son, Ken Ringle, has written about the break-in based on what his mother remembered about it. See Ken Ringle, "What Dad Did Before the War," *Washington Post Magazine*, Dec. 6, 1981, 54–62. Unfortunately, neither Japanese Foreign Ministry nor Japanese Navy Ministry records relating to this case are available.

3. This information dealt with an ONI report on the target practice of a ten-thousand-ton cruiser in the Pacific (J. E. Hoover to Adolf A. Berle Jr., Assistant Secretary of State, FBI memorandum, May 14, 1941, RG 59, NA). After the Japanese attack on Pearl Harbor, Al Blake sold an exclusive, self-serving account of his role as an ONI informant to a popular detective magazine. See Al Blake, "Me, Jap Agent for Uncle Sam," *Official Detective Stories*, Feb. 1942, 8–11, 41–43; March 1942, 6–9, 36–37; April 1942, 12–14, 36–38; and June 1942, 13–16, 40–41. To dramatize the Tachibana espionage case as a heinous instance of treason, Blake erroneously—but no doubt purposely—identified Kōno Toraichi as an American-born Japanese.

4. Sanematsu Yuzuru, *Maboroshi no Saigo Tsūchō* (Tokyo: Satsuki Shobō, 1995), 71–84. As the former chief of the Office of Japanese Naval Attachés, Sanematsu recalls that he and his staff were naively unaware of the ONI and FBI sting operation and therefore were taken by complete surprise when Tachibana was arrested.

5. Documents relating to Lieutenant Commander Okada Sadatomo, including FBI reports, can be found in Box 5901, RG 59, NA. These documents also include material relating to another Japanese naval officer on the East Coast who was arrested along with Okada. This officer was Engineer Lieutenant Yamada Wataru.

6. For example, the *Los Angeles Examiner*, June 10, 1941, headlined its story, "Japanese Spy Plot Believed Smashed Here." The headline of the *Los Angeles Times*, June 10, 1941, read, "Japanese Navy Officer Held in Spy Plot." *Time*, June 23, 1941, ran its story under the caption, "Espionage—Secret Agent," with a picture of Al Blake.

7. For biographical data on Dr. Furusawa Takashi and Sachiko see Endō Shirō, *Minami Kashū Okayama Kenjin Hattenshi* (Los Angeles: Minami Kashū Okayama Kenjin Hattenshi Hensanjo, 1941), 3–4; Kazahaya Katsu'ichi, *Minami Kashū Okayama Kenjin Hattenshi* (Los Angeles: Minami Kashū Okayama Kenjin Hattenshi Hensanjo, 1955), 227–28; Nakagawa Mushō, *Zaibei Tōshiroku* (Los Angeles:

Hakubundō Shoten, 1932), 360–63; Matsumoto Honkō, *Kashū Jimbutsu Taikan* (Los Angeles: Shōwa Jihōsha, 1929), 101–2; Matsumoto Honkō, *Fukkō Senjō ni Odoru Kikan Dōhō* (Los Angeles: Rafu Shoten, 1946), 262–63; and Rafu Shimpōsha, *Kigen Nisen Roppyakunen Hōshuku Kinen Taikan* (Los Angeles: Rafu Shimpōsha, 1940), 58. See also Senoo Sadao, *Enyō Kōkai Yowa* (Kamakura: Yama-tokai Shuppanbu, 1971), 86–98; and Enemy Alien Case Files, Box 23, File 15942/ 359, Sachiko Furusawa, RG 85, NA Branch Depository, Pacific Southwest Region, Laguna Niguel.

8. For information about the Japanese Navy Association I have relied heavily on Nippon Kaigun Kyōkai, Box 5901, RG 59, NA.

9. *Umi no Nippon*, no. 168, April 1, 1939, 8.

10. The prospectus was titled "Nihon Kaigun Kyōkai no Shimei" [The Mission of the Japanese Navy Association]. A copy can be found in ONI Security Classified Administrative Correspondence, 1942–1946, Box 218, Record Group 38, National Archives.

11. The most detailed FBI report on the Japanese Navy Association and Dr. and Mrs. Furusawa is by Agent A. P. LeGrand, July 9, 1941, in RG 59, NA.

12. The two Nisei girls were young and attractive. Mitsuyo Kuriki was born in 1917, Teruko Kiyomura in 1919. Kuriki had already graduated from Roosevelt High School, while Kiyomura was a senior during the 1937–38 school year. Both were selected to accompany Mrs. Furusawa and Mrs. Murase because they were attractive young girls who had a good command of spoken Japanese. In addition, Kiyomura was an accomplished Japanese dancer. Mrs. Furusawa felt that the presence of these two Nisei girls would help to cheer up the sick and wounded Japanese soldiers in the military hospitals they were scheduled to visit. Teruko Kiyomura Nakao, interview by Yuji Ichioka, Nov. 17, 1997; and Mitsuyo Kuriki Kimberly to author, May 26, 1998.

13. *Miyako Shimbun*, April 3, 8, 1938; *Yomiuri Shimbun*, April 2, 8, 1938; *Kokumin Shimbun*, April 3, 7, 1938; *Tōkyō Nichinichi Shimbun*, April 2, 1938; *Tōkyō Asahi Shimbun*, April 2, 8, 1938.

14. For example, see *Nagoya Shimbun*, April 13, 14, 1938; *Kyōto Hinode Shimbun*, April 16, 1938; and *Gōdō Shimbun*, April 22, 1938.

15. *Miyako Shimbun*, July 15, 1938.

16. *Rafu Shimpō*, Aug. 1, 1938; *Sangyō Nippō*, Aug. 1, 1938; and *Kashū Mainichi*, Aug. 1, 1938.

17. Mutō Shōgo's articles pertaining to Mrs. Furusawa and her group appeared in the *Rafu Shimpō*, Feb. 23, March 12, April 4, 8, 9, 25–27, May 2, 17, 1938.

18. Furusawa Sachiko, "Nihon ni Tsukai Shite," *Rafu Shimpō*, April 28–30, 1938; "Yorokobimukaerarete Tada Kangeki to Namida no Tabi," *Rafu Shimpō*, June 3, 1938; and "Sensen ni Tsukai Shite Tada Kangeki to Namida no Tabi," *Rafu*

Shimpō, June 20–22, 1938. See also "Jin'ei to Byōin nite Yūshi no Gantan," *Rafu Shimpō*, Jan. 1, 1939.

19. *Rafu Shimpō*, Aug. 18, 1938; and *Kashū Mainichi*, Aug. 16, 1938.

20. FBI agent F. J. Holmes, Report, Aug. 26, 1941, in Box 5901, RG 59, NA.

21. *Rafu Shimpō*, May 27, 1939, May 27, 28, 1940.

22. Holmes, Report (see note 20).

23. Office of Naval Intelligence, Counter Subversion Section, "Japanese Intelligence and Propaganda in the United States During 1941," Dec. 4, 1941, in Box 5897, RG 59, NA.

24. Nobuo Tsuboi, interview by Yuji Ichioka, June 29, 1996.

25. Lt. Commander C. H. Coggins, "Japanese Undercover Organization—14th Naval District, July, 1941–May, 1942," May 15, 1942, in Records of the Office of the Chief of Naval Operations, Office of Naval Intelligence, Sabotage Espionage, Counterespionage Section (SEC), Oriental Desk (Op 16-B-7-o), 1936–46, "Japanese Organization and Intelligence in US," Box 1, RG 38, NA.

26. [Kenneth Ringle], "The Japanese in America: The Problem and the Solution," *Harper's Magazine*, Oct. 1942, 491.

27. "FBI Memorandum Re: Japanese Espionage, November 17, 1941," in Box 5899, RG 59, NA.

28. *Rafu Shimpō*, June 10, 1941.

29. Ibid.

30. *Rafu Shimpō*, May 11, 1941

31. *Rafu Shimpō*, June 15, 1941.

32. Ibid.

33. *Rafu Shimpō*, June 12, 1941.

34. *Rafu Shimpō*, June 22, 1941.

35. Kaname Wakasugi and M. M. Hamilton, "Arrest of Lieutenant Commander Tachibana," memorandum of conversation, June 18, 1941, Box 5903, RG 59, NA; M. M. Hamilton, "Arrest of Lieutenant Commander Tachibana," confidential memorandum, June 18, 1941, Box 5903, RG 59, NA. See also Nomura Kichisaburō, *Beikoku ni Tsukai Shite: Nichibei Kōshō no Kaikō* (Tokyo: Iwanami Shoten, 1946), 64–65. The intercepted "Magic Cables" have virtually nothing on the Tachibana case, except for references to Ambassador Nomura's protest visit to the State Department on June 14 and Tachibana's departure from the United States on June 21. See U.S. Department of Defense, *The "Magic" Background of Pearl Harbor* (Washington, DC: GPO, 1978), 2: appendix, A-46 and A-154.

36. Frank Knox to Rear Admiral Charles A. Blakely, June 27, 1941, in Naval Districts and Shore Establishments, Eleventh Naval District, Commandant's Headquarters, San Diego, Folder S.F.-64, Jan. 1935–Dec. 1941, Box 125, RG 181, NA Branch Depository, Pacific Southwest, Laguna Niguel.

37. The best treatment of Kōno's relationship to Chaplin can be found in the biographical study of Chaplin by David Robinson, *Chaplin: His Life and Art* (New York: McGraw-Hill, 1985). Gerith von Ulm, *Charlie Chaplin: King of Tragedy* (Caldwell: Caxton Printers, 1940), claims to present Kōno's inside view of Chaplin. In his autobiography Chaplin only mentions Kōno with regard to his tour of Japan in 1932. See Charles Chaplin, *My Autobiography* (New York: Simon and Schuster, 1964), 371–73. A special series on the life of Kōno Toraichi recently appeared in a Japanese newspaper under the title *Chapurin no Kagebōshi* [The Shadow of Chaplin]. See *Chūgoku Shimbun*, Jan. 15, 22, 29, Feb. 5, 12, 19, 26, March 5, 12, 19, 26, and April 2, 1997.

38. Secretary of Navy Frank Knox strenuously objected to the release of Kōno, saying that "it is regretted that he will not be brought to trial and convicted." Since Kōno would not be placed on trial, Knox recommended that he "be apprehended and deported as an undesirable alien." Frank Knox to State Department, June 27, 1941, in Box 5903, RG 59, NA. However, the Justice Department advised that it had no basis for deporting Kōno.

39. In 1953 Dr. Furusawa suffered a fatal heart attack several minutes after greeting Crown Prince Akihito at the Ambassador Hotel in Los Angeles. The heart attack was brought on by apparent overexcitement at meeting the crown prince. See *Rafu Shimpō*, Oct. 1, 1953. Mrs. Furusawa died in 1959 in Atami, Japan. See *Rafu Shimpō*, Feb. 21, 1959. Attesting to her enduring attachment to the Japanese navy, she left 1.2 million yen or $3,333 to the Japan Self-Defense Navy in her will. See Senoo, *Enyō Kōkai Yowa*, 273. Both are buried in the Evergreen Cemetery in East Los Angeles.

40. Yuji Ichioka, "Japanese Immigrant Nationalism: The Issei and the Sino-Japanese War, 1937–1941," *California History* 69 (1990): 260–75, 310–11.

41. The Justice Department recognized this fact in the case of at least two individuals. Murase Akiko was arrested as a "potentially dangerous" enemy alien. She had accompanied Mrs. Furusawa to Japan in 1938 as a so-called *imonshi*. The FBI report on Murase indicated that she was a supporting member of the Japanese Navy Association and wife of Dr. Murase Masakazu, a member of the Sakura Kai. See R. A. Garvey, Report, Dec. 31, 1941, re: Murase, in Enemy Alien Case Files, Box 32, File 15942/531, Akiko Murase, RG 85, NA Branch Depository, Pacific Southwest Region, Laguna Niguel. On March 17, 1942, the Justice Department reclassified her and paroled her to the custody of an American. Later she was interned at the Manzanar Internment Camp. See Enemy Alien Case Files, Box 32, File 15942/531, RG 85, NA Branch Depository, Pacific Southwest Region, Laguna Niguel.

Like Murase, Hiratsuka Masuo had been a member of the Japanese Navy Association and, in his case, arrested as a dangerous enemy alien. He had been employed by Minami Yaemon and doubtless joined the association under his influence. The FBI report on Hiratsuka placed his membership in the association as the primary reason for his arrest. See E. J. Thaney, Report, Jan. 9, 1942, re: Hiratsuka, in Box 14, File 15942/166, Masuo Hiratsuka, RG 85, NA Branch Depository, Pacific Southwest Region, Laguna Niguel. On May 18, 1942, the Justice Department reclassified him at his hearing in Fort Missoula, Montana, and released him on parole. Permitted to go to Salt Lake City, he resided there for the duration of the war. A graduate of Rikkyō University, Hiratsuka was a devout Christian who knew prominent white Christians. Many of them vouched for him, convincing INS officials that he deserved to be reclassified and released. See Box 14, File 15942/166, Masuo Hiratsuka, RG 85, NA Branch Depository, Pacific Southwest Region, Laguna Niguel. Ironically, his wife and Nisei children were interned at Gila, Arizona, while he was a free man in Salt Lake City.

TEN

"Attorney for the Defense"

Yamato Ichihashi and Japanese Immigration

Yamato Ichihashi (1878–1965) was one of the first scholars of Japanese descent to teach at an American university. From 1913 to 1943 he was a professor of Japanese studies at Stanford University. Ichihashi is best known as the author of *Japanese in the United States*. Published in 1932, his book remained the standard work on Japanese immigration history for many years.[1] When it first appeared, a few reviewers characterized Ichihashi as playing "the role of the attorney for the defense."[2] Japanese immigration had been a controversial political issue between 1900 and 1924, when the anti-Japanese exclusion movement occurred and climaxed with the enactment of the 1924 Immigration Act, which terminated all Japanese immigration.[3] Although Ichihashi's book was published eight years after the restrictive legislation, it still had the purpose of refuting the arguments advanced against Japanese immigration during the period before 1924. Throughout his career at Stanford, Ichihashi was attached to the Japanese Foreign Ministry. Thus he acted in a dual capacity. He was at once a Stanford professor and an unofficial Japanese government spokesman. Here the Japanese term *shoku-taku* is applicable. This term designates the employment status of a person hired temporarily to do a specific job for a set time period. In the case of the Foreign Ministry, such a person was not a career employee who had passed the formal examination for entry into the ministry. Ichihashi's close association with the Foreign Ministry began with the special circumstances of his appointment at Stanford.

Ichihashi was a native of Aichi Prefecture, situated in central Japan. He was born on April 15, 1878, the third son of Ichihashi Hiromasa and Ichihashi Ai. During the Tokugawa period the Ichihashi family had samurai ranking as retainers of the Owari fief, one of three Tokugawa family domains. Ichihashi had eight siblings, six brothers and two sisters. From 1884 to 1892 he attended public school in the city of Nagoya, completing four years more of education than the compulsory four-year elementary school requirement. Ichihashi was among the many ambitious Japanese youth who left Japan in the late nineteenth century to study in the United States. He landed in San Francisco in 1894 at the age of sixteen. His oldest brother had preceded him. He attended the public schools of San Francisco and eventually graduated from Lowell High School in 1902. In 1903 he matriculated into Stanford University, from which he received two degrees in economics: an AB in 1907 and an AM in 1908. From 1908 to 1910 he served as an assistant in the Economics Department at Stanford and as a special agent of the United States Immigration Commission. In the latter capacity he conducted field studies of Japanese immigrants under Harry A. Millis, who directed the commission's investigation of Japanese immigrants living throughout the western United States. In 1910 Ichihashi went to Harvard University and obtained his PhD three years later.[4]

Ichihashi's personal relationship to Stanford president David Starr Jordan was an important factor behind his initial appointment to Stanford. Jordan was something of a Japanophile. Very much a man of his time, he believed that human progress had a biological basis.[5] All races were not equal; some were genetically superior to others, and the Nordic people constituted the most superior race of mankind. According to Jordan the Japanese people also ranked quite high. He believed they were descendants of the Ainu, a branch of the Aryan race that had fallen into decadence but whose blood flowed through the veins of the Japanese, particularly aristocratic Japanese. Jordan attributed the great strides Japan had made in industry, science, and education since the Meiji Restoration to this biological factor.

Personal experience strengthened his belief. Jordan's first contacts with Japanese people were through the students who attended Stanford. Indeed, two Japanese were members of the first class of 1891. Significantly, both served as domestic servants in Jordan's household, and one was among his first students in zoology. These two students were followed by many others in the ensuing years. Jordan had a high opinion of the Japanese students, describing them as "nearly all of the impoverished samurai (feudal retainer)

Figure 13. Yamato Ichihashi in his Stanford office. Reproduced
from Gordon H. Chang, *Morning Glory, Evening Shadow:
Yamato Ichihashi and His Internment Writings, 1942–1945*
(Stanford: Stanford University Press, 1997). Courtesy of
Special Collections, Green Library, Stanford University.

class who had worked their way upward by sheer energy and persistence."[6]
Several later visits to Japan brought him into contact with high Japanese government officials, prominent businessmen, and leading scholars. Jordan relished his visits and, according to a biographer, "delighted in the beautiful
scenery, in the benign climate, and in the charming ways of the cultivated
classes. The stage of advancement of science, of industry, and of education
impressed him profoundly."[7] In short, Jordan's experience with Japanese
people reinforced his belief in their superior racial qualities.

The relationship of Ichihashi to Jordan dated back to the younger man's student days at Stanford. From the outset of that relationship Ichihashi always exhibited deference toward Jordan. Later, as a senior at Stanford, Ichihashi wanted to continue his studies on the East Coast, but he needed financial assistance. In 1907, with Jordan's support, he applied unsuccessfully for a graduate fellowship at Columbia University. In expressing his gratitude to Jordan, Ichihashi wrote, "I am very grateful to you and in case I succeed in getting one I shall endeavor to make the best use of it, hoping . . . to repay you by becoming a man not only for this but also for the benefits I received at Stanford."[8] In 1908 he applied for another graduate scholarship, this time at Wisconsin University, but was not too optimistic about his chances of receiving it. His option was to become an assistant under Professor Allyn A. Young in the Economics Department. Ichihashi solicited Jordan's advice:

> Now on [the] supposition that I shall be unable to go East, Dr. Young asked me if I would like to be an assistant in his Department and do some research work on any subject I may choose. I have not yet given him my answer for I am very anxious to ask your opinion on this. On the other hand, I have been contemplating . . . going out to work for a year or two, so that I may be enabled to go East with certainty.
>
> Under the circumstance would you advise me to stay here another year or so or seek work elsewhere?[9]

By soliciting advice in such a manner, Ichihashi no doubt appealed to Jordan's sense of self-importance. He ingratiated himself with the president in order to strengthen his option with the Economics Department. When Ichihashi did not receive a graduate scholarship from Wisconsin, Jordan, not surprisingly, appointed him as an assistant in the Economics Department for the academic year 1908–9. Ichihashi wrote "Thanking you again and again" in a note to Jordan, which he signed "Your Affectionate Student."[10]

After Ichihashi went to Harvard in 1910 as a graduate student, he continued to correspond with Jordan. In 1911 he applied for the California-Harvard Scholarship and asked Jordan to be kind enough "to help me to get it if you think I am the most deserving of the candidates."[11] Besides soliciting his help, Ichihashi also flattered Jordan. On Jordan's return from a trip to Japan in 1911, Ichihashi wrote to the Stanford president:

I learn through the newspaper that you and Mrs. Jordan are back from the trip to Japan. The papers and magazines that I get from Japan were unanimous in welcoming you and your message of peace. From this I can easily see that you have done a great good to the Japanese people on one side, and the American people on the other. I feel sure that your sojourn in Japan was a pleasant one. I have read an account of the reception tendered in your honor by Count Okuma. . . . I also wish to express my small personal appreciation of your great work and join, at least, in spirit in welcoming you home again.[12]

After his return to the United States Jordan was awarded the Second Class of the Order of the Sacred Treasure by the Meiji emperor. In this connection Ichihashi wrote:

I learned sometime ago that you had been decorated by the Japanese Emperor. The news was not a surprise to me, for I have been anticipating it now for quite a while. I do not know whether you think much of that sort of thing or not. But from our standpoint, the decoration was the best expression of our appreciation and gratitude through our ruler of your humanitarian services. The Japanese people know what you have done for them and their nation. Please accept my humble congratulations.[13]

Ichihashi's personal relationship to Jordan paid dividends. In 1913 Jordan appointed Ichihashi as an instructor in Japanese history and government at Stanford. This position was funded temporarily by the Japanese government under special circumstances. During Jordan's 1911 trip to Japan a luncheon was given in his honor by Asano Sōichirō, president of the Oriental Steamship Company. At this luncheon, according to Jordan's account, a discussion occurred relating to the state of Japanese-American relations and the many misunderstandings Americans had of Japan and Japanese immigration. To dispel the misunderstandings, Jordan suggested that Japan would do well to dispatch an educator to teach Japanese studies at an American university. Shiraishi Motojirō, managing director of the Oriental Steamship Company, welcomed this suggestion, and he and his business associates expressed a willingness to endow a professorship in Japanese studies at Stanford University. Shiraishi made no concrete commitment at the time. The discussion ended with an understanding that time would be required to generate sufficient funds for an endowed professorship, which, ideally, should be established on a permanent basis.[14]

With Ichihashi in mind for the possible professorship, Jordan informed him of Shiraishi's tentative offer. In early 1912 Ichihashi inquired of Jordan if "you have not heard from Mr. Shiraishi about the suggestion you made to him. Do you think that there is any hope of realizing that scheme?" Ichihashi anticipated obtaining his PhD from Harvard and told Jordan of his earnest wish to become a professor at an American university:

> I have been encouraged by two . . . Stanford professors to prepare myself to teach in this country. They felt sure and so did I, perhaps blindly, that there would be a chance for me to teach and thus I have been studying quite a while. I wanted to be a scholar before I started teaching for two reasons— first, I am a Japanese and must, therefore, be above the average and secondly, because I have seen not a few young men start teaching without knowing a good deal about their subjects.

As a Japanese, however, Ichihashi realized that it was not going to be easy to secure a teaching post. He appraised his prospects in the following way:

> I may be wrong but I feel now that I know [a] little about Economics, Sociology and the history of civilizations, enough, at least, to start teaching with. I notice here that many young men of mediocre scholarship start teaching. I began to wonder, of late, why and how these men, many of them foreigners, . . . get jobs easily while I could not get any at all. Now, if the fact of my being a Japanese disqualifies me as a teacher, that settles the question. Yet I cannot feel that that is quite true.

Ichihashi appealed to Jordan for a teaching job at Stanford, saying that "I am not particular about rank or salary so long as I get an opportunity to teach and [earn] a living."[15]

Less than two weeks later, Ephraim D. Adams, head of the History Department, and Harry A. Millis, faculty member in the Economics Department, made a proposal to Jordan regarding the prospective Japanese-funded professorship in Japanese studies. They suggested that Stanford accept a temporarily funded one-year professorship in lieu of a permanently endowed chair. They also proposed that Ichihashi be appointed to this temporary post.

> Mr. Millis and I believe that, if any such chair is to be established, it ought to be endowed with a sum sufficient to pay an adequate salary and to provide for a general library equipment. This cannot be done at once, it must be

gradually arranged for. In the meantime, it has been suggested that a tempo-rary trial of the plan might be made in securing from the Japanese . . . a gift for one year only. It so happens that there is a Japanese student, formerly of Stanford and now at Harvard University, who is well equipped to make a trial of the work. This is Mr. Ichihashi.

It is our recommendation to you, therefore, that Mr. Millis be authorized to approach the Japanese consul in San Francisco and others interested and suggest to them that, if they will provide a fund of $1,600 for the academic year 1912–1913, the Board of Trustees will be asked to appoint for one year Mr. Ichihashi as an instructor in history to give courses in the history of Japanese civilization.[16]

President Jordan endorsed this proposal.

Ichihashi returned to San Francisco toward the end of the summer of 1912. He had completed all his requirements for a PhD at Harvard, except for his dissertation. Since his dissertation was going to cover Japanese immi-gration, he chose to research and write it in California. In the fall he called on Consul Nagai Matsuzō of San Francisco to ascertain the status of the original Shiraishi offer. Much to his chagrin, he learned that nothing had materialized. Highly disappointed, he conveyed his sense of frustration and indignation to Jordan:

> On my way here I met Professor Millis and learned from him about the plan that you and he were kindly trying to carry out for me. Upon . . . interviewing . . . Mr. Nagai [he] informed me that Mr. Shiraishi had failed to write him so far. Mr. Nagai added that while he was still hoping, so far as he saw, the plan would not materialize in a short time. And naturally, while I did not anticipate materialization of the plan easily, I was more or less disappointed at the outcome.
>
> And my disappointment was not without some reasons. In the first place, I thought that the establishment of the hoped for chair would be of some good service both to America and Japan. In the second place, I was more or less prepared to take up the work. Finally, under the circumstances I shall have to return to Japan. I have no aspiration other than an academic career, but it is denied me here in America because I am a Japanese. America is evidently no place for educated Japanese. Thus though it is against my will, I am compelled to go home.[17]

Without any prospect of a teaching job, Ichihashi felt for the moment that he had no alternative but to return to his homeland.

In the meantime he finished his dissertation and obtained his PhD. In 1913 he applied for a position at the University of Wisconsin for which Harvard had recommended him. The opening was an instructorship in Japanese politics in the Department of Political Science, headed by Paul Reinsch, a close friend of Jordan. On behalf of Ichihashi, Jordan wrote a glowing letter of recommendation.[18] When Jordan sent off his letter in early May, the idea of an endowed professorship at Stanford was being resuscitated by Numano Yasutarō, the newly designated acting consul of San Francisco. Sometime in mid-May Ichihashi met with Numano, who informed him that he was checking out the possibility of such a professorship, but he was not considering a permanently endowed chair. Ichihashi was reluctant to commit himself to a temporary appointment and even doubted whether such an arrangement would materialize. He reported his disappointment to Jordan, concluding that "if the proposed chair at Wisconsin, which is not an endowment chair, should be offered to me[,] I should accept it rather than the one planned at your university."[19]

The 1913 California Alien Land Act was behind the revival of the idea of an endowed professorship. Consul Numano had assumed his post in April just as the state legislature was deliberating on the Alien Land Bill. Directed specifically against Japanese immigrant farmers, this measure would prohibit "aliens ineligible to citizenship" from purchasing agricultural land and from bequeathing or transferring such land to each other. In addition, it would limit the leasing of agricultural land to three years. The legislature passed the bill in early May, and Governor Hiram Johnson signed it into law on May 19. Almost immediately after, the Japanese Foreign Ministry launched "a campaign of education" to present factual information about Japan and Japanese immigration to the American public in order to counteract the unfounded allegations of anti-Japanese exclusionists. One method of achieving this goal was to have American institutions of higher learning establish professorships in Japanese studies.

On May 20, the day after the governor signed the alien land legislation, Consul Numano wired the Foreign Ministry. He had visited President Jordan on May 17, and Jordan had assured him that Stanford was prepared to establish a chair in Japanese studies and to appoint Ichihashi to it. Only the lack of funds held Stanford back. Numano suggested that Tokyo fund such a chair. It would require three thousand dollars for one year, of which twelve hundred dollars would be earmarked for Ichihashi's salary and eighteen hundred dollars to cover the expenses he would incur in the local consulate's campaign of education. Numano added that he would disburse the twelve hundred dollars to Stanford in the name of a nominal donor. Because of Ichihashi's pending job application with Wisconsin, he urged the Foreign Ministry to give this matter top priority.[20] A day later Tokyo approved his request and allocated three thousand dollars.[21]

Numano quickly notified Jordan that "a number of his countrymen" were willing to contribute fourteen hundred dollars (twelve hundred dollars for salary and two hundred dollars for a book fund) for a chair in Japanese studies on a one-year trial basis. "While I am not in a position to give any positive assurances as to the continuance of financial support beyond the first year," he wrote, "I have no reason to doubt that such support will be forthcoming provided the work of the proposed Chair meets the expectations of its patrons."[22] Numano later identified the representatives of the so-called patrons as T. Isaka and J. Fujihira, the branch heads of the Oriental Steamship Company and the Yokohama Specie Bank in San Francisco.[23] Whether Wisconsin ever offered Ichihashi the instructorship in Japanese politics is unknown. What is known is that Stanford accepted the fourteen hundred dollars and quickly appointed Ichihashi as an instructor in Japanese history and government. In sum, Stanford was able to hire Ichihashi with funds ostensibly donated by private Japanese businessmen but in fact provided by the Japanese government through its San Francisco consulate.

Subsequently, the Foreign Ministry contributed additional funds for Ichihashi's reappointment. With the approval of new Stanford president John C. Branner, Ephraim D. Adams of the History Department, in November 1913, queried Consul Numano about the future intent of the "Japanese donors." Ichihashi had been appointed only for the 1913–14 academic year, and Adams believed that another one-year appointment would be unsatisfactory. In order to give Ichihashi a measure of security, he requested that the donors consider contributing enough money for a three-year appointment:

> . . . Simply to make again a grant of funds for Mr. Ichihashi for one year only is not advisable. It puts him upon a very misfortunate basis, and makes it difficult for the History Department to plan its work. I would suggest therefore that the best solution would be to place in the hands of the Board of Trustees an amount sufficient to cover Mr. Ichihashi's salary and library purchases for say three years. This would give Mr. Ichihashi a sense of security.

The original idea of a permanently endowed professorship had called for the appointment of an established scholar of distinction. Adams admitted that Ichihashi did not fit this bill but believed the young man had the potential of becoming such a scholar. To justify a three-year appointment, Adams lauded that potential in effusive terms:

> Permit me to add a few words in regard to Mr. Ichihashi himself. He is a young man, and naturally, therefore, does not fulfill the requirements of a scholar of proved and established reputation, such as it was intended to appoint under the original plan of an endowed Chair of Japanese History. But Mr. Ichihashi, in my opinion, might become later such a scholar, for he has the keenness of intellect, the breadth of interest, and the ability in instruction, and in writing, that are necessary to such scholarship. In short, he has the promise of distinction, but has yet to give evidence of it. The Department of History is greatly pleased with the teaching he is now doing, his students are enthusiastic, while his personality is attractive to all whom he meets. If my suggestion is followed that the generous donors of the present fund make provision for Mr. Ichihashi for a three year period, it would give time for Mr. Ichihashi to show more clearly his worth.[24]

A three-year appointment, Adams stated, would require a contribution of five thousand dollars to the Stanford trustees.

Consul Numano endorsed this recommendation in a report to the Foreign Ministry. The Stanford instructorship in Japanese studies, he believed, had started auspiciously. Ichihashi possessed "a keen intellect," in his opinion. "Enthusiastic in his teaching at Stanford, he is very popular among faculty and students. He is recognized as a promising scholar and has a very bright future ahead of him."[25] In addition to the five thousand dollars, Numano asked the Foreign Ministry to allocate three thousand dollars to supplement Ichihashi's salary for any work that he might do on behalf of the consulate. In January 1914 the Foreign Ministry approved Numano's recommendation and instructed him to donate the five thousand dollars allocated for Ichihashi's salary in the "name of private donors."[26]

Consul Numano donated the five thousand dollars in the names of the same businessmen who had ostensibly contributed the funds for the first year. The Foreign Ministry attached three conditions, which Consul Numano ascribed to the nominal donors. He told Stanford that the donors asked that Ichihashi's salary be fixed at fourteen hundred dollars during the first year and increased to fifteen hundred dollars in the second and to sixteen hundred dollars in the third. Second, the donors wanted Stanford in time to pay his salary out of regular university funds and make his position permanent. Third, the donors requested that Ichihashi "be utilized to the fullest extent by the University and that he be given every opportunity to lecture and teach on any subject pertinent to Japanese civilization." They desired that he "be utilized in any Department of the University where he can work to advantage, and that his activities be not necessarily confined to specialization in history."[27] This third condition was in keeping with the Foreign Ministry's campaign of education. Japanese officials did not want Ichihashi confined either to the field of history or to the History Department. They wanted him to be free to lecture on and teach any subject pertaining to Japan, including current issues in Japanese-American relations, and in other departments as well.

The Stanford trustees acknowledged all three conditions and accepted the funds. President Branner relayed to Numano the trustees' acceptance of the third condition using identical language. "It is understood," he wrote, "that Mr. Ichihashi shall be given every opportunity to lecture and teach on any subject pertinent to Japanese Civilization, his services while primarily under the Department of History, being utilized in any department of the University where he can work to advantage."[28] Under the terms actually set down by the Foreign Ministry, Ichihashi was reappointed in this manner at Stanford for a three-year period running from 1914 to 1917.

This arrangement inevitably meant that Ichihashi had close ties to the Japanese government. To expedite his educational work on behalf of the Foreign Ministry, the local consul liberally supplemented his salary with a fifty-dollar monthly allowance, travel expenses, and a book-purchasing fund. In 1914 the Foreign Ministry sent him to Japan at its expense for six months. This trip was arranged to enable Ichihashi to deepen his knowledge of Japan, giving him a chance to catch up on recent developments in his homeland and to acquaint himself with as many prominent Japanese leaders as possible. Ichihashi dutifully submitted reports on his activities to the local Japanese consul. His report at the conclusion of the 1914–15 academic year cited the benefits he had derived from his trip to Japan:

I feel that the sojourn of six months in Japan benefited me immeasurably. I have seen Japan of to-day. I have met the representative men of to-day at home. I have learned their ambition. Besides, I have brought back with me more than three hundred volumes of "authoritative" Japanese books. These will form the nucleus of our Japanese library, and will render me invaluable service. I now lecture with confidence which I did not possess before.[29]

In this particular report Ichihashi dwelt mostly on his classes and the students enrolled in them. During the second semester, he had taught three classes: a seminar on "Current Political Questions in Japan" and two lecture courses on "Modern Japanese Civilization" and "Immigration and the Race Problem." His students, he reported, were keenly interested in his classes. For the edification of the consul he attached course syllabi to his report and listed every talk he presented outside of the classroom before campus clubs and civic bodies.

In December 1915 Ichihashi filed a similar report. Covering the six-month period from June to December, it described his classes and listed all of his outside speaking engagements. He had been "trying to build a circle of friends," he noted, and his students would be "the nucleus of such a circle." The personal relationships he had formed were of "value" to him "and [would be] to Japanese interests sometime."[30] This time Ichihashi enumerated the various professional associations and civic bodies he had joined to "expand" his "contact with Americans." They included the American Economic Association, American Historical Association, Cosmopolitan Club, International Politics Club, Stanford Faculty Club, Stanford Union, and the Japan Society of America.

The scheduled expiration of Ichihashi's three-year appointment at the end of the 1916–17 academic year became a matter of concern in 1916. In May Ephraim D. Adams broached the subject with Ichihashi himself. He assured him that the History Department wished to retain his service, but he believed that it was unrealistic to expect the Stanford trustees to pick up his entire salary. As a compromise Adams proposed that the Japanese donors be approached again and told that Stanford was prepared to match any contributions they would make in order to continue the professorship in Japanese studies. For example, if the donors created a fund that would yield an annual interest of one thousand dollars, the trustees would be asked to appropriate a one-thousand-dollar match so that there would be the total of two thousand dollars available to maintain the position. In this way the professorship could be made permanent. Adams had cleared this proposal with President Ray L. Wilbur.[31]

Ichihashi took it on himself to convey Adams's proposal to the acting consul of San Francisco. He estimated that a fund of twenty-five thousand dollars would be necessary to bear an annual interest of one thousand dollars. Feeling that this sum might be too high, Ichihashi came up with an alternative plan. He proposed that the "donors" contribute one thousand dollars per year for at least ten years instead of a fund of twenty-five thousand dollars. "I suggest ten years," he said, "because I am afraid that a shorter period might cause the University to drop the plan entirely." Above all else, Ichihashi wanted some assurance of permanency: "No person can work with enthusiasm, the prerequisite for success, unless he can see his way clear a little ahead." And he reminded the acting consul of the paramount importance of his "social position" as a university professor and the "splendid opportunity" the Stanford offer afforded him to continue his educational work.[32]

The matter eventually fell on the lap of Hanihara Masanao, the new consul of San Francisco, who assumed his post a month later, in June 1916. He fully reviewed Ichihashi's case, met with Stanford officials, and interviewed Ichihashi, and concluded that the chair in Japanese studies should be extended, with Ichihashi continuing to fill the position. Hanihara held Ichihashi in high esteem, regarding him as "an erudite scholar" and "a diligent and industrious" man who had the "goodwill and trust of students and faculty alike." Moreover, Ichihashi's off-campus activities were invaluable. "During university holidays," Hanihara told his superiors, Ichihashi "has always accepted invitations from people in this area to lecture on Japan and Japanese-American relations, working in this way in our campaign of education. His achievements have been outstanding."[33] Forecasting greater future results, Hanihara recommended that the Foreign Ministry adopt either Adams's proposal or Ichihashi's alternative plan. In either case he requested that Tokyo allocate an additional annual sum of six hundred dollars to supplement Ichihashi's salary.

The Foreign Ministry elected to continue its previous arrangement. It committed itself to another three-year period with an additional donation of fifty-four hundred dollars, which again was funneled through the local Japanese consulate and contributed in the name of the same "private donors." It also allocated one thousand dollars per year for three years to cover Ichihashi's travel, social, book, and other expenses.[34] Stanford accepted the new three-year grant. Supplementing the fifty-four hundred dollars with two hundred dollars per year, the school reappointed Ichihashi as an assistant professor at an annual salary of two thousand dollars.[35] Although no doubt relieved that he was reappointed, Ichihashi was not altogether pleased with his new three-year appointment. He still aspired to occupy a permanent chair with a substantial endowment, one as high as one hundred thousand dollars. So, while on sabbatical leave in 1919–20, he visited Japan to see if he could negotiate such an endowment himself. "He asserted at the time he left," Adams recalled, "that he would not return here on the old basis of a three year endowment."[36]

In April 1919 Ōta Tamekichi, the new consul in San Francisco, revived the idea of a permanently endowed chair. It was "highly desirable," in his opinion, because Ichihashi played an important role in "the campaign of education." Ōta was aware that the second three-year grant would expire in June 1920. In the light of a resurgence of anti-Japanese agitation, he placed an even greater value on Ichihashi's position than his predecessors had. Thus Ōta urged the Foreign Ministry to donate an endowment fund of twenty-five thousand dollars in order to place the professorship on a permanent footing. Such a fund would yield an annual interest of one thousand dollars. According to Ōta the Stanford trustees were prepared to supplement this interest with one thousand dollars annually in order to pay Ichihashi's annual salary of two thousand dollars.[37] No less a personage than Baron Gotō Shimpei endorsed Ōta's recommendation. A former minister of home affairs and foreign minister, Gotō stopped off in San Francisco en route to Europe. In a letter to Foreign Minister Uchida Yasuya he asserted that Ichihashi was "an effective agent who is supported by the Imperial Government to engage in indirect propaganda." In order to make the professorship permanent, Gotō suggested that the Foreign Ministry negotiate with the Finance Ministry for the necessary funds.[38]

Available sources do not reveal what kind of negotiations took place. What is known is that an endowment of $37,500 was ultimately created. Ichihashi informed Adams in August 1920 that Stanford would be offered this sum of money if it was willing to meet a condition.[39] An endowment of $37,500 would yield an annual interest of $1,500. Stanford had to match this interest, so that a total of $3,000 would be available to establish the professorship on a permanent basis. Sometime toward the end of the year, Shibusawa Eiichi, a prominent banker-financier active in Japanese-American affairs in a private capacity, tendered the offer to President Ray L. Wilbur. In all likelihood Shibusawa was the nominal donor, as the other private businessmen had been in the previous donations. The timing of his offer was significant. The post–World War I period witnessed a resurgence of anti-Japanese agitation centered in California. In 1920 the initiative campaign to amend the 1913 Alien Land Act occurred. Designed to drive Japanese immigrants out of California agriculture, the initiative measure appeared on the November ballot. In 1919 Consul Ōta had recommended that the Foreign Ministry place Ichihashi's position on the permanent footing. The renewed anti-Japanese tide made it seem imperative that it do so. Thus the Foreign Ministry, in all probability, disbursed the $37,500 itself and funneled this money through Shibusawa.[40] President Wilbur accepted Shibusawa's offer in January 1921 and shortly after reappointed Ichihashi as an assistant professor to the now permanently endowed chair in Japanese studies.[41]

Because of the special circumstances under which he was appointed at Stanford, Ichihashi invariably had to tiptoe along a very narrow path throughout his early academic career. On the one hand, he had no security of employment for many years. He was not promoted to associate professor and given tenure until 1928. With the exception of his initial one-year appointment, he was reappointed repeatedly for three-year periods, first as an instructor and then as an assistant professor. Each appointment had to be negotiated with no guarantee that it would be renewed. As far as Stanford was concerned, the continued support of the History Department and the university president was absolutely essential. At a minimum Ichihashi had to please his senior colleagues and preserve his reputation as a conscientious teacher among his students. On the other hand, he had to satisfy the Japanese government. After all, the Foreign Ministry contributed the funds that made his appointments possible. Japanese officials expected Ichihashi to be active on and off the Stanford campus. His task was to educate as many Americans as possible about Japan, both past and present, including those issues currently causing friction in Japanese-American relations. The Japanese immigration question, of course, was one of the burning issues at the time.

Consequently, Ichihashi was always caught between two sets of competing demands. A Stanford set required that he be scholarly and nonpartisan as a professor specializing in Japanese history and civilization. Lest he be accused of being a propagandist in disguise, he had to carefully avoid any semblance of being one-sided or unfairly pro-Japan. A Foreign Ministry set of demands dictated that he enlighten Americans about Japan so that they

would become understanding of and sympathetic to the country and its people. The Foreign Ministry connection also dictated that he present and
defend the Japanese side of political issues in line with the ministry's policy.
These two sets of demands placed Ichihashi in a difficult and sometimes
untenable position, forcing him to strike a delicate balance between them.

The two sets clashed in the preliminary discussion regarding the donation of the $37,500 to endow Ichihashi's chair on a permanent basis. The
Japanese "donors" hinted that they wanted the name of the chair changed
to "American-Japanese Relations." As head of the History Department,
Ephraim D. Adams objected strenuously to such a change. Payson J. Treat,
a senior member of the department, was a specialist in Far East diplomacy
and U.S.-Japan relations. Adams believed that Treat had "a prior right" to
this field, and if the chair was so renamed, Ichihashi would encroach on it.
"Mr. Ichihashi's field," he insisted adamantly, "has been specified as that of
Japanese History and Civilization." Parenthetically, Adams added that "I
very much doubt the expediency of appointing any Japanese scholar" to the
field of Japanese-American relations.[42] In other words, this field was the
province of an American scholar like Treat, not of a foreign scholar like
Ichihashi.

Ichihashi had an inflated sense of his own self-importance. He placed no
stock in the ability of Japanese immigrant leaders to contribute toward
improving Japanese-American relations. Japanese associations, established
throughout the Pacific Coast and in the adjacent western states, were the
principal political organizations of Japanese immigrants. The Japanese
Association of America, the leading association, had "proved most ineffi-
cient" in Ichihashi's opinion. His harsh judgment was that "not a single contribution" had "ever been made by it." He considered it a "pity" that someone like Ushijima Kinji, commonly known as George Shima, the Potato
King, had been made its president. "If no better substitute could be found,"
Ichihashi observed, "the presidency of the Association should be made
inconspicuous." To control more effectively the associations, the consul, he
advised, should "further bureaucratize" them:

> They should be put under the absolute control of the Consulate . . . and
> should be guided to do what they should and to avoid what they should.
> . . . This is a confession of one who has prized democracy above all things,
> and has watched with a keen interest for the last twenty years its evolution

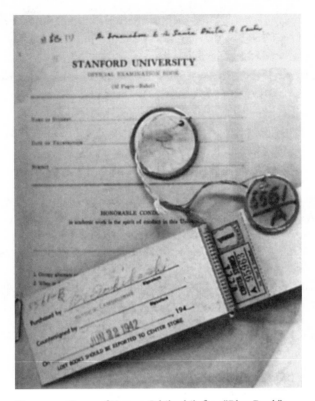

Figure 14. Cover of Yamato Ichihashi's first "Blue Book"
diary, his ticket book, and his identification tag from Santa
Anita Assembly Center. Reproduced from Gordon H.
Chang, *Morning Glory, Evening Shadow: Yamato Ichihashi
and His Internment Writings, 1942–1945* (Stanford: Stanford
University Press, 1997). Courtesy of Special Collections,
Green Library, Stanford University.

among the Japanese here. They are by nature not democratic, and there are
no stimuli to make them so. They are at least twenty years behind the intelligent Japanese at home, and lord only knows how [many] years they are
behind the intelligent Americans. They have not been in touch with the
progress here or at home. They must be ruled from above.[43]

Ichihashi expressed this elitist view in another way during World War II.
From the Santa Anita Assembly Center he wrote to Payson J. Treat, his

Stanford History Department colleague, telling him that it was "very painful for cultured persons" like himself to be confined like "animals" with "lowly, uncouth rustics," that is, his fellow Japanese immigrants.[44]

Ichihashi had an equally low opinion of Japanese officialdom, particularly those functionaries who had been sent by the Japanese government to participate in the 1915 Panama Pacific International Exposition held in San Francisco. From his standpoint the Japanese participation in the exposition had accomplished nothing. The fundamental reason was the inability of Japanese officials to speak English:

> It is amusing to recall their confidence and egoism with which they presented themselves to the Japanese public here, and will likely do so upon their return home. . . . With the exception of one, none of the officials could handle English intelligently. In an English speaking community, persons unable to speak English [are] helpless as [the] deaf and dumb so far as Americans are concerned. . . . Americans are very peculiar in that they have no confidence in foreigners who cannot speak English.[45]

For this reason Japanese delegates at the exposition had failed to fulfill their mission of educating Americans about Japan.

Yet proficiency in English, though necessary, was not sufficient. To be truly influential, a Japanese also had to possess what Ichihashi called "social position." He equated social position with high social standards that few, if any, Japanese could meet. "Our so-called representative Japanese here are far below the accepted social standard, and in my humble opinion many years must be consumed before they can attain that social standard." The unfortunate result was that "there are no qualified spokesmen . . . on behalf of the Japanese and their interests here and at home." University professors were the exception, for they commanded social respect. Somewhat immodestly, Ichihashi evaluated his own worth:

> Now, university professors[,] though financially poor[,] enjoy social position. I despise self-advertisement, but even [though I am] a Jap[,] because of my university position[,] I enjoy social position and take advantage of it in carrying [on] my campaign of education. No one seems to refuse to take me in. This fact convinces me that the securing of social position is the fundamental pre-requisite before a positive campaign of any sort could effectively be conducted. Hence I believe . . . that there should

be stationed here as many Japanese as possible in dignified positions. Otherwise, our campaign will remain non-vital.[46]

Because of his own "dignified position," Ichihashi believed that he was qualified to speak on behalf of all Japanese to Americans.

The difficulty of Ichihashi's dual role was compounded by publicity surrounding the source of his salary. In late 1920 Kuno Yoshisaburō of the University of California publicly accused Ichihashi of being a spokesman for Japanese interests. Kuno taught Japanese in the Department of Oriental Languages at Berkeley. The timing of his accusation was very significant. The 1920 alien land initiative generated a political tempest. As it was raging in October, Kuno published a series of articles entitled *A Survey of the Japanese Situation* in the *Oakland Tribune.*[47] In this series he alleged that Japanese consulates controlled the Japanese associations and that Japanese immigrants had managed to evade the 1913 Alien Land Law. In one installment he charged specifically that Ichihashi was "paid by the Japanese consulate in San Francisco." Later Kuno asked President Ray L. Wilbur in a private letter to identify the actual source of Ichihashi's salary.[48] Wilbur identified the source as "certain gentlemen in Japan."[49]

Dissatisfied with Wilbur's answer, Kuno issued an "Open Letter," addressed to the Stanford president. Before submitting it to the *Tribune* for publication, he assured the newspaper's assistant manager: "I shall conclusively prove that Mr. Ichihashi . . . is nothing more than a talking machine for Japanese interests."[50] He even informed the arch-exclusionist V. S. McClatchy of his intention to do so.[51] In his open letter Kuno cited the Stanford alumnus and the *Annual Report of the President* as proof of his contention that Ichihashi was paid by Japanese interests rather than Stanford. These publications contained items announcing that "Japanese donors" had supplied money as "gifts" through the local Japanese consulate. The *Tribune* carried the open letter under the caption "Professor at Stanford Paid by Japanese; Kuno Takes Issue with President Wilbur."[52] Wilbur refused to be drawn into a public debate with Kuno. Instead, he sent a private memorandum to him in which he presented a history of the various "gifts" donated through the consulate and named J. Fujihira as one of the original donors.[53] Kuno disputed the veracity of Wilbur's account, contending that "Fujihira and others . . . are . . . merely dummies, as the money does not come from their pockets."[54]

Kuno also impugned Ichihashi's qualifications to teach Japanese studies. Admittedly, Ichihashi possessed an excellent command of English and a sound Occidental education, but his knowledge of Japanese history was woefully lacking. His graduate training and expertise were in economics and modern labor problems, not Japanese history. His knowledge of Japanese was also inadequate for the study of Japanese history. Because he had left Japan in his youth, his Japanese-language reading proficiency was rather low. In terms of his education and experience in the United States, Ichihashi was eminently qualified to teach American studies in Japan but not to teach Japanese studies in the United States. In Kuno's opinion Ichihashi was a charlatan masquerading as an expert in Japanese history.

A month before his articles appeared in the *Tribune*, Kuno had written to Payson J. Treat, openly denigrating Ichihashi and other Japanese scholars like him:

> Sometimes scholars of this type study their native history or political conditions through Occidental books and give addresses to American audiences. Because of their splendid Occidental education and command of English, they naturally impress their hearers and are highly complimented. Becoming thus inflated and forgetting how very little they really know, such men pose as authorities and bring great trouble to the Japanese cause by their propaganda and misrepresentations. You need not look very far for an example of this kind. Stanford harbors one.[55]

Along the same vein, Kuno wrote to President Wilbur:

> The point which I desired to emphasize was not the source of the fund donated by the Japanese, but the use of Stanford University for the purpose of Japanese propaganda. In this connection, I would like to call your attention to the kind of education Mr. Ichihashi has received. . . . Although he received the degree of Ph.D. from Harvard University, this degree was conferred because of his research work in Economics and Labor Problems. While he is undoubtedly very capable as a teacher in these subjects, it is a matter of great surprise to those who know him to open the Stanford Register and find him giving courses in Old Japanese Law . . . because he has never had any systematic instruction either in this line or in any [other aspect] of the history of Japan in any recognized institution of learning.

"Is the public far wrong, then," Kuno rhetorically asked, "in surmising that Mr. Ichihashi gives lectures at Stanford in the interest of the Japanese?"[56]

Whatever Kuno's motives were in attacking Ichihashi,[57] he cast a cloud of suspicion over the Stanford assistant professor in the public mind. Kuno did not pursue the matter further, but the suspicion he cast necessarily placed Ichihashi in a more precarious position and made it much harder for him to fulfill his dual role.

Ichihashi formulated the basic framework of *Japanese in the United States* during the anti-Japanese exclusion movement period. At the beginning of 1913, as he was completing his dissertation, he was commissioned to write a pamphlet by the Japanese Association of America. In Ichihashi's own words, the pamphlet was to be "an unbiased statement of the more obvious facts relative to the Japanese in California" in order to counteract the falsehoods disseminated by anti-Japanese exclusionists.[58] Issued under the title *Japanese Immigration: Its Status in California*, it was published and distributed before the enactment of the 1913 Alien Land Law. David Starr Jordan wrote a brief introduction to the pamphlet extolling Ichihashi's qualifications. Divided into four parts, the pamphlet covered the number, types, and geographical distribution of Japanese immigrants; their occupational breakdown in California; their capacity to assimilate into American society; and the anti-Japanese exclusion movement.

In taking up the defense of Japanese immigrants, Ichihashi stressed factual data and endeavored to rebut the allegations advanced against Japanese immigrants by citing so-called authoritative sources. He first demonstrated statistically that Japanese immigration had always been limited in scope and number and that the Gentlemen's Agreement of 1907–8 was being honored faithfully by the Japanese government. Second, he argued that Japanese immigrants were generally not of the "coolie" laboring class or "scums" of Japan as charged. They were young men and women who brought as much capital to this country as European immigrants and who, moreover, were the most literate among all the foreign-born people living in the United States. Third, Ichihashi presented statistics showing that Japanese immigrants were concentrated heavily in agriculture and in certain city trades but were never in direct competition with Americans "to the detriment of the general standard of living." Finally, and most significant, Ichihashi upheld the assimilability of the Japanese. One of the fundamental arguments raised against Japanese immigrants was that they could never be assimilated into American society. According to Ichihashi the educational, political, and even religious institutions of the immigrants all promoted assimilation. He wrote that the

immigrants "are eager and make strenuous effort to learn of American institutions and to speak, read and write English. In fact, they 'have made unusu-
ally good progress' in this regard. They are practically free from criminal acts
and pauperism. They impose no burden upon the community."[59] Note that
this sanguine view contrasted sharply with the low opinion in which Ichihashi privately held his fellow immigrants. By way of conclusion Ichihashi
appealed for "the granting of the right of naturalization" as "the fundamental
and permanent solution to the so-called Japanese problem." "Justice and fairness have to be accorded to [the] Japanese," he argued, "and this is all we ask
of fair-minded Americans."[60] Originating as a defense of the Japanese in the
midst of the exclusion movement, this pamphlet became the fundamental
framework of Ichihashi's later writings on Japanese immigration.

In 1915 the pamphlet was reissued. This second edition had the identical
structure and purpose of the 1913 version. It only differed slightly in several
respects. To give it a greater mantle of authority, Ichihashi often cited two
new studies: Sidney L. Gulick, *The American Japanese Problem* (New York:
Scribner, 1914), and H. A. Millis, *The Japanese Problem in the United States*
(New York: Macmillan, 1915). The former was a major study, authored by
the foremost opponent of Japanese exclusionists, which argued cogently
against Japanese exclusion, whereas the latter summarized the empirical
findings of the United States Immigration Commission's investigation of
Japanese immigrants living in the western United States. In addition to citing these two new studies, Ichihashi provided information on the enactment
of the 1913 Alien Land Law and its unjust character. He also restated Gulick's
and Millis's proposals for specific reforms in immigration statutes in order to
limit future immigration in a way that would not discriminate against any
nation. Finally, he appended a selected bibliography of sources on the
Japanese immigration issue. As he had in 1913, he ended with an appeal for
the right of naturalization, which, he believed, would enable Japanese immigrants to "make contributions to American civilization as its loyal citizens."[61]

Ichihashi's dissertation was an expanded academic version of the 1913
pamphlet. Entitled "Emigration from Japan and Japanese Immigration into
the State of California," it was composed of thirteen chapters. As introductory chapters, the first three presented historical summaries of pre-Meiji emigration, modern immigration to countries besides Hawaii and the United
States, and the colonization of Hokkaido, Taiwan, south Manchuria, Korea,
and the southern half of Sakhalin Island. The heart of the dissertation

consisted of chapters 4 through 9. Dealing mainly with the Japanese in California, these chapters were divided into four parts, exactly as the 1913 pamphlet was: the number, types, and character of Japanese immigrants to Hawaii and the United States; their occupational distribution in California; their assimilation into American society; and the anti-Japanese exclusion movement.

Like the 1913 pamphlet, the dissertation defended Japanese immigrants. Of the four parts, the first was heavily statistical. As before, Ichihashi demonstrated that Japanese immigration to the United States had been limited. It was not numerous, not composed on the whole of "coolie" laborers, and not uncontrolled. Ichihashi differentiated between the Japanese immigrants who immigrated to Hawaii and those who came to the continental United States. In the nineteenth century, contract labor was legal on the Hawaiian Islands. It was not banned until 1900, when American immigration statutes became applicable to the newly annexed territory. Between 1885 and 1900 the overwhelming majority of the Hawaii-bound immigrants had been contract laborers. On the other hand, contract labor had been outlawed on the continental United States since 1885. This meant that all Japanese immigration to the United States necessarily had been "voluntary." "Under the circumstance," Ichihashi reasoned, there was "no possibility for the 'scums' of Japan to directly emigrate to the United States."[62] Hawaii had many "undesirable" lower-class laborers, Ichihashi admitted, but this was not true for the continental United States. And since the majority of the immigrants to the United States did not originate as contract laborers, they were of a better class of Japanese, with much higher moral character.

The other three parts of the dissertation also paralleled the 1913 pamphlet. In the second part Ichihashi presented a breakdown of the occupational distribution of Japanese immigrants in California, showing again that they were concentrated in agriculture and in certain city trades. Based on his own fieldwork as a special agent of the United States Immigration Commission, this part was detailed and the most original. In the third part Ichihashi examined in greater detail the various educational, religious, and political organizations of Japanese in terms of their role in promoting the assimilation of the immigrants into American society. They were so effective, Ichihashi wrote, that, contrary to popular belief, "the degree of Japanese assimilation . . . is not inferior to that of . . . the Europeans."[63] In the fourth part he presented a detailed account of the Japanese exclusion movement.

In three additional chapters Ichihashi treated other related topics. Chapter 10 dealt with the causes of Japanese emigration and argued that the principal motivation was "an economic aspiration" held by emigrants "to better their economic condition." Chapter 11 analyzed possible links between population growth and emigration and concluded that no causal relationship existed between the two; emigration had not developed as a solution to problems of overpopulation. Chapter 12 presented the "positive" effects of Japanese emigration on Japan, the immigrants themselves, and the United States. A final chapter contained Ichihashi's summary and conclusions. He ended with his familiar appeal for the right of naturalization as "an easy solution of the so-called Japanese problem in California."[64]

Japanese in the United States was an updated version of the 1913 dissertation. One can only speculate why Ichihashi waited so long to publish it. If the book had appeared before 1924, it could have served to counteract the exclusion movement, but publication did not come until 1932. Ichihashi perhaps felt that his reputation and credibility as a scholar had been so tarnished by Kuno's public attack that earlier publication might have cast more suspicion on him and prompted hostile anti-Japanese reviews. Moreover, if the book were interpreted as Japanese propaganda, it would have added fuel to the exclusion movement. According to documents obtained through the Freedom of Information/Privacy Acts, Ichihashi came under investigation of the Bureau of Investigation and the Office of Naval Intelligence as "a Japanese propagandist" in September 1921.[65] At this time Ichihashi was in Washington, DC, participating in the Washington Conference on the Limitation of Armaments as an official delegate of the Japanese government. If he were aware of this investigation, it might have helped convince him to maintain a low profile and forgo early publication. Moreover, after participating in this conference, he devoted himself to writing a book about it, which was eventually published in 1928 by Stanford University Press as *The Washington Conference and After*. This first book became the basis on which he was promoted to associate professor and given the security of employment that he had sought at Stanford for fifteen years.

Although *Japanese in the United States* was published in 1932, it retained the same purpose and organization as the 1913 dissertation. Chapter 1 was an abbreviated chapter. Chapters 2 to 5 presented statistics on the number and character of Japanese immigrants to Hawaii and the United States. Chapter 6, on the causes of Japanese emigration, reached a conclusion identical to that of the dissertation. Revised in parts, chapters 7 to 13 provided a geographical and occupational breakdown of Japanese immigrants, with particular focus on California. Chapter 14 discussed the question of assimilation and concluded that "the attitude of Japanese immigrants has been to assimilate themselves to the best of their ability and as rapidly as possible."[66] Chapters 15 to 19 narrated the major events in the Japanese exclusion that culminated in the passage of the 1924 Immigration Act. Aside from chapters 1 and 6, these chapters represented the same four basic divisions found in the 1913 dissertation. Chapters 20 to 22 constituted a new section devoted to the American-born second generation. Nothing in this section, however, was original with Ichihashi. He relied exclusively on studies by Reginald Bell, William C. Smith, Marvin L. Darsie, and Eliot G. Mears.[67] In two final chapters he assessed the outlook for amendments to the 1924 Immigration Act and repeated the material in his dissertation on population and emigration.

In previous writings Ichihashi had appealed for the right of naturalization. This time, however, he made no such plea. The United States Supreme Court in 1922 had settled the question when it ruled in the Takao Ozawa case that Japanese were ineligible for citizenship under existing naturalization statutes.[68] Ichihashi now appealed for amendments to the 1924 Immigration Act. The act sought to control the racial composition of the American population by setting a ceiling on annual admissions under a quota system that lopsidedly favored immigration from northern and western Europe. Singling out the Japanese (and other Asians) as inferiors and unwanted immigrants, it barred the entry of any alien ineligible for citizenship. To erase this stigma of racial undesirability, Ichihashi proposed that the act be amended to place Japan on the quota system reserved for European nations. In the book's final paragraph he summarized his defense of Japanese immigration: "The writer has done his best to present facts on the subject of Japanese immigrants and their children with an unbiased mind, and has refrained as much as possible from injecting his own personal views. He prefers to have his readers draw their own conclusions so long as they judge by facts and not by hearsay."[69]

Defense attorneys are obliged to argue the best possible case that they can make on behalf of their clients. Ichihashi took up the defense of Japanese immigrants. The indictment against them was that they were a fundamental menace to American society. According to the exclusionists, Japanese immigration consisted of so-called coolie laborers who worked for cheap wages. With a low standard of living, such laborers were able to compete with American workmen and undermine their higher standard of living. Contrary to its purported intent, the Gentlemen's Agreement of 1907–8 did not halt the immigration of Japanese laborers. Disguised as wives of Japanese residents, many female laborers were admitted in violation of the spirit and intent of the agreement. Unlike European immigrants, Japanese immigrants could not be Americanized. Their language, culture, religion, and morals were so far removed from American civilization that they could never be assimilated. Even their American-born children were unassimilable. As non-whites, both the immigrants and their descendants would forever constitute a dangerous alien element in American society.

Ichihashi's defense strategy was straightforward and uncomplicated. He adopted a factual approach to exonerate the Japanese immigrants of the exclusionists' indictment. He addressed himself to each allegation and pre-sented contrary evidence. His heavy reliance on statistical data was in keep-ing with his factual approach. His strategy precluded the airing of anything detrimental to either the Japanese government or the immigrants them-selves. He was beholden to the Foreign Ministry for his professorship at Stanford University, and he was active in the ministry's campaign of educa-tion. As such, he was in no position to be critical of the Japanese govern-ment. Nor was he in a position to criticize publicly his fellow immigrants. Committed to their defense, he omitted or glossed over unsavory features of Japanese immigrant life in order to project a positive public image. Ichihashi's strategy also precluded the filing of an aggressive counterindict-ment of racism in American society. He never endeavored to link up the Japanese immigrant experience with that of other racial minorities. *Japanese in the United States* was a product of this strategy with all its limitations. It was a kind of legal brief submitted in defense of Japanese immigrants.

Any final assessment of *Japanese in the United States* must place the author within the context of the anti-Japanese era in which he lived. On the one hand, Japanese immigrants constituted a powerless racial minority. Denied the right of naturalization, they were unable to participate in the American political process in order to defend themselves. On the other hand, the anti-Japanese forces commanded overwhelming power and influence. They included among their number organized labor, the American Legion, vari-ous nativist groups, local Granger organizations, many local and state politi-cians, and much of the news media. In the face of such racist opposition, often of a violent nature, Japanese immigrants could only appeal to an abstract sense of American justice and fair play. Ichihashi made such appeals, though his position as an unofficial spokesman of the Japanese government left him vulnerable to public attacks like that of Kuno and subject to surveillance by American intelligence agencies. In engaging in the Japanese government's campaign of education, he had to be extremely careful. Given these considerations, Ichihashi's approach and treatment of the Japanese immigration issue probably could not have been otherwise.

Notes

1. Ichihashi, *Japanese in the United States*. General histories of American immigration rely heavily on Ichihashi's work for their treatment of Japanese immigration. For example, see such works as Maldwyn A. Jones, *American Immigration* (Chicago, IL: University of Chicago Press, 1960); Carl Wittke, *We Who Built America* (Cleveland: Press of Case Western Reserve University, 1967); and Alan M. Kraut, *The Huddled Masses* (Arlington Heights, IL: Harlan Davidson, 1982).

2. See R. D. McKenzie, review of *Japanese in the United States*, by Yamato Ichihashi, *Pacific Historical Review* 2 (1933): 347–48; and William C. Smith, review of *Japanese in the United States*, by Yamato Ichihashi, *Social Science* 10 (1935): 82.

3. Roger Daniels, *The Politics of Prejudice* (Berkeley: University of California Press, 1962).

4. Information regarding Ichihashi's early life has been pieced together from several sources: Yamato Ichihashi Papers, University Archives, Stanford University; the Japanese family registry of Ichihashi Hiromasa, Nagoya city government office; FBI files on Ichihashi obtained through the Freedom of Information/Privacy Acts; and "Fukuinkai Enkaku Shiryō, Sanki no Bu (C), October 1895–December 1897," Japanese American Research Project Collection, University of California, Los Angeles. The Ichihashi Papers, unfortunately, contain very little that bears directly on the heart of this essay. During World War II Ichihashi (along with his wife) was incarcerated first at the Santa Anita Assembly Center and then at Manzanar. Later he was transferred to Tule Lake to enable him to join his son, Woodrow. The FBI "arrested" Ichihashi at Tule Lake and "interned" him separately as a so-called dangerous enemy alien. Soon after, the FBI reclassified him as a harmless enemy alien and "released" him to the custody of the War Relocation Authority, which placed him back into the Tule Lake Camp. In 1943 Ichihashi was transferred to Amache, Colorado. Stanford University gave him credit for service during the wartime years so that by June 1943 he had accumulated thirty years of service with Stanford. In April 1943 he turned sixty-five years old, which entitled him to draw his retirement benefits on completing thirty years of

service. At the beginning of 1943 his name appeared on a list of Japanese nationals eligible for repatriation to Japan on the second exchange ship, but he refused repatriation. In 1945 he returned to Stanford, where he lived in retirement until his death in 1965. For a full biography of his life see the recent study by Gordon H. Chang, "Yamato Ichihashi: A Biographical Essay," in Chang, *Morning Glory, Evening Shadow*, 9–87.

5. Edward M. Burns, *David Starr Jordan: Prophet of Freedom* (Stanford, CA: Stanford University Press, 1953), 61–66.

6. David Starr Jordan, *The Days of a Man* (New York: World Book, 1922), 2:7–8.

7. Burns, *David Starr Jordan*, 65.

8. Ichihashi to Jordan, March 8, 1907, David Starr Jordan Papers (hereafter cited as DSJ), University Archives, Stanford University.

9. Ichihashi to Jordan, Sept. 16, 1907, and Ichihashi to Jordan, April 17, 1908, DSJ.

10. Ichihashi to Jordan, July 2, 1908, DSJ.

11. Ichihashi to Jordan, Feb. 6, 1911, DSJ.

12. Ichihashi to Jordan, Nov. 5, 1911, DSJ.

13. Ichihashi to Jordan, Feb. 22, 1912, DSJ.

14. Jordan, *Days of a Man*, 2:373–74.

15. Ichihashi to Jordan, Feb. 22, 1912, DSJ.

16. Adams and Millis to Jordan, March 5, 1912, DSJ.

17. Ichihashi to Jordan, Sept. 7, 1912, DSJ.

18. Jordan to Reinsch, May 10, 1913, DSJ.

19. Ichihashi to Jordan, May 20, 1913, DSJ.

20. Numano to Makino, May 20, 1913, in Cecil H. Uyehara, *Checklist of Archives in the Japanese Ministry of Foreign Affairs, Tokyo, 1868–1945* (Washington, DC: Photoduplication Service, Library of Congress, 1954), reel no. 746.

21. Makino to Numano, May 21, 1913, in ibid.

22. Numano to Jordan, May 21, 1913, in ibid.

23. Numano to Clark, June 4, 1913, in ibid.

24. Adams to Numano, Nov. 5, 1913, in ibid.

25. Numano to Makino, Nov. 20, 1913, in ibid.

26. Makino to Numano, Jan. 14, 1914, in ibid.

27. Numano to Treat, March 4, 1914, in ibid.

28. Branner to Numano, April 2, 1914, in ibid.

29. Ichihashi to Numano, May 25, 1915, in ibid.

30. Ichihashi to Numano, Dec. 28, 1915, in ibid.

31. Adams to Ichihashi, May 4, 1916, in ibid.

32. Ichihashi to Yamasaki, May 17, 1916, in ibid.

33. Hanihara to Terauchi, Nov. 1, 1916, in ibid, reel 747.

34. Honno to Hanihara, Jan. 12, 1917, in ibid.

35. Wilbur to Hanihara, March 3, 1917, in ibid.

36. Adams to Wilbur, Aug. 20, 1920, Ray Lyman Wilbur Papers (hereafter cited as Wilbur Papers), University Archives, Stanford University.

37. Ōta to Uchida, April 21, 1919, in Uyehara, *Checklist*, reel no. 747.

38. Gotō to Uchida, April 20, 1919, in ibid. Gotō actually visited Stanford University on this trip. See Tsurumi Yūsuke, *Gotō Shimpei*, 4 vols. (Tokyo: Gotō Shimpei haku Denki Hensankai, 1937), 4:10.

39. Adams to Wilbur, Aug. 20, 1920, Wilbur Papers.

40. This interpretation seems strengthened by the fact that there are no documents relating to the endowment in the published Shibusawa Eiichi papers. All projects in which Shibusawa was involved directly are documented heavily. The only reference to the endowment is a newspaper article announcing that he had donated $37,500 to Stanford University. See Shibusawa Seien Kinen Zaidan Ryūmansha, *Shibusawa Eiichi Denki Shiryō*, 58 vols. (Tokyo: Shibusawa Eiichi Denki Shiryō Kankōkai, 1955–66), 40:360.

41. Wilbur to Shibusawa, Jan. 7, 1921, and Shibusawa to Wilbur, May 16, 1921, Wilbur Papers.

42. Adams to Wilbur, Aug. 20, 1920, Wilbur Papers.

43. Ichihashi to Numano, Dec. 28, 1915, in Uyehara, *Checklist*, reel no. 746.

44. Ichihashi to Treat, June 7, 1942, Payson J. Treat Papers (hereafter cited as Treat Papers), Hoover Institution, Stanford University.

45. Ichihashi to Yamasaki, May 17, 1916, in Uyehara, *Checklist*, reel no. 746.

46. Ibid.

47. *Oakland Tribune*, Oct. 25–31, 1920.

48. Kuno to Wilbur, Nov. 6, 1920, Wilbur Papers.

49. Wilbur to Kuno, Nov. 29, 1920, Yoshi S. Kuno Papers (hereafter cited as Kuno Papers), Bancroft Library, University of California, Berkeley.

50. Kuno to L. S. Levy, Nov. 22, 1920, Kuno Papers.

51. Kuno to McClatchy, Nov. 22, 1920, Kuno Papers.

52. *Oakland Tribune*, Dec. 2, 1920.

53. Wilbur to Kuno, Dec. 27, 1920, Kuno Papers.

54. Kuno to Wilbur, Dec. 31, 1920, Wilbur Papers.

55. Kuno to Treat, Sep. 17, 1920, Treat Papers.

56. Kuno to Wilbur, Dec. 31, 1920, Wilbur Papers. Kuno published this letter in the *Oakland Tribune* on Jan. 16, 1921.

57. In all likelihood there were several reasons for Kuno's vicious attack on Ichihashi. Kuno, like Ichihashi, was a native of Aichi Prefecture; indeed, he was also from the city of Nagoya. During the Tokugawa period his father was a daimyō within the Owari fief, placing the Kuno family much higher in social

ranking than the Ichihashi clan. With a more illustrious family background, Kuno doubtlessly looked down on Ichihashi as a social inferior. (For Kuno's family background see Mori Shingen, *Kunozan: Seianji Bochi Yori* [Nagoya: Kuno Ayako, 1969].) In addition Kuno was thirteen years older than Ichihashi, and the age disparity probably reinforced Kuno's attitude. Professional jealousy likely added to Kuno's hostility, for he did not have a doctoral degree. He obtained a BS degree in civil engineering and an MS degree in astronomy and mathematics from the University of California. In 1911 he was appointed an instructor in the Department of Oriental Languages, and nine years later he was promoted to assistant professor. Compared to Ichihashi, Kuno ranked lower in the academic hierarchy. Kuno had graduated from a Japanese middle school, which he equated with a German gymnasium. He considered his education in Japan in the Japanese classics and history incomparably superior to Ichihashi's Japanese education. Yet Ichihashi had a higher status at Stanford University and taught classes in Japanese history and civilization. This rankled Kuno. (For Kuno's educational background see "Yoshi Saburo Kuno, 1865–1941," *University of California: In Memoriam, 1941*, 13–15 [Available at the Online Archive of California: http://texts.cdlib.org/xtf/view ?docId=hb3199n7tr&doc.view=entire_text, accessed Aug. 13, 2005].) There was probably another reason for Kuno's hostility toward Ichihashi. Kuno was at odds, well before 1920, with Ichihashi and others who participated in the campaign directed by the local Japanese consul to educate Americans about Japan and Japanese immigration. Kuno considered them all "propagandists" for the Japanese government. Besides Ichihashi he included Kawakami Kiyoshi, Kanzaki Kiichi, and Inui Kiyosue in this category. Kawakami was the director of the Pacific Press Bureau, a news agency that had been set up in 1914 by the Japanese Foreign Ministry. Kanzaki was the secretary general of the Japanese Association of America, and Inui was the secretary of the Japan Society of Northern California and later lecturer at Occidental College and the University of Southern California. In 1916 Kuno accused them of plotting to seek his removal from his instructorship at the University of California. According to Kuno they resented his refusal to teach Japanese history as they dictated and objected to his public criticism of their defense of Japan and Japanese immigration (Kuno to Benjamin Ide Wheeler, March 22, 1916; Kuno to Henry R. Hatfield, March 25, 1916; and Kuno to David P. Barrows, Oct. 30, 1916; these letters can be found in both the Kuno Papers and Benjamin Ide Wheeler Papers, Bancroft Library, University of California, Berkeley). Kuno so despised these men that in private correspondence he referred to them as the "San Francisco Japs." (See Kuno to Toshi, Oct. 11, 1920, Kuno Papers. *Toshi* was Kuno's contraction of the first name of Tanaka Toshitarō, who was his dentist.)

58. Ichihashi to Jordan, March 28, 1913, Jordan Papers.

59. Yamato Ichihashi, *Japanese Immigration: Its Status in California* (San Francisco: Japanese Association of America, 1913), 44.

60. Ibid., 48.

61. Yamato Ichihashi, *Japanese Immigration: Its Status in California* (San Francisco: Marshall Press, 1915), 64.

62. Yamato Ichihashi, "Emigration from Japan and Japanese Immigration into the State of California" (PhD diss., Harvard University, 1913), 327–28.

63. Ibid., 260.

64. Ibid., 418.

65. For example, see Bureau of Investigation, Special Agent, Reports of Sep. 13–15, 17, 20, 26, Oct. 6, 10, 21, 1921. In reply to an inquiry from the Bureau of Investigation, Stanford president Wilbur attested to Ichihashi's character. He wrote that "we have found him a good teacher, a scholar and a gentleman. As far as I know there has been no suspicion of propaganda in regard to him. I think he is a very highminded Japanese who understands America and its attitude on Oriental problems. I feel that he can be of the greatest of service at the Conference on Limitation of Armaments" (Wilbur to Guy M. Walker, Sep. 29, 1921, Wilbur Papers). This Wilbur letter was quoted almost verbatim by the Bureau of Investigation report of October 6, 1921.

66. Ichihashi, *Japanese in the United States*, 215.

67. Reginald Bell, "A Study of Certain Phases of the Education of Japanese in Central California" (MA thesis, Stanford University, 1928); Marvin L. Darsie, *The Mental Capacity of American-Born Japanese Children* (Baltimore: Williams and Wilkins, 1926); Eliot G. Mears, *Resident Orientals on the American Pacific Coast* (Chicago: University of Chicago Press, 1928); William C. Smith, "Born American But—," *Survey Graphic*, May 1, 1926, 167–68; and William C. Smith, *The Second-Generation Oriental in America* (Honolulu: Institute of Pacific Relations, 1927).

68. Yuji Ichioka, "The Early Japanese Immigrant Quest for Citizenship: The Background of the 1922 Ozawa Case," *Amerasia Journal* 4, no. 2 (1977): 1–22.

69. Ichihashi, *Japanese in the United States*, 400.

ELEVEN

The Death of Dr. Honda Rikita

A Tragic Wartime Story

Introduction

Dr. Honda Rikita was among those *Issei* of Southern California who were arrested on December 7, 1941, as so-called dangerous enemy aliens. In his specific case he was picked up by the Moneta Police Department and sent to the detention facility of the Immigration and Naturalization Service located on Terminal Island. There he was confined in a solitary cell, where FBI agents interrogated him about his prewar, pro-Japan activities. Exactly a week later, early on the morning of December 14 in the hospital ward where Dr. Honda had been transferred temporarily, he was reported to have committed suicide by slashing his arm with a razor. During the Pacific War some Issei cast doubts on whether Dr. Honda really committed suicide, alleging instead that he had actually been beaten to death by his FBI interrogators.

I first learned of Dr. Honda's death as I was conducting research on Issei nationalism during the 1930s. The fact that he had died in the custody of the FBI on Terminal Island raised disturbing questions in my mind. With doubts about the official suicide explanation of his death, I decided to look into the matter for myself. I read existing wartime and postwar Issei accounts of what had happened to Dr. Honda. I also read newspaper accounts. I obtained a copy of the Los Angeles County Coroner's report. I requested and received Dr. Honda's redacted FBI file through the Freedom of Information/Privacy Acts. I contacted Mrs. Yasuko Utsumi, the eldest daughter of Dr. Honda,

Figure 15. Dr. Honda Rikita, ca. 1937. Yuji Ichioka Papers.

and interviewed her regarding her childhood recollections. Since she herself was trying to solve the riddle of her father's death, I shared with her what information I had collected. Most recently, I uncovered Dr. Honda's "Enemy Alien Case File," deposited at the National Archives, Pacific Southwest Region, in Laguna Niguel. Based on all of these and other materials, I would like to unravel the tragic wartime story of the death of Dr. Honda.

Background

A native of Yamagata Prefecture, Dr. Honda was born on February 1, 1893. He received his medical training at the prestigious Chiba Medical College, from which he graduated in 1918. After his graduation he served in the Medical Corps of the Japanese army from 1918 to 1920. He immigrated to the United States in 1921. In 1924 he opened his medical practice in Oakland, and then shortly after he became the head of the Fresno Japanese Hospital. From 1925 to 1928 he conducted medical research at the University of Pennsylvania and the University of Colorado. After he submitted his research findings to Tokyo Imperial University, he obtained a Doctorate of Medicine in 1931 from that institution. His prewar medical office was located in the heart of Little Tokyo of Los Angeles at 129½ East 1st St. He was married to a Nisei woman, with whom he had four children. His residence was located in Moneta, or present-day Gardena.[1]

Dr. Honda was a prominent person in the prewar Japanese community. As a physician he enjoyed high social status. At one time or another he was the president of the Japanese Medical Society and the Yamagata Prefectural Association. An avid sports fan, he was affiliated with sumō, kendō, and judō associations and was himself an accomplished kendō fencer. As a former member of the Japanese Army Medical Corps, he was also the founder and commander of the *Nanka Teikoku Gunyū Dan*, a fraternal organization of Japanese veterans dedicated to supporting the Japanese army. Because of Dr. Honda's involvement with this last group, the FBI placed him under close surveillance before the war and eventually arrested him as a so-called dangerous enemy alien on Pearl Harbor Day.[2]

Cause of Death

The precise cause of Dr. Honda's death remains unclear. The inspector in charge at the Terminal Island detention facility gave the following causal explanation of his death to the Los Angeles County coroner:

> On the morning of the 14th instant at about 6 A.M., the guard on duty in his rounds of the detention rooms, discovered that Mr. Honda had slashed his wrists and upper arms in an attempt to commit suicide. First aid was immediately given and the United States Public Health doctor was called immediately, but due to the fact that the alien had lost so much blood, nothing could be done to save his life.[3]

The Los Angeles FBI field office gave a slightly different account in notifying FBI headquarters in Washington, DC, of Honda's death. Its teletype of December 14 read:

Dr. Rikita Honda in custodial detention, immigration office, Terminal Island, California, committed suicide at five fifty five A.M. today by cutting veins with razor. Honda, subject of custodial detention card, was picked up December seven last or early morning of December eight last by police in Moneta, California. Detained in hospital ward separate from others where he was treated for diabetes. Doctors believe shock from cutting body in three places rather than loss of blood was responsible for death.[4]

Similarly, the Los Angeles County coroner's register recorded that the cause of death was "hemorrhage and shock—incision of deep vessels left ante cubital fossa," meaning a deep gash in the left forearm.[5] Despite disagreeing on the exact cause of death, whether it was by bleeding or hemorrhage or shock, all official documents concur that Dr. Honda committed suicide.

Japanese Wartime Propaganda

An alternative explanation of Dr. Honda's death originated within the context of the propaganda warfare waged by the Japanese government against the United States during the Pacific War. An Issei, Nakazawa Ken, was the first person to publicly question the suicide explanation. In fact, he went much further and charged that Dr. Honda had actually been beaten to death. Nakazawa made this allegation in 1942 shortly after he returned to Japan aboard the first exchange ship. Before the war Nakazawa had been a staff member of the Los Angeles Japanese Consulate, ostensibly as an educational adviser but in reality as an unofficial Japanese government spokesman who defended Japanese policy before the American public. Indeed, he had performed this role of spokesman continuously since 1928.[6] Nakazawa also had been a part-time lecturer in Oriental Studies at the University of Southern California and with the Los Angeles County Museum, positions that had given him extra credibility when he spoke before American audiences. Nakazawa was arrested by the FBI, too, but, unlike the typical arrested Issei, he was among those who were allowed to return to Japan in exchange for Americans who had been arrested and detained by the Japanese government.

The first exchange ship arrived in Yokohama in late August 1942.[7] To interview the returnees aboard the ship, newspaper reporters converged on the docks. Many of the first returnees recounted grim stories of ill treatment received at the hands of American authorities to the reporters. A *Japan Times and Advertiser* story of an internee, for example, was headlined "Brutal U.S. Treatment Scored—Japanese Herded like Criminals, Exposed to Countless Humiliations and Denied Bare Necessities of Life, Says Internee."[8] In a statement released to foreign correspondents on September 11 a spokesman of the Japanese government officially charged the United States government with "unfair, unjustifiable, and inhuman treatment" of "Japanese evacuees and internees."[9] At the same time, the Japanese government intensified its anti-American propaganda campaign by accusing the American side of adopting an official government policy of "persecuting" Japanese nationals and Japanese Americans and of committing numerous acts of "brutality" and "atrocities" against them.

Nakazawa took part in this anti-American propaganda campaign. He first gave an account of how Dr. Honda had been tortured to death to the Japanese press.[10] Later he participated in a special NHK Radio series entitled *Disclosures of American Inhumanity*. As evidence for his version of Honda's death, he reported that Dr. Honda's wife, when shown her husband's corpse, was unable to identify it as her husband because the face had been so disfigured and the body so badly mangled. As a result, Nakazawa said, Mrs. Honda had gone insane. Other returnees told similar tales of horror in this special radio series, which aired from September 9 through September 21, 1942.[11]

The *Japan Times and Advertiser*, in an editorial entitled "American Atrocities" on September 24, catalogued a list of "acts of insane persecution" committed by the "barbarous inhumanity of the American authorities" against Japanese nationals. This list included the "murder" of Dr. Honda. Drawing from Nakazawa's version of Dr. Honda's death, this editorial said the following: "[The] worst of all has been the treatment accorded Japanese who have been held for examination by the American authorities. Inhumane third degree methods have resulted in the murder of at least one victim by the American officials, as for instance in the classic case of Dr. Honda, a physician of San Pedro who was mistreated by the American authorities until he died."[12] NHK Radio broadcast this editorial in its entirety on the same date.[13] The U.S. Foreign Broadcast Intelligence Service monitored NHK shortwave radio broadcasting, so American authorities were fully aware of this Japanese interpretation of Dr. Honda's death.

In 1943 Nakazawa published a book in which he recounted his own experience of arrest and detention. He had been initially detained on Terminal Island, too. The title of his book was *Amerika Gokuchū Yori Dōhō ni Tsugu* [Report to My Compatriots from an American Prison]. In it Nakazawa explained the reason for his utter disbelief in the suicide explanation of Dr. Honda's death. He described Honda as a kind of person who was the least likely to commit suicide. According to Nakazawa he was an intelligent, robust, outgoing, and active man with a zest for life. Indeed, he had been an expert kendō fencer who loved sports of all kinds. Given his personality, Nakazawa asserted that it was impossible for him to believe that Dr. Honda had committed suicide and reiterated his belief that Honda had been beaten to death.[14]

Ebina Kazuo echoed Nakazawa's views. Ebina was another Issei who had lived in California for many years, working as a newspaperman for Japanese immigrant newspapers. He had been employed variously by the *Nichibei*, *Rafu Nichibei*, *Hokubei Asahi*, and *Shin Sekai Asahi*. The outbreak of the Pacific War found Ebina in Tokyo because he had returned to Japan in November 1941. At the beginning he was employed part-time by NHK Radio to write anti-American radio scripts and served as a commentator on the arrest and detention of Issei leaders and the eventual mass internment of the entire West Coast Japanese population. During the course of the war, he emerged as an active figure in the "Ei-Bei kichiku undō," a propaganda campaign through which the Japanese government cast Anglo-Americans in the image of subhuman beasts.[15]

Like Nakazawa Ken, Ebina published a book in 1943. Entitled *Karifuonia to Nihonjin* [California and the Japanese], this book rehashed the history of anti-Japanese racism in California and attributed the internment of the West Coast Japanese population to this very same racism. Indeed, in chapter 9, entitled "*Beikoku Kanken no Bōgyaku*" [Official American Atrocities], Ebina insisted that all the arrested and detained Issei leaders were "innocent non-combatants" who were victims of "vicious revenge." Having suffered a string of defeats at the hands of the Japanese military, Americans had retaliated by "handcuffing Issei like common criminals and hounding them into prisons." Using the metaphor of evil demons, Ebina said that "the hands of the American demon now extend over all Japanese in the United States." And he stated his own conviction that Dr. Honda had been tortured to death.[16]

Postwar Perspectives

During the postwar years other Issei offered somewhat different perspectives on Dr. Honda's death. Bishop Fukuda Yoshiaki of the Konkōkyō Church, for example, did not deny that Dr. Honda had committed suicide. Rather he claimed that Honda received such harsh third-degree treatment that FBI agents caused him to take his own life.[17] Similarly, the biographer of Dr. Tashiro Kikuo, a prewar Issei medical colleague of Dr. Honda, explained Dr. Honda's suicide as the result of grueling FBI interrogation.[18] Fujioka Shirō provided still another perspective. A longtime Issei staff writer of the *Rafu Shimpō*, he published a voluminous work on the Issei generation in 1957. In it he wrote about his own experience of being arrested, detained, and interrogated by the FBI at Terminal Island during which, he recalled, he heard disturbing rumors to the effect that "Dr. Honda either had committed suicide in his solitary cell or had been tortured and beatened [*sic*] to death."[19] Without assessing either the source or reliability of these rumors, Fujioka left the cause of death up in the air.

Enemy Alien Case File

Dr. Honda's enemy alien case file sheds light on the cause of death. This file includes eight short notes written by Dr. Honda himself during his confinement at the Terminal Island detention facility. Dr. Honda scribbled these notes, mostly in Japanese, on his own office pad with the letterhead clearly printed "Rikita Honda, M.D., Ph.D. (Tokyo Imperial University), Physician and Surgeon." The address and telephone number of his office and residence appear on either upper corner. The notes were addressed to himself or to specifically named persons. Except for one, the notes are all undated.

The notes provide evidence that Dr. Honda contemplated suicide. One note more than hints at this in these words: "A doctor's vocation is to save lives. In order to save lives, it is a doctor's highest honor to sacrifice himself. I dedicated myself to Japanese-American friendship. Now Japan and America are at war. I could not prevent it. I wish to make amends by taking my own life." Another addressed to his Nisei wife, Mae, reads: "Do the best you can for the children. And please do what you think is best for

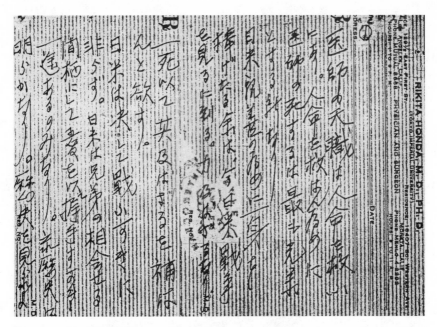

Figure 16. Honda's suicide note (translation in the text), December 1941. Enemy Alien Case Files (RG 85), National Archives, Pacific Southwest Region.

yourself, Mae. I will live forever through my descendants. Nothing bothers me now. I am content. There is no greater love than to sacrifice one's own life [literally, 'hito sono inochi wo sasageru yori dainaru ai wa nashi']. I'm grateful to God for giving me the opportunity to undertake this worthy endeavor."

Two other notes state Dr. Honda's suicidal intent even more explicitly, with an added motive. In the first one he wrote, "As a Japanese officer, I cannot remain a prisoner of war. I have no alternative but to commit suicide" (literally, "jiketsu no itto aru nomi"). In the second, addressed to a younger man by the name of "Ōkubo-kun," dated December 13, that is, the day before Dr. Honda's actual death, this same suicidal intent is expressed in identical language. But this note closes with the final words: "Look after things for me" (literally, "banji tanomu"), with Dr. Honda asking Ōkubo to attend to his personal affairs after his death.

The Japanese military code of conduct taught Japanese soldiers that it was a disgrace to be taken prisoner. Inasmuch as Dr. Honda had served in the Japanese army in the Medical Corps, he must have known this code of con-

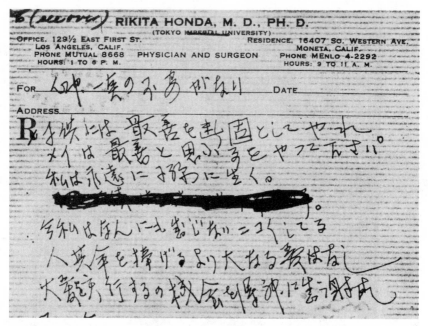

Figure 17. Honda's suicide note (translation in the text), December 1941. Enemy Alien Case Files (RG 85), National Archives, Pacific Southwest Region.

duct from firsthand experience. The latter two notes reveal that Dr. Honda still retained an identity as a Japanese officer. Moreover, they show that he equated his arrest and detention as tantamount to being "a prisoner of war." Under the circumstances, he believed he had only one option open to him to remove the implied stigma of shame captivity had brought on him. That option was to commit suicide, an extreme but nonetheless understandable act for someone like Dr. Honda, for it was in keeping with the Japanese military code of conduct.

Only one note refers to his interrogation by FBI agents. With a touch of indignation, combined with exasperation, it reads: "I told nothing but the truth, but was told I told only lies. I am at a loss. Only God knows." No note gives any evidence that Dr. Honda had been subjected to harsh third-degree treatment. Taken together, all of the notes indicate rather convincingly that, in all probability, Dr. Honda, contrary to the allegation that he had been beaten to death, actually took his own life.[20]

Conclusion

This conclusion does not preclude the possibility that some high-pressure methods might have been employed by FBI agents in interrogating Dr. Honda. A Russo-Japanese War veteran, Ōkura Momota was one of the vice commanders of the Nanka Teikoku Gunyū Dan and a close friend of Dr. Honda. Along with other members of the Gunyū Dan, he was also arrested on December 7, 1941, and detained on Terminal Island. According to his son, K. Patrick Okura, his father told him that he had been intensely inter-rogated over many days about his prewar, pro-Japan activities, but he was never threatened nor inflicted with bodily harm.[21] Dr. Honda probably underwent similar intense and prolonged interrogation, but his interroga-tion cannot be said to have been the primary cause of his suicide. The FBI looked on Dr. Honda's establishment and leadership of the Nanka Teikoku Gunyū Dan with great suspicion because of its avowed purpose of strength-ening the Japanese army and because of its membership consisting of Japanese army veterans. Like so many other prewar Issei organizations, the Gunyū Dan patriotically rallied behind Japan in the Sino-Japanese War with monetary contributions and other forms of support.[22] But it was not an organization that engaged in espionage as alleged by Senator Guy M. Gillette of Iowa shortly after Dr. Honda's death.[23] Indeed, the FBI reports on Dr. Honda make no reference to any espionage activities. Most Issei arrested as dangerous enemy aliens were not confined in solitary cells. That Dr. Honda was placed in such a cell means that he had been singled out for spe-cial treatment.

The FBI considered the Nanka Teikoku Gunyū Dan as dangerous as the *Nippon Kaigun Kyōkai*, which was dedicated to the goal of strengthening the Japanese navy. On June 7, 1941, the FBI had arrested Lieutenant Commander Tachibana Itaru, a Japanese naval officer, on the charge of espi-onage in Los Angeles.[24] Tachibana was closely connected to the Nippon Kaigun Kyōkai and its Issei leaders. As a result the FBI conducted a thor-ough investigation of the leaders and members well before Pearl Harbor Day.[25] Subsequent to Tachibana's arrest, the FBI searched his hotel room in Little Tokyo, and among the material found was a 1940 pamphlet explain-ing the purpose of the Nanka Teikoku Gunyū Dan. From this point in time the FBI had members of this group under strict surveillance, considering them a threat to national security on a par with the members of the Nippon Kaigun Kyōkai.[26] Hence the arrest of Dr. Honda and his confinement in a solitary cell. The Second World War spawned many tragedies on both sides of the Pacific. The suicide of Dr. Honda Rikita should be counted among the tragedies on the American side.

Notes

1. Biographical information on Honda Rikita has been culled from Rafu Shimpōsha, *Kigen Nisen Roppyakunen Hōshuku Kinen Taikan* (Los Angeles: Rafu Shimpōsha, 1940), 72; and "Rikita Honda," in Enemy Alien Case Files, Box 36, File 15942/624, RG 85, NA Branch Depository, Pacific Southwest Region, Laguna Niguel.

2. E. J. Thaney, FBI Report, Jan. 27, 1942, "Dr. Rikita Honda," in Enemy Alien Case Files, Box 36, File 15942/624, RG 85, NA Branch Depository, Pacific Southwest Region, Laguna Niguel.

3. Trent Doser, Inspector in Charge, to Office of the County Coroner, December 17, 1941, in Enemy Alien Case Files, Box 36, File 15942/624, RG 85, NA Branch Depository, Pacific Southwest Region, Laguna Niguel.

4. Los Angeles FBI Field Office to FBI Headquarters, Washington, DC, teletype, Dec. 14, 1941, in Rikita Honda, File no. 100-49480, Federal Bureau of Investigation, Freedom of Information/Privacy Acts release.

5. Los Angeles County Coroner's Register, File no. 97077, Rikita Honda.

6. Nakazawa did not have the status of a regular Japanese diplomat. He was hired by the Los Angeles Consulate in 1928 as a temporary staff member expressly for the purpose of educating Americans about Japan. A graduate of the University of Oregon with a PhD in English literature, he was fluent in English and a polished speaker, which made him a valuable and effective spokesman. Officially, he was listed as an educational adviser who assisted Japanese students, but he was in reality a consular staff member (*tai-Bei keihatsuin*) who worked to educate Americans about Japanese government policy. He was initially paid $100 per month. By 1937 his salary had risen to $135 per month. See Consul Hori Kōichi to Foreign Minister Satō Naotake, June 1, 1937, "Shōwa Jūninen Shigatsu Tsuitachi Genzai Shiyōnin Hōkokusho Teishutsu no Ken," DRO; and Consul Nakauchi Kenji to Foreign Minister Konoye Fumimaro, April 11, 1941, Japanese Foreign Ministry, Diplomatic Records Office. For FBI reports on Nakazawa see General Records of the Department of State, Decimal File, 1940–44, 894.20211, Nakazawa Ken File, Box 5900, RG 59, NA.

7. For a study of the exchange ships see Murakawa Yōko and Kumei Teruko, *Nichibei Senji Kōkansen, Sengo Sōkansen "Kikokusha" ni Kansuru Kisoteki Kenkyū—*

Nikkei Amerikajin no Rekishi no Shiten kara (Tokyo: Toyota Zaidan, 1992). See also P. Scott Corbett, *Quiet Passages: The Exchange of Civilians Between the United States and Japan During the Second World War* (Kent, OH: Kent State University Press, 1987).

8. *Japan Times and Advertiser*, Sep. 29, 1942.

9. *Japan Times and Advertiser*, Sep. 11, 1942.

10. U.S. Foreign Broadcast Intelligence Service, Transcript of NHK Shortwave Broadcasts, 1940–45, Sep. 8, 11, 1942.

11. Kitayama Setsurō, *Daitōa e no Michi*, vol. 2 of *Rajio Tōkyō Senji Taiseika Nihon no Taigai Hōsō* (Tokyo: Tabata Shoten, 1988), 205–7.

12. "American Atrocities," *Japan Times and Advertiser*, Sep. 24, 1942.

13. U.S. Foreign Broadcast Intelligence Service, Transcript of NHK Shortwave Broadcasts, 1940–45, Sep. 24, 1942.

14. Nakazawa Ken, *Amerika Gokuchū Yori Dōhō ni Tsugu* (Tokyo: Sonshobō, 1943), 34–37.

15. Kitayama, *Daitōa e no Michi*, 216–17. According to Kiyosawa Kiyoshi, the well-known diplomatic historian and onetime Issei himself, former Issei residents of the United States played leading roles in the anti-Anglo-American campaign. Besides Ebina, Mutō Shōgo was very active. Mutō had been the Tokyo correspondent of the *Rafu Shimpo* of Los Angeles before the war. See Kiyosawa Kiyoshi, *Ankoku Nikki* (Tokyo: Hyōronsha, 1959), 454.

16. Ebina Kazuo, *Karifuonia to Nihonjin* (Tokyo: Taiheiyō Kyōkai, 1943), 241–45.

17. Fukuda Yoshiaki, *Yokuryū Seikatsu Rokunen* (San Francisco: Konkōkyō Church, 1957), 57–58. Bishop Fukuda claimed that Dr. Honda was his friend, but he mistakenly identified him as Honda Nobuta rather than Honda Rikita. Fukuda also incorrectly wrote Honda's surname in Japanese. Instead of writing the "da" of Honda with the Chinese character meaning "many," he mistakenly wrote it with the character meaning "field." These mistakes make one wonder how much of a friend Dr. Honda actually was to Bishop Fukuda.

18. Hasegawa Shin, *Nihon Dasshutsuki: Rosanjierusu no Tashiro Dokutā* [Exodus from Japan: Dr. Tashiro of Los Angeles] (Tokyo: Seijisha, 1978), 306.

19. Fujioka Shirō, *Ayumi no Ato* (Los Angeles: Ayumi no Ato Kankō Iinkai, 1957), 187. Others, however, attribute Dr. Honda's death to suicide, without any reference to his interrogation. See, e.g., Matsumoto Honkō, *Fukkō Senjō ni Odoru Kikan Dōhō* (Los Angeles: Rafu Shoten, 1949), 15; and Nanka Nikkeijin Shōgyō Kaigisho, *Minami Kashū Nihonjin Nanajūnenshi* (Los Angeles: Nanka Nikkeijin Shōgyō Kaigisho, 1960), 523.

20. All of these notes are in "Rikita Honda," in Enemy Alien Case Files, Box

36, File 15942/624, RG 85, NA Branch Depository, Pacific Southwest Region, Laguna Niguel.

21. K. Patrick Okura, interview by Yuji Ichioka, June 22, 1997.

22. For a discussion of the Issei's prewar patriotic activities vis-à-vis Japan see Chapter 8.

23. *New York Times*, Dec. 19, 1941; *Los Angeles Times*, Dec. 19, 1941.

24. For details of the Tachibana espionage case see Chapter 9 above; see also Pedro Loureiro, "The Imperial Japanese Navy and Espionage: The Itaru Tachibana Case," *Intelligence and Counterintelligence* 3, no. 1 (1989): 105–21.

25. For detailed FBI reports on the Nippon Kaigun Kyōkai and its leaders and members see Agent A. P. LeGrand, Report, July 9, 1941; and Agent F. J. Holmes, Report, Aug. 26, 1941, both in General Records of the Department of State, Decimal File, 1940–44, 894.20211, Box 5901, RG 59, NA. See also Chapter 9 herein.

26. In 1943 the Office of Naval Intelligence compiled comprehensive lists of "subversive" Japanese organizations. The ONI's "A" list consisted of organizations "deemed to constitute an actual threat to the internal security of the United States." Both the Teikoku Gunyū Dan and Nippon Kaigun Kyōkai appeared on this A list. See "Subversive Japanese Organizations in the U.S.," April 1, 1943, in Records of the Office of the Chief of Naval Operations, Office of Naval Intelligence, Sabotage, Espionage, Counterespionage Section (SEC), Oriental Desk (Op 16-B-7-o), 1936–46, Japanese Organization and Intelligence in US, Box 1, RG 38, NA.

PART THREE

TWELVE

The Future of Japanese American Studies

*Prospect of Comparative Historical Perspectives
on Nikkei in North and South America*

Introduction

In the United States Japanese American Studies have reached a kind of turning point. There is a plethora of sociohistorical studies on Japanese Americans,
but such studies are confined to the United States. While many of them are
worthwhile, they all share the limitation of being only about the *Nikkei*
[people of Japanese ancestry] in the United States. The sole exception to this
generalization is the few extant comparative studies of the wartime internment of Japanese Americans and Japanese Canadians. There are also numerous sociohistorical studies of the Nikkei in Canada, Brazil, Peru, and other
Latin American countries in English, Portuguese, Spanish, and Japanese.
Such studies likewise place their Nikkei subjects within the context of
specific national histories or view them within the framework of modern
Japanese history. Few studies, if any, historically compare the Nikkei experience across national boundaries. As a new direction in Japanese American
Studies, I believe that comparative historical studies of the Nikkei in North
and South America can be a fruitful departure from past insular approaches.[1]
For such studies hold out the prospect of bringing comparative perspectives
to bear on the Nikkei experience in order to formulate new interpretations
of that experience and to advance not only the field of Japanese American
Studies but also the field of Nikkei studies as a whole.

In my opinion one broad question should be addressed in any comparative historical framework: What was the historical process through which

Japanese immigrants (including Okinawans) became Nikkei in North and South America? In raising this central question I am assuming that the Japanese who emigrated abroad, whether to North or South America (or elsewhere for that matter), were fundamentally the same, with the single exception of the Okinawans, who constituted a special subset of Japanese immigrants. Regardless of whether the Japanese emigrants left Japan during the Meiji, Taisho, or early Showa periods, they shared a common Japanese identity and culture and adhered to a common set of Japanese values. They all started out as *dekasegi* laborers who left Japan with the intent of returning home on the completion of their temporary sojourn abroad. But through force of circumstances these people ended up living out their lives and raising families in their respective immigrant lands. On the other hand, I am not assuming that their descendants—the present-day Nikkei in North and South America—are all the same. Quite the contrary, I am assuming that, although we are all no longer Japanese, we differ considerably as Nisei, Sansei, and Yonsei (and even Gosei in the case of Hawaii) living in different countries. The explanation for the differences is to be sought in the historical process through which Japanese immigrants became Nikkei.

Broadly speaking, this process occurred during the crucial years between 1930 and 1960, spanning the three decades of the prewar, wartime, and immediate postwar years. During the prewar decade the Issei occupied positions of dominance in every Japanese immigrant society, with the Nisei still relegated to subordinate roles. The outbreak of the Pacific War radically altered the relationship between the two generations. In every Japanese immigrant society the war generated an intense crisis of identity, characterized in part by a growing breach between the Issei and Nisei generations. This breach formed the essential background to the postwar transition from Japanese to Nikkei, marked by the demise of the Issei generation and the ascendancy of the Nisei generation.

Prewar Years

During the prewar years the countries of North and South America differed widely in their reception and treatment of Japanese immigrants, ranging from overt racial hostility to general receptivity. In comparing the Issei generation, I would begin by asking how the host societies received Japanese immigrants and compare how the immigrants themselves, similarly and/or dissimilarly, adapted to their new immigrant lands. These questions are of course related to problems of identity, language, culture, values, and adaptation faced by all Issei regardless of where they immigrated to. In addition to comparing the adaptation of the Issei, I would also compare how they perceived the future of their children. Generally speaking, the so-called problem of the second generation came to the forefront in the 1930s in both North and South America (admittedly, somewhat earlier in the case of the United States and Canada). From an Issei perspective this problem also entailed fundamental questions relating to the retention of the Japanese language, values, culture, and identity on the part of the Nisei. It also involved questions relating to the desired degree to which, the Issei believed, the Nisei should adapt themselves and assimilate to their native countries.

The 1930s witnessed the rise of militarism in Japan, which vastly complicated all questions of adaptation and assimilation. As a general rule, regardless of where the Issei resided, they patriotically identified with their homeland and supported Japan's military actions in China. They purchased Japanese National Defense Bonds, collected and sent War Relief Funds, and also collected and sent so-called *imonbukuro*, or care packages, earmarked for Japanese soldiers on the China warfront. The Issei in Hilo, Hawaii; Los Angeles, California; and Lima, Peru, also collected and donated funds for military aircraft. The patriotic zeal of the Issei found expression through literature, poetry, music, and other cultural forms. Issei patriotism initially surfaced in the aftermath of the Manchurian Incident of 1931; progressively intensified during the decade, but especially after the commencement of the Sino-Japanese War in July 1937; and culminated in the first conference of overseas Japanese held in Tokyo in November 1940. Whether in South or North America, the Issei identification with Japan's cause in Asia strongly influenced their assessment of their own immigrant status and that of their Nisei descendants.

In contrast to the Issei generation, I would ask and compare how the Nisei themselves perceived their own problems of language, culture, identity, and gender in the 1930s. Their own assessment invariably hinged on the question of how and to what degree they felt it necessary to integrate themselves into their native countries. Put in another way, it depended on the question of how much they thought they should endeavor to become full participating members of their own societies. In the United States this assessment was complicated by the presence of so-called *Kibei-Nisei*, that is, those Nisei who had been reared and educated, in whole or in part, in Japan but who had returned to their native land, the United States. In Brazil, on the other hand, questions relating to the Nisei were complicated by the presence of so-called proto-Nisei (*jun-Nisei*) who had accompanied their parents to Brazil either in infancy or early childhood and had been raised and educated there. Such persons were neither true Issei nor true Nisei; they were what Korean Americans today call the 1.5 generation. A comparison of the initial debate among Nisei leaders in North and South America regarding solutions to their problems undoubtedly will reveal sharp differences, reflecting the different positions the Nisei occupied in their respective societies and their relationship to the Issei generation on the eve of Pearl Harbor.

The Second World War

The outbreak of the Pacific War accelerated and intensified the prewar division between the Issei and Nisei generations. It goes without saying that the Issei and Nisei experienced the Second World War differently in North and South America. All Nikkei in the Western Hemisphere were not interned, and when they were, their experiences were not uniform. Internment was confined to the Japanese in the United States, Canada, and Mexico, plus the Peruvian deportees who were interned under special circumstances in the United States. Unlike most countries in the Western Hemisphere, the Brazilian government did not declare war against the Axis Powers until the summer of 1942 and did not adopt harsh repressive measures against its Japanese population. The government only ordered the closure of all privately operated Japanese-, German-, and Italian-language schools. While the Peruvian government itself did not intern all Japanese Peruvians, it did collaborate with the American government in the arrest and detention of selected Japanese Peruvians and adopted stringent repressive measures against the remainder of the Japanese population.

Notwithstanding the differences between North and South America, however, the Pacific War raised new questions of loyalty, nationalism, and politics under wartime conditions that widened the gap between the Issei and Nisei generations. Here I would ask how the Issei comparatively experienced the Pacific War and how that shaped their shifting views of the Nisei.

Similarly, I would ask how the Nisei comparatively experienced the war and how their own experience shaped their answers to ongoing questions relating to identity, language, culture, and the larger question of loyalty engendered by the Pacific War. Although each generation in North and South America experienced the Second World War in similar and dissimilar ways, I believe that the war had the overall effect of widening the gap between the Issei and Nisei generations, convincing many Nisei leaders that their future was inextricably tied to their own respective countries and not to their parents' homeland.

Postwar Period

What the Pacific War started, the postwar years completed. The postwar years witnessed the demise of the Issei generation and the complete ascendancy of the Nisei generation. Stated somewhat differently, the transition from Japanese to Nikkei occurred in the aftermath of the Second World War. Here I am assuming that the historical process was not identical in North and South America. Indeed, I believe that it took different twists and turns depending on how the Nikkei experienced the wartime years and the postwar conditions in their respective countries. Nevertheless, regardless of country, the postwar years witnessed a renewed, vigorous debate among the Nisei regarding the fundamental question of how far they should adapt and assimilate to their native lands. The differences in the substance of the debate and the actual postwar assimilation of the Nisei go far to explain the transition from Japanese to Nikkei and the ensuing differences that emerged among the Nikkei in North and South America.

I realize the new postwar Japanese immigrants to Brazil, Argentina, Bolivia, and Paraguay do not fit neatly into this research time frame because of their later arrival in Latin America. Yet these Japanese are now going through a similar process of transforming themselves from being Japanese to becoming Nikkei, albeit without the cataclysmic impact of the Pacific War. This process itself can be examined on a comparative basis with the antecedent Nikkei experience as a historical example. I am also aware of the recent "rediscovery" of Japanese and Okinawan identities among Nikkei in North and South America, in part the by-product of Japan's emergence as an economic superpower, the reverse labor migration of Nikkei from Latin

America to Japan, and the reaffirmation of ethnicity in both North and South America. But this rediscovery and reaffirmation of so-called Japanese-ness and Okinawanness are really no more than new permutations of pre-existing Nikkei identities.

It is a truism to say that it is vital to examine the relationship between the homeland government and the immigrant nation in any interpretation of Japanese immigrants and their descendants. Japan's diplomatic relations with the United States, Canada, Brazil, Peru, Argentina, Paraguay, Bolivia, and Mexico all differed over time and, accordingly, have had, and continue to have, a differential impact on Japanese communities. The relationship of Japan to any one of these nations cannot be equated with its relationship to any other. Moreover, the Japanese government has aided and continues to aid many Japanese communities in Latin America through the Japan International Cooperation Agency. In sum, it is well-nigh impossible to understand the Nikkei experience, whether in North or South America, without comparing and grasping the different and changing diplomatic rela-tions Japan has had over the years down to the present with the various countries to which the Issei immigrated.

Conclusion

From my knowledge of the available primary sources in North and South America, I would say that they are sufficiently abundant to undertake this kind of research. In my mind comparative historical studies will enhance greatly our understanding of the Nikkei experience, for they offer the real prospect of adding to our historical knowledge of how Japanese immigrants became Nikkei and of highlighting what present-day Nikkei in North and South America share in common and what differences set them apart.

Over and beyond the prospect of giving us comparative insights into the Nikkei experience, comparative historical studies will also add to our store-house of knowledge regarding the pliability of the Japanese as a people. Such studies will show, in opposition to Japanese racial thinking (and in unequiv-ocal terms I believe), that there is no such thing as an immutable Japanese racial trait or national character transmitted by blood from one generation to another. Japanese racial thinking would have us believe the adage "Once a Japanese, always a Japanese." Comparative historical studies of the Nikkei should not only give the lie to this adage but also suggest the necessity of an expanded definition of the meaning of Japanese in the globalized world in which all of us now live.

Notes

Editor's note: This essay was completed before the publication of Hirabayashi et al., eds., *New Worlds, New Lives: Globalization and People of Japanese Descent in the Americas and from Latin America in Japan* (Stanford, CA: Stanford University Press, 2002).

    1. Yuji Ichioka, "Nikkei in the Western Hemisphere," *Amerasia Journal* 15, no. 2 (1989): 175–77.

THIRTEEN

A Historian by Happenstance

I shy away from describing myself as a professional historian. The reason is quite simple. Unlike most professional historians, I did not become a historian through the conventional process of completing a PhD program in history at an established university. True, at one time I had aspired to be a historian of modern China, but I quickly divested myself of this idea when I dropped out of Columbia University in 1963 after less than a year in graduate school. My brief exposure to graduate studies persuaded me that a doctoral program was not my cup of tea. Nor did I become a historian by long-term, personal design. My public-school education did everything but instill in me an interest in history. Indeed, it is not too far-fetched to say that on my graduation from Berkeley High School in 1954 I was the veritable embodiment of ignorance in all matters relating to history. I came upon my interest in Asian American history much later in life through force of circumstances within the context of the civil rights and anti–Vietnam War movements.

Circumstantial Beginning

Thirty-one years ago, in the spring of 1969 at UCLA, I taught the first class in what we now call Asian American Studies under the title "Orientals in America." I was invited to teach this class by UCLA student activists who were spearheading the push for Asian American Studies on their campus.

They had heard of my political activities in Northern California. In the spring of 1968 I had founded the Asian American Political Alliance, a political action group in Berkeley. The students contacted me and asked if I would consent to have them submit my name as a potential instructor. I gave them the go-ahead, and once I was approved as the instructor, I accepted a part-time, one-quarter lectureship that marked the beginning of my personal involvement with Asian American Studies. Thus my entrance into the academy was different from that of my colleagues. I began my career under these special circumstances without standard academic credentials.

The atmosphere at UCLA was politically charged from the outset. The San Francisco State Third World Strike had erupted in November 1968, followed by the Berkeley Third World Strike in January 1969. Both strikes had a profound impact on racial minorities on the campus. Charles E. Young, the youngest chancellor in the history of the University of California system, assumed his post at UCLA on July 1, 1968, and he immediately found himself under great political pressure. Black, Latino, and Asian students were clamoring for the appointment of third world faculty and classes in Ethnic Studies. Angela Davis, then a young professor in the Philosophy Department and a self-proclaimed member of the American Communist Party, was one of the most popular lecturers on the UCLA campus. Once the Board of Regents learned of her communist background, however, it decided to dismiss her, forcing Young to defend her in the name of academic freedom. In January 1969 a shoot-out occurred on the campus between members of the Black Panther Party and US, Ron Karenga's African nationalist group. Two Black Panthers were killed. Some have charged that this incident was instigated by FBI provocateurs. Whether true or not, a pervasive sense of crisis enveloped the campus.

The UCLA students who invited me had decided on the class outline in advance of my appointment. In this sense I was the nominal rather than the actual instructor (although I did make a few changes once the class got under way). Approximately 150 students enrolled. The class format mainly featured small sections, led by the student organizers, in which weekly discussions of politics and identity dominated. At the time, many, if not most, of the enrolled students were wrestling with their own identity problems revolving around the question of what it meant to be an Asian in American society. Inasmuch as I had never faced a class in my life, this class became my baptism into teaching.

With scant knowledge of the history of Asians in the United States, I realized that I had to educate myself to prepare for the class. I quickly read the "classics" in Asian American Studies for the first time: Mary Coolidge, *Chinese Immigration* (1909); Bruno Lasker, *Filipino Immigration to the Continental United States and to Hawaii* (1931); Yamato Ichihashi, *The Japanese in the United States* (1932); Hilary Conroy, *The Japanese Frontier in Hawaii, 1868–1898* (1953); and Rose Hum Lee, *The Chinese in the United States* (1960). I also examined the two standard works on the anti-Chinese and anti-Japanese exclusion movements: Elmer C. Sandmeyer, *The Anti-Chinese Movement in California* (1939); and Roger Daniels, *The Politics of Prejudice* (1962); as well as the standard work on California labor history: Ira A. Cross, *A History of the Labor Movement in California* (1935). And I set about reviewing the then already voluminous literature on the wartime internment of Japanese Americans.

My interest in Japanese American history was reinforced by the Japanese American Research Project (JARP). Sponsored by the Japanese American Citizens League, JARP had been launched in 1962 as a sociohistorical study of Japanese immigrants and their descendants. In 1969 it was still an ongoing research project based on the UCLA campus. One of its research assistants was Yasuo Sakata, a former classmate of mine and a doctoral candidate in the UCLA History Department. In 1962 we had graduated together as history majors from UCLA, I as a young Nisei and he as a foreign student from Japan. From him I learned that JARP had collected a sizable body of primary sources in the Japanese language on Japanese immigration history. I also learned (and much to my dismay I might add) that the collection was in an unorganized state, the material still stored in dusty cartons. Yet I didn't have to look at everything in order to arrive at a reasonable judgment as to the worth of the collection. A cursory inspection sufficed to confirm Sakata's view that it, indeed, contained many primary sources of immense historical value relating to Japanese immigration history.

The Asian American Studies Center at UCLA was established on July 1, 1969. Those of us who were involved in the first class in Asian American Studies had drafted the proposal for the establishment of the center. I served as the associate director in the first year. From its inception, the center had, among its multiple purposes, the goal of doing research on Asians in American society in the past and present. At the time the director of JARP had no plans to organize the JARP collection. I consulted with Yasuo Sakata.

Because he and I both agreed on its historical value, we decided to undertake the accession work of organizing and annotating the Japanese-language material in the collection. So in 1971, with the support of the Asian American Studies Center, we commenced the tedious and dirty work of going through the dusty boxes in which the material had been stored. Our labor bore fruit three years later with the publication of *A Buried Past: An Annotated Bibliography of the Japanese American Research Project Collection* (1974).

My work on the bibliography laid the foundation for my research work. A reading of the secondary literature on Japanese American history convinced me of the accuracy of Roger Daniels's observation, made in 1966, that Asians had been studied only because they had been objects of exclusion. Studies of prewar Japanese American history almost exclusively concentrated on what had happened to the Issei generation. They focused on the anti-Japanese exclusion movement and the exclusionists, but rarely, if ever, did they touch on how the excluded, the Issei, felt, thought, and reacted to being excluded. In general, researchers assumed that Japanese immigrants left no records of their American experience; and even when researchers assumed otherwise, they failed to look into the records, often using the difficulty of reading the Japanese language as a convenient excuse. What resulted was a skewed view of the Issei as mere objects of exclusion. That is why I selected the title *A Buried Past* for our bibliography. In my opinion Issei history remained an unexhumed past.

The accession work opened my eyes to the existence of Japanese-language sources by and about the Issei. The JARP Collection included the microfilm records of the Japanese Foreign Ministry on overseas Japanese immigration and the Japanese exclusion movement; Japanese immigrant newspapers and periodicals; Japanese Association records; numerous general, regional, and local histories, as well as histories of religious institutions and other community organizations; biographies, memoirs, and autobiographies; published works of fiction and poetry; rich personal papers of prominent Issei; and photographic albums and other material. Taken together, these Japanese language sources constituted a rich treasure trove never before tapped by past historians.

Today, it is no longer a question of the availability of Japanese-language sources. Rather, it is the question of the ability of researchers to use such sources, now even more abundantly available than when we annotated the

JARP Collection. In the introduction to the JARP bibliography I wrote that the interest in the history of racial minorities should entail "the debunking of old distortions and myths, the uncovering of hitherto neglected or unknown facts, and the construction of a new interpretation of that past." I came away from the accession work with the firm conviction that research in the Japanese-language sources in the JARP Collection offered the best possibility of accomplishing all three tasks as far as Japanese American history was concerned. This conviction became the cornerstone of my research work and later efforts to collect additional sources to enhance the JARP Collection.

Fits and Starts

In 1969 my knowledge of Japanese was not good enough to do in-depth historical research. I was a typical postwar Nisei who grew up ignorant of the Japanese language. I never attended a Japanese-language school, and I only spoke broken Japanese at home. When I graduated from high school, my speaking ability was, at best, at a kindergarten level. It goes without saying that I had absolutely no reading or writing ability. My introduction to Chinese characters took place in Chinese-language classes I took in connection with my early aspiration to become a historian of modern China, which ended abruptly when I dropped out of graduate school. Subsequently, I took a job as far removed from East Asian Studies as possible. I became a Youth Parole Worker with the New York State Training School for Boys, a social-service agency working with so-called delinquent youth. I worked a year in an institutional setting in Warwick, New York, and another year as a parole worker in New York City.

While employed as a parole worker, I began to study Japanese in preparation for a trip to Japan. I studied on my own for the most part but had some help from a few Japanese friends. One couple had come to New York City from Tokyo to do a book on Malcolm X. Unable to understand the colloquial expressions in the speeches and writings of Malcolm X, they sought help from me. In exchange for my assistance they offered to give me private Japanese lessons. I accepted their offer and studied with them for about six months. In the winter of 1966 I sailed to Yokohama aboard the *Argentina Maru*, an old Osaka Steamship Company vessel that had transported many

Japanese immigrants to Latin America. Since I booked steerage passage, I shared quarters with many people, many of whom were Japanese immigrants returning to their homeland after long sojourns in Brazil. For the first time in my life I found myself in an all-Japanese-speaking environment. What little Japanese I had studied until that time proved to be woefully wanting. I still could not adequately communicate my thoughts and feelings in the language. I often felt like an imbecile among my shipmates, with whom I shared crammed quarters during the 11-day transpacific passage. This experience, at once disappointing and exasperating, motivated me to continue learning Japanese during my subsequent three-month stay in Japan.

On my return to the States I worked as a warehouseman until the winter of 1967, when I entered the East Asian Studies MA program at the University of California at Berkeley. I enrolled in a few classes in Japanese literature and culture, but most of my classes were in history, especially modern Japanese history. Under the guidance of Professor Yamaguchi Kōsaku, a visiting professor of history from Japan, I did my MA thesis on Takayama Chōgyū, a Meiji writer and conservative political thinker. While pursuing my MA degree, I made special efforts to socialize with native Japanese speakers with the goal of improving my spoken Japanese. I also served as an occasional, unofficial interpreter for members of the Japanese Council Against the A- and H-Bomb (Gensuikin) who came to participate in anti–Vietnam War rallies and activities in the San Francisco Bay Area. The council was an official organ of the Japanese Socialist Party.

In this way I improved my Japanese proficiency, but it still was not good enough to do research in Japanese immigration history. I was unable to easily read or fully comprehend Japanese written in late Meiji times, not to mention hand transcriptions of Japanese diplomatic cables and reports. Nor could I read with facility early Japanese immigrant newspapers and periodicals. Fortunately, I had Yasuo Sakata as my mentor. As we worked together on the accession work of organizing and annotating the JARP Collection, he taught me about the characteristics of Meiji-style writing, the meaning of old idiomatic expressions, and the secret of deciphering difficult passages. The accession work was my on-the-job training, so to speak. I learned a new grammar, a new vocabulary, and new idioms, all related, directly or indirectly, to Japanese immigration history, which prepared me for my future research work. Through these circumstances I became keenly interested in

Japanese American history, to the extent that I began to entertain the idea of doing research on the topic myself.

The field of Japanese American Studies was wide open. Except for studies of the prewar Japanese exclusion movement and the wartime internment of Japanese Americans, there were no historical studies of any merit. During the early 1970s, under the influence of the civil rights movement, most Japanese Americans were self-absorbed in reassessing their wartime internment experience. While this was perfectly understandable, it had the unintended effect of promoting a myopic view of Japanese American history, at least as I saw it at the time. With so much attention paid to the internment years, it was as if Japanese American history had begun with the Second World War, consigning the half century or more of prewar history to a state of almost complete oblivion. If I decided to do historical research, I promised myself that I would stay clear of the wartime years. I would take advantage of the opportunity afforded by the JARP Collection and study the prewar years, especially the Issei generation during the late nineteenth century and early twentieth.

Research and Related Work

I commenced research in earnest after the publication of our annotated bibliography. I published my first essay, on Issei socialists and anarchists, in 1971 in the second issue of *Amerasia Journal*. The research and writing for this piece predated my work on the JARP annotation project and originated in my first encounter with the late Karl Yoneda, the longtime Japanese American leftist. Although I had heard of Karl prior to 1967, I never had had the privilege of meeting him. I met him for the first time in the summer of 1967. Almost immediately after, I read his Japanese book on the history of Japanese workers in the United States. From my reading I learned, much to my surprise and joy, that there had been Issei socialists and anarchists at the turn of the century in the San Francisco Bay Area. I felt an immediate kinship with them because they, too, had struggled against racism, political oppression, and economic exploitation. I felt an even greater kinship as I learned that one of the anarchists, Ueyama Jitarō, was the father of Dr. Hajime Ueyama. Dr. Ueyama was our family doctor, who lived and practiced medicine a block from our home in Berkeley. Despite the fact that I grew up with Dr. Ueyama's son, I had been unaware that his grandfather had been a member of the Social Revolutionary Party, the Issei anarchist organization formed in Oakland in 1906. With my curiosity whetted, I decided to do my piece on the Issei socialists and anarchists. In retrospect I think I selected this topic because it enabled me to link the Japanese American past, in a very personal way, to what I was doing politically in Berkeley at the time.

My subsequent writings consisted of essays on other topics in Japanese American history. In doing the research for them, I used the Japanese-language sources in the JARP Collection, sometimes supplementing them with other sources. With no clear book in mind, I moved from one topic to another, with each essay standing on its own. My initial focus was on Issei laborers. I worked on such topics as the Japanese labor contracting system and American railroads and the United Mine Workers of America and Japanese coal miners in Rock Springs, Wyoming. Working as I was in new research terrain, I always faced the challenge of having to start more or less from scratch in writing my essays. For example, when I began research on the landmark 1922 Takao Ozawa naturalization test case, I discovered that no one had bothered to examine the Japanese immigrant background to the case. The extant secondary works only covered the legal issues it raised. So I reconstructed the Japanese immigrant background from my reading of the Japanese immigrant press, Japanese Foreign Ministry cables and reports, and other Japanese-language sources. Similarly, when I started asking myself questions about the adverse effects of the California alien land laws, I discovered that very little had been produced on how the Japanese immigrants themselves perceived and reacted to the laws. Some researchers, without examining Japanese-language sources, maintained that the laws had no real negative effects. To refute this unfounded claim, I wrote about the effects as evidenced by how Japanese immigrants actually reacted to the enactment and enforcement of the alien land laws. Eventually, I put all of my essays into a coherent narrative in book form as *The Issei: The World of the First-Generation Japanese Immigrants, 1885–1924* (1988).

Alongside my research work I did other related things. For one, I suggested to Karl Yoneda that he should write an autobiography, believing that it was important for people to read the story of his life of struggle as a trade-unionist, communist, writer, and political activist. Karl hesitated at first because he thought his English was inadequate to the task. Though born in the United States, he had been educated—except for a year in an elementary school in Glendale, California—entirely in Japan. Understandably, Japanese was his first language. Once he agreed to my suggestion, however, he approached the job of writing in English with characteristic dogged determination. Using his index fingers in a hunt-and-peck manner, he knocked out a draft on an old typewriter. I assumed the job of editing. As much as possible, I retained the flavor of his original English but made deletions and recommended additions wherever I thought they would improve the draft. In 1983, after considerable give-and-take, the Asian American Studies Center published the autobiography under the title *Ganbatte: Sixty-Year Struggle of a Kibei Worker*. Attracting a wide readership, the book sold out in a very short time.

I also worked to expand the JARP Collection. Convinced that some Japanese American families still had personal records of their Issei parents or grandparents, I sought out such families. Many of these families, unable to read Japanese, were not aware of the historical value of what they possessed. The JARP Project officially had ended in 1972. I persuaded families with personal papers to donate them to UCLA through the Asian American Studies Center. Among the most significant ones are the Sakai Yoneo Papers, Karl Yoneda Papers, Abiko Family Papers, Fujita Akira Papers, Togawa Akira Papers, and Fujii Ryōichi Papers, all rich in Japanese-language manuscript material. Sakai Yoneo (1900–1978) was an Issei newspaperman affiliated with the *Rafu Shimpō* before the Second World War; Fujita Akira (1920–1988) was a Kibei writer who was a prominent figure in the Nanka Bungei, a postwar literary group in Southern California; Togawa Akira (1903–1980) was an Issei poet and member of the Nanka Bungei as well; and Fujii Ryōichi (1905–1983) was an Issei newspaperman and founder of the *Chicago Shimpō*. The Abiko Family Papers primarily consist of the papers of Abiko Yonako (1880–1944), the Issei wife of Abiko Kyūtarō, founder and publisher of the *Nichibei Shimbun* of San Francisco. I have already identified Karl Yoneda (1906–1999). Besides the foregoing papers we also acquired the Edison Uno Papers, Charles Kikuchi Papers, and T. Scott Miyagawa Papers, papers of three prominent Nisei.

Both the registries of each of the papers and the papers themselves are available at the Department of Special Collections in the UCLA Charles E. Young Research Library, where the entire JARP Collection is deposited. *Fading Footsteps of the Issei: An Annotated Check List of the Manuscript*

Holdings of the Japanese American Research Project Collection (1992), compiled by Yasuo Sakata, is an annotated bibliography of the manuscript holdings of the original JARP Collection. *A Buried Past II: A Sequel to the Annotated Bibliography of the Japanese American Research Project Collection* (1999), which I most recently compiled with Eiichiro Azuma, is an annotated bibliography of all the new Japanese-language material added to the JARP Collection since 1973, including numerous new studies on Japanese immigration history published in Japan. Combined with the original collection, this new material makes the JARP Collection unrivaled. It is without a doubt the finest collection of primary and secondary sources in the United States in the Japanese language on Japanese immigrants and their descendants.

Finally, I presented many public lectures. From the beginning the staff of the Asian American Studies Center committed itself to forging ties with the Asian American communities of Southern California and making some kind of contributions to them. Accordingly, I taught community classes on Japanese American history over an eight-year period. These classes were held in the evenings at churches, temples, and other community institutions and were attended, for the most part, by Japanese Americans. Many were Sansei and Yonsei who were probing into their own family roots and were therefore especially eager to learn about the Japanese American past. Older Nisei attendees often shared their knowledge and life experiences with class members, providing unanticipated but important personal lessons in history from which everyone in the classes benefited. No instructor could have asked for a better group of motivated, engaged, and attentive students.

Japanese Academic Studies

During the last twenty-five years I have followed closely Japanese researchers and their writings on Japanese Americans. From about the late 1970s an interest in overseas Japanese arose in academic and other circles in Japan. This interest was stimulated, in part, by the 1978 commemorative events marking the seventieth anniversary of Japanese immigration to Brazil. In Saõ Paulo, the president of Brazil and the crown prince of Japan participated in the weeklong events carried out with great fanfare. The Japanese news media gave wide coverage to all of the events, the effect of which was to generate a popular interest in Japanese Brazilians and other Nikkei living outside of

Brazil. At the beginning there were only a handful of researchers who studied overseas Japanese, but the number of such people increased dramatically during the 1980s, so much so that in 1991 the Nihon Imin Gakkai, or Japanese Association for Migration Studies, was established. From the association's inception the membership, now exceeding three hundred members, comprised people in the social sciences and humanities conducting research on Japanese emigration abroad, particularly to North America. The official organ of the association, the *Imin Kenkyū Nenpō* ["The Annual Review of Migration Studies"], has been published since 1995.

Throughout the years I have met many Japanese researchers. My relationship to them has not been always cordial. On the one hand, I have met researchers who have a sincere interest in Nikkei and have produced admirable studies. These persons have my respect and gratitude. On the other hand, I have come across others whom I have found, to put it bluntly, rather hard to stomach. My first research trip to Japan occurred in 1974. After seeing *A Buried Past* through publication I decided to go to Tokyo to search for more Japanese-language sources. On this my second trip to Japan, I met Itō Kazuo, a well-known Japanese writer on Japanese American history. In 1969 he had published *Hokubei Hyakunen Zakura*, an edited collection of Issei reminiscences about prewar life and labor in the Pacific Northwest, on which his reputation rested. Itō impressed me as an arrogant, conceited Japanese male. Draping himself in a mantle of authority, he was a self-anointed "expert" on Japanese American history.

Apart from dislikable personalities, I am critical of Japanese researchers for other reasons. I have long advocated that sources in Japanese American history should be deposited in public institutions accessible to all bona fide researchers. This belief has served as my guiding principle in my work of expanding the JARP Collection. Hence I have opposed sources going into private hands, especially into Japanese hands for exclusive usage in Japan. After all, the Issei made history in the United States, and the records of that history should remain in this country as a part of our historical heritage. Nonetheless, some Japanese researchers have managed to get their hands on sources, sometimes by methods bordering on thievery, and then have carted them off to Japan.

The *Yuta Nippō* of Salt Lake City once had valuable source material accumulated since the day it was launched back in 1914. When I paid a call on the newspaper office, I was shocked to find that the office shelves had been picked clean of books and other material. The Nisei daughter of the deceased publisher informed me that Japanese visitors, who visited the office periodically, had taken everything away. In my opinion these visitors took advantage of the fact that this daughter did not know what the office shelves held because she could not read Japanese. Then there is the case of the personal library of the Reverend Tamai Yoshitaka, the longtime Buddhist minister of the Tri-State Buddhist Church of Denver. When he passed away, Nakagaki Masami of Ryūkoku University, a onetime Buddhist minister himself, obtained the library and took it to Kyoto. Today, this library is not accessible to outside researchers. This is why I appealed to the family of Asano Shichinosuke not to donate his personal papers to Japan as soon as I learned that he, too, had passed away. Asano was an Issei newspaperman affiliated with the prewar *Nichibei Shimbun* and the postwar *Nichibei Jiji*. I feared that, like the Tamai library, his personal papers would be irretrievably lost to us if they fell into Japanese hands.

Members of the Japanese Association for Migration Studies are drawn to the study of overseas Japanese primarily because it is a new field offering more research opportunities than older established fields of study. Many members have had no personal contacts with or experience living among overseas Japanese. With little empathy for their subjects, they study the Nikkei as mere "objects" of investigation, at times with paternalistic condescension, sometimes with thinly disguised contempt. Tamura Norio of Tokyo Keizai University is an example. He heads a research group which has studied Japanese immigrant newspapers over the years. He is a founding member of the Japanese Association for Migration Studies and onetime past president. He invited me to join his research team in 1984 after he received a Toyota Foundation grant. The grant required American participation because his research project had been funded as a joint international undertaking. While I was a member, I took part in two symposia. In fact, I organized the second symposium, held in Los Angeles in 1985, with partial support from the Times-Mirror Foundation. I also contributed an essay to an anthology.

In 1987 I withdrew from Tamura's research group. I reached the conclusion that Tamura had little respect for Nikkei people as a whole. On the surface he voices concern for the past and present welfare of Japanese Americans, but his attitude and behavior invariably belie such sentiments. Like many insular Japanese, Tamura cannot accept and embrace the fact that, by definition, Nikkei are not Japanese. Nor can he acknowledge that we have our own raison d'être equally as valid as being Japanese. Consequently, he looks down on us, often in a patronizing manner, at other times in amused contempt, but always with a presumption of superiority. To him Japanese immigrant newspapers are "objects" of academic research. In this sense, Japanese Americans are means to an end—research fodder as it were—with the end being the professional advancement of Tamura and the members of his research team. His group has also collected sources in Canada and the United States, but he does not permit outsiders to see or use them, an objectionable practice rooted in Japanese academic insularity.

In some cases different research approaches make disputes between Japanese researchers and me all but a foregone conclusion. Some Japanese researchers study overseas Japanese emigration as an integral aspect of modern Japanese history and overseas Japanese immigrant communities as extensions of Japanese society. In direct contrast I anchor Japanese American history and communities firmly within the boundaries of American history and society. Other Japanese researchers, explicitly or implicitly, study overseas Japanese within the framework of the question, What is a Japanese? This question is rooted in contemporary Japanese society and its obsession with the meaning of *Japanese*. Again, in direct contrast I place Japanese Americans within the framework of the question, What is an American? Given these and other contrasting approaches, setting aside my stated objections to Japanese researchers, I bear in mind that there are unavoidable disagreements over interpretations of Japanese American history between Japanese historians in Japan and someone like me in the United States.

Present and Future Status

Looking back over the last three decades, no one can deny that there has been progress in the writing of Asian American history. We now know much more about our past than we did thirty years ago, validating the adage that historical knowledge is cumulative. And we should not forget that we would not know what we know today had it not been for the emergence and development of Asian American Studies. In recent years many scholars have made noteworthy contributions to Japanese American history. Among these scholars, however, only a handful have researched Japanese-language sources to produce their studies. To correct the past and present imbalance in writings on Japanese American history, based as it is almost exclusively on English-language sources, many more monographs using Japanese-language sources are needed.

There is no question that further research into Japanese-language sources can enhance our understanding of Japanese American history. We still lack a study of the small but vocal Japanese American left in the 1920s and 1930s. The Karl Yoneda Papers, with an almost complete set of leftist publications in Japanese, provide ample sources. We also lack studies of Japanese Americans in Japan and Asia during the 1930s and 1940s. As an initial foray into this topic I edited and contributed to "Beyond National Boundaries: The Complexity of Japanese-American History," a special issue of *Amerasia Journal* 23, no. 3 (1997–98). Future studies should examine in much greater detail the role of the Issei and Nisei in the service of the Japanese government and military before and during the Second World War.

We know virtually nothing about Issei and Kibei literary writings, except for a few anthologies of Issei poetry translated into English. This sad state of affairs is not due to a dearth of sources. The Togawa Akira Papers in the JARP Collection lend themselves to the writing of several doctoral dissertations on this topic. These papers include Togawa's complete writings and his fifty-seven-volume diary spanning the years 1921 to 1978; many albums of Japanese immigrant newspaper clippings on art and literature from 1925 to 1978; the best collection of Issei poetry anthologies and literary writings; and almost complete sets of the *Shūkaku, Tessaku, Dotō, Posuton Bungei, Nanka Bungei*, and other literary journals. Combined with the Fujita Akira Papers, these sources can be the basis of in-depth studies of Issei and Kibei poets and authors. Their writings, now preserved in the JARP Collection, only await a competent literary historian to give them their rightful voice and place in Japanese American literature and history.

Studies of the wartime internment can also profit from the use of Japanese-language sources. In my reading of the existing literature one thing has always struck me: the conspicuous slighting of the Issei, equally so of those interned in Justice Department internment camps, as well as those interned in so-called WRA Relocation Camps.[1] This slighting has taken many different forms. To cite but one example, autobiographical and biographical accounts of internment in Japanese by and about Issei (and Kibei for that matter) have never been incorporated into the wartime internment studies. This glaring omission and others must be corrected by future researchers. To give readers some idea of such accounts, I have appended a representative annotated bibliography at the end of this chapter.[2] Beyond more research into Japanese language sources, we need to broaden our research focus. One possible area of fruitful inquiry is interethnic relationships. Japanese immigrants and their descendants interfaced and interacted not with only white Americans but with other racial and ethnic minorities as well. Depending on the locale, they lived, and often worked, alongside Chinese, Koreans, Filipinos, Asian Indians, Mexicans, Armenians, Afro-Americans, Jews, and other people. Their relationships to these groups were often competitive and hostile but sometimes amicable. Past studies of race relations, commencing with the Race Relations Survey by Robert E. Park in the 1920s, have stressed the centrality of Japanese-white relations, ignoring the relationships Japanese immigrants and their descendants had with other racial and ethnic minorities. The prizewinning essay by Eiichiro Azuma on Japanese-Filipino relations in the San Joaquin River Delta during the 1930s is an excellent example of what can be done on this neglected topic.[3]

The histories of the Issei in Hawaii and on the mainland warrant reconsideration. So far the two have been treated apart from each other under the assumption that geographical separation led to distinctive histories. This assumption has precluded the examination of connections between the Issei in Hawaii and their counterparts on the mainland, not to mention shared experiences in their presumed separate histories. I can think of many linkages yet to be explored. In 1928 a sensational racial incident occurred on the islands. Myles Yutaka Fukunaga, a poor, working-class Hawaii-born Nisei, kidnapped and murdered the ten-year-old son of a prominent white Honolulu banker.[4] According to his confession, racial resentment and revenge played a role in his premeditated crime. Fukunaga's trial and execution had a dramatic impact, not only on the Japanese in Hawaii, but on the mainland as well. The mainland Japanese immigrant press covered the case closely. Mainland Issei leaders were stunned by what they called this "heinous" crime, and they asked themselves the logical question, Could such a crime be repeated on the Pacific Coast? This question was not an idle one, for the first signs of juvenile delinquency and youth gangs had already surfaced on the mainland. The news of the Fukunaga Incident forced the leaders to pay closer attention to the looming problems of the second-generation and rededicate themselves to imparting Japanese moral values to Nisei youngsters to avert a similar happening on the Pacific Coast. Their reactions illustrate how the histories of the Issei in Hawaii and the mainland are closely interrelated.

Comparison of the Nikkei experience in North and South America should also be considered as a new line of research. Japanese immigration to Latin America began with Mexico in 1897, Peru in 1898, Brazil in 1908, and in later years to other countries. Today significant Nikkei populations live in Brazil, Peru, Argentina, Bolivia, Peru, and Mexico. Brazil has the largest population of approximately 1.2 million, far outnumbering the combined Japanese American population of Hawaii and the continental United States. In my view one broad question should be addressed in any comparative historical research: What was the historical process through which Japanese immigrants (including Okinawans) became Nikkei in North and South America? Regardless of whether Japanese immigrants left Japan during the Meiji, Taisho, or early Showa periods, they generally shared a common Japanese identity and culture and adhered to a common set of Japanese values. Today, as descendants of Japanese immigrants, we are all no longer Japanese, but we differ considerably as Nisei, Sansei, and Yonsei (and even Gosei in the case of Hawaii) living in different countries in the Western Hemisphere. The explanation for the differences lies in the historical process through which Japanese immigrants became Nikkei.

Comparative historical studies will add to our storehouse of knowledge about the Nikkei by highlighting what we in North and South America have in common and what we do not. The International Nikkei Research Project, recently launched by the Japanese American National Museum of Los Angeles, marks a small but significant beginning. Funded by the Nippon Foundation, this three-year project [1998–2001] is an initial attempt at comparative research of Nikkei in the Western Hemisphere. Comparative historical studies will require research in English-, Japanese-, Portuguese-, and Spanish-language sources, no small challenge for future researchers.

Final Thoughts

Arif Dirlik has reexamined the purposes and scope of Asian American Studies in the light of the changes brought about by the post-1965 Asian immigration and transnational capital.[5] Rightfully, he places me among the founders of Asian American Studies dedicated to claiming our legitimate place in American history and society. Asian American Studies has undergone many changes in its short history. I have welcomed most of them, but I find it difficult to go along with the present shift to cultural studies dressed up in so-called postmodern and postcolonial language. Most of us who established the initial programs in Asian American Studies began with the political agenda of critiquing American society and of promoting and advancing the welfare of Asian Americans within it. I fail to see how postmodern cultural studies relate to these purposes. Try as I might, I find myself unable to comprehend most of the studies because they are written in such arcane language. I ask myself, If I cannot understand them, how can the vast majority of ordinary educated people who live outside of university circles understand them? It seems to me Asian American Studies is now producing cultural studies decipherable to only a handful of ivory tower academics. In this sense our field has gone astray.

Although bilingual and bicultural, I identify myself as an American committed to politically changing our country for the better. At the same time, I believe in the old-time practice of doing narrative history, of telling a story in ordinary language based on substantive research in primary sources. Such are the views of this Asian American historian who entered the historical profession by happenstance and who still insists on practicing the craft in his "old-fashioned" way.

Notes

1. Admittedly, there are some exceptions to this generalization. The recent publication of Gordon Chang, ed., *Morning Glory, Evening Shadow: Yamato Ichihashi and His Internment Writings, 1942–1945* (Stanford, CA: Stanford University Press, 1997), is a major contribution to the wartime internment literature, but it is based on the original English writings of Professor Yamato Ichihashi. Similarly, Lane Ryo Hirabayashi, ed., *Inside an American Concentration Camp: Japanese American Resistance at Poston* (Tucson: University of Arizona Press, 1995), presents the English writings on camp life by Richard S. Nishimoto, an Issei. Louis Fiset, ed., *Imprisoned Apart: The World War II Correspondence of an Issei Couple* (Seattle: University of Washington Press, 1997), reprints the wartime correspondence (some originally in Japanese) of Matsushita Iwao with his wife, Hanaye. Teruko Imai Kumei, "'Skeleton in the Closet': The Japanese American Hokoku Seinen-dan and Their 'Disloyal' Activities at the Tule Lake Segregation Center During World War II," *Japanese Journal of American Studies* 7 (1996): 67–

102, is an outstanding recent example of the use of Japanese-language sources. Patsy Sumie Saiki, *Ganbare: An Example of the Japanese Spirit* (Honolulu: Kisaku, 1982), takes a look specifically at those Issei in Hawaii who were classified as so-called dangerous enemy aliens and interned in Justice Department camps. Other studies of Justice Department internees include Paul F. Clark, "Those Other Camps: An Oral History Analysis of Japanese Alien Enemy Internment During World War II," MA thesis, California State University, Fullerton, 1980; Tetsuden Kashima, "American Mistreatment of Internees During World War II: Enemy Alien Japanese," in *Japanese Americans: From Relocation to Redress*, ed. Roger Daniels, Sandra C. Taylor, and Harry H. L. Kitano, 52–56 (Salt Lake City: University of Utah Press, 1986); John J. Culley, "The Santa Fe Internment Camp and the Justice Department Program for Enemy Aliens," in ibid., 57–71; John J. Culley, "Trouble at the Lordsburg Internment Camp," *New Mexico Historical Review* 60 (1985): 225–48; and Carol Van Valkenburg, *An Alien Place: The Fort Missoula, Montana, Detention Camp, 1941–1944* (Missoula, MT: Pictorial Histories Publishing, 1995). Violet Kazue De Cristoforo, ed., *May Sky: There Is Always Tomorrow, An Anthology of Japanese American Concentration Kaiko Haiku* (Los Angeles: Sun and Moon Press, 1997), an anthology of haiku poems composed by Issei during the war, is an excellent example of what we can learn from Issei poetry in translation. Bunyu Fujimura, *Though I Be Crushed* (Los Angeles: Nembutsu Press, 1985), and Claire Gorfinkel, ed., *The Evacuation Diary of Hatsuye Egami* (Pasadena, CA: Intentional Productions, 1995), are two brief autobiographical accounts of internment in English. There are a few English translations of other autobiographies: Fukuda Yoshiaki, *My Six Years of Internment: An Issei's Struggle for Justice* (San Francisco: Konkō Church, 1990), an autobiography by the Bishop of the Konkōkyō Mission, originally published as *Yokuryū Seikatsu Rokunen* (San Francisco: Konkōkyō San Furanshiko Kyōkai, 1957); Minoru Kiyota, *Beyond Loyalty: The Story of a Kibei* (Honolulu: University of Hawaii Press, 1997), originally published in the third person as *Nikkei Hangyakuji* (Tokyo: Nihon Hanbai Kabushiki Kaisha, 1990); James Oda, *Heroic Struggles of Japanese Americans: Partisan Fighters from America's Concentration Camps* (Los Angeles: Privately printed, 1981), originally published as *Aru Nikkei Beihei no Shuki* (Los Angeles: Privately printed, 1973); and Seiichi Higashide, *Adios to Tears: The Memoirs of a Japanese-Peruvian Internee in U.S. Concentration Camps* (Honolulu: E and E Kudo, 1993), originally published as *Namida no Adios: Nikkei Perū Imin, Beikoku Kyōsei Shūyō no Ki* (Tokyo: Sairyūsha, 1981). Howard Schonberger, "Dilemmas of Loyalty: Japanese Americans and the Psychological Warfare Campaigns of the Office of Strategic Services, 1943–45," *Amerasia Journal* 16, no. 1 (1990): 20–38, discusses the wartime service of Issei in the OSS. A few earlier works round out this short list of English-language material on the Issei: Eleanor Hull, *Suddenly the Sun: A Biogra-*

phy of Shizuko Takahashi (New York: Friendship Press, 1957); Takeo Kaneshiro, comp., *Internees: War Relocation Center Memoirs and Diaries* (New York: Vantage Press, 1976); Daisuke Kitagawa, *Issei and Nisei: The Internment Years* (New York: Seabury Press, 1967); and Zuigaku Kodachi, with Jan Keikkala (trans.) and Janet Cormack (ed.), "Portland Assembly Center: Diary of Saku Tomita," *Oregon Historical Quarterly* 81 (1980): 149–71.

　　2. For some Issei and Kibei autobiographies and biographies, see the list of references following the notes. A few nonimmigrant Japanese, who returned to Japan aboard the first exchange ship, also published noteworthy accounts of their own arrest and internment: see Taguchi Shūji, *Senjika Amerika ni Kokyū Suru* (Tokyo: Shōwa Tosho Kabushiki Gaisha, 1942); Hoshino Jigorō, *Amerika Seikanki* (Tokyo: Kōkoku Seinen Kyōiku Kyōkai, 1942); Katō Masuo, *Beikoku Tokuhain Kichō Hōkoku—Tekikoku Amerika* (Tokyo: Dōmei Tsūshinsha, 1942); Nakano Gorō, *Sokoku ni Kaeru* (Tokyo: Shin Kigensha, 1943); Akasaka Seisaku, *Amerika Kankin Seikatsuki* (Tokyo: Nippon Shuppansha, 1943).

　　3. Eiichiro Azuma, "Racial Struggle, Immigrant Nationalism, and Ethnic Identity: Japanese and Filipinos in the California Delta, 1930–1941," *Pacific Historical Review* 67, no. 2 (1998): 163–99.

　　4. For this incident see Miwa Haruie, *Tensaiji Fukunaga Yutaka* (Honolulu: Matsuzakaya Shoten, 1929); Kihara Ryūkichi, *Hawai Nihonjin Shi* (Tokyo: Bunseisha, 1935), 770–75; Sōga Yasutarō, *Gojūnenkan no Hawai Kaiko* (Honolulu: Gojūnenkan no Hawaii Kaiko Kankōkai, 1953), 431–38; Makino Kinzaburō Den Hensan Iinkai, *Makino Kinzaburō Den* (Honolulu: Makino Michie, 1965), 65–67; Ozawa Gijō, ed., *Hawai Nihongo Gakkō Kyōiku Shi* (Honolulu: Hawai Kyōiku Kai, 1972), 153–54; Dennis M. Ogawa, *JAN KEN PO: The World of Hawaii's Japanese Americans* (Honolulu: Japanese American Research Center, 1973), 112–49; Roland Kotani, *The Japanese in Hawaii: A Century of Struggle* (Honolulu: Hawaii Hochi, 1985), 71–76; and Eileen Tamura, *Americanization, Acculturation, and Ethnic Identity: The Nisei Generation in Hawaii* (Urbana: University of Illinois Press, 1994), 81–84, 168.

　　5. Arif Dirlik, "Asians on the Rim: Transnational Capital and Local Community in the Making of Contemporary Asian America," *Amerasia Journal* 22, no. 3 (1996): 1–24.

References

Akiya Kāru, *Jiyū e no Michi: Taiheiyō wo Koete—Aru Kibei Nisei no Jiden* (Kyoto: Kōrosha, 1996). An autobiography of a Kibei. Includes his internment at Tanforan and Topaz and wartime service with the OSS.

Aoki Hisa, *Dai-Niji Kōkansen Teia-Maru no Hōkoku* (Tokyo: Maeda Shobō, 1944). An account of internment and return to Japan aboard the second exchange ship by a Japanese-language schoolteacher and prewar columnist for the *Kashū Mainichi*.

Asano Shichinosuke, *Zaibei Yonjūnen: Watakushi no Kiroku* (Tokyo: Yūki Shobō, 1962). An autobiography of an Issei newspaperman that includes his accounts of internment at Tanforan and Topaz.

Ebina Kazuo, *Karifuonia to Nihonjin* (Tokyo: Taiheiyō Kyōkai, 1943). A wartime propaganda account of wartime internment by an Issei newspaperman who had returned to Japan before Pearl Harbor.

Fujioka Shirō, *Ayumi no Ato* (Los Angeles: Ayumi no Ato Kankō Kōenkai, 1957). A comprehensive history of the Japanese in the United States by an Issei newspaperman that includes an account of the author's arrest and interrogation by FBI agents and internment at Ft. Missoula.

Furuya Kumaji (Suikei), *Haisho Tenten* (Honolulu: Hawai Taimusu-sha, 1964). A Hawai'i Issei's account of internment at Ft. Missoula and Santa Fe.

Hashimoto Masaharu, *Nankin Rokunen* (Tenri-shi: Hashimoto Kiyoshi, 1953–1954), 2 vols. A Tenrikyō minister's diary of internment at Lordsburg and Santa Fe.

Ikeda Kandō, *Senjika Nikkeijin to Beikoku no Jitsujō—Nikkeijin no Ketsurui Jitsushi to Dai-Niji Taisen Rimenshi* (Oakland: Daireikyō Kenkyūjo, 1950–1951), 2 vols. An Issei conservative's interpretation of the wartime internment of Japanese Americans.

Itō Kazuo, *Nakagawa Yoriaki no Sokuseki* (Tokyo: Nichibō Shuppan-sha, 1974). A biography of an Issei Japanese-language schoolteacher in Seattle. Includes his arrest and internment at Ft. Missoula and Minidoka.

Koide Jō, *Aru Zaibei Nihonjin no Kiroku* (Tokyo: Yūshindo, 1967, 1970), 2 vols. An autobiography of an Issei communist. Volume 2 covers his internment at Santa Anita and Heart Mountain and wartime service with the OSS.

Nakamura Kenta, *Kōkansen* (Tokyo: Shinwasha, 1966). An Issei account of internment at Santa Fe and Lordsburg and repatriation to Japan aboard the second exchange ship.

Nakazawa Ken, *Amerika Gokuchū Yori Dōhō ni Tsugu* (Tokyo: Sonshobō, 1943). A propagandistic account of internment and repatriation aboard the first exchange ship by a prewar staff member of the Los Angeles Japanese Consulate.

Nishi Shigeki (pseud.), *Kenedei Shūyōjo* (New York: Privately printed, 1983). A Peruvian Issei's account of internment at Kennedy, Texas. The author's real name is Nishioka Shigeyuki.

Noda Kasen, *Posuton Tenjūki* (Los Angeles: Nippon Shoten, 1968). An Issei account of internment at Poston.

Noda Nobuo, ed., *Hokujin, Nagumo Shōji no Ikō* (Tokyo: Takagi Reiko, 1978). Autobiographical essays by Nagumo Shōji, an Issei leader of the Southern California Gardeners Federation. Includes accounts of internment at Pomona and Heart Mountain.

———, *Manzanā no Arashi* (Los Angeles: Privately printed, 1971). An Issei account of the so-called Manzanar Incident of December 6, 1942.

Oka Naoki et al., eds., "Sokoku wo Teki to Shite," in *Nihon Heiwaron Taikei* (Tokyo: Nihon Tosho Sentā, 1994), vol. 17, 273–478. A reprint of a biography of Oka Shigeki, a longtime Issei socialist, printer, and newspaper publisher. Includes an account of his internment at Heart Mountain and wartime service with the British government in India.

Sasaki Shūichi (Sasabune), *Yokuryūsho Seikatsu* (Los Angeles: Rafu Shoten, 1950). An Issei newspaperman's account of internment primarily at Ft. Missoula.

Shirai Noboru, *Karifuorunia Nikkeijin Kyōsei Shūyōjo* (Tokyo: Kawade Shobō Shinsha, 1981). An account of internment at Tule Lake.

Sōga Yasutarō (Keihō), *Tessaku Seikatsu* (Honolulu: Hawaii Times, 1948). The Nippu Jiji Issei editor's account of internment at Lordsburg and Santa Fe.

Sugimachi Yaemitsu, *Amerika ni Okeru Nihongo Kyōiku* (Pasadena, CA: Sugimachi Mitsue, 1968). An autobiography of a Japanese-language schoolteacher in Southern California. Includes his wartime arrest and internment at Lordsburg and Seagoville.

Susuki Sakae, *Zuiri Kaiko Gojūnen* (Los Angeles: W. M. Hawley, 1959). An autobiography with illustrations by an Issei physician commonly known as Dr. P. M. Suski. Includes accounts of his wartime internment at Santa Anita and Heart Mountain.

Tana Daishō, *Santa Fē Rōzubāgu Yokuryūsho Nikki* (Tokyo: Tana Tomoe, 1976, 1978, 1980, 1985), 4 vols. A Buddhist minister's diary of internment at Santa Fe and Lordsburg.

Yamamoto Asako (pseud.), *Ibara Aru Hakudō* (n.p.: Privately printed, 1952). A diary of internment at Santa Anita and Gila covering the period from December 7, 1941, to July 31, 1943. The diarist returned to Japan aboard the second exchange ship. Her real name is Aoki Hisa (see above).

Yamashiro Masao, *Tōi Taigan* (Tokyo: Gurōbyūsha, 1984). Autobiographical essays by a Kibei writer. Includes accounts of his internment at the Tule Lake Segregation Camp and his assessment of the Kibei there.

Yoneda Kāru, *Manzanā Kyōsei Shūyōjo Nikki* (Tokyo: PMC Shuppan, 1988). A diary of a Kibei communist interned at Manzanar, covering the period from December 7, 1941, to December 17, 1942.

Epilogue

Remembering Yuji

GORDON H. CHANG

In reflecting on the lifework of a historian, or of any intellectual, it is perilous to try to separate the personal from the political, or even the personal from the academic. It is not just dangerous to try to do so in writing about Yuji but, in fact, impossible.

Features of Yuji's singular personality are embedded throughout his many contributions to Asian American Studies and to the study of history generally. As anyone who had even the most cursory contact with Yuji knows, he was a passionate person: he always had, and expressed, strong opinions, whether they were about the current NBA season, events in the world, or a recently published work in his field. Would we all be so fortunate to live as fully and as energetically as Yuji, to live with as much feeling and intellectual intensity as he?

Yuji's scholarship is inseparable from his own personal qualities and his political commitments, which were as important to him as his academic work. His efforts to uncover a "buried past," to use his own perfectly chosen words, served the broader purpose of intellectually exposing and opposing racism and empowering those who had suffered such oppression. He had no patience with scholarship that pretended to be nonpolitical or solely dispassionate. But at the same time, he had no use for cant, superficial or trendy analysis, or intellectualism that masqueraded as committed politics. He demanded honesty. Yuji was also not afraid to let his strong opinions be known, and he was therefore not without those who found him difficult. No matter. Yuji wasted little time fretting about what may have been said about him.

He saw no contradiction between engaging in the most rigorous and truthful scholarship and political principle. For Yuji, true history advanced the politics of antiracism and social justice; and in turn, he believed that such political values guided his own historical work. At the same time, he respected what he believed was good scholarship, that is, writing that was smart, grounded in solid research, and truthful. That was the type of work he himself pursued. He described his scholarship as "old school," history that focused on uncovering new information and new narratives based on the given record. As he would say, he liked to tell good stories in a language that could be widely read and understood. He was eminently successful. His publications have had good legs; they continue to stand firmly and, I suspect, are consulted as widely (perhaps even more so) today than when they appeared over the course of his more-than-three-decades career.

Yuji and I had only sporadic contact from the late 1960s, when we first met, until the latter 1980s, when we began to see each other more regularly. He would sometimes send some of his writing for comment, and I would do the same. But in the early 1990s I approached him with a serious proposal: to collaborate on a study of Yamato Ichihashi, the Stanford professor who during the interwar years wrote about Japanese Americans and Pacific relations. Yuji had been the first to rekindle interest in Ichihashi in a published essay and then in several pages of his now classic book *The Issei*. Ichihashi had slipped into obscurity after World War II, but in the prewar years Ichihashi had been one of the most prominent Japanese intellectuals in America. Yuji's opinion, though, was highly critical, even scathing, of Ichihashi—his arrogance toward fellow Japanese Americans, as well as his almost sycophantic relationship with the Japanese government, angered Yuji. The title of Yuji's essay reflected this contempt of Ichihashi: he was an "attorney for the defense," an apparatchik who used his academic position to advance the purposes of the imperial government. Even Ichihashi's outspoken defense of Japanese immigrants against the anti-Japanese movement did not redeem him in Yuji's eyes, since privately the samurai-descended Ichihashi frequently expressed disdain toward the dirt farmers and laborers he publicly defended. It was not that Ichihashi served political purposes that so irked Yuji, but it was the sometimes hidden political purposes to which Ichihashi was dedicated. Yuji declined to collaborate. "I have twenty years of Ichihashi's diaries," I tried to entice him. But Yuji would not change his mind. "I have had enough of him," he said. And that was that. Yuji wanted to move on.

I completed the Ichihashi project a few years later, with Yuji's research help along the way. He was generous with his time and support. He warmly endorsed the published volume, happy, I think, that it was out *and* that someone other than himself had spent the time on it.

But Yuji's work on Ichihashi in some way had signaled the beginning of a shift in his own intellectual attention. Yuji's first work emphasized the difficulties and hardships the Issei suffered in America. The early history of Japanese immigrants in the United States, he wrote, was above all, "a history of a racial minority struggling to survive in a hostile land." "It was also labor history," he added. Yuji's historical interests nicely coincided with his own commitments to racial justice and sympathy with working people. But in the mid-1980s Yuji moved his attention to the post-1924 period and away from writing "history from the bottom up." He began to write increasingly about identifiable community leaders and writers among the Japanese in America. He was less interested in how the Issei established organizations, struggled against discrimination, and made their lives as immigrants but more and more interested in how the Issei and Nisei understood their cultural and political relationship to a hostile America and to an expansionist Japan.

To be sure, aspects of his work in the latter 1980s and 1990s still exhibited his earlier concerns. He continued to be personally interested in the fortunes, and tragedies, of Japanese American revolutionaries, such as Karl Yoneda and some of his communist comrades, but he actually wrote little about them. Yuji kept in touch with Yoneda until Karl's death. Yuji also wrote respectfully about the sometimes maligned Japanese American social scientists involved in the Japanese Evacuation and Resettlement Project. (See *Views from Within: The Japanese American Evacuation and Resettlement Study.*) But increasingly, Yuji began to work on topics that he believed were important to confront but which also troubled him. For the last ten years or so, Yuji explored the problem of the ties, emotional and formal, Japanese Americans developed with militarist Japan, from the 1920s to the 1940s. He hated militarism and chauvinism of any sort, and it was disturbing to him to reveal the various ways a good number of Japanese Americans supported Japanese expansionism in Asia in the interwar years. He wrote less and less about liberals, workers, and leftists and more and more about rightists and others who maintained or developed attachments with imperial Japan.

Yuji's interpretations properly placed these individuals in the context of the times: the long-standing ostracism of Japanese in the United States. But it is clear that he felt a need to understand the Japanese nationalist sentiment of the prewar years. This was probably not easy for him to do psychologically or intellectually. Yuji originally attended graduate school to study Chinese history, and he well knew the brutality of Japanese aggression against China in the 1930s and of Japanese colonial rule over Korea. He had great sympathy for the victims of Japanese aggression.

Yuji also knew he was treading into sensitive terrain. Other scholars were also working on what might be called a "revisionist" approach to the interwar years, an approach that was not preoccupied with Nisei Americanism, which has dominated the writing of Japanese American history. But as undeniable as was that part of the history, so was the difficult story of those who crafted their lives around the fortunes of imperial Japan. And this is what Yuji increasingly addressed. He called for an appreciation of the "complexity of Japanese American history," by which in part he meant the need to go beyond the geographic borders of America to understand the Japanese American experience. He was interested in the transnational and diasporic connections—the Nikkei in the Americas, those who went to Japan for their careers in the 1930s, and so forth. But more important, he urged the need to confront the thorny and controversial problem of political identities. He asked us to think about "the meaning of loyalty in a racist society." (See the issue of *Amerasia Journal* edited by Yuji, entitled *Beyond National Boundaries: The Complexity of Japanese-American History* [winter 1997].) He certainly would never have wanted his work to be seen in any way as justifying internment, which he and his family had suffered. Never. But his own political and intellectual integrity pressed him to address awkward questions that begged discussion.

Yuji never got to finish this intellectual journey, although he was well on his way when he died. Before his decline in health, Yuji had gathered together a number of his published and unpublished essays that explored the issue of Japanese American "loyalty" and political identity in characteristically provocative and substantive ways. The subjects of these efforts were no longer workers or unassuming farmers; they were journalists, prominent community leaders, and even agents of Japan in America. He even completed a brief introduction to this collection and asked me for my comment. Not knowing how weakened he was, I suggested that his introduction could benefit from some expansion of the ideas he tentatively raised. He wrote back, saying he agreed and would tackle the challenge soon, after he had regained some strength. But it was not to be. A few days later Yuji passed away.

I first met Yuji (and Emma) in the summer of 1969 in Berkeley. Yuji had recently coined the term *Asian American*, a contribution he always claimed proudly. Yuji and Emma were simultaneously helping found the academic field of Asian American Studies and the political project called the Asian American movement. It feels like those heady days were a lifetime ago. Or, was it just yesterday?

September 20, 2002

REFERENCE MATTER

Select Bibliography of Japanese Americans During World War II

Bibliographies

Barnhart, Edward N. *Japanese American Evacuation and Resettlement; Catalog of Material in the General Library*. Berkeley: University of California, General Library, 1958.

Cheung, King-kok, and Stan Yogi. *Asian American Literature: An Annotated Bibliography*. New York: Modern Language Association, 1988.

Cummings, Orpha, and Helen E. Hennefrund. *Bibliography on the Japanese in American Agriculture*. Washington, DC: GPO, 1943.

Hansen, Arthur A., Debra G. Hansen, and Sue Kunitomi Embrey. *An Annotated Bibliography for Manzanar National Historic Site*. Fullerton: California State University Oral History Program, Japanese American Project, 1995.

Ichioka, Yuji, Yasuo Sakata, Nobuya Tsuchida, and Eri Yasuhara. *A Buried Past: An Annotated Bibliography of the Japanese American Research Project Collection*. Berkeley: University of California Press, 1974.

Okamura, Raymond. "The Concentration Camp Experience from a Japanese American Perspective: A Bibliographical Essay and Review of Michi Weglyn's Years of Infamy." In *Counterpoint: Perspectives on Asian America*, ed. Emma Gee, 27–30. Los Angeles: Asian American Studies Center, UCLA, 1976.

Ölschleger, Hans Dieter, Eva König, and Barbara Ölschleger. *Japaner in der Neuen Welt: Eine teilannotierte Bibliographie von Werken zu japanischen Einwanderern in Nordamerika in europaischen Sprachen*. München: Deutsches Institut für Japanstudien, 1997.

Sakata, Yasuo. *Fading Footsteps of the Issei: An Annotated Check List of the*

Manuscript Holdings of the Japanese American Research Project Collection. Los Angeles: Asian American Studies Center, UCLA, 1992.

Spicer, Edward H., Asael T. Hansen, Katherine Luomala, and Marvin K. Opler. "Annotated Bibliography of the Community Analysis Section." In *Impounded People: Japanese-Americans in the Relocation Centers,* prep. by Edward H. Spicer, 301–16. Tucson: University of Arizona Press, 1969.

———. "A Bibliography of Life in the War Relocation Centers." In *Impounded People: Japanese-Americans in the Relocation Centers,* prep. by Edward H. Spicer, 317–31. Tucson: University of Arizona Press, 1969.

Sugimoto, Howard H. "A Bibliographical Essay on the Wartime Evacuation of Japanese from the West Coast Areas." In *East Across the Pacific,* ed. Hilary Conroy and T. Scott Miyakawa, 140–50. Santa Barbara, CA: Clio Press, 1972.

Thompson, William Takamatsu. "Amache: A Working Bibliography on One Japanese American Concentration Camp." *Amerasia Journal* 19, no. 1 (1993): 153–59.

U.S. War Relocation Authority. *Bibliography of Japanese in America.* 3 vols. Washington, DC: GPO, 1942–45.

———. *Bibliography on War Relocation Authority: Japanese and Japanese Americans.* Washington, DC: GPO, 1944.

The 1930 Background

STUDIES OF PREWAR JAPANESE AMERICANS

Adamic, Louis. "A Young American with a Japanese Face." In *From Many Lands,* by Louis Adamic, 185–234. New York: Harper, 1940.

Azuma, Eiichiro. "Interethnic Conflict Under Racial Subordination: Japanese Immigrants and Their Asian Neighbors in Walnut Grove, California, 1908–1941." *Amerasia Journal* 20, no. 2 (1994): 27–56.

———. "Racial Struggle, Immigrant Nationalism, and Ethnic Identity: Japanese and Filipinos in the California Delta, 1930–1941." *Pacific Historical Review* 67, no. 2 (1998): 163–99.

Bell, Reginald. *Public School Education of Second-Generation Japanese in California.* Stanford, CA: Stanford University Press, 1935.

Burrows, Edwin G. *Chinese and Japanese in Hawaii During the Sino-Japanese Conflict.* Honolulu: Institute of Pacific Relations, 1939.

Daniels, Roger. "Japanese America, 1930–1941: An Ethnic Community in the Great Depression." *Journal of the West* 64, no. 4 (1985): 35–49.

Halsted, Ann L. "Sharpened Tongues: The Controversy over the 'Americanization' of Japanese Language Schools in Hawaii, 1919–1927." PhD diss., Stanford University, 1988.

Heuterman, Thomas H. "'We Have the Same Rights as Other Citizens': Coverage of Yakima Japanese Americans in the 'Missing Decades' of the 1920s and 1930s." *Journalism History* 14, no. 4 (1987): 94–103.

Hunter, Louise H. *Buddhism in Hawaii: Its Impact on a Yankee Community.* Honolulu: University of Hawaii Press, 1971.

Ichihashi, Yamato. *Japanese in the United States.* Stanford, CA: Stanford University Press, 1932.

Ichioka, Yuji. "Japanese Immigrant Nationalism: The Issei and the Sino-Japanese War, 1937–1941." *California History* 69, no. 3 (1990): 260–75, 310–11.

———. "*Kengakudan*: The Origin of Nisei Study Tours of Japan." *California History* 73, no. 1 (1994): 30–43, 87–88.

———. "The Meaning of Loyalty: The Case of Kazumaro Buddy Uno." *Amerasia Journal* 23, no. 3 (winter 1997–98): 44–71.

———. "A Study in Dualism: James Yoshinori Sakamoto and the *Japanese American Courier*, 1928–1942." *Amerasia Journal* 13, no. 2 (1986–87): 49–81.

———. "'Unity in Diversity'; Louis Adamic and Japanese Americans." *Working Papers*, Asia-Pacific Institute, Duke University, 1987.

Kurashige, Lon. "The Problem of Biculturalism: Japanese American Identity and Festival before World War II." *Journal of American History* 86, no. 4 (March 2000): 1632–54.

La Violette, Forrest E. "The American-Born Japanese and the World Crisis." *Canadian Journal of Economics and Political Science* 7 (1941): 517–27.

———. *Americans of Japanese Ancestry: A Study of Assimilation in the American Community.* Toronto: Canadian Institute of International Affairs, 1945.

Matsubayashi, Yoshihide. "The Japanese Language Schools in Hawaii and California, from 1892–1941." PhD diss., University of San Francisco, 1984.

Matsumoto, Valerie J. "Desperately Seeking 'Deirdre': Gender Roles, Multicultural Relations, and Nisei Women Writers of the 1930s." *Frontiers* 12 (1991): 19–32.

———. "Redefining Expectations: Nisei Women in the 1930s." *California History* 73, no. 1 (1994): 44–53, 88.

Miyamoto, S. Frank. "Immigrants and Citizens of Japanese Origin." *Annals of American Academy of Political and Social Science* 223 (Sep. 1942): 107–13.

———. "Social Solidarity Among the Japanese in Seattle." *University of Washington Publications in the Social Sciences* 11, no. 2 (Dec. 1939): 57–130.

Morimoto, Toyotomi. "Language and Heritage Maintenance of Immigrants: Japanese Language Schools in California, 1903–1941." PhD diss., University of California, Los Angeles, 1989.

O'Brien, Robert W. "Reaction of the College Nisei to Japan and Japanese Foreign

Policy from the Invasion of Manchuria to Pearl Harbor." *Pacific Northwest Quarterly* 36 (1945): 19–28.

Okihiro, Gary Y. *Cane Fires: The Anti-Japanese Movement in Hawaii, 1865–1945.* Philadelphia: Temple University Press, 1991.

Park, Robert E. *Race and Culture.* New York: Free Press, 1964.

Smith, William C. *Americans in Process: A Study of Our Citizens of Oriental Ancestry.* Ann Arbor, MI: Edwards Bros., 1937.

———. *Americans in the Making: The Natural History of the Assimilation of Immigrants.* New York: Appleton-Century, 1939.

Spickard, Paul R. "Not Just the Quiet People: The Nisei Underclass." *Pacific Historical Review* 68, no. 1 (1999): 78–94.

Stephan, John. "Hijacked by Utopia: American Nikkei in Manchuria." *Amerasia Journal* 23, no. 3 (winter 1997–98): 1–42.

Strong, Edward K. *Japanese in California.* Stanford, CA: Stanford University Press, 1933.

———. *The Second-Generation Japanese Problem.* Stanford, CA: Stanford University Press, 1934.

———. *Vocational Aptitudes of Second-Generation Japanese in the United States.* Stanford, CA: Stanford University Press, 1933.

Takahashi, Jere. "Japanese American Responses to Race Relations: The Formation of Nisei Perspectives." *Amerasia Journal* 9, no. 1 (1982): 29–57.

———. *Nisei/Sansei: Shifting Japanese American Identities and Politics.* Philadelphia, PA: Temple University Press, 1997.

Tamura, Eileen H. *Americanization, Acculturation, and Ethnic Identity: The Nisei Generation in Hawaii.* Urbana: University of Illinois Press, 1994.

———. "The English-Only Effort, the Anti-Japanese Campaign, and Language Acquisition in the Education of Japanese Americans in Hawaii, 1915–40." *History of Education Quarterly* 33, no. 1 (1993): 37–58.

Yamamoto, Eriko. "Cheers for Japanese Athletes: The 1932 Los Angeles Olympics and the Japanese American Community." *Pacific Historical Review* 69, no. 3 (August 2000): 399–430.

———. "Miya Sannomiya Kikuchi: A Pioneer Nisei Woman's Life and Identity." *Amerasia Journal* 23, no. 3 (winter 1997–98): 73–101.

Yoo, David. "Enlightened Identities: Buddhism and Japanese-Americans of California, 1924–1941." *Western Historical Quarterly* 27, no. 3 (1996): 281–301.

———. *Growing Up Nisei: Race, Generation, and Culture Among Japanese Americans of California, 1924–49.* Urbana: University of Illinois Press, 2000.

———. "'Read All About It': Race, Generation, and the Japanese American Ethnic Press, 1925–41." *Amerasia Journal* 19, no. 1 (1993): 69–92.

"SPIES" AND INTELLIGENCE

Chambers, Whitman. *Invasion!* New York: Dutton, 1943.

Herzig, John A. "Japanese Americans and MAGIC." *Amerasia Journal* 11, no. 2 (1984): 47–65.

Hynd, Alan. *Betrayal from the East: The Inside Story of Japanese Spies in America.* New York: Robert M. McBride, 1943.

Kumamoto, Bob. "The Search for Spies: American Counterintelligence and the Japanese American Community, 1931–1942." *Amerasia Journal* 6, no. 2 (1979): 45–75.

Munson, Curtis B. "Report on the Japanese on the West Coast." In *Hearings*, U.S. Congress, Joint Committee on the Investigation of the Pearl Harbor Attack, Part 6, 2682–96. Washington, DC: GPO, 1946.

[Ringle, Kenneth D.] "Japanese in America: The Problem and the Solution." *Harper's Magazine*, Oct. 1942, 489–97.

Sayers, Michael, and Albert E. Kahn. *Sabotage!—The Secret War Against America.* New York: Harper, 1942.

Seth, Ronald. *Secret Servants: A History of Japanese Espionage.* New York: Farrar, Straus, and Cudahy, 1957.

Singer, Kurt. *Spies and Traitors of World War II.* New York: Prentice-Hall, 1945.

Pearl Harbor

Bergamini, David. *Japan's Imperial Conspiracy.* New York: William Morrow, 1971.

Borg, Dorothy, and Shumpei Okamoto, eds. *Pearl Harbor as History: Japanese-American Relations, 1931–1941.* New York: Columbia University Press, 1973.

Butow, Robert J. C. *Tojo and the Coming of the War.* Princeton, NJ: Princeton University Press, 1961.

Clarke, Thurston. *Pearl Harbor Ghosts: A Journey to Hawaii Then and Now.* New York: William Morrow, 1991.

Conroy, Hillary, and Harry Wray, eds. *Pearl Harbor Reexamined: Prologue to the Pacific War.* Honolulu: University of Hawaii Press, 1990.

Dower, John W. *War Without Mercy: Race and Power in the Pacific War.* New York: Pantheon, 1986.

Feis, Herbert. *The Road to Pearl Harbor: The Coming of the War Between the United States and Japan.* New York: Atheneum, 1965.

Honan, William H. *Visions of Infamy: The Untold Story of How Journalist Hector C. Bywater Devised the Plans That Led to Pearl Harbor.* New York: St. Martin's, 1991.

Herzog, James H. *Closing the Open Door: American-Japanese Diplomatic Negotiations, 1936–1941.* Annapolis: Naval Institute Press, 1973.

Ienaga, Saburo. *The Pacific War, 1931–1945.* New York: Pantheon, 1978.

Ike, Nobutaka. *Japan's Decision for War: Records of the 1941 Policy Conferences.* Stanford, CA: Stanford University Press, 1967.

Iriye, Akira. *Power and Culture: The Japanese-American War, 1941–1945.* Cambridge, MA: Harvard University Press, 1981.

Layton, Edwin T. *"And I Was There": Pearl Harbor and Midway—Breaking the Secrets.* New York: William Morrow, 1989.

Kimmell, Husband E. *Admiral Kimmel's Story.* Chicago: H. Regnery, 1955.

Martin, James J. *Beyond Pearl Harbor: Essays on Some Historical Consequences of the Crisis in the Pacific in 1941.* Little Current: Plowshare Press, 1981.

Millis, Walter. *This Is Pearl: The United States and Japan—1941.* New York: William Morrow, 1947.

Pelz, Stephen E. *Race to Pearl Harbor: The Failure of the Second London Naval Conference and the Onset of World War II.* Cambridge, MA: Harvard University Press, 1974.

Morley, James W., ed. *Japan's Road to the Pacific War.* 5 vols. New York: Columbia University Press, 1976–87. Vol. 1: *Japan Erupts: The London Naval Conference and the Manchurian Incident, 1928–1932*; Vol. 2: *The China Quagmire: Japan's Expansion on the Asian Continent, 1933–1941*; Vol. 3: *Deterrent Diplomacy: Japan, Germany, and the U.S.S.R., 1935–1940*; Vol. 4: *Fateful Choice: Japan's Advance into South Asia, 1939–1941*; Vol. 5: *The Final Confrontation: Japan's Negotiations with the United States, 1941.*

Prange, Gordon W. *At Dawn We Slept: The Untold Story of Pearl Harbor.* New York: Penguin, 1982.

———. *Pearl Harbor: The Verdict of History.* New York: McGraw-Hill, 1986.

Slackman, Michael. *Target—Pearl Harbor.* Honolulu: University of Hawaii Press, 1990.

Stephan, John J. *Hawaii Under the Rising Sun: Japan's Plans for Conquest After Pearl Harbor.* Honolulu: University of Hawaii Press, 1984.

Stillwell, Paul, ed. *Air Raid: Pearl Harbor: Recollections of a Day of Infamy.* Annapolis: Naval Institute Press, 1981.

Toland, John. *Infamy: Pearl Harbor and Its Aftermath.* New York: Doubleday, 1982.

Weintraub, Stanley. *Long Day's Journey into War: December 7, 1941.* New York: Dutton, 1991.

Wohlstetter, Roberta. *Pearl Harbor: Warning and Decision.* Stanford, CA: Stanford University Press, 1962.

General Histories

Bloom, Leonard, and Ruth Riemer. *Removal and Return: The Socio-Economic Effects of the War on Japanese Americans.* Berkeley: University of California Press, 1949.

Bosworth, Allan R. *America's Concentration Camps.* New York: Norton, 1967.

Broom, Leonard, and John I. Kitsuse. *The Managed Casualty: The Japanese-American Family in World War II.* Berkeley: University of California Press, 1956.

Conroy, Hilary, and Sharlie Conroy Ushioda. "A Review of Scholarly Literature on the Internment of Japanese Americans During World War II: Toward a Quaker Perspective." *Quaker History* 83, no. 1 (1994): 48–52.

Daniels, Roger, ed. *American Concentration Camps: A Documentary History of the Relocation and Incarceration of Japanese Americans, 1942–1945.* 9 vols. New York: Garland, 1989.

Daniels, Roger. *Concentration Camps: North America; Japanese in the United States and Canada During World War II.* Rev. ed. Malabar, FL: Robert E. Krieger, 1981.

———. *Concentration Camps USA: Japanese Americans and World War II.* New York: Holt, Rinehart, and Winston, 1971.

———. *Prisoners Without Trial: Japanese Americans in World War II.* New York: Hill and Wang, 1993.

Daniels, Roger, Sandra C. Taylor, and Harry H. L. Kitano, eds. *Japanese Americans: From Relocation to Redress.* Salt Lake City: University of Utah Press, 1986.

Davis, Daniel S. *Behind Barbed Wire: The Imprisonment of Japanese Americans During World War II.* New York: Dutton, 1982.

Drinnon, Richard. *Keeper of Concentration Camps: Dillon S. Myer and American Racism.* Berkeley: University of California Press, 1987.

Fisher, Anne R. *Exile of a Race.* Seattle: F and T Publishers, 1965.

Foote, Caleb. *Outcasts! The Story of America's Treatment of Her Japanese American Minority.* New York: Fellowship Publications, 1944.

Fukei, Budd. *The Japanese American Story.* Minneapolis, MN: Dillon Press, 1976.

Fussell, Paul. *Wartime: Understanding and Behavior in the Second World War.* New York: Oxford University Press, 1989.

Gerhard, Paul F. *The Plight of the Japanese Americans During World War II: A Study of Group Prejudice.* Wichita, KS: University of Wichita Press, 1963.

Girdner, Audrie, and Anne Loftis. *The Great Betrayal: The Evacuation of the Japanese-Americans During World War II.* New York: Macmillan, 1969.

Grodzins, Morton. *The Loyal and the Disloyal: Social Boundaries of Patriotism and Treason.* Chicago: University of Chicago Press, 1956.

Inada, Lawson, ed. *Only What We Could Carry: The Japanese American Internment Experience.* Berkeley, CA: Heyday Books, 2000.

Isserman, Maurice. *Which Side Were You On? The American Communist Party During the Second World War.* Middletown, CT: Wesleyan University Press, 1982.

Kitagawa, Daisuke. *Issei and Nisei: The Internment Years.* New York: Seabury Press, 1967.

Koppes, Clayton R., and Gregory D. Black. *Hollywood Goes to War: How Politics,*

Profits, and Propaganda Shaped World War II Movies. Berkeley: University of California Press, 1990.

Mackey, Mike, ed. *Guilt by Association: Essays on Japanese Settlement, Internment, and Relocation in the Rocky Mountain West*. Powell, WY: Western History Publications, 2001.

McWilliams, Carey. *Prejudice: Japanese Americans; Symbol of Racial Intolerance*. Boston: Little, Brown, 1944.

Nakanishi, Don T. "Surviving Democracy's 'Mistake': Japanese Americans and the Enduring Legacy of Executive Order 9066." *Amerasia Journal* 19, no. 1 (1993): 7–35.

Nash, Gerald D. *The American West Transformed: The Impact of the Second World War*. Bloomington: Indiana University Press, 1985.

National Japanese American Historical Society. *Americans of Japanese Ancestry and the American Constitution, 1787–1987*. San Francisco, CA: National Japanese American Historical Society, 1987.

O'Brien, David J., and Stephen S. Fugita. *The Japanese American Experience*. Bloomington: Indiana University Press, 1991.

Petersen, William. *Japanese Americans: Oppression and Success*. New York: Random House, 1971.

Renne, Louis O. *Our Day of Empire—War and the Exile of Japanese Americans*. Glasgow: Strickland Press, 1954.

Roche, John P. *The Quest for the Dream: The Development of Civil Rights and Human Relations in Modern America*. New York: Macmillan, 1963.

Smith, Bradford. *Americans from Japan*. Philadelphia, PA: Lippincott, 1948.

Smith, Page. *Democracy on Trial: The Japanese American Evacuation and Relocation*. New York: Simon and Schuster, 1995.

Spickard, Paul R. *Japanese Americans: The Formation and Transformations of an Ethnic Group*. New York: Twayne, 1996.

Sundquist, Eric J. "The Japanese-American Internment: A Reappraisal." *American Scholar* 36 (autumn 1988): 529–47.

Walker, Samuel. *In Defense of American Liberties: A History of the ACLU*. New York: Oxford University Press, 1990.

Wax, Rosalie Hankey. "The Development of Authoritarianism: A Comparison of the Japanese-American Relocation Centers and Germany." PhD diss., University of Chicago, 1951.

Weglyn, Michi. *Years of Infamy*. New York: William Morrow, 1976.

Causal Interpretations

Bird, Kai. *The Chairman John J. McCloy: The Making of the American Establishment*. New York: Simon and Schuster, 1992.

Conn, Stetson. "The Decision to Evacuate the Japanese from the Pacific Coast." In *Command Decisions*, ed. Kent R. Greenfield, 105–9. New York: Harcourt, Brace, 1960.

———. "Japanese Evacuation from the West Coast." In *Guarding the United States and Its Outposts*, ed. Stetson Conn, Rose C. Engelman, and Byron Fairchild, 115–49. Washington, DC: GPO, 1964.

Daniels, Roger. *The Decision to Relocate the Japanese Americans*. Philadelphia, PA: Lippincott, 1975.

———. "The Decision to Relocate the North American Japanese: Another Look." *Pacific Historical Review* 51 (1982): 71–77.

———. "Incarcerating Japanese Americans: An Atrocity Revisited." In Mackey, *Remembering Heart Mountain*, 17–33.

Grodzins, Morton. *Americans Betrayed: Politics and the Japanese Evacuation*. Chicago: University of Chicago Press, 1949.

Hirabayashi, Lane Ryo, and James Hirabayashi. "A Reconsideration of the United States Military's Role in the Violation of Japanese-American Citizenship Rights." In *Ethnicity and War*, ed. Winston A. Van Horne and Thomas V. Tonnesen, 87–100. Milwaukee: University of Wisconsin System American Ethnic Studies Coordinating Committee/Urban Corridor Consortium, 1984.

Iiyama, Patricia. "American Concentration Camps: Racism and Japanese-Americans During World War II." *International Socialist Review* 34, no. 4 (1973): 24–33.

Irons, Peter. *Justice at War*. New York: Oxford University Press, 1983.

Izumi, Kiyotada. "The Japanese Evacuation of 1942." *Journal of Asian and African Studies* 17, nos. 3–4 (1982): 266–75.

Miyamoto, S. Frank. "The Forced Evacuation of the Japanese Minority During World War II." *Journal of Social Issues* 29, no. 2 (1973): 11–32.

Okihiro, Gary Y., and Julie Sly. "The Press, Japanese Americans, and the Concentration Camps." *Phylon* 44 (1983): 66–83.

Petonito, Gina. "Constructing the Enemy: Justifying Japanese Internment During World War II." PhD diss., Syracuse University, 1992.

Shaffer, Robert. "Opposition to Internment: Defending Japanese American Rights During World War II." *Historian* 61 (spring 1999): 597–619.

Slackman, Michael. "The Orange Race: George S. Patton, Jr.'s Japanese-American Hostage Plan." *Biography* 7 (1984): 1–49.

Smith, Geoffrey S. "Racial Nativism and Origins of Japanese American Relocation." In Daniels, Taylor, and Kitano, *Japanese Americans*, 79–87.

Stanley, Gerald. "Justice Deferred: A Fifty-Year Perspective on Japanese Internment Historiography." *Southern California Quarterly* 74, no. 2 (1992): 181–206.

Suzuki, Peter T. "For the Sake of Inter-University Comity: The Attempted

Suppression by the University of California of Morton Grodzins' *Americans Betrayed.*" In *Views from Within: The Japanese American Evacuation and Resettlement Study*, ed. Yuji Ichioka, 95–123. Los Angeles: Asian American Studies Center, UCLA, 1989.

ten Broek, Jacobus, Edward Norton Barnhart, and Floyd W. Matson. *Prejudice, War, and the Constitution.* Berkeley: University of California Press, 1954.

U.S. Department of War. "Evacuation—Its Military Necessity." In *Final Report: Japanese Evacuation from the West Coast, 1942*, 1–38. Washington, DC: GPO, 1943.

Legal and Constitutional Issues

Barnhart, Edward N. "The Individual Exclusion of Japanese Americans in World War II." *Pacific Historical Review* 29 (1960): 111–30.

Chuman, Frank F. *The Bamboo People: The Law and Japanese-Americans.* Del Mar, CA: Publisher's Inc., 1976.

Dembitz, Nanette. "Racial Discrimination and the Military Judgement: The Supreme Court's Korematsu and Endo Decisions." *Columbia Law Review* 45 (1944): 175–239.

Detlefsen, Robert R. "The Wartime Internment Cases Reconsidered: Peter Irons' *Justice at War.*" *Journal of Contemporary Studies* 8, no. 4 (1985): 13–23.

Fine, Sidney. "Justice Murphy and the Hirabayashi Case." *Pacific Historical Review* 33 (1964): 195–210.

Irons, Peter. *Justice at War.* New York: Oxford University Press, 1983.

Irons, Peter. *Justice Delayed: The Record of the Japanese American Cases.* Middletown, CT: Wesleyan University Press, 1989.

———. "Race and the Constitution: The Case of the Japanese American Internment." *Constitution* 13 (1986): 18–26.

Konvitz, Milton F. *The Alien and the Asiatic in American Law.* Ithaca, NY: Cornell University Press, 1946.

Kutulas, Judy. "In Quest of Autonomy: The Northern California Affiliate of the American Civil Liberties Union and World War II." *Pacific Historical Review* 67, no. 2 (1998): 201–31.

Rostow, Eugene. "The Japanese American Cases—A Disaster." *Yale Law Review* 54 (1945): 489–533.

———. "Our Worst Wartime Mistake." *Harper's Magazine*, Sep. 1945, 193–201.

ten Broek, Jacobus, Edward Norton Barnhart, and Floyd W. Matson. *Prejudice, War and the Constitution*, Berkeley: University of California Press, 1954.

Tsuchida, Nobuya. *American Justice: Japanese American Evacuation and Redress Cases.* Minneapolis: Asian/Pacific American Learning Resource Center, University of Minnesota, 1988.

Yamamoto, Eric K. *Race, Rights, and Reparation: Law and the Japanese American Internment*. Gaithersburg, MD: Aspen Law and Business, 2001.

United States Government Agencies

WAR RELOCATION AUTHORITY

Myer, Dillon S. "Japanese American Relocation: Final Chapter." *Common Ground* 6, no. 1 (1945): 61–66.

———. *Uprooted Americans: The Japanese Americans and the War Relocation Authority During World War II*. Tucson: University of Arizona Press, 1970.

Wallinger, Michael J. "Dispersal of the Japanese-Americans: Rhetorical Strategies of the War Relocation Authority, 1942–1945." PhD diss., University of Oregon, 1975.

War Relocation Authority. *Administrative Highlights of the WRA Program*. Washington, DC: GPO, 1946.

———. *Community Government in War Relocation Centers*. Washington, DC: GPO, 1946.

———. *Education in the War Relocation Centers*. Washington, DC: GPO, 1945.

———. *The Evacuated People: A Quantitative Description*. Washington, DC: GPO, 1946.

———. *Evacuees of Tule Lake*. Washington, DC: GPO, 1943.

———. *Legal and Constitutional Phases of the WRA Program*. Washington, DC: GPO, 1946.

———. *Myths and Facts About the Japanese-Americans*. Washington, DC: GPO, 1945.

———. *The Relocation Program*. Washington, DC: GPO, 1946.

———. *Segregation of Persons of Japanese Ancestry in Tule Lake Relocation Center*. Washington, DC: GPO, 1943.

———. *Wartime Exile: The Exclusion of the Japanese Americans from the West Coast*. Washington, DC: GPO, 1946.

———. *Wartime Handling of Evacuee Property*. Washington, DC: GPO, 1946.

———. *WRA: A Story of Human Conservation*. Washington, DC: GPO, 1946.

OTHER AGENCIES

Daniels, Roger. "The Bureau of the Census and the Relocation of Japanese Americans: A Note and Document." *Amerasia Journal* 9, no. 1 (1982): 101–5.

Okamura, Raymond. "The Myth of Census Confidentiality." *Amerasia Journal* 8, no. 2 (1981): 111–20.

Taylor, Sandra C. "The Federal Reserve Bank and the Relocation of the Japanese in 1942." *Public Historian* 5, no. 1 (1983): 9–30.

Specific Japanese Communities

Brown, Betty F. "The Evacuation of the Japanese Population from a California Agricultural Community." MA thesis, Stanford University, 1944.

Culley, John H. "Relocation of Japanese Americans: The Hawaiian Experience." *Air Force Law Review* 24 (spring 1984): 176–83.

Culley, John J. "World War II and a Western Town: The Internment of Japanese Railroad Workers of Clovis, New Mexico." *Western Historical Quarterly* 13 (1982): 43–61.

Droker, Howard A. "Seattle Race Relations During the Second World War." *Pacific Northwest Quarterly* 67, no. 4 (1976): 163–74.

Fukuyama, Yoshio. "Citizens Apart: A History of the Japanese in Ventura County, Including: The Japanese in Oxnard, California, 1898–1945." *Ventura County Historical Society Quarterly* 39, no. 1 (1994–95): 1–31.

Gardner, Dudley. "World War II and the Japanese of Southwest Wyoming." *Wyoming History Journal* 68 (spring 1996): 22–32.

Hosokawa, Bill. "When Seattle's Japanese Vanished." *Annals of the Chinese Historical Society of the Pacific Northwest* (1984): 90–94.

Masumoto, David Mas. *Country Voices: The Oral History of a Japanese American Family Farm Community*. Del Rey, CA: Inaka Publications, 1987.

Matsumoto, Valerie J. *Farming the Home Place: A Japanese American Community in California*. Ithaca, NY: Cornell University Press, 1993.

McDonald, Archie. *The Japanese Experience in Butte County, California*. Chico, CA: Association for Northern California Records and Research, 1993.

Naske, Claus-M. "The Relocation of Alaska's Japanese Residents." *Pacific Northwest Quarterly* 74 (1983): 124–32.

Ng, Wendy Lee. "Collective Memory, Social Networks, and Generations: The Japanese-American Community in Hood River, Oregon." PhD diss., University of Oregon, 1989.

Noda, Kesa. *Yamato Colony: 1906–1960*. Livingston, CA: Livingston-Merced JACL Chapter, 1981.

Olmstead, Timothy. "Nikkei Internment: The Perspective of Two Oregon Weekly Newspapers." *Oregon Historical Quarterly* 85 (1984): 5–32.

Pursinger, Marvin G. "Oregon's Japanese in World War II: A History of Compulsory Relocation." PhD diss., University of Southern California, 1961.

Rawitsch, Mark Howland. *No Other Place: Japanese American Pioneers in a Southern California Neighborhood*. Occasional Monographs of the Department of History, University of California, Riverside, 1983.

Russell, Andrew. "A Fortunate Few: Japanese-Americans in Southern Nevada, 1905–1945." *Nevada Historical Society Quarterly* 31 (1988): 32–52.

Saiki, Patsy Sumie. *Ganbare!—An Example of Japanese Spirit*. Honolulu: Kisaku, 1982.

Sato, Susie. "Before Pearl Harbor: Early Japanese Settlers in Arizona." *Journal of Arizona History* 14 (1973): 317–34.

Schlenker, Gerald. "The Internment of the Japanese of San Diego County During the Second World War." *Journal of San Diego History* 18, no. 1 (1972): 1–9.

Sims, Robert C. "'Fearless, Patriotic, Clean-Cut Stand': Idaho's Governor Clark and Japanese American Relocation in World War II." *Pacific Northwest Quarterly* 70 (1979): 75–81.

———. *Japanese-American Contributions to Idaho's Economic Development*. Boise, ID: Boise State University, Center for Research, Grants, and Contracts, 1977.

Tamura, Linda. *The Hood River Issei: An Oral History of Japanese Settlers in Oregon's Hood River Valley*. Urbana: University of Illinois Press, 1993.

Yamashita, Kanshi Stanley. "Terminal Island: Ethnography of an Ethnic Community: Its Dissolution and Reorganization to a Non-Spatial Community." PhD diss., University of California, Irvine, 1985.

Yasui, Barbara. "The Nikkei in Oregon, 1834–1940." *Oregon Historical Quarterly* 76, no. 3 (1975): 225–57.

Separate Camp Histories

Arrington, Leonard J. *The Price of Prejudice: The Japanese-American Relocation Center in Utah During World War II*. Logan: Utah State University, 1962.

Bailey, Paul D. *City in the Sun: The Japanese Concentration Camp at Poston, Arizona*. Los Angeles: Westernlore Press, 1971.

Bearden, Russell. "The False Rumor of Tuesday: Arkansas's Internment of Japanese-Americans." *Arkansas Historical Quarterly* 41 (1982): 327–39.

———. "Life Inside Arkansas's Japanese-American Relocation Centers." *Arkansas Historical Quarterly* 48, no. 2 (1989): 169–96.

Brown, Robert L. "Manzanar—Relocation Center." *Common Ground* 3, no. 1 (1942): 27–32.

Caruso, Samuel T. "After Pearl Harbor: Arizona's Response to the Gila River Relocation Center." *Journal of Arizona History* 14 (1973): 335–46.

Cates, Rita Takahashi. "Comparative Administration and Management of Five War Relocation Authority Camps: America's Incarceration of Persons of Japanese Descent During World War II." PhD diss., University of Pittsburgh, 1980.

Clark, Paul F. "Those Other Camps: An Oral History Analysis of Japanese Alien Enemy Internment During World War II." MA thesis, California State University, Fullerton, 1980.

Culley, John J. "The Santa Fe Internment Camp and the Justice Department Program for Enemy Aliens." In Daniels, Taylor, and Kitano, *Japanese Americans*, 57–71.

———. "Trouble at the Lordsburg Internment Camp." *New Mexico Historical Review* 60 (1985): 225–48.

Feeley, Francis. *A Strategy of Dominance: The History of an American Concentration Camp, Pomona, California*. New York: Brandywine Press, 1995.

Friedlander, E. J. "Freedom of the Press Behind Barbed Wire: Paul Yokota and the Jerome Relocation Center Newspaper." *Arkansas Historical Quarterly* 44 (1985): 303–13.

Friedlander, Jay. "Journalism Behind Barbed Wire, 1942–44: An Arkansas Relocation Center Newspaper." *Journalism Quarterly* 62 (1985): 243–46, 271.

Garrett, Jessie A., and Ronald C. Larson, eds. *Camp and Community: Manzanar and the Owens Valley*. Fullerton: California State University Oral History Program Japanese American Project, 1977.

Hansen, Arthur A. "Representations of an Imprisoned Poston Past." *Journal of Orange County Studies* 3–4 (1989–90): 102–8.

Hansen, Arthur A., and David A. Hacker, "The Manzanar Riot: An Ethnic Perspective." *Amerasia Journal* 2, no. 2 (1974): 112–57.

Jackman, Norman R. "Collective Protest in Relocation Centers." *American Journal of Sociology* 63 (1957): 264–72.

Jacoby, Harold S. *Tule Lake: From Relocation to Segregation*. Grass Valley, CA: Comstock Bonanza, 1996.

Johnson, Melyn. "At Home in Amache: A Japanese-American Relocation Camp in Colorado." *Colorado Heritage* 1 (1989): 2–11.

Kumei, Teruko Imai. "'Skeleton in the Closet': The Japanese American *Hokoku Seinen-dan* and Their 'Disloyal' Activities at the Tule Lake Segregation Center During World War II." *Japanese Journal of American Studies*, no. 7 (1996): 67–102.

Lehman, Anthony L. *Birthright of Barbed Wire: The Santa Anita Assembly Center for the Japanese*. Los Angeles: Westernlore Press, 1970.

Leighton, Alexander H. *The Governing of Men: General Principles and Recommendations Based on Experience at a Japanese Relocation Camp*. Princeton, NJ: Princeton University Press, 1945.

Mackey, Mike. *Heart Mountain: Life in Wyoming's Concentration Camp*. Powell, WY: Western History Publications, 2000.

———, ed. *Remembering Heart Mountain: Essays on Japanese American Internment in Wyoming*. Powell, WY: Western History Publications, 1998.

Miyamoto, S. Frank. "Resentment, Distrust, and Insecurity at Tule Lake." In Ichioka, *Views from Within*, 127–40.

———. "The Career of Intergroup Tensions: A Study of the Collective Adjustments of Evacuees to Crises at the Tule Lake Relocation Center." PhD diss., University of Chicago, 1950.

Nelson, Douglas W. *Heart Mountain: The History of an American Concentration Camp*. Madison, WI: Logmark Editions, 1976.

Nishimoto, Richard S. *Inside an American Concentration Camp: Japanese American Resistance at Poston, Arizona*. Ed. Lane Ryo Hirabayashi. Tucson: University of Arizona Press, 1995.

Nudd, Jean. "Japanese Internment Camps in Arizona: Sources for Original Documents." *Casa Grande Valley Histories* (1992): 29–41.

Okihiro, Gary Y. "Japanese Resistance in America's Concentration Camps: A Re-evaluation." *Amerasia Journal* 2, no. 1 (1973): 20–34.

———. "Tule Lake Under Martial Law: A Study in Japanese Resistance." *Journal of Ethnic Studies* 5, no. 3 (1977): 71–85.

Sakoda, James M. "Minidoka: An Analysis of Changing Patterns of Social Interaction." PhD diss., University of California, Berkeley, 1949.

———. "The 'Residue': The Unresettled Minidokans, 1943–1945." In Ichioka, *Views From Within*, 247–84.

Sims, Robert C. "The Japanese American Experience in Idaho." *Idaho Yesterday* 22, no. 1 (1978): 2–10.

Spencer, Robert F. "The Relocation Center at Rivers, Arizona: Concentration Camp or Community?" *Casa Grande Valley Histories* (1992): 7–20.

Taylor, Sandra C. "Interned at Topaz: Age, Gender, and Family in the Relocation Experience." *Utah Historical Quarterly* 59, no. 4 (1991): 380–94.

———. "Japanese Americans and Keetley Farm: Utah's Relocation Colony." *Utah Historical Quarterly* 54 (1986): 328–44.

———. *Jewel of the Desert: Japanese American Internment at Topaz*. Berkeley: University of California Press, 1993.

Thomas, Dorothy S., and Richard S. Nishimoto. *The Spoilage*. Berkeley: University of California Press, 1946.

Turner, Stanton B. "Japanese-American Internment at Tule Lake, 1942–1946." *Journal of the Shaw Library* 2, no. 1 (1987): 1–34.

Uchida, Yoshiko. "Topaz City of Dust." *Utah Historical Quarterly* 48, no. 3 (1980): 234–43.

Van Valkenburg, Carol. *An Alien Place: The Fort Missoula, Montana Detention Camp, 1941–1944*. Missoula, MT: Pictorial Histories, 1995.

Wada, George, and James C. Davies. "Riots and Rioters." *Western Political Quarterly* 10 (1957): 864–74.

Yatsushiro, Toshio. "Political and Socio-Cultural Issues at Poston and Manzanar Relocation Centers—A Thermal Analysis." PhD diss., Cornell University, 1953.

Camp Life

RESISTANCE OR RIOTS

Embrey, Sue Kunitami. *Manzanar Martyr: An Interview with Harry Y. Ueno.*
Fullerton: California State University Oral History Program Japanese American
Project, 1986.

Emi, Frank. "Resistance: The Heart Mountain Fair Play Committee's Fight for
Justice." *Amerasia Journal* 17 (1991): 47–51.

Hansen, Arthur A. "Cultural Politics in the Gila River Relocation Center, 1942–
1943." *Arizona and the West* 27 (1985): 327–61.

Hohri, William Minoru, and Mits Koshiyama. *Resistance: Challenging America's
Wartime Internment of Japanese-Americans.* Lomita, CA: Epistolarian, 2001.

Inouye, Frank T. "Immediate Origins of the Heart Mountain Draft Resistance
Movement." In Mackey, *Remembering Heart Mountain,* 121–39.

Kurashige, Lon. "Resistance, Collaboration, and Manzanar Protest." *Pacific
Historical Review* 70 (2001): 387–417.

Muller, Eric L. *Free to Die for Their Country: The Story of the Japanese American
Draft Resisters in World War II.* Chicago: University of Chicago Press, 2001.

Okihiro, Gary Y. "Religion and Resistance in America's Concentration Camps."
Phylon 45 (1984): 220–33.

———. "Tule Lake Under Martial Law: A Study in Japanese Resistance." *Journal of
Ethnic Studies* 5, no. 3 (1977): 71–85.

THE ROLE OF SOCIAL SCIENTISTS

Adams, William Y. "Edward H. Spicer, Historian." *Journal of the Southwest* 32, no.
1 (1990): 18–26.

Brown, G. Gordon. "War Relocation Authority, Gila River Project, Rivers,
Arizona, Community Analysis Section, May 12 to July 7, 1945: Final Report."
Applied Anthropology 4, no. 4 (1945): 1–49.

Chang, Gordon H. *Morning Glory, Evening Shadow: Yamato Ichihashi and His
Internment Writings, 1942–1945.* Stanford, CA: Stanford University Press,
1997.

de Cristoforo, Violet Kazue. "J'Accuse." *Rikka* 13, no. 1 (1992): 16–36.

Embree, John F. N. "Community Analysis—An Example of Anthropology in
Government." *American Anthropologist* 46 (1944): 277–91.

Hansen, Arthur A. "An Interview with James M. Sakoda." In *Japanese American
World World II Oral History Project: Part III: Analysts,* ed. Arthur A. Hansen,
341–457. Munich: K. G. Saur, 1994.

———. "An Interview with Robert F. Spencer." In *Japanese American World World II*

Oral History Project: Part III: Analysts, ed. Arthur A. Hansen, 175–340. Munich: K. G. Saur, 1994.

———. "Political Ideology and Participant Observation: Nisei Social Scientists in the Evacuation and Resettlement Study, 1942–1945." In Mackey, *Guilt By Association*, 119–44.

Hansen, Asael T. "Community Analysis at Heart Mountain Relocation Center." *Applied Anthropology* 5, no. 3 (1946): 15–25.

———. "My Two Years at Heart Mountain: The Difficult Role of an Applied Anthropologist." In Daniels, Taylor, and Kitano, *Japanese Americans*, 33–37.

Hirabayashi, Lane Ryo. *The Politics of Fieldwork: Research in an American Concentration Camp*. Tucson: University of Arizona Press, 1999.

Hirabayashi, Lane Ryo, and James Hirabayashi. "The 'Credible' Witness: The Central Role of Richard S. Nishimoto in JERS." In Ichioka, *Views from Within*, 65–94.

Ichioka, Yuji. "JERS Revisited: Introduction." In Ichioka, *Views from Within*, 3–27.

———, ed. *Views from Within: The Japanese American Evacuation and Resettlement Study*. Los Angeles: Asian American Studies Center, UCLA, 1989.

Kikuchi, Charles. "Through the JERS Looking Glass: A Personal View from Within." In Ichioka, *Views from Within*, 179–95.

Luomala, Katherine. "Community Analysis Outside the Centers—A War Relocation Experience." *Applied Anthropology* 6, no. 1 (1947): 25–31.

Miyamoto, S. Frank. "Dorothy Swaine Thomas as Director of JERS: Some Personal Observations." In Ichioka, *Views from Within*, 31–63.

———. "Reminiscences." In Ichioka, *Views from Within*, 141–55.

Murray, Stephen O. "The Rights of Research Assistants and the Rhetoric of Political Suppression: Morton Grodzins and the University of California Japanese-American Evacuation and Resettlement Study." *Journal of the History of the Behavioral Sciences* 27, no. 2 (1991): 130–56.

Nishimoto, Richard S. *Inside an American Concentration Camp: Japanese American Resistance at Poston, Arizona*. Ed. Lane Ryo Hirabayashi. Tucson: University of Arizona Press, 1995.

Officer, James E. "Edward H. Spicer and the Application of Anthropology." *Journal of the Southwest* 32, no. 1 (1990): 27–35.

Provinse, John H., and Solon T. Kimball. "Building New Communities During War Time." *American Sociological Review* 11 (1946): 396–410.

Redfield, Robert. "The Japanese-Americans." In *American Society in Wartime*, ed. William F. Ogburn, 143–64. Chicago: University of Chicago Press, 1943.

Sakoda, James M. "Reminiscences of a Participant Observer." In Ichioka, *Views from Within*, 219–45.

Spencer, Robert F. "Gila in Retrospect." In Ichioka, *Views from Within*, 157–74.

Spicer, Edward H. "Anthropologists and the War Relocation Authority." In *The Uses of Anthropology*, ed. Walter Goldschmidt, 217–37. Washington, DC: American Anthropological Association, 1979.

———. "Early Applications of Anthropology in North America." In *Perspectives on Anthropology, 1976*, ed. Anthony F. C. Wallace, 116–41. Washington, DC: American Anthropological Association, 1977.

———. "The Use of Social Scientists by the War Relocation Authority." *Applied Anthropology* 5, no. 2 (1946): 16–36.

Spicer, Rosamond B. "A Full Life Well Lived: A Brief Account of the Life of Edward H. Spicer." *Journal of the Southwest* 32, no. 1 (1990): 3–17.

Starn, Orin. "Engineering Internment: Anthropologists and the War Relocation Authority." *American Ethnologist* 13, no. 4 (1986): 700–720.

Suzuki, Peter T. "Anthropologists in the Wartime Camps for Japanese Americans: A Documentary Study." *Dialectical Anthropology* 6, no. 1 (1981): 23–60.

———. "Case Study: A Retrospective Analysis of a Wartime 'National Character Study.'" *Dialectical Anthropology* 5, no. 1 (1980): 33–46.

———. "Planned Communities in Wartime America: A Province for the New Urban History." Unpublished essay.

———. "The University of California Japanese Evacuation and Resettlement Study: A Prolegomenon." *Dialectical Anthropology* 10 (1986): 189–213.

Takagi, Dana. "Life History Analysis and JERS: Reevaluating the Work of Charles Kikuchi." In Ichioka, *Views from Within*, 197–216.

Wakayama, Edgar. "Passing the Torch from Father to Son Because It Should Never Happen Again." *UNR Times* 7 (winter 1989–90): 5–8.

Wax, Rosalie H. "The Destruction of a Democratic Impulse." *Human Organization* 12, no. 1 (1953): 11–21.

———. "Fieldwork in the Japanese American Relocation Centers, 1943–1945." In *Doing Fieldwork: Warnings and Advice*, by Rosalie H. Wax, 59–174. Chicago: University of Chicago Press, 1971.

EDUCATION

George, Robert C. L. "The Granada Colorado Relocation Center Secondary School." MA thesis, University of Colorado, 1944.

Hirabayashi, Lane Ryo. "The Impact of Incarceration on the Education of Nisei Schoolchildren." In Daniels, Taylor, and Kitano, *Japanese Americans*, 44–51.

James, Thomas. "The Education of Japanese Americans at Tule Lake, 1942–1946." *Pacific Historical Review* 56 (1987): 25–58.

———. *Exile Within: The Schooling of Japanese Americans, 1942–1945*. Cambridge, MA: Harvard University Press, 1987.

————. "'Life Begins with Freedom': The College Nisei, 1942–1945." *History of Education Quarterly* 25 (1985): 155–74.

Light, Jerome. "The Development of a Junior-Senior High School Program in a Relocation Center for People of Japanese Ancestry During the War With Japan." PhD diss., Stanford University, 1947.

Mossman, Robert A. "Japanese American War Relocation Centers as Total Institutions with Emphasis on the Educational Program." EdD diss., Rutgers University, 1978.

O'Brien, Robert W. *The College Nisei.* Palo Alto, CA: Pacific Books, 1949.

Okihiro, Gary Y. *Storied Lives: Japanese American Students and World War II.* Seattle: University of Washington Press, 1999.

Tajiri, Vincent, ed. *Through Innocent Eyes: Writings and Art from the Japanese American Internment by Poston I Children.* Los Angeles: Keiro Services Press, 1990.

Wollenberg, Charles. "Schools Behind Barbed Wire." *California Historical Quarterly* 55, no. 3 (1976): 210–17.

Yumiba, Carole K. "An Educational History of the War Relocation Center at Jerome and Rohwer, Arkansas, 1942–1945." PhD diss., University of Southern California, 1979.

Zeller, William D. *An Education Drama: The Educational Program Provided the Japanese Americans During the Relocation Period, 1942–1945.* New York: American Press, 1969.

ART AND LITERATURE

Blicksilver, Edith. "The Japanese-American Woman, the Second World War, and the Relocation Camp Experience." *Women's Studies International Forum* 5 (1982): 351–53.

de Cristoforo, Violet Kazue. *May Sky: There Is Always Tomorrow: An Anthology of Japanese American Concentration Kaiko Haiku.* Los Angeles: Sun and Moon Press, 1997.

de Cristoforo, Violet Kazue Matsuda. "There Is Always Tomorrow: An Anthology of Wartime Haiku." *Amerasia Journal* 19, no. 1 (1993): 93–115.

Eaton, Allen H. *Beauty Behind Barbed Wire: The Arts of the Japanese in Our War Relocation Camps.* New York: Harper, 1952.

Edmiston, James. *Home Again.* Garden City: Doubleday, 1955.

Ehrlich, Gretel. *Heart Mountain.* New York: Viking, 1988.

Gesensway, Deborah, and Mindy Roseman. *Beyond Words: Images from America's Concentration Camps.* Ithaca, NY: Cornell University Press, 1987.

Guterson, David. *Snow Falling on Cedars.* New York: Vintage Books, 1995.

Fukuhara, Henry. *Portfolio of 50 Scenes of the Relocation Centers.* New York: Plantin Press, 1944.

Hewes, Laurence. *Boxcar in the Sand.* New York: Alfred Knopf, 1957.

Higa, Karin M. *The View from Within: Japanese American Art from the Internment Camps, 1942–1945.* Los Angeles: Japanese American National Museum, 1992.

Hill, Kimi Kodani. *Topaz Moon: Chiura Obata's Art of the Internment.* Berkeley: Heyday Books, 2000.

Hudson, Helen. *A Temporary Residence.* New York: G. P. Putnam's Son, 1988.

Ikeda, Stewart David. *What the Scarecrow Said.* New York: Regan Books, 1996.

Ishigo, Estelle. *Lone Heart Mountain.* Los Angeles: Anderson, Ritchie, and Simon, 1972.

Kubo, Sadajirō, ed. *Hokubei Nihonjin no Shūyōjo.* Tokyo: Sōbunsha, 1981 [a catalog of wartime paintings by Henry Sugimoto].

Matsuoka, Jack. *Camp II, Block 211: Daily Life in an Internment Camp.* San Francisco: Japan Publications, 1974.

Means, Florence C. *The Moved Outers.* Boston: Houghton-Mifflin, 1945.

Miyakawa, Edward. *Tule Lake.* Waldport, OR: House by the Sea, 1979.

Mueller, Marnie. *The Climate of the Country.* Willimantic, CT: Curbstone Press, 1999.

Nakagawa, George. *Seki-Nin (Duty Bound).* Fullerton: California State University Oral History Program Japanese American Project, 1989.

Nakano, Jiro, and Kay Nakano, eds. and trans. *Poets Behind Barbed Wire.* Honolulu: Bamboo Ridge Press, 1983.

Okada, John. *No-No Boy.* Rutland, VT: Charles E. Tuttle, 1957.

Okubo, Mine. *Citizen 13660.* New York: Columbia University Press, 1946.

———. *Mine Okubo: An American Experience.* Oakland, CA: Oakland Museum, 1972.

Opler, Marvin, and F. Obayashi. "Senryu Poetry as Folk and Community Expression." *Journal of American Folklore* 58 (1945): 1–11.

Rizzuto, Rahna Reiko. *Why She Left Us.* New York: Perennial, 2000.

Robertson, Georgia D. *The Harvest of Hate: A Novel of the Japanese American Evacuation.* Fullerton: California State University Oral History Program Japanese American Project, 1986.

Schweik, Susan. "The 'Pre-Poetics' of Internment: The Example of Toyo Suyemoto." *American Literary History* 1, no. 1 (1989): 89–109.

Steel, Danielle. *Silent Honor.* New York: Delacorte Press, 1966.

Suzuki, Peter T. "Wartime Tanka (Classical Japanese Poetry of 31 Syllables): Issei and Kibei Contributions to a Literature East and West." *Literature East and West: Journal of World and Comparative Literature* 21 (1977): 242–54.

Yamamoto, Traise. *Masking Selves, Making Subjects: Japanese American Woman, Identity, and the Body.* Berkeley: University of California Press, 1999.

CULTURE AND RELIGION

Gantite, Nancy J. "Survived Behind Barbed Wire: The Impact of Imprisonment on Japanese-American Culture During World War II." *Maryland Historian* 19, no. 2 (1988): 15–32.

Mondello, Salvatore. "The Integration of Japanese Baptists in American Society." *Foundations* 20, no. 3 (1977): 254–63.

Okada, Victor N. *Triumphs of Faith: Stories of Japanese-American Christians During World War II.* Los Angeles: Japanese-American Internment Project, 1998.

Opler, Marvin K. "Japanese Folk Belief and Practices, Tule Lake, California." *Journal of American Folklore* (October/December, 1950): 385–97.

———. "A Sumo Tournament at Tule Lake Center." *American Anthropologist* 47 (1945): 134–39.

———. "Two Japanese Religious Sections." *Southwestern Journal of Anthropology* 6, no. 1 (1950): 69–78.

Shaffer, Robert. "Opposition to Internment: Defending Japanese American Rights During World War II." *Historian* 61 (spring 1999): 597–619.

Spencer, Robert F. "Japanese Buddhism in the United States, 1940–1946: A Study in Acculturation." PhD diss., University of California, Berkeley, 1946.

Suzuki, Lester E. *Ministry in the Assembly and Relocation Centers of World War II.* Berkeley, CA: Yardbird, 1979.

Suzuki, Peter T. "The Ethnolinguistics of Japanese Americans in the Wartime Camps." *Anthropological Linguistics* 18 (1976): 416–27.

Toelken, Barre. "Cultural Maintenance and Ethnic Intensification in Two Japanese-American Internment Camps." *Oriens Extremus* 33, no. 2 (1990): 69–94.

FAMILY

Bloom, Leonard. "Familial Adjustment of Japanese-Americans to Relocation: First Phase." *American Sociological Review* 8, no. 5 (1943): 551–60.

Broom, Leonard, and John I. Kitsuse. *The Managed Casualty: The Japanese-American Family in World War II.* Berkeley: University of California Press, 1956.

Fernandes, Marjorie M. "I Don't Like Japan, Mommy. I Want to Go Back to America." *San Jose Studies* 14, no. 2 (1988): 8–30.

Matsumoto, Valerie J. "Japanese American Women During World War II." *Frontiers* 8 (1984): 6–14.

———. "Nisei Women and Resettlement During World War II." In *Making Waves: An Anthology of Writings by and About Asian American Women*, ed. Asian American Women United of California, 115–26. Boston: Beacon Press, 1989.

Nakano, Mei. *Japanese American Women: Three Generations, 1890–1990.* Berkeley, CA: Mina Press, 1990.

Taylor, Sandra C. "Interned at Topaz: Age, Gender, and Family in the Relocation Experience." *Utah Historical Quarterly* 59, no. 4 (1991): 380–94.

Tsuchida, Nobuya, ed. *Reflections: Memoirs of Japanese American Women in Minnesota.* Covina, CA: Pacific Asia Press, 1994.

Japanese American Citizens League

Chin, Frank. "Come All Ye Asian American Writers of the Real and the Fake." In *The Big Aiiieeeee!—An Anthology of Chinese American and Japanese American Literature*, ed. Jeffrey P. Chan Lawson Inada, 1–92. New York: Meridian Books, 1991.

Daniels, Roger. "The Japanese." In *Ethnic Leadership in America*, ed. John Higham, 36–63. Baltimore: Johns Hopkins University Press, 1978.

Hosokawa, Bill. *JACL: In Quest of Justice.* New York: Morrow, 1982.

———. *Nisei: The Quiet Americans: The Story of a People.* New York: Morrow, 1969.

Japanese American Citizens League. *The Case for the Nisei: Brief of the Japanese American Citizens League.* Salt Lake City, UT: JACL, 1945.

Japanese American Citizens League. "Minutes of San Francisco Emergency Meeting, March 8–10, 1942." Repr. Los Angeles: Southern California JACL Office, 1972.

Lim, Deborah. *The Lim Report: A Research Report on Japanese Americans in American Concentration Camps During World War II.* Kearney, NE: Morris, 1990.

Masaoka, Mike. *They Call Me Moses Masaoka.* New York: William Morrow, 1987.

Spickard, Paul R. "The Nisei Assume Power: The Japanese [American] Citizens League, 1941–1942." *Pacific Historical Review* 52 (1983): 147–74.

Wilson, Robert A., and Bill Hosokawa. *East to America: A History of the Japanese in the United States.* New York: Morrow, 1980.

Zelko, Frank. *Generation, Culture, and Prejudice: The Japanese American Decision to Cooperate with Evacuation and Internment During World War II.* Victoria, Australia: Department of History, Monash University, 1992.

Nisei Soldiers

Ano, Masaharu. "Loyal Linguists: Nisei of World War II Learned Japanese in Minnesota." *Minnesota History* 45, no. 7 (1977): 273–87.

Bittner, Eric. "'Loyalty . . . Is a Covenant': Japanese-American Internees and the Selective Service Act." *Prologue* 23 (1991): 248–52.

Cary, Otis, ed. *War-Wasted Asia; Letters. 1945–46.* Tokyo: Kodansha, 1975.

Chan, Won-joy. *Burma: The Untold Story.* Novato, CA: Presidio Press, 1986.

Chang, Thelma. *"I Can Never Forget": Men of the 100th/442nd.* Honolulu: Sigi Productions, 1991.

Choy, Peggy. "Racial Order and Contestation: Asian American Internees and Soldiers at Camp McCoy, Wisconsin, 1942–1943." In *Asian Americans: Comparative and Global Perspectives*, ed. Shirley Hune, Stephen S. Fujita, and Amy Ling, 87–102. Pullman: Washington State University Press, 1991.

Crost, Lyn. *Honor by Fire: Japanese Americans at War in Europe and the Pacific*. Novato, CA: Presidio Press, 1994.

Deane, Hugh, ed. *Remembering Koji Ariyoshi: An American GI in Yenan*. Los Angeles: U.S.-China Peoples Friendship Association, 1978.

Duus, Masayo. *Unlikely Liberators: The Men of the 100th and 442nd*. Honolulu: University of Hawaii Press, 1987.

Fujishin, Sam. "Nisei Soldiers: Their Contribution to Post–World War II Japanese American Rights." In Mackey, *Remembering Heart Mountain*, 141–51.

Fujita, Frank "Foo." *Foo, a Japanese-American Prisoner of the Rising Sun*. Denton: University of North Texas Press, 1993.

Hansen, Arthur. "Sergeant Ben Kuroki's Perilous 'Home Mission': Contested Loyalty and Patriotism in Japanese American Detention Centers." In Mackey, *Remembering Heart Mountain*, 153–75.

Harrington, Joseph D. *Yankee Samurai: The Role of Nisei in America's Pacific Victory*. Detroit, MI: Pettigrew Enterprises, 1979.

Hawaii Nikkei History Editorial Board. *Japanese Eyes, American Heart: Personal Reflections of Hawaii's World War II Nisei Soldiers*. Honolulu: Tenri Educational Foundation, 1998.

Ichinokuchi, Tad. *John Aiso and the M.I.S.: Japanese-American Soldiers in the Military Intelligence Service, World War II*. Los Angeles: Military Intelligence Club of Southern California, 1988.

Ishimura, Stone S. *The Military Intelligence Language School U.S. Army Fort Snelling, Minnesota*. Los Angeles: TecCom Productions, 1991.

Kiyosaki, Wayne S. *A Spy in Their Midst: The World War II Struggle of a Japanese-American Hero*. Lanham, MD: Madison Books, 1995.

Kotani, Roland. "The Nisei Soldier." In *The Japanese in Hawaii: A Century of Struggle*, by Roland Kotani, 107–22. Honolulu: Oahu Kanyaku Imin Centennial Committee, 1985.

Lind, Andrew. *Hawaii's Japanese*. Princeton, NJ: Princeton University Press, 1946.

Martin, Ralph G. *A Boy from Nebraska*. New York: Harper, 1946.

Mashbir, Sidney F. *I Was an American Spy*. New York: Vantage Press, 1953.

Menton, Linda K. "Research Report: Nisei Soldiers at Dachau, Spring 1945." *Holocaust and Genocide Studies* 8, no. 2 (1994): 258–74.

Military Intelligence Service of Northern California and National Japanese American Historical Society. *The Pacific War and Peace: Americans of Japanese Ancestry in Military Intelligence Service, 1941 to 1952*. San Francisco, CA: NJAHS, 1991.

Murphy, Thomas D. *Ambassadors in Arms: The Story of Hawaii's 100th Battalion.* Honolulu: University of Hawaii Press, 1954.

Nakasone, Edwin M. *The Nisei Soldier: Historical Essays on World War II and the Korean War.* White Bear Lake, MN: J-Press, 1999.

Nishimura, Hiro. *Trials and Triumphs of the Nikkei.* Mercer Island, WA: Fukuda Publishers, 1993.

Oda, James. *Heroic Struggles of Japanese Americans: Partisan Fighters from America's Concentration Camps.* Los Angeles: Privately printed, 1980.

———. *Secret Embedded in Magic Cables.* Los Angeles: Privately printed, 1993.

100th Infantry Battalion Committee. *Remembrances.* Honolulu: 100th Infantry Battalion Committee, 1992.

Rademaker, John A. *These Are Americans: The Japanese Americans in Hawaii in World War II.* Palo Alto, CA: Pacific Books, 1951.

Ringle, Ken. "The Troops America Forgot: A World War II Correspondent's History of Unsung Japanese American Heroes." *Washington Post,* February 15, 1995.

Shibutani, Tamotsu. *The Derelicts of Company K.* Berkeley: University of California Press, 1978.

Shirey, Orville C. *Americans: The Story of the 442nd Combat Team.* Washington, DC: Infantry Journal Press, 1947.

Steidl, Franz. *Lost Battalions: Going for Broke in the Vosges, Autumn 1944.* Novato, CA: Presidio Press, 1997.

Suzuki, Peter T. "Suicide Prevention in the Pacific War (WWII)." *Suicide and Life-Threatening Behavior* 21, no. 3 (1991): 291–97.

Tsuchida, William S. *Wear It Proudly.* Berkeley: University of California Press, 1947.

Wakamatsu, Jack K. *Silent Warriors: A Memoir of America's 442nd Regimental Combat Team.* New York: Vantage Press, 1995.

Renunciants

Christgau, John. "Collins v. the World: Wayne Collins, Sr. and the Tadayasu Abo Case." *Historical Reporter* 3, no. 1 (1983): 2–14.

———. "Collins Versus the World: The Fight to Restore Citizenship to Japanese-American Renunciants of World War II." *Pacific Historical Review* 54 (1985): 1–31.

———. "Hiro: Japanese-American Relocation and the End of Internment." In *"Enemies": World War II Alien Internment,* by John Christgau, 144–81. Ames: Iowa State University Press, 1985.

Collins, Donald E. *Native American Aliens: Disloyalty and the Renunciation of Citizenship by Japanese Americans During World War II.* Westport, CT: Greenwood Press, 1985.

Corbett, P. Scott. *Quiet Passage: The Exchange of Civilians Between the United States and Japan During the Second World War.* Kent, OH: Kent State University Press, 1987.

Grodzins, Morton. "Making Un-Americans: A Pathology of Disloyalty." In *The Loyal and the Disloyal: The Social Boundaries of Patriotism and Treason,* by Morton Grodzins, 105–31. Chicago: University of Chicago Press, 1956.

Ishida, Gladys. "The Japanese American Renunciants of Okayama Prefecture: Their Accommodation and Assimilation to Japanese Culture." PhD diss., University of Michigan, 1955.

Resettlement

Albert, Michal D. "Japanese American Communities in Chicago and the Twin Cities." PhD diss., University of Minnesota, 1980.

Bailey, Sydney D. "The Problem of the Japanese-Americans." *India Quarterly* 2 (1946): 366–70.

Boesen, Victor. "The Nisei Come Home." *New Republic,* April 26, 1948, 16–19.

Bogardus, Emory S. "Japanese Return to the West Coast." *Sociology and Social Research* 31 (1947): 226–33.

Brooks, Charlotte. "In the Twilight Zone Between Black and White: Japanese American Resettlement and Community in Chicago, 1942–1945." *Journal of American History* 86, no. 4 (March 2000): 1655–87.

Cullum, Robert W. "Japanese American Audit—1948." *Common Ground* 9 (1949): 87–92.

Inoue, Miyako. "Japanese-Americans in St. Louis: From Internees to Professionals." *City and Society* 3, no. 2 (1989): 142–52.

Kashima, Tetsuden. "Japanese American Internees Return, 1945–1955: Readjustment and Social Amnesia." *Phylon* 41 (1980): 107–15.

Leonard, Kevin. "'Is That What We Fought For?'—Japanese Americans and Racism in California; The Impact of World War II." *Western Historical Quarterly* 22, no. 4 (1990): 463–82.

Linehan, Thomas M. "Japanese American Resettlement in Cleveland During and After World War II." *Journal of Urban History* 20 (Nov. 1993): 54–80.

Luomala, Katherine. "California Takes Back Its Japanese Evacuees: The Readjustment of California to the Return of the Japanese Evacuees." *Applied Anthropology* 5, no. 3 (1946): 25–39.

Matsumoto, Valerie. "Nisei Women and Resettlement During World War II." In *Making Waves: An Anthology of Writings by and About Asian American Women,* ed. Asian American Women United of California, 115–126. Boston: Beacon Press, 1989.

Morita, Yukio. "The Japanese-Americans in the United States Between 1945 and 1965." MA thesis, Ohio State University, 1967.

Nishi, Setsuko. *Facts About Japanese-Americans.* Chicago: American Council on Race Relations, 1946.

Oakes, Vanya. "Test Case for Democracy." *Asia* 45 (March 1945): 147–50.

Oyama, Mary T. "Nisei Report from Home: My Return to Los Angeles." *Common Ground* 6, no. 2 (1946): 26–28.

Philip, Kenneth R. "Dillon S. Myer and the Advent of Termination." *Western Historical Quarterly* 19 (1988): 37–59.

Sawada, Mitziko. "After the Camps: Seabrook Farms, New Jersey, and the Resettlement of Japanese Americans, 1944–47." *Amerasia Journal* 13, no. 2 (1986–87): 117–36.

Schwartz, Harvey. "A Union Combats Racism: The ILWU's Japanese-American 'Stockton' Incident of 1945." *Southern California Quarterly* 62, no. 2 (1980): 161–76.

Seabrook, John. "The Spinach King: American Dreams and Nightmares at Seabrook Farms." *New Yorker,* Feb. 20 and 27, 1995, 222–31.

Shimada, Koji. "Education, Assimilation, and Acculturation: A Case Study of a Japanese-American Community in New Jersey," PhD diss., Temple University, 1975.

Shimano, Eddie. "Blueprint for a Slum." *Common Ground* 3, no. 4 (1943): 78–85.

Smith, Elmer R. "Resettlement of Japanese-Americans." *Far Eastern Survey,* May 18, 1949, 117–18.

Stevenson, Janet. "Before the Colors Fade: The Return of the Exiles." *American Heritage* 20, no. 4 (1969): 22–24, 96–99.

Tajiri, Larry. "Democracy Corrects Its Own Mistakes." *Asia and the Americas* 43 (1943): 213–16.

———. "Farewell to Little Tokyo." *Common Ground* 4, no. 2 (1944): 90–95.

Taylor, Sandra C. "Japanese Americans and Keetley Farms: Utah's Relocation Colony." *Utah Historical Quarterly* 54 (1986): 328–45.

———. "Leaving the Camps: Japanese American Resettlement in Utah and the Intermountain West." *Pacific Historical Review* 60 (1991): 169–94.

Thomas, Dorothy S. *The Salvage.* Berkeley: University of California Press, 1952.

Worden, William L. "The Hate That Failed." *Saturday Evening Post,* May 4, 1946.

Yatsushiro, Toshio, Iwao Ishino, and Yoshihara Matsumoto. "The Japanese-American Looks at Resettlement." *Public Opinion Quarterly* 8 (1944): 188–201.

Autobiographies and Biographies

IN ENGLISH

Biddle, Francis. *In Brief Authority.* New York: Doubleday, 1962.

Bird, Kai. *The Chairman John J. McCloy: The Making of the American Establishment.* New York: Simon and Schuster, 1992.

Cray, Ed. *Chief Justice: A Biography of Earl Warren.* New York: Simon and Schuster, 1997.

Current, Richard N. *Secretary Stimson: A Study in Statecraft.* New Brunswick, NJ: Rutgers University Press, 1954.

Davidson, Sue. "Aki Kato Kurose: Portrait of an Activist." *Frontiers* 7, no. 1 (1983): 91–97.

Duus, Masayo. *Tokyo Rose: Orphan of the Pacific.* Tokyo: Kodansha, 1979.

East Bay Japanese for Action. *Our Recollections.* Berkeley: East Bay Japanese for Action, 1986 [in Japanese as Wantō Nikkei Shakai Hōshidan, *Watakushitachi no Kiroku*].

Eisenhower, Milton S. *The President Is Calling.* New York: Doubleday, 1974.

Emmerson, John K. *The Japanese Thread: A Life in the U.S. Foreign Service.* New York: Holt, Rinehart, and Winston, 1978.

Fiset, Louis. *Fields Under Snow: Letters from Behind Barbed Wire Fences, 1941–1944.* Seattle: University of Washington Press, 1997.

———. *Imprisoned Apart: The World War II Correspondence of an Issei Couple.* Seattle: University of Washington Press, 1998.

Fujimura, Bunyu. *Though I Be Crushed.* Los Angeles: Nembutsu Press, 1985.

Fukuda, Yoshiaki. *My Six Years of Internment: An Issei's Struggle for Justice.* Trans. Konkō Church of San Francisco and the Research Information Center of the Konkō Churches of North America. San Francisco: Konkō Church, 1990. Originally published as *Yokuryū Seikatsu Rokunen* (San Francisco: Konkōkyō San Furanshisuko Kyōkai, 1957).

Gorfinkel, Claire, ed. *The Evacuation Diary of Hatsuye Egami.* Pasadena, CA: Intentional Productions, 1995.

Hansen, Arthur A., ed. *Japanese American World War II Evacuation Oral History Project.* 5 vols. Westport, CT: Meckler, 1991–92. Vol. 1: *Internees*; Vol. 2: *Administrators*; Vol. 3: *Analysts*; Vol. 4: *Resisters*; Vol. 5: *Guards and Townspeople*.

———. "Oral History and the Japanese American Evacuation." *Journal of American History* 82, no. 2 (1995): 625–39.

———. "A Riot of Voices: Racial and Ethnic Variables in Interactive Oral History Interviewing." In *Interactive Oral History Interviewing*, ed. Eva M. McMahan and Kim Lacy Rogers, 107–39. Hillsdale, NJ: Lawrence Erlbaum, 1994.

Hansen, Arthur A., and Betty E. Mitson, eds. *Voices Long Silent: An Oral Inquiry into the Japanese American Evacuation*. Fullerton: California State University Oral History Program Japanese American Project, 1974.

Hansen, Arthur A., Betty E. Milton, and Sue Kunitomi Embrey. "Dissident Harry Ueno Remembers Manzanar." *California History* 64 (1985): 58–64, 77.

Harris, Catherine Embree. *Dusty Exile: Looking Back at Japanese Relocation During World War II*. Honolulu: Mutual Publishing, 1999.

Harth, Erica. "Children of Manzanar." *Massachusetts Review* (autumn 1994): 367–91.

Hosokawa, Bill. *Out of the Frying Pan: Reflections of a Japanese American*. Boulder: University Press of Colorado, 1998.

Houston, Jeanne Wakatsuki, and James D. Houston. *Farewell to Manzanar: A True Story of Japanese American Experience During and After the World War II Internment*. Boston: Houghton Mifflin, 1973.

Howe, Russell Warren. *The Hunt for "Tokyo Rose."* Lanham, MD: Madison Books, 1990.

Hull, Eleanor. *Suddenly the Sun: A Biography of Shizuko Takahashi*. New York: Friendship Press, 1957.

Kalman, Laura. *Abe Fortas: A Biography*. New Haven, CT: Yale University Press, 1990.

Kaneshiro, Takeo, comp. *Internees: War Relocation Center Memoirs and Diaries*. New York: Vantage Press, 1976.

Katcher, Leo. *Earl Warren: A Political Biography*. New York: McGraw-Hill, 1967.

Kessler, Lauren. *Stubborn Twig: Three Generations in the Life of a Japanese American Family*. New York: Random House, 1993.

Kiyota, Minoru. *Beyond Loyalty: The Story of a Kibei*. Honolulu: University of Hawaii Press, 1997.

Lamson, Peggy, and Roger Baldwin. *Founder of the American Civil Liberties Union*. Boston: Houghton Mifflin, 1976.

Levine, Ellen. *A Fence Away from Freedom: Japanese Americans and World War II*. New York: Putnam's Sons, 1995.

Lipton, Dean. "Wayne M. Collins and the Case of Tokyo Rose." *Journal of Contemporary Studies* 8, no. 4 (1985): 25–41.

MacDonald, Dwight. "In Defense of Everybody." *New Yorker*, July 11, 1953, 31–55, and July 18, 1953, 29–59.

McWilliams, Carey. *The Education of Carey McWilliams*. New York: Simon and Schuster, 1978.

Maeda, Laura. "Life at Minidoka: A Personal History of the Japanese-American Relocation." *Pacific Historian* 20 (1976): 379–87.

Matsumoto, Toru. *Beyond Prejudice: A Story of the Church and Japanese Americans.* New York: Friendship Press, 1946.

Mitson, Betty E. "Looking Back in Anguish: Oral History and Japanese-American Evacuation." *Oral History* (1974): 24–51.

Modell, John, ed. *The Kikuchi Diary: Chronicle from an American Concentration Camp.* Urbana: University of Illinois Press, 1973.

Newman, Roger K. *Hugo Black: A Biography.* New York: Pantheon, 1994.

Oishi, Gene. *In Search of Hiroshi: A Japanese-American Odyssey.* Rutland, VT: Charles E. Tuttle, 1988.

Rawls, James J. "The Earl Warren Oral History Project: An Appraisal." *Pacific Historical Review* 56 (1987): 87–97.

Rhoads, Esther B. "My Experience with the Wartime Relocation of Japanese." In *East Across the Pacific*, ed. Hilary Conroy and T. Scott Miyakawa, 127–40. Santa Barbara, CA: Clio Press, 1972.

"Rites of Passage: The Commission Hearings, 1981." *Amerasia Journal* 8, no. 2 (1981): 53–105.

Sano, Iwao Peter. *1,000 Days in Siberia: The Odyssey of a Japanese-American POW.* Lincoln: University of Nebraska Press, 1997.

Sone, Monica. *Nisei Daughter.* Boston: Little, Brown, 1953.

Sprague, Claire D. "Till You Come Back." *Pacific Historian* 24, no. 2 (1980): 192–95.

Stanley, Jerry. *I Am an American: A True Story of Japanese Internment.* New York: Crown, 1994.

Steel, Ronald. *Walter Lippmann and the American Century.* New York: Vintage, 1980.

Stimson, Henry. *On Active Service in Peace and War.* New York: Harper, 1947.

Tateishi, John. *And Justice for All: An Oral History of the Japanese American Detention Camps.* New York: Random House, 1984.

Uchida, Yoshiko. *Desert Exile: The Uprooting of a Japanese American Family.* Seattle: University of Washington Press, 1982.

Uyeda, Clifford I. "A Final Report and Review: The Japanese American Citizens League National Committee for Iva Toguri." Occasional Monograph Series, no. 1, University of Washington, Asian American Studies Program, 1980.

———. "The Pardoning of 'Tokyo Rose': A Report on the Restoration of American Citizenship to Iva Ikuko Toguri." *Amerasia Journal* 5, no. 2 (1978): 69–93.

Warren, Earl. *The Memoirs of Earl Warren.* New York: Doubleday, 1977.

Weglyn, Michi, and Betty E. Mitson, eds. *Valiant Odyssey: Herbert Nicholson In and Out of America's Concentration Camps.* Upland: Brunk's Printing, 1978.

White, G. Edward. *Earl Warren: A Public Life.* New York: Oxford University Press, 1982.

———. "The Unacknowledged Lesson: Earl Warren and the Japanese Relocation Controversy." *Virginia Quarterly Review* 55, no. 4 (1979): 613–29.

Yamazaki, James N. *Children of the Atomic Bomb*. Durham, NC: Duke University Press, 1995.

Yashima, Mitsu. "Letters to Mako to Meet Again." *Common Ground* 9, no. 3 (1949): 41–46.

Yoneda, Karl. *Ganbatte: Sixty-Year Struggle of a Kibei Worker*. Ed. Yuji Ichioka. Los Angeles: Asian American Studies Center, UCLA, 1983.

Yoshino, Ronald W. "Barbed Wire and Beyond: A Sojourn Through Internment— A Personal Recollection." *Journal of the West* 34 (Jan. 1996): 34–43.

Kodachi, Zuigaku, with Jan Keikkala (trans.) and Janet Cormack (ed.). "Portland Assembly Center: Diary of Saku Tomita." *Oregon Historical Quarterly* 81 (1980): 149–71.

IN JAPANESE

Akiya Kāru Ichirō. *Jiyū e no Michi: Taiheiyō wo Koete: Aru Kibei Nisei no Jiden*. Kyoto: Kōrosha, 1996.

———. "Kobe kara Yuta-shū Topāzu Made no Michi." *Pan* 3 (1986): 120–65.

Asano Shichinosuke. *Zaibei Yonjūnen*. Tokyo: Yūki Shobō, 1962.

Fukuda Yoshiaki. *Yokuryū Seikatsu Rokunen*. San Francisco: Konkōkyō San Furanshisuko Kyōkai, 1957.

Furuya Kumatsugu [Suikei]. *Haisho Tenten*. Honolulu: Hawai Taimusu Sha, 1964.

Hashimoto Masaharu. *Nankin Rokunen*. 2 vols. Tenri: Hashimoto Haru, 1954–55.

Higa Tarō. *Aru Nisei no Wadachi*. Tokyo: Nichibō Shuppansha, 1982.

Higashide, Seiichi. *Namida no Adios: Nikkei Perū Imin: Beikoku Kyōsei Shūyō no Ki*. Tokyo: Sairyūsha, 1981.

Ikeda Kandō. *Senjika Nikkeijin to Beikoku no Jitsujō*. 2 vols. Oakland, CA: Dairei Kenkyūjo, 1950–51.

Itō Kazuo, ed. *Nakagawa Yoriaki no Sokuseki*. Tokyo: Mrs. Nakagawa, 1972.

Kiyota Minoru. *Nikkei Hangyakuji*. Tokyo: Nihon Hanbai Kabushiki Kaisha, 1990.

Kodaira Naomichi. *Amerika Kyōsei Shūyōjo*. Tokyo: Tamagawa Daigaku Shuppanbu, 1980.

Koide Jō. *Aru Zaibei Nihonjin no Kiroku*. 2 vols. Tokyo: Yushindo, 1967, 1970.

Kuwahara Henri. *Tetsujōmō Kara no Shiganhei*. Tokyo: Tairyūsha, 1981.

Nagae Yoshimichi. *Nikkeijin no Yo Ake: Zaibei Issei Jyānarisuto Asano Shichinosuke no Shōgen*. Morioka: Iwate Nippōsha, 1987.

Nishi Shigeki. *Kenedei Shūyōjo*. New York: Nishioka Shigeki, 1983.

Oda James. *Aru Nikkei Beihei no Shuki*. Tokyo: Ayumi Shuppansha, 1973.

Otani Isao. *Japan Bōi: Nikkei Amerikajintachi no Taiheiyō Sensō*. Tokyo: Kadokawa Shoten, 1983.

Sasaki Shūichi (Sasabune). *Yokuryūjo Seikatsu*. Los Angeles: Rafu Shoten, 1950.

Shimojima Tetsurō. *Amerika Kokka Hangyakuzai*. Tokyo: Kōdansha, 1993.

Shirai Noboru. *Karifuorunia Nikkeijin Kyōsei Shūyōjo*. Tokyo: Kawade Shobō Shinsha, 1981.

Sōga Yasutarō. *Tessaku Seikatsu*. Honolulu: Hawaii Times, 1948.

Sugimachi Yaemitsu. *Amerika ni Okeru Nihongo Kyōiku*. Pasadena, CA: Privately printed, 1968.

Takemura Yoshiaki. *Issei Paionia: Uchiyama Shunsuke*. Fowler: Uchiyama Toshi, 1974.

Tana Daishō. *Santa Fē, Rōzubāgu Yokuryūjo Nikki*. 2 vols. Tokyo: Sankibō Butsushorin, 1976, 1978.

Yamamoto Asako [pseud.]. *Ibara Aru Hakudō*. N.p.: Privately printed, 1952.

Yamashiro Masao. *Tōi Taigan: Aru Kibei Nisei no Kaisō*. Tokyo: Gurōbyūsha, 1984.

Yoneda Kāru. *Amerika Ichi Jōhōhei no Nikki*. Tokyo: PMC Shuppan, 1989.

———. *Manzanā Kyōsei Shūyōjo Nikki*. Tokyo: PMC Shuppan, 1988.

Photographic Albums

Adams, Ansel. *Born Free and Equal: Photographs of the Loyal Japanese-Americans at Manzanar Relocation Center, Inyo County, California*. New York: U.S. Camera, 1944.

Adams, Ansel, and Toyo Miyatake. *Two Views of Manzanar: An Exhibition of Photographs*. Los Angeles: Frederick S. Wight Art Gallery, 1978.

Anon. "Inside Wyoming." *Annals of Wyoming* 61, no. 1 (1989): 47–54.

———. "Uprooted: A Portfolio of Japanese-Americans in World War II." *Colorado Heritage* 1 (1989): 12–27.

Armor, John, and Peter Wright. *Manzanar*. New York: New York Times, 1988.

Conrat, Maisie, and Richard Conrat. *Executive Order 9066: The Internment of 110,000 Japanese Americans*. San Francisco: California Historical Society, 1971.

Danovitch, Sylvia E. "The Past Recaptured—The Photographic Record of the Internment of Japanese-Americans." *Prologue* 12 (1980): 91–103.

Ohrn, Karin B. "What You See Is What You Get: Dorothea Lange and Ansel Adams at Manzanar." *Journalism History* 4, no. 1 (1977): 15–22.

Okihiro, Gary. *Whispered Silences: Japanese Americans and World War II*. Seattle: University of Washington Press, 1996.

Szasz, Ferenc M., and Patrick Nagatani. "Constricted Landscapes: The Japanese-American Concentration Camps, a Photographic Essay." *New Mexico Historical Review* 71 (April 1996): 157–87.

Tanaka, Chester. *Go for Broke: A Pictorial History of the Japanese American 100th Infantry Battalion and the 442d Regimental Combat Team*. Richmond, CA: Go for Broke, 1982.

Redress and Reparation

Baker, Lillian. *The Concentration Camp Conspiracy: A Second Pearl Harbor*. Lawndale, CA: AFHA Publications, 1981.

———. *Dishonoring America: The Collective Guilt of American Japanese*. Medford, OR: Webb Research Group, 1988.

Chin, Rocky. "The Long Road: Japanese-Americans Move on Redress." *Bridge* 7, no. 4 (1981–82): 11–29.

Daniels, Roger. "Japanese Relocation and Redress in North America: A Comparative View." *Pacific Historian* 26, no. 1 (1982): 2–13.

DeSoto, Hisaye Yamamoto. "Pilgrimage." *Amerasia Journal* 19, no. 1 (1993): 61–67.

Dubro, Alec. "The Japanese-American Internment." *California Lawyer* 3, no. 8 (1983): 24–31.

Fiset, Louis. "Redress for Public Employees of Japanese Ancestry in Washington State After World War II." *Pacific Northwest Quarterly* 88, no. 1 (1996): 21–32.

Hatamiya, Leslie T. *Righting a Wrong: Japanese Americans and the Passage of the Civil Liberties Act of 1988*. Stanford, CA: Stanford University Press, 1993.

Hohri, William. *Repairing America: An Account of the Movement for Japanese American Redress*. Pullman: Washington State University Press, 1988.

Irons, Peter, and Ken Masugi. "Japanese Americans During WWII: Two Views on Redress." *New Perspectives* 18, no. 1 (1986): 2–13.

Iyeki, Marc H. "The Japanese American Coram Nobis Cases: Exposing the Myth of Disloyalty." *Review of Law and Social Change* 13 (1984–85): 199–221.

Kitayama, Glen. "Japanese Americans and the Movement for Redress: A Case Study of the Grassroots Activism in the Los Angeles Chapter of the National Coalition for Redress/Reparation." MA thesis, University of California, Los Angeles, 1993.

Maki, Mitchell T., Harry H. Kitano, and Megan Berthold. *Achieving the Impossible Dream: How Japanese Americans Obtained Redress*. Urbana: University of Illinois Press, 1999.

Murray, Alice Yang. " 'Silence No More': The Japanese American Redress Movement, 1942–1992." PhD diss., Stanford University, 1994.

Nagata, Donna K. *Legacy of Injustice: Exploring the Cross-Generational Impact of the Japanese American Internment*. New York: Plenum Press, 1993.

Nash, Philip T. "Movement for Redress," *The Yale Law Journal* 94 (1985): 743–55.

Oishi, Gene. "The Anxiety of Being a Japanese-American." *New York Times Magazine*, April 28, 1985.

Okihiro, Gary Y. "Justice and Japanese-Americans." *Oral History Review* 13 (1985): 137–44.

Smith, Geoffrey S. "Doing Justice: Relocation and Equity in Public Policy." *Public Historian* 6, no. 3 (1984): 83–97.

Takezawa, Yasuko I. *Breaking Silence: Redress and Japanese-American Ethnicity.* Ithaca, NY: Cornell University Press, 1995.

Tanaka, Richard K. *America on Trial.* New York: Carlton Press, 1987.

Trager, James G. "Haunting Echoes of the Last Round-Up." *Perspectives* 12, no. 2 (1980): 8–15.

U.S. Commission on Wartime Relocation and Internment of Civilians. *Personal Justice Denied.* Washington, DC: GPO, 1982.

U.S. Congress. House. Committee on the Judiciary. *Japanese-American and Aleutian Wartime Relocation: Hearing Before the Subcommittee on Administrative Law and Governmental Relations.* 98th Cong., 2nd sess., June and Sep. 1984. Washington, DC: GPO, 1985.

Beyond Redress

Barkan, Elazar. *The Guilt of Nations: Restitution and Negotiating Historical Injustices.* New York: Norton, 2000.

Brooks, Roy L., ed. *When Sorry Isn't Enough: The Controversy over Apologies and Reparations for Human Justice.* New York: New York University Press, 1999.

Nakanishi, Don T. "Surviving Democracy's 'Mistake': Japanese Americans and the Enduring Legacy of Executive Order 9066," *Amerasia Journal* 19, no. 1 (1993): 7–35.

Robinson, Randall. *The Debt: What America Owes to Blacks.* New York: Dutton, 2000.

Yamamoto, Eric K. *Interracial Justice: Conflict and Reconciliation in Post–Civil Rights America.* New York: New York University Press, 1999.

———. "What's Next? Japanese American Redress and African Americans." *Amerasia Journal* 25, no. 2 (1999): 1–17.

Miscellaneous

Banse, Walter R. *Adjudications of the Attorney General of the United States, Vol. I: Precedent Decisions Under the Japanese-American Evacuation Claims Act, 1950–1956.* Washington, DC: GPO, 1956.

Chang, Gordon H. "'Superman is about to visit the relocation centers' and the Limits of Wartime Liberalism." *Amerasia Journal* 19, no. 1 (1993): 37–59.

Chiasson, L. "Japanese-American Relocation During World War II: A Study of California Editorial Reactions." *Journalism Quarterly* 68, no. 1 (1991): 263–72.

Chiasson, Lloyd E., Jr. "An Editorial Analysis of the Evacuation and Encampment of the Japanese-Americans During World War II." PhD diss., Southern Illinois University, 1983.

Fox, Stephen. *The Unknown Internment: An Oral History of the Relocation of Italian Americans During World War II.* Boston: Twayne, 1990.

Greenberg, Cheryl. "Black and Jewish Responses to Japanese Internment." *Journal of American Ethnic History* 14, no. 2 (winter 1995): 3–37.

Hayashi, Haruo. "Self-Identity of the Japanese-Americans During the Internment Period: An Archival Research." PhD diss., University of California, Los Angeles, 1983.

Krammer, Arnold. "Japanese Prisoners of War in America." *Pacific Historical Review* 52 (1983): 67–91.

———. *Undue Process: The Untold Story of America's German Alien Internees.* London: Rowman and Littlefield, 1997.

Nagata, Donna K. "The Japanese American Internment: Exploring the Transgenerational Consequences of Traumatic Stress." *Journal of Traumatic Stress* 3, no. 1 (1990): 47–69.

Okamura, Raymond K. "The American Concentration Camps: A Cover-up Through Euphemistic Terminology." *Journal of Ethnic Studies* 10, no. 3 (1982): 95–108.

Shibutani, Tamotsu. "The Circulation of Rumors as a Form of Collective Behavior." PhD diss., University of Chicago, 1948.

Spickard, Paul R. "Injustice Compounded: Amerasians and Non-Japanese Americans in World War II Concentration Camps." *Journal of American Ethnic History* 5 (1986): 5–22.

Takamoto, Janis S. "The Effects of World War II and Wartime Sentiment on Japanese and Japanese American 'Voluntary' Evacuees." MS thesis, California State University, Long Beach, 1991.

Whitney, Helen E. "Care of Homeless Children of Japanese Ancestry During Evacuation and Relocation." MA thesis, University of California, Berkeley, 1948.

Yoo, David. "Captivating Memories: Museology, Concentration Camps, and Japanese American History." *American Quarterly* 48, no. 4 (1996): 680–99.

Japanese-Peruvians

Barnhart, Edward N. "Citizenship and Political Tests in Latin American Republics in World War II." *Hispanic American Historical Review* 42 (1962): 297–332.

———. "Japanese Internees from Peru." *Pacific Historical Review* 31 (1962): 169–78.

Ciccarelli, Orazio. "Peru's Anti-Japanese Campaign in the 1930s: Economic

Dependency and Abortive Nationalism." *Canadian Review of Studies in Nationalism* 9 (1982): 113–33.

Emmerson, John K. "Japanese and Americans in Peru, 1942–1943." *Foreign Service Journal* 54, no. 5 (1977): 40–47, 56.

Fukumoto, Mary. *Hacia Un Nuevo Sol: Japoneses y Sus Descendientes en El Perú.* Lima: Asociación Peruano Japonesa Del Perú, 1997.

Gardiner, C. Harvey. *The Japanese and Peru, 1873–1973.* Albuquerque: University of New Mexico Press, 1975.

———. *Pawns in a Triangle of Hate: The Peruvian Japanese and the United States.* Seattle: University of Washington Press, 1981.

Higashide, Seiichi. *Adios to Tears: The Memoirs of a Japanese-Peruvian Internee in U.S. Concentration Camps.* Honolulu: E and E Kudo, 1993. Originally published as *Namida no Adios: Nikkei Perū Imin, Beikoku Kyōsei Shūyō no Ki* (Tokyo: Sairyūsha, 1981).

Nishi, Shigeki. *Kenedei Shūyōjo.* New York: Nishioka Shigeyuki, 1983.

Japanese-Canadians

Adachi, Ken. *The Enemy That Never Was: A History of the Japanese Canadians.* Toronto: McClelland and Stewart, 1976.

Bernard, Elaine. "A University at War: Japanese Canadians at UBC During World War II." *BC Studies* 35 (1977): 36–55.

Bolaria, B. Singh, and Peter S. Li. *Racial Oppression in Canada.* Toronto: Garamond Press, 1985.

Broadfoot, Barry. *Years of Sorrow, Years of Shame: The Story of the Japanese Canadians in World War II.* Toronto: Doubleday, 1977.

Cohn, Werner. "The Persecution of Japanese Canadians and the Political Left in British Columbia, December 1941–March 1942." *BC Studies* 68 (winter 1985–86): 3–22.

Fisher, Galen M. "Japanese Evacuation in Canada." *Far Eastern Survey*, June 29, 1942, 145–50.

Iwaasa, David B. "The Japanese in Southern Alberta, 1941–1945." *Alberta History* 24, no. 3 (1976): 5–19.

Kitagawa, Muriel. *This Is My Own: Letters to Wes and Other Writings on Japanese Canadians, 1941–1948.* Vancouver: Talon Books, 1985.

Makabe, Tomoko. "Canadian Evacuation and Nisei Identity." *Phylon* 41, no. 2 (1980): 116–25.

Nakano, Takeo U. *Within the Barbed Wire Fence: A Japanese Man's Account of His Internment in Canada.* Seattle: University of Washington Press, 1981.

National Association of Japanese Canadians. *Economic Losses of Japanese Canadians After 1941.* Winnipeg: National Association of Japanese Canadians, 1985.

Oiwa, Keibo, ed. *Stone Voices: Wartime Writings of Japanese Canadian Issei.* Montreal: Vehicule Press, 1991.

Roy, Patricia E. "The Soldiers Canada Didn't Want: Her Chinese and Japanese Citizens." *Canadian Historical Review* 59, no. 3 (1978): 341–58.

Roy, Patricia E., J. L. Granatstein, Masako Iino, and Hiroko Takamura. *Mutual Hostages: Canadians and Japanese During the Second World War.* Toronto: University of Toronto Press, 1990.

Stovall, G., ed. *The Left Bank #1 Writing and Fishing in the Northwest.* Hillsboro, OR: Blue Heron, 1991.

Sunahara, M. Ann. "Historical Leadership Trends Among Japanese Canadians: 1940–1950." *Canadian Ethnic Studies* 11, no. 1 (1979): 1–16.

———. "The Japanese American and Japanese Canadian Relocation in World War II: Historical Records and Comparisons." *Canadian Ethnic Studies* 10, no. 1 (1978): 126–28.

———. "The Japanese Experience in North America." *Canadian Ethnic Studies* 8, no. 2 (1976): 106–8.

———. *The Politics of Racism: The Uprooting of Japanese Canadians During the Second World War.* Toronto: James Lorimer, 1981.

Sunahara, M. Ann, and Glenn T. Wright. "The Japanese-Canadian Experience in World War II: An Essay on Archival Resources." *Canadian Ethnic Studies* 11, no. 2 (1979): 78–87.

Tanaka, June K. "Fruit of Diaspora: The Japanese Experience in Canada." *Japan Interpreter* 12, no. 1 (1978): 110–17.

Ward, Peter W. "British Columbia and the Japanese Evacuation." *Canadian Historical Review* 57, no. 3 (1976): 289–309.

Ujimoto, Victor K. "Contrasts in the Prewar and Postwar Japanese Community in British Columbia: Conflict and Change." *Canadian Review of Sociology and Anthropology* 13, no. 1 (1976): 80–89.

Manuscript Collections, Charles E. Young Research Library, UCLA

UCLA Special Collections
    Fujii Ryoichi Papers
    Fujita Akira Papers
    Japanese American Research Project Collection
    Charles Kikuchi Papers
    Ralph Merritt Papers
    Togawa Akira Papers
    Edison Uno Papers
    Karl Yoneda Papers

Papers of the U.S. Commission on Wartime Relocation and Internment of Civilians. 35 reels. Frederick, MD: University Publications of America, 1985.

Japanese American Newspapers (published in "Assembly Centers and Relocation Camps"). 22 reels.

A Collection of Publications Issued by the War Relocation Authority. 21 reels.

Index

Page numbers in italics indicate material in figures.

Nisei wartime experience and, 169; patriotism and, 111; physical appearance and, 140; Sakamoto on, 96–97, 118–19; Uno and, 161–62, 164, 166–69. *See also* Anti-Japanese sentiment; Exclusionism
Radio: anti-American broadcasts on, 262, 263; Sakamoto and, 106; shortwave Japanese broadcasting on, 193; Tokyo Rose and, 148; Uno and, 157, 167–68, 171n6, 175n51
Rafu Shimpō: dinner/reception of, 160; Fujioka and, 79; on Fukunaga Incident, 85–86; on Furusawa Sachiko, 210; and Sino-Japanese War, 186–89; on Tachibana Incident, 216–17; Uno and, 41, 158, 159, 162
Redress and reparations movement, xxiii, 204
Red Scare, 94
Reinsch, Paul, 234
Rescript on Education, *see* Imperial Rescript on Education
Resettlement policy, 144
Rikkōkai, 34
Ringle, Kenneth, 6, 115–16, 215, 222n2
Roosevelt, Franklin D., 99, 197
Roosevelt, Theodore, 56
Russo-Japanese War (1904–5), 198, 212

Sagitani Seiichi, 188
Saito, John T., 160
Saitō Hiroshi, 29, 106
Saitō Jirō, 166
Saitō Miki, 166
Sakai Yoneo, 288
Sakamoto, James Yoshinori, xviii, xxii–xxiii, 92–119; Adamic and, 111–12, 134–35, 138; Americanism of, 8, 30, 47, 92–93, 95–100, 106, 135 (*see also* superpatriotism of); background of, 93–94; and bridge of understanding, 8, 30, 93, 100–109; on communism, 98, 100; and cooperation with American intelligence, 116; dualism of, 92–119; FBI investigation of, 122n49; and JACL, 97, 112–16; as *Japanese American Courier* founder, 92; and Japanese language, 103; Japan promoted by, 29–30, 104–9; on labor unions, 98–100; Nisei and, 117–18; and Nisei study tours, 103–4; on Pearl Harbor, 92, 117; on racism, 96–97, 118–19; superpatriotism of, 109–17; writing of, 118
Sakamoto, Misao, 92

Sakamoto, Shizume, 59, 63
Sakata, Yasuo, 282–83, 285, 289
Sakura Kai, 212–14, 220, 225n41
Sandmeyer, Elmer C., 282
San Francisco, California, pro-Japan activities in, 183
San Francisco State Third World Strike, 281
Sannomiya, Miya, 26, 42, 68, 69, 70, 71, 191
Sano Kazō, 86
Sansei, 274, 289, 295
Sasaki, Shizuko, 31
Sasaki Masami, 218
Satō Yuki, 122n49
Scherer, James A. B., 56
Seattle, Washington, pro-Japan activities in, 183
Seattle Federation of Japanese Christian Churches, 103
Seattle girls, Nisei visit by, 25–26, 58
Seattle Progressive Citizens' League, 19
Second-generation problem: Adamic and, 112, 127, 136–39; background of, 10; dualism and, 93; education and, 10–24; emergence of, 53; in immigration context, 112, 127, 138–39; Issei perspective on, 10, 14, 17–18, 24; Kibei-Nisei problem, 43–45; Nisei perspective on, 45; North versus South American, 275; Park's study of, 140–41; post-1924 aspects of, 24–32; recognition of, 12; Sino-Japanese War influence on, 36–43; study in Japan, 32–36. *See also* New Americans
Senninbari, 37, 181
Setchūron, 14
Shanghai Evening Post and Mercury (newspaper), 157, 166
Shanghai Times (newspaper), 109
Shibusawa Eiichi, 26, 63, 240–41, 255n40
Shidehara Kijūrō, 63, 106
Shiga Shigetaka, 17
Shima, George, 242
Shimada Saburō, 17
Shimano Kōhei, 20
Shimanouchi, Henry Toshirō, 41–42, 191
Shimanouchi Yoshinobu, 191, 202n38
Shin Sekai Asahi (newspaper), 39–41, 155, 158, 159, 188–90
Shin Sekai (newspaper), 11–12, 14, 75, 88, 138, 158

ASIAN AMERICA SERIES

*Japanese Pride, American Prejudice: Modifying the Exclusion Clause of the
1924 Immigration Act*
IZUMI HIROBE, 2001

Chinese San Francisco, 1850-1943: A Trans-Pacific Community
YONG CHEN, 2000

*Dreaming of Gold, Dreaming of Home: Transnationalism and Migration
Between the United States and South China, 1882-1943*
MADELINE Y. HSU, 2000

Imagining the Nation: Asian American Literature and Cultural Consent
DAVID LEIWEI LI, 1998

*Morning Glory, Evening Shadow: Yamato Ichihashi and His Internment
Writings, 1942-1945*
EDITED, ANNOTATED, AND WITH A BIOGRAPHICAL ESSAY BY GORDON H.
CHANG, 1997

Dear Miye: Letters Home From Japan, 1939-1946
MARY KIMOTO TOMITA, EDITED, WITH AN INTRODUCTION AND NOTES, BY
ROBERT G. LEE, 1995

Beyond the Killing Fields: Voices of Nine Cambodian Survivors in America
USHA WELARATNA, 1993

Making and Remaking Asian America
BILL ONG HING, 1993

*Righting a Wrong: Japanese Americans and the Passage of the Civil Liberties
Act of 1988*
LESLIE T. HATAMIYA, 1993